{ THE STRANGE GENIUS OF MR. O }

THE STRANGE GENIUS OF MR.

The World of the United States' First Forgotten Celebrity

CAROLYN EASTMAN

Published by the
OMOHUNDRO INSTITUTE OF
EARLY AMERICAN HISTORY AND CULTURE,
Williamsburg, Virginia,
and the
UNIVERSITY OF NORTH CAROLINA PRESS,
Chapel Hill

The Omohundro Institute of Early American History and Culture
is sponsored by the College of William and Mary. On November 15, 1996,
the Institute adopted the present name in honor of a bequest from
Malvern H. Omohundro, Jr.

Cover illustration: *Don Quixote*. Engraving, 1823.
Courtesy of the Maryland Historical Society, MS194

Library of Congress Cataloging-in-Publication Data
Names: Eastman, Carolyn, author. | Omohundro Institute of
Early American History & Culture, publisher.
Title: The strange genius of Mr. O : the world of the United States'
first forgotten celebrity / Carolyn Eastman.
Description: Williamsburg, Virginia : Omohundro Institute of Early American
History and Culture ; Chapel Hill : University of North Carolina Press, 2021. |
Includes bibliographical references and index.
Identifiers: LCCN 2020032959 | ISBN 9781469660516 (cloth ; alk. paper) |
ISBN 9781469660523 (ebook)
Subjects: LCSH: Ogilvie, James, 1760–1820. | Orators—United States—
Biography. | Oratory—United States—History—19th century. | Oratory—
Social aspects—United States. | Celebrities—United States.
Classification: LCC B931.O44 E195 2021 | DDC 191—dc23
LC record available at https://lccn.loc.gov/2020032959

The University of North Carolina Press has been a
member of the Green Press Initiative since 2003.

MIX
Paper from
responsible sources
FSC
www.fsc.org   FSC® C008955

For Kevin

{ CONTENTS }

{ ILLUSTRATIONS }

{ THE STRANGE GENIUS OF MR. O }

{ INTRODUCTION }
A Celebrity in the Early Republic

They arrived early, trying to get seats close to the stage. Each ticket cost a dollar, the equivalent of a full day's wages for a laborer, and those able to spend that kind of money wanted to have a good view. They wore their best clothes, even if in some cases they hadn't been fashionable in years. Having read rapturous reports about James Ogilvie's performances in larger towns and cities elsewhere in the country, they knew he'd seen bigger crowds and had socialized with wealthier and more stylish people. How would they compare? As they alighted from their carriages at Captain Whidden's Assembly House in Portsmouth, New Hampshire, some found themselves self-conscious of how they might perform for this celebrity performer.

Walking upstairs, the attendees could feel proud of the Assembly Room's elegance, for it highlighted Portsmouth's aspirations. The largest room in the city, it was used for all large gatherings: meetings, dances and dancing lessons, Fourth of July banquets, and the ventriloquist who also performed sleight of hand magic tricks. Three decades earlier, the newly elected George Washington had called this space "one of the best I have seen anywhere in the United States" when he made a tour of the nation in 1789. At about eighteen hundred square feet, it featured sparkling chandeliers hanging from high ceilings. Sconces on the walls for additional candles accentuated the gilded wall decorations carved to look like bouquets of flowers. In anticipation of Ogilvie's many attendees, the building's owner had packed the room with benches, easily removed on other nights for dances. Just weeks earlier on the Fourth of July, they had decorated the room with a red, white, and blue canopy and the very chair Washington had sat in when he visited, all bringing attention to a full-length portrait of the president. Now, as townspeople moved inside, they sought to avoid sitting next to the two or three men who were already intoxicated. Ogilvie had spent a lot of money lighting the room with more candles than usual, and he would be able to see who in the audience misbehaved, looked bored, or started snoring.[1]

The room quieted shortly after seven o'clock as he stepped on the stage. Ladies fanned themselves, trying to maintain the appearance of feminine delicacy in the room's collective heat. They knew already that Ogilvie was tall and very thin, for they'd seen him in town for weeks beforehand as he had made arrangements for the talks. As they waited for him to begin, he appeared even more awkward, cold despite the room's warmth. He grew still for a moment, perhaps mustering

1

his energy. Would this performance be as masterful as they had heard? Would he have full range of what he called his powers? In those few moments before he started speaking, the audience seemed to hold its breath.

But when his deep, sepulchral voice sounded through the room, his body seemed to transform and loosen. Watching the gracefulness of his movements reminded them of what they had read about the great orators of the classical world—Cicero, Seneca—as Ogilvie's physical posture onstage conveyed authority, self-possession, moral certainty. He began with no preface, none of the usual thanks to the audience, no humble comments about hoping to be worthy of their attendance; he simply leapt into his subject. "When we review and analyze our pleasures and our pains," he began, looking around the room, even "the most vulgar mind" must see "the scantiness and evanescence of the former, [and] the multiplicity, variety and permanence of the latter." Evidence of the world's pains was everywhere, he said. Consider the pages of history: a "black catalogue of corrosive calamities," he continued. The alliteration of hard Cs cut like the cracks of an electrical storm through the room, undergirded by the roll of the Rs in *corrosive* delivered in his Scottish accent. Consider, too, evidence from our own lives: "How many moments of exquisite agony?" With that, some in the audience flashed to the illnesses and deaths of loved ones, children, spouses. As he delivered the words "exquisite agony," his thin hand delicately touched his heart, accentuating the poignancy of the sentiment.[2]

Moving across the stage, his gestures and facial expressions helped to build the dark mood of the subjects he discussed. In one moment, he reached out toward his listeners and looked at them entreatingly with his soft blue eyes, as if he knew they might resist his argument. Alternately, he might cast his eyes down or scowl with a ferocity that made his eyes appear almost black, forcing his listeners to feel along with him the worlds of suffering he described, those existential pains. A few lines later, his assertion that "man is but a shadow and life but a dream" seemed so melancholically eloquent, so Shakespearean, that it raised goosebumps on the arms of the gentlemen and brought several of the ladies' mouths to open unconsciously. Their nervousness had left them. Their silence was complete.[3]

They began to realize that Ogilvie was going to ask the audience to feel sympathy for those tormented by suicidal thoughts—a stunning position that challenged the moral, religious, and legal oppositions to suicide.

And with that, they were hooked.

James Ogilvie may be the earliest and most significant American celebrity you've never heard of. His career revealed many of the hallmarks of celebrity we recognize from later eras: glamorous circles of friends, eccentric clothing, scandal-

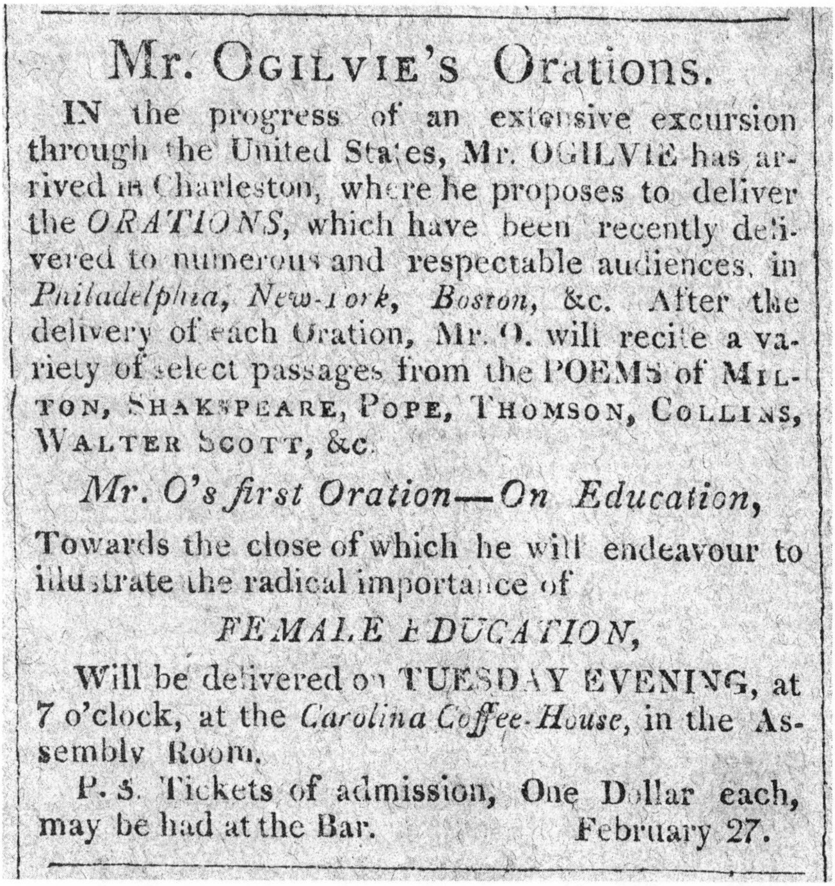

Mr. OGILVIE's Orations.

IN the progress of an extensive excursion through the United States, Mr. OGILVIE has arrived in Charleston, where he proposes to deliver the *ORATIONS*, which have been recently delivered to numerous and respectable audiences, in *Philadelphia, New-York, Boston, &c.* After the delivery of each Oration, Mr. O. will recite a variety of select passages from the POEMS of MILTON, SHAKSPEARE, POPE, THOMSON, COLLINS, WALTER SCOTT, &c.

Mr. O's first Oration—On Education,

Towards the close of which he will endeavour to illustrate the radical importance of

FEMALE EDUCATION,

Will be delivered on TUESDAY EVENING, at 7 o'clock, at the *Carolina Coffee-House*, in the Assembly Room.

P. S. Tickets of admission, One Dollar each, may be had at the Bar. February 27.

Figure 1. "Mr. Ogilvie's Orations." From Charleston Courier (S.C.), Mar. 2, 1811, [3].
One of Ogilvie's advertisements, revealing the alliteration of Ogilvie and oration, a long O
that perhaps even evoked the audience's propensity to ogle this talented speaker.
Courtesy of the American Antiquarian Society, Worcester, Mass.

ous religious views, narcissism, and a reputation for the habitual use of narcotics. He had quirks: the tendency to neglect his personal hygiene and to tell acquaintances that he would ultimately inherit an earldom in Scotland. Despite his idiosyncrasies, he enjoyed the friendship and patronage of some of the most important men in the nation, including Thomas Jefferson, John Quincy Adams, the physician Benjamin Rush, and the novelist Washington Irving. Influential society women were equally vital to his success, including him in evening soirees and parlor gatherings and introducing him to networks of family and friends—potential supporters all. He became so familiar in the years after 1808 that newspapers referred to him simply as Mr. O, a long O that mirrored the same sound in the word *oratory* and even mimicked the shape of an open mouth. Yet some of the same Americans who admired him most fervently during his heyday came to forget him during the decades after his death in 1820—a purposeful forgetting that now seems so notable because the names of his supporters still resonate more than two hundred years later.[4]

It was Ogilvie's genius for eloquence that made him a household name—or, to use the words that appeared most frequently describing him, his *peculiar genius*. Commentators regularly proclaimed "Mr. Ogilvie's genius" as "elegant and original" and repeated the insistence on his genius several times in the course of a single review. "Standing forth in all the proud originality of his genius," a Philadelphia admirer proclaimed, Ogilvie had offered an "exhibition of superior talents." They used *peculiar* in two ways. Reviewers usually used it to indicate that he possessed distinctive talents for public speech; his oratory was unlike anyone else's. "His style is peculiar, without affected imitation, sufficiently varied with his subject, clear, nervous, splendid," a reviewer in Salem, Massachusetts, offered approvingly. A newspaper in Washington, D.C., commended his "peculiar powers" for bringing together "finished compositions, beaming with intellect, rich in research, illuminated with the dazzling splendors of classic lore," and declared that he had cast "magic spells" on "the minds and hearts of his auditors." But the same review also used *peculiar* to suggest strangeness, oddness: "In his recitations, too, he is sometimes peculiarly happy," the writer continued. To underline the point, friends and critics alike called him *eccentric*. Most of all, they insisted, it was impossible to describe adequately "the force, or the brilliancy of his colloquial talents." "To those who had not witnessed them," one writer explained, they "appear like exaggeration." These characterizations sought to set Ogilvie's talents apart, to claim that his performances offered something rare, distinctive, confounding, magical.[5]

One of the things that distinguished Ogilvie from many of his contemporaries was the extent to which he traveled, a pursuit that was expensive and time-consuming but permitted him to see an extraordinary amount of the United States in its infancy. Usually on horseback, he visited seventeen of the nation's nineteen states, as well as the District of Maine, the Indiana and Illinois Territories, and Montreal and Quebec across the northern border in Lower Canada. He found it comparatively easy to make his way up and down parts of the East Coast, during which he stopped five times each in Philadelphia and New York, the country's two largest cities. Getting to the farthest corners of the nation was harder. To reach Tennessee and Kentucky required weeks of walking his horse on rutted, rocky bridle paths every day with the hope of encountering a house along the way where he might prevail on the inhabitants for a meal and a place to sleep. On occasion he could take advantage of water routes, as when he sped up the

Hudson River from New York to Albany on a steamboat. But to continue north from Albany toward Montreal—another 250 miles—returned him to creeping along at about 4 or 5 miles per hour. The new United States was both geographically vast and overwhelmingly rural, and many of the people who flocked to his performances encountered him as a rarity: a worldly cosmopolitan who had seen so much. Understanding his celebrity requires entering into that vast world and engaging seriously with the women and men who resided there.[6]

This book follows Ogilvie and his talent for the spoken word through the pathways of the country he adopted and the people he encountered. That so many of his contemporaries found him a powerful performer makes his career all the more illustrative of his time, for talent often rests in the eyes of the beholders. What they saw in him—and what they did not see—illuminates the aspirations, assumptions, and priorities of the era. Equally revelatory are the controversies and scandals that erupted around him, often spearheaded by people resistant to his charms, people who had goals of their own. Taken together, they paint a portrait of a United States in the midst of invention.[7]

Ogilvie was hardly the first person to win acclaim in America, but his celebrity looks different from that of political figures like George Washington and Alexander Hamilton, religious leaders like George Whitefield and Lorenzo Dow, or those who won acclaim for their writing or expertise, such as Benjamin Franklin, the poet Phillis Wheatley, and the physician Benjamin Rush.[8] Many of these individuals ambitiously sought fame at the same time that they offered public service, and, like Ogilvie, they believed that, as long as a person sought to be "instrumental in promoting the progress of society," they might also crave public honors and accolades. But who conferred those honors, and who fueled a person's fame? Ogilvie represented a newer form of celebrity fanned into a flame, not by years of public service, but by the combined efforts of a growing print media and members of an anonymous public who usually knew him only as a famous figure rather than personally.[9] With the public and the media providing the foundation, his celebrity could be more fragile, more liable to be exposed as illegitimate or undermined by scandal. The potential fickleness of public and press adoration threatened Ogilvie's form of celebrity. As dramatically as the media might characterize his precipitous rise, they could also make his fall from grace appear absolute.[10]

Celebrities hold up a mirror to culture, displaying not just who we admire but also who we are and what we hope to become. It can also display the media technologies that construct those forms of identification. Tracing the emergence of this new form of celebrity in the early nineteenth-century United States permits us to see other elements of the history of that era through fresh eyes, including contradictions in how various media disseminated information. In an era before talent agents, publicists, and paparazzi, a man eager to build his fame required different tools to find his audience. Seeing how Ogilvie used social and family networks can suggest a nation crisscrossed by webs of association in which well-connected individuals promoted the career of the itinerant orator in ways that both displayed and enhanced their own reputations. At other times, however, the lapses and lacunae in communication shaped Ogilvie's fate. A controversy in one city might fail to register in the next, making it possible for Ogilvie to whipsaw from failure to triumph simply by traveling ninety miles up the road. Ogilvie built his celebrity by using the intense yet profoundly uneven spread of information through the vast early American Republic.

Ogilvie's celebrity rested on his genius for another medium of communication: his eloquence. He performed oratory at a moment in the early nineteenth century when the spoken word seemed uniquely significant to the nation. If he had shown a special talent in a related area—acting or writing, to take two examples—he likely would not have achieved such success. Contemporaries called this "the golden age of American oratory" to capture the ways that the performance of eloquence became increasingly important in many areas of American society and politics.[11] Scrutinizing Ogilvie's talent for the spoken word helps to reveal the origins of this golden age and the importance of this form of media. To the men and women who found him so compelling, he offered a vision of a culture united by eloquence, just as the classical republics of Rome and Greece had been shepherded by great orators with thoughtful and discerning publics listening carefully as they assessed those leaders' arguments. In a country divided along many lines—by regions that appeared socially and culturally incompatible, by two political parties deeply and diametrically opposed, by the urban-rural divide, by the political conflicts that blossomed into the War of 1812, and over matters of religion and belief, all subjects that appear in vivid relief throughout this book—Ogilvie's performances could help his audiences spin a fantasy of a more unified United States even as his appearances might remind them how provincial and isolated they were. By lecturing on matters of civic concern, he sought to model how members of a heterogeneous public might think together and engage in collective deliberation. But some recoiled from his popular and often emotional performances. No one yet used the derogatory term *fans* (short for *fanatics*), but some worried that an infant nation overly entranced by a magnetic figure could become vulnerable to demagoguery.[12]

National unity might have been illusory, but the broader drama of Ogilvie's celebrity itself offered a topic for many to share. More often than not, print media facilitated those exchanges. Whether they loved or hated him, he provoked common conversation. The story of his rise and increasing popularity gave a diverse readership a reason to pay attention to the growing number of mentions of his

career in the press. When he made errors of judgment, the scrum of public discussion gave a divided public an early taste of schadenfreude in observing a public downfall. At one point, many Americans seemed to join together in insisting
that they would reject this false prophet; they would not be so gullible in the
future. They revealed an ambivalence about celebrity—that intense combination
of love and hate, fascination and revulsion—that still inflects our relationships
to celebrities. Americans forgot about Ogilvie in the decades after his death, and,
in doing so, they enacted one final familiar ritual with celebrities: after celebrating them, they unceremoniously and collectively choose to put their former infatuation behind them.[13]

In each of these ways, Ogilvie's celebrity serves less as the primary subject
than as a nexus where so many elements of early national life crossed. It draws
connections from print and oral media to social networks, rumor, letter writing, and parlor conversations, all of which might bolster his reputation. It links
Ogilvie's ambitious attempts to build his career and fashion an appealing persona to the ways that his supporters and lecture attendees sought to reflect back
to him their own respectability and discernment. Following him in his final years
to England and Scotland, where his successes were more modest, highlights
the differences in culture, media, and society that prevailed across the Atlantic. Finally, viewing this form of celebrity through the people who celebrated or
criticized him, spread across a diverse social, political, and religious landscape
of the early United States, grants us a surprisingly expansive view of a national
culture in the making.

Focusing on the career of a single individual also gives us glimpses of the
effects of celebrity on the self. The radical vacillations of public love and hate,
and the toll they might take on someone's emotional life, might be familiar subjects to a twenty-first-century audience but were much less common two hundred years ago. Just as Ogilvie took sole control over his appearances, his travels,
and the arc of his career, so he stood alone in managing his own health and
spirits. His choices about how to weather the storm of public scrutiny ultimately
offers unexpected insights into the culture he inhabited and reminds us of the
importance of viewing the triumphs and survival strategies of people in the past
on their own terms.

People who spent their lives on the move are hard to track. James Ogilvie never
remained in a single place for long, and no collection of his own personal papers
survives. More sedentary individuals might have retained diaries, letters, and
financial records throughout their lives, but itinerants with few possessions had
no desk or attic or trunk in which to preserve them. By the time Ogilvie was
twenty-one, he had lived in three different parts of Scotland as well as in north-

Figure 2. Zachariah Poulson. By James Peale. 1808. In this portrait of the
Philadelphia printer and newspaper editor, he holds a copy of his own paper;
underneath are manuscript pages of advertisement submissions that have yet
to be printed. Courtesy of the Library Company of Philadelphia

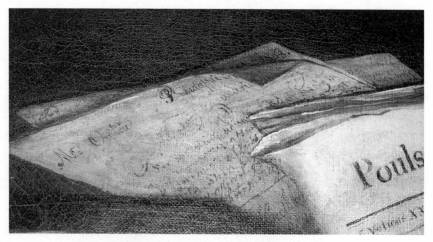

Figure 3. Detail of Zachariah Poulson. By James Peale. 1808.
The manuscript page is a proposed advertisement from Mr. Ogilvie.
Courtesy of the Library Company of Philadelphia

ern England and had recently emigrated to Virginia to work as a schoolteacher. For the next fifteen years he lived in at least six parts of the state to take teaching jobs. When he abandoned the schoolroom in favor of a career as an itinerant lecturer, he spent the rest of his life traveling. It is a testament to Ogilvie's celebrity—and a measure of his ambition—that so many records about his life survive, scattered in archives throughout the United States, Quebec, and Great Britain and documented in his published writings, an autobiographical narrative, and hundreds of newspaper accounts and advertisements.[14]

Evidence of Ogilvie's career appears in archives on both sides of the Atlantic, sometimes hiding in plain sight. Take a portrait of the Philadelphia newspaper editor Zachariah Poulson that hangs in the Reading Room at the Library Company of Philadelphia. The artist James Peale portrayed Poulson holding a copy of his own newspaper, *Poulson's American Daily Advertiser*, with a few manuscript pages lying on the desk below. If you turn the portrait upside down and squint your eyes, you can see that the manuscript page is titled "Mr. Ogilvie"—a proposed submission for the newspaper, dating from a moment in October 1808 when the orator's success in the city seemed most assured and *Poulson's* proclaimed his performances to be "elegant and instructive." Peale completed the portrait only days before a scandal shattered Ogilvie's triumph in that city.[15]

Other sources proved confounding or wrong. Despite a respectable amount of information about Ogilvie's father, a Scottish minister and poet, his biographers rarely mentioned his son's career—marking an odd divide between the father's eminence as a literary and religious figure and his son's renown for a different

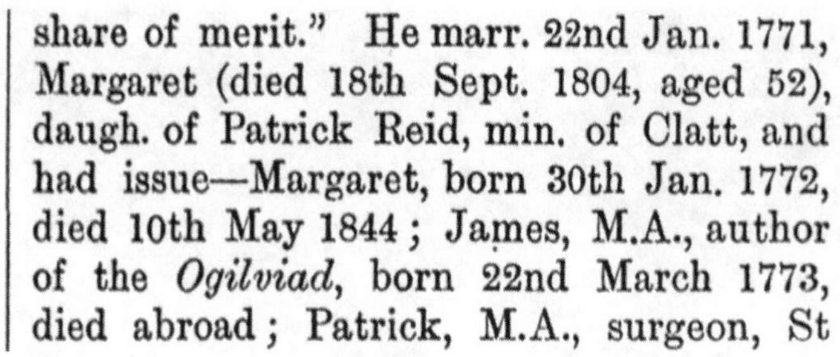

share of merit." He marr. 22nd Jan. 1771,
Margaret (died 18th Sept. 1804, aged 52),
daugh. of Patrick Reid, min. of Clatt, and
had issue—Margaret, born 30th Jan. 1772,
died 10th May 1844; James, M.A., author
of the *Ogilviad*, born 22nd March 1773,
died abroad; Patrick, M.A., surgeon, St

Figure 4. Detail from Hew Scott, Fasti Ecclesiae Scoticanae: The Succession of Ministers in the Church of Scotland from the Reformation, new ed. (Edinburgh, 1926), VI, 108. This biographical dictionary of Scottish clergymen contains an entry on Rev. John Ogilvie of Midmar, Scotland. His eldest son, James, is erroneously described as having "died abroad," but it distinguishes him as the author of The Ogilviad. Courtesy of the Library of Virginia, Richmond

form of eloquence. One late nineteenth-century account of the Reverend John Ogilvie erroneously explained that he had three sons (actually, he had eight), none of whom was named James. But another, published fifty years later, contained a brief note explaining that his son James was the author of *The Ogilviad*. That tantalizing reference was the single clue to a remarkable document. Today many rare printed materials appear in digital editions online, making historical research infinitely easier, but this one still does not. Only a single known copy still exists in a library, far in the northeast of Scotland, and the last time anyone seemed to notice it was in 1887.[16]

If you have ever wondered what motivates historians to undertake their research, imagine turning the rag paper pages of a long-forgotten eighteenth-century pamphlet and finding yourself grinning. Despite its seemingly epic title, *The Ogilviad* brims over with wit and the ingenious banter of eighteenth-century college students. It sings of personal ambition and rumbles with festering grudges. For, as we shall see, *The Ogilviad* not only tells the tale of a fight between two boys; it represents the continuation of that fight in poetry—a battle of words between students who otherwise spent their time learning that eloquence could achieve more than fists.

CHAPTER 1

The Ogilviad; or, Two Students at King's College Fight a Duel in Poetry,

1786–1793

The fight began on the grounds of King's College in Aberdeen on the far north-eastern coast of Scotland. It was winter. This close to the Arctic Circle, Aberdonians ate their breakfast of bread with milk in the dark, saw morning light emerge sometime before nine in the morning, and found the sun fading by three in the afternoon. In fact, they probably wouldn't have used the word *sun* at all, because no one knew better than the Scots how many winter days saw nothing but heavy clouds and cold, wet precipitation. Aberdeen was often called the Grey City for the locally quarried gray granite used to build the city's homes, businesses, and municipal buildings; its winter days with its half-lit skies made this landscape appear in grayscale only—and against this backdrop, the college boys' red gowns appeared like targets. The temptation to hurl a snowball or stuff a wad of cold, wet slush down the back of another boy's gown could be overwhelming.

Conflicts between the students were so common that the college had installed elaborate rules to punish the offenders. Even the choice of red gowns was intentional. Nearly a century earlier the British Parliament had insisted that all Scottish college students wear scarlet gowns to discourage bad behavior, reasoning that the color made the boys hard to miss in a crowd; "therby the students may be discurraged from vageing or vice." A glimpse at the lists of rules suggests, however, that putting them in scarlet had not solved the problem. A few years before James Ogilvie arrived at King's, the students had rioted. Most of the students ranged between the ages of thirteen and nineteen—in the 1780s, college students in both Britain and America usually finished by their late teens—and fighting was endemic. If the college had caught Ogilvie fighting with Grigor Grant, the boys would have received fines, and Ogilvie, at least, didn't have the money to spare.[1]

Why sixteen-year-old Ogilvie knocked Grigor Grant into the snow has been lost to history. But we do know how the fight proceeded, because rather than follow through with fists the two boys decided to continue their fight in poetry. By the end, they were so pleased with themselves that they published their poem with a grandiose title: *The Ogilviad*, or song of Ogilvie, a title that mimics Homer's *The Iliad* (song of Ilion). But if *The Iliad* told of great battles, *The Ogilviad* is itself a battle. The two teenaged authors took turns insulting each other and claiming superior wit and intelligence for themselves rather than recounting heroic feats. In attack-and-reply fashion, they mocked each other's intelligence, poetic skill, clothing, and hygiene. It is, in essence, an eighteenth-century duel fought at ten syllables per line.

Reading *The Ogilviad* reveals more than just the Scottish youth of a man who would eventually become celebrated in the United States. This document illuminates the power of words during an age of revolutions. Grant and Ogilvie wrote it to show off their linguistic chest-puffing, but along the way they demonstrated their ambitions using the syntax they learned from their college classes: ambition robed in the language of Greek heroes, the panache of Roman orators, and the slashing wit of early eighteenth-century British poets. Neither of these teens came from privilege, and both knew their opportunities after graduation were limited. Learning to speak and write with eloquent power could raise their chances. Their educations taught them to dream of displaying their talents and rising to positions of public importance, all on the basis of their power with words. *The Ogilviad* is only sixteen pages long, but it opens up a larger world of the marriage between eloquence and ambition.

> A Poem now presents itself to view,
> Replete with many wonders strange and true;
> Ye critics, stare not, nor with partial eye
> View the prowess of *great* Ogilvie.

These lines by Grigor Grant opened the poem and set its tone and could easily be mistaken as serious. But the italics referring to "*great* Ogilvie" were intended to signal sarcasm, not admiration. Although the title seems to invoke Homer's epic, actually the two boys mimicked Alexander Pope's mock-heroic poem, *The Dunciad* (1728–1743, or song of the Dunce), a classic of literary satire well known to readers of the day. Pope wrote the poem to attack his critics, characterizing them as a confederacy of dunces and hacks who worshipped the goddess Dullness and sought to flood the nation with stupidity and tastelessness. *The Dunciad* proved wildly influential, prompting more than two hundred imitators over the decades who used titles ending with -*iad* and deployed withering mockery to goad their enemies and establish themselves as talented wits. The vogue even crossed the Atlantic, leading to a *Jeffersoniad* in 1801 and two *Hamiltoniads*, both published in 1804, among others. When these two boys published their *Ogilviad*, none of their readers would have missed the debt to Pope's poem.[2]

In the hands of an author like Pope, the weapon of poetic satire could be merciless as it poked at the foibles of his critics. This kind of poem positions readers as potential allies: it seeks to persuade them to join the author in laughing at

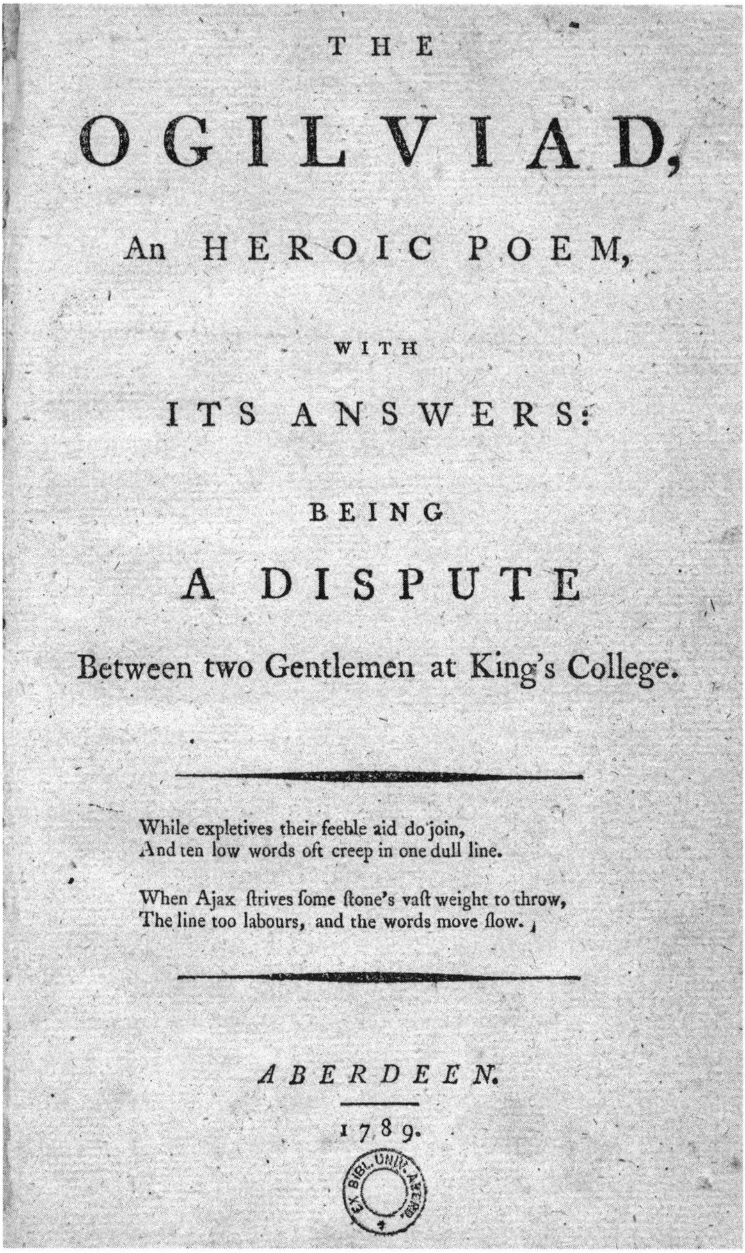

THE
OGILVIAD,

An HEROIC POEM,

WITH

ITS ANSWERS:

BEING

A DISPUTE

Between two Gentlemen at King's College.

While expletives their feeble aid do join,
And ten low words oft creep in one dull line.

When Ajax ſtrives ſome ſtone's vaſt weight to throw,
The line too labours, and the words move ſlow.

ABERDEEN.

1789.

Figure 5. Title page of [Grigor Grant and James Ogilvie], The Ogilviad,
an Heroic Poem . . . (Aberdeen, U.K., 1789). The witty lines quoted here come from
Alexander Pope's Essay on Criticism (1711) so that, in case a reader missed the title's
homage to Pope's Dunciad (1728–1743), they'd be reminded. Courtesy of the Special
Collections Centre, Sir Duncan Rice Library, University of Aberdeen

a target by showing off the author's humorous, linguistic dexterity. Achieving that goal could be tricky. After all, if you seek to convince readers that the object of fun is a vulgar dunce, you need to avoid any indication that you, too, might be tasteless or foolish; it requires a careful balance of pitch-perfect humor lest readers start to feel sympathy for the target. The job becomes even more difficult if the poem features two authors trying to duke it out for superiority. As Ogilvie and Grant took turns throwing punches in the course of The Ogilviad, neither exactly triumphed in the end. Grant got the chance to start the poem, but Ogilvie got the last word. Who was the hero, and who was the dunce?[3]

Grant's opening lines established the tone as mock heroism, setting up Ogilvie as a Don Quixote-like comical figure who foolishly believed he was the hero. "Without delay great Ogilvie did stride / Within the College wall, elate with pride, / To all that met him he the feat did tell / Of that important day the battle fell." After a little more than a printed page of Grant's verse, Ogilvie offered an answer of about the same length. Ultimately, each wrote three sections of attack of roughly equal length. Throughout, they charged each other of being scoundrels and poor poets. Even as they accused each other of plagiarism, both lifted phrases liberally from the poetry they studied in their college classes and most of all from Alexander Pope himself. Ogilvie charged Grant of being a coward who showed himself "unequal for the fight"; Grant retaliated by describing Ogilvie as a "pseudo-poet" who lived inside a "dirty den." As The Ogilviad moved back and forth between the two authors, both boys sought to land effective blows—barbs that might win applause from their classmates, likely the most important witnesses to the battle.[4]

If boys hurling insults at one another can appear a timeless practice, the fight displayed in The Ogilviad very much illustrates a specific moment in time and the power of words for college boys.

Start with the insults themselves and what they reveal about an eighteenth-century culture of honor among gentlemen. *Liar, scoundrel,* or *coward* (as well as *puppy,* another insult levied several times in The Ogilviad, likening a man to a dog): these were fighting words, capable of causing deep, even unforgivable offense between men. Terms like these humiliated a man in the eyes of others. They hacked away at his position in society, his manliness, his gentility. Men did not hurl such words at another without understanding that consequences would follow: a challenge, a demand for a public apology, even a duel with pistols, for the only way to resuscitate one's reputation after being offended was to stand up manfully and demand retraction. In the United States, for example, when Alexander Hamilton accused James Monroe of being a liar, Monroe called Hamilton a scoundrel, and the challenges ratcheted up from there. "I will meet you like a Gentleman," Hamilton followed, showing he was man enough to address the challenge; "get your pistols," Monroe replied. After several tense weeks of negotiations, they resolved their differences without meeting on the dueling ground, each believing his reputation had survived intact—a resolution achieved largely through delicate mediation by Monroe's friend, Aaron Burr, who would kill Hamilton in a duel of their own several years later. Most affairs of honor between gentlemen likewise ended without bloodshed, but within this culture men could feel they had regained their honor only by showing themselves willing to stand up to the insults. When Ogilvie and Grant engaged in a war of words, they played at being adults, trying on the attitudes and manners of the men they wanted to become. In many ways, The Ogilviad represented a rehearsal for manhood in which the boys learned the power of insults and the appropriate manly behavior in response.[5]

When Grant and Ogilvie delivered their insults via the medium of poetic mockery, they added another layer to their attempts at one-upmanship: a command of language, a facility for deploying words and arguments that could reveal their social polish and advanced educations. To win this fight clearly required displaying linguistic panache. Ogilvie took his turn in their poetic battle by writing:

> Ignoble coward, I've read thy jingling verse,
> Which vainly strives a combat to rehearse;
> Yourself, ev'n conscious of inferior fame,
> Sent forth your empty rhymes without a name,
> Attack'd your foe beneath the gloom of night,
> And shew'd yourself unequal for the fight.

It was bad enough for Grant to offer up these verses anonymously (and what could be more cowardly than anonymity?); Ogilvie also charged him with writing "jingling verse" and "empty rhymes," all indicative of his "inferior fame." Just as they adopted masculine stances in fending off insults like *coward* and *puppy*, they sought to show off their superior knowledge, humor, and poetic eloquence, all in the hope of winning in the court of the opinion of their friends.[6]

An eighteenth-century college education sought to teach a gift for speech backed up by knowledge, and the gentlemanly bearing that accompanied both. Boys arrived in Aberdeen having learned from their tutors or grammar schools a solid grounding in Latin and at least an introduction to Greek, but they had just begun to learn to carry themselves like men accustomed to respect from others. In addition to the classics, geography, rhetoric, mathematics, natural history, logic, and metaphysics they learned at King's College, boys needed to learn politeness and civility, qualities that would mark them as distinct from uneducated Scots.[7]

Figure 6. A South East View of Kings College, Old Aberdeen 1785. Watercolor. *The college sat about a mile up the road from the thriving city center of Aberdeen, an area still called Old Aberdeen. Courtesy of the Special Collections Centre, Sir Duncan Rice Library, University of Aberdeen*

Scottish college students learned in no uncertain terms that they needed to perfect their command of the English language in both writing and speech to distinguish themselves as intellectual equals to their English neighbors to the south. This message came explicitly from their professors. In an era when many rural Scottish people still spoke the Scots language—the language that the Scottish poet Robert Burns was just beginning to romanticize in his poetry and in songs like *Auld Lang Syne* during the 1780s—college dons saw nothing romantic about it. For them and for other educated members of the literary elite, Scots was improper, uncouth, even barbaric. To these figures, dropping Scoticisms into one's speech, like to say *isnae* instead of *isn't*, or *do you ken* instead of *do you know*, identified you as someone who insisted on clinging to crude markers of the untaught and the provincial. One of the most renowned Aberdeen professors of the day, James Beattie, worried that eliminating those words posed a nearly impossible task. He lamented that no education in the English language could teach Scots to attain "a perfect purity of English style. We may avoid gross improprieties, and vulgar idioms; but we never reach that neatness and vivacity of expression which distinguish the English authors." Even the best Scottish writers,

Beattie believed, "have always something of the stifness and awkwardness of a man handling a sword who has not learned to fence"—and he reluctantly admitted that his own writing suffered. In his courses he urged his students to study English authors in order to improve their command of the written and spoken language. He even handed out lists of some two hundred Scots words that "must be avoided, because they are barbarous, and because to an English ear they are very offensive, and many of them unintelligible," as he explained in a lecture. (And, in fact, James Ogilvie left no evidence that he ever used Scoticisms in his writing or his speech.) Beattie also advised students to try to learn to speak with "the English accent or tone" and as much as possible abandon "what is most disagreeable in his national or provincial accent." How should a Scottish boy learn such an accent? By "conversing with strangers, or with those who speak better than himself."[8]

Beattie particularly held up as a model the elegant language of the early eighteenth-century magazine The Spectator, a periodical so influential that thousands of miles away in the American colonies the teenaged printer's apprentice Benjamin Franklin would use it to teach himself a fluid, authoritative style. Just as Franklin saw the perfection of his writer's skills as one key to a brighter future for a poor boy born in the American provinces, so Scottish college students scrupulously studied their command of English and learned to rid themselves of provincial linguistic habits because their professors assured them they would never win esteem otherwise.[9]

The Ogilviad illustrates boys' seeking respect from their peers through words—and not just any words, but through the epic (and mock-epic) poetry that had such an important place in their educations. Colleges taught boys to admire and emulate great men of the past. From the very beginning of their years at King's College, students scrutinized the speeches of Cicero, the great Roman senator, whose oratory revealed the highest ideals of a man mobilizing his vast stores of knowledge for noble purposes: to steer the Republic forward on the right path. They venerated the model of the righteous orator, the good and admirable man who used convincing arguments and appeals to both reason and emotion rather than sheer power to persuade his fellow citizens in matters of civic importance. In short, they learned how important it was to speak forcefully and well and in all aspects of their manner and speech to display their intellectual accomplishments—perhaps even more so because of the prevailing sense that Scottish college students had something to prove in contrast to their English neighbors.[10]

Perhaps it was that sense of a chip on their shoulder that had led Scottish theorists to become so influential in the eighteenth-century British elocution movement, which sought to transform how people spoke and sought to persuade one another. Elocutionists believed that infusing all forms of public speech with the energy of new forms of presentation would have manifest benefits for the public at large. Dynamic ministers would attract and retain parishioners, exciting their religious convictions; well-spoken businessmen and shopkeepers could be more successful in their enterprises with the ability to win clients and sell goods; eloquent political figures could pick up the mantle of classical oratorical heroes like Cicero as they deployed reason and persuasion in their speeches or debates. Scottish college professors from Adam Smith to David Hume published important works on the subject of eloquence and taught their students to perform their recitations with animation and emotion. It didn't hurt to have a good voice. Another King's College student recalled that, "having a good ear and a sonorous voice, I was esteemed the best reciter in our class" for lessons that required students to recite poetry by British greats like John Milton and James Thomson (and decidedly not the Scots romantic, Robert Burns). The elocution movement ultimately swept through British education at all levels and was swiftly adopted by American educators, becoming fundamental to schools around the Anglo-Atlantic world by the time Ogilvie entered school. It inspired poor boys like him to imagine they could lift themselves up from obscurity, using the powers of their knowledge, a strong voice, and an ability to move the feelings and change the minds of their listeners.[11]

Elocution thus played an important role in encouraging youth in the late eighteenth century to believe they could advance themselves in life by displaying their merit. Scottish elocutionists knew that everyone needed the ability to speak well, even if they didn't aim for a profession that privileged formal public speech. Farmers would gain an advantage in selling their crops if they knew something of the arts of persuasion. Poorer girls and boys learned they could appear more respectable on the marriage market if they carried themselves well and spoke in ways that signaled intelligence. Even before the rise of narratives of self-made men and inspirational rags-to-riches autobiographies, and despite cultural assumptions about Scottish inferiority in contrast to the English, Scottish college boys believed that a gift for speech could help them rise in society, no matter how modest their beginnings.

Not that Scottish college students allowed the boys from humble backgrounds to forget their place in a social hierarchy. Studying the soaring eloquence and heroism of classical orators might have encouraged them to improve themselves, but, as one of the scholarship students, James Ogilvie lived in a college culture highly attuned to the differences in wealth and status among boys.

Grigor Grant didn't just mock Ogilvie's intellect in The Ogilviad; he also made fun of his clothes. "The hero's dress I'll now describe, / But not by any means deride," he began with a big wink to their readers, for he saw here an easy way to get a laugh:

> With sky blue ribbons decking both his knees,
> He proudly struts with unaffected ease.
> The tiny buttons his green coat adorn
> That by his sires in former times was worn.
> The coat itself was bought at second hand,
> And half a crown was the immense demand;
> The boots an ornament to him not mean,
> Their fiftieth year, I'm confident, have seen.
> From sire to son preserv'd with reverend care,
> They now adorn great Ogilvie the bear.

What was worst: the fifty-year-old boots, the coat with at least two previous owners, or the "sky blue ribbons" decorating the knees of his breeches? Even his red college gown couldn't conceal the riot of outdated color underneath and the lack of family money that these clothes represented.[12]

Ogilvie's father and grandfathers on both sides had received college educations and served as parish ministers, all in the broader Aberdeenshire region of northeast Scotland, and as such enjoyed much higher levels of education and social status than most of the population. But that wasn't saying much for their salaries at this point in Scottish history. Obtaining a post as a minister in the Church of Scotland guaranteed a man a modest annual living that protected him against the vicissitudes of other common forms of work, making it a perfect profession for men unlikely to inherit much from their families. Whereas farmers stood at the mercy of the weather and businessmen at the mercy of the markets, ministers, like the Reverend John Ogilvie, could trust that their modest income would always appear. Ogilvie's living allowed him and his wife, Margaret Reid, to raise their young family of eleven children, nine of whom survived to adulthood. The size of that annual income varied widely by parish, and was disdained by one contemporary writer as "narrow." On average, Scottish ministers made fifty-two pounds per year in the late eighteenth century, though some earned as little as twenty-five pounds, far below the legal minimum of forty-four pounds. In many parishes the salary had remained the same for a century, despite the rise in the cost of living. In Midmar, where John Ogilvie ministered to the locals for more than fifty years, the pay was better than a schoolmaster's and certainly better than an agricultural laborer's, but still too low to allow him to amass much to pass on to his children. With all those mouths to feed, there was little left to purchase new clothes.[13]

They might not have had much money, but the Reverend Ogilvie nevertheless benefited from high standing in his community. In this unremarkable stretch of Scottish agricultural country about twenty miles west of Aberdeen—Midmar remains such a rural place today that you don't find signs directing you there until you've already arrived—an eminence like Ogilvie stood out from the tenant farmers who made up the majority of his parishioners, and even from some of the landowning gentry. He had earned a reputation as a poet and writer, ultimately publishing eight books of poetry and another eight volumes of sermons and essays. One poetry collection appeared in at least six editions, and his *Day of Judgment: A Poem* (1753) proved appealing enough to get translated into German for a Leipzig edition. Editors frequently selected another of his most popular (and shorter) poems, *An Ode to Melancholy* (1759), for use in anthologies throughout his life and into the nineteenth century. His career as a poet permitted him to travel occasionally to London to visit his publisher and other literary acquaintances. Although few eighteenth-century writers made much money on their published works, Ogilvie's prolific career enhanced his reputation and burnished his role as a minister in a remote hamlet.[14]

In later years, some writers would downplay Reverend Ogilvie's achievements and characterize him as a stereotypically dour Scottish clergyman, the kind of humorless figure who served as the straight man for far snappier wits. One biographer characterized his life as distinctively quiet. "With the exception of the publication of a book and an occasional visit to London, the life of Dr. Ogilvie was marked by hardly any incident." Another often-repeated assessment had it that "he was less luminous than voluminous" as a writer, publishing a great deal that was quickly forgotten. English writers in particular found him an entertaining target for barbs about the Scots. During a dinnertime conversation with the English writer Samuel Johnson, for example, Ogilvie praised Scotland's dramatic Highland landscapes and its "noble wild prospects," prompting Johnson to retort, "Sir, let me tell you, the noblest prospect which a Scotchman sees is the high-road that leads him to England." If English contemporaries saw this as a hilarious jab, it reveals as much about their snobbery as Ogilvie's character.[15]

His sons might not have followed him by becoming clergymen, but listening to their father's weekly sermons familiarized them with the power of the spoken word. One didn't have to be a college student to recognize that, in the eighteenth century, leadership and a facility for public speech often went together. Reverend Ogilvie's social standing in Midmar came in large part because of his enactment of public speech, sermons that carefully explored the wisdom and lessons of biblical verses in ways that resonated with his parishioners. In fact, the scene of his small church with him at the forefront exemplified the organization of social power at the time. Few questioned the authority of the man standing in front of

Figure 7. Midmar Stone Circle. Some of the standing stones in the stone circle where Rev. John Ogilvie had his new church built in Midmar, Scotland, in 1787. Photograph by the author

his congregation speaking to them of faith with his learned understanding of theology, just as they accepted the power of their parliamentary representatives. Those weekly sermons would have undergirded James Ogilvie's growing knowledge of the Greek and Roman orators gleaned from his studies, texts that likewise illustrated the power of public speakers who sought to lead the people.[16]

Reverend Ogilvie made the most of his quiet life in Midmar. When he became fascinated by the ancient circle of standing stones positioned on a hill nearby, he delved into historical research on the people who had lived in the region in prehistoric times, ultimately publishing a long poem, *The Fane of the Druids* (1787). When his congregation expanded in 1787, he insisted they build the new Midmar church next to the stone circle, juxtaposing those inscrutable stones with his neat new Christian building. He also earned enough income from his publications to pay tuition for grammar school and college when one of his sons failed to win a scholarship. Of his six sons who survived to adulthood, five attended college in Aberdeen, following in the footsteps of their father and grandfathers. Higher education was in their blood, even if a life in the church was not; none of the Ogilvie boys became ministers. Not all of them did well in college, either. James's younger brother Walter struggled through his four years, a period when his professors recorded occasional brief notes assessing their students' progress. One professor described one of Walter's classmates as "tolerable"; others were described as "indifferent" or "bad." About Walter, a professor wrote in screechy all caps: "PESSIMUM," or Latin for "THE WORST." (Walter earned his degree nevertheless.)[17]

When it came to providing their children with educations, Scottish parents lacking in wealth like the Ogilvies had one major advantage over those in England or America: an impressive number of scholarships endowed by wealthy Scottish lords smoothed the path to college for talented boys—even those, like Walter Ogilvie, who ultimately disappointed their tutors. For nearly a century, commentators had marveled at the frequency of poorer and middling Scottish children attending grammar schools where they learned Latin. "It has been often said, that the people of Scotland give too many of their children a grammar-school education; and some of our manufacturers have been loud in this complaint: they wish boys rather to be employed in carding, spinning, or picking ropes, till they are fit for harder labour," one writer explained. But this author dismissed those manufacturers' complaints as "mere selfishness," a desire for an underclass of poorly paid, uneducated laborers. "Does not the parent therefore act wisely, if his circumstances permit, when he gives his son such an education as can hurt him in no sphere of life, and may be useful, and even necessary to him in many occupations?"[18]

At a time when only a tiny minority of American college students received scholarships, almost half of Aberdeen's college student populations benefited from these awards. When James Ogilvie arrived at King's College in 1786, sixteen of the thirty-three students in his first-year class were bursars, as they called scholarship students. (Those whose families paid full price for tuition were called libertines.) In some cases, the college awarded the scholarships as a result of a competition among eligible boys. In others, the donor had stipulated from the outset that the funds would support students with particular surnames, boys from indigent or tenant farming families, or students eager to study particular subjects like philosophy or theology. The Redhyth bursary, which James Ogilvie received, had been so well endowed by Walter Ogilvie of Redhyth in 1678 that it supported twenty boys of a range of ages at any given time. First, the funds allowed them to board at a school in Fordyce on the northern coast of Scotland, more than fifty miles from Aberdeen—a grammar school that would teach them Latin and prepare them for the rigors of college life. ("An excellent school" with "a good teacher," another student recalled.) From the age of eight, they spent five years in Fordyce before moving to Aberdeen to enter college at the age of thirteen. The Redhyth bursary specifically benefited talented boys who were "poor and such as are not able to be educate by their own Means." It was not, however, wholly based on need or merit; the donor stipulated that it first be offered to boys named Ogilvie on either their father's or mother's side.[19]

Considering that half of Ogilvie's class comprised scholarship students, one might suspect that Scottish colleges fostered a spirit of equality between rich and poor. This was decidedly not true. To be sure, King's College no longer required bursars to wear black gowns to contrast with the libertines' red ones as a "mark of inferiority"; they had ended that practice at least two decades earlier. Still, distinctions between rich and poor appeared everywhere at the college. Libertines had the money to buy themselves new gowns and adorn them with velvet collars. Poor students wore secondhand gowns that fit poorly and were covered with patches "like that of Joseph, of 'many colours,'" as one remembered. Bursars sat at the second table at dinner, where they received meals that paled in comparison with the much better food served to faculty and libertines. Because they resented the way the wealthier students "hold up their heads, and look down on the poor bursars," bursars often elected to retaliate: to "pelt them with snowballs, and treat them with contempt, to shew how little they value these aristocrats." The college, however, reminded them regularly of the differences between the two groups of students. Not only did it levy fines against students in order to maintain discipline (six pence for snowballing, a shilling for damaging the fabric of another student's gown, and half a guinea for carrying a bludgeon and uttering threats), but fines were doubled for scholarship students "because [they] ought to set an Example of good order and Diligence to the rest." Repeat offenders could even lose their bursaries.[20]

The process of obtaining a scholarship, too, could require enacting the role of grateful subordinate before wealthy donors. Bursaries often still remained in the hands of a family heir who selected among the applicants. The earl of Findlater, whose name was also James Ogilvie, had inherited the power to oversee the distribution of the Redhyth scholarship to worthy boys whose fathers wrote to him entreating for favor. One of these letters emphasized pride in the Ogilvie family name as he begged the earl for a spot for his son. "He has the Honour to be of the same name as the Noble Family of Findlater," wrote one of the earl's tenants in 1776. Moreover, this father entreated, after raising several other sons he simply had nothing left to offer this boy except the promise that "he should have something of a tollerable education." When Grigor Grant's uncle, Sir John Grant, requested that his young nephew receive a Redhyth bursary, the earl of Findlater appears to have rejected the request—perhaps because he believed that another titled landowner ought to provide the funds for his own kin. In turn, the earl retained the right to endow each scholarship with a grandiose presentation, which began and ended with elaborate statements regarding his power to act the noble patron. "Having undoubted right to the Patronage of the Mortification and Bursaries founded by the Deceased Walter Ogilvie of Redhyth," he began with a flourish, "do hereby nominate and present to you the principal, Master, and members of the Kings College of Aberdeen." No one who received a bursary would fail to understand the importance of gratitude to men like Findlater for their largesse, nor their relative place in society.[21]

Each of the bursaries came with subsidies to pay for room, books, and board, not to mention fees to pay for exams at the end of each year, but the amounts varied by scholarship. One student might be able to pay for a few extras while another struggled to pay the bare minimum. The cost of fees for classes with the professor of Greek alone was £1 11s. 6d. and represented a serious dent in a student's total scholarship. Another student recalled in his memoir that, even with a limited amount of money to spend, he was still able to buy occasional lollypops from an old woman named Sweety Nell and shuttlecocks for badminton games. He also paid a Highland sergeant for lessons in fighting with the broad sword and still had a little left to pay fines for snowball fights and being late to roll call. Other students had to subsist without luxuries; sometimes the bursary didn't even cover the basics. No scholarship student could afford new clothes without help from home. Moreover, a student could not graduate without paying additional fees, so only about half the entrants of any given class received a degree even when they completed all the coursework.[22]

James Ogilvie's Redhyth bursary covered a bit more than the most parsimonious scholarships, but not enough to cover the many small pleasures enjoyed by the King's College libertines. It was one thing to wear a secondhand green coat and fifty-year-old boots, and another to miss out on all the other pleasures of the city of Aberdeen that he couldn't afford. Compared to the tiny village of Midmar, Aberdeen was an exciting metropolis of more than twenty thousand, an active center for manufacturing, commerce, shipping, shipbuilding, and banking, and featured a second college in the center of the city, Marischal (pronounced *Marshall*). College boys could swarm throughout the city visiting taverns, buying sweets, taking drawing or French classes, and going to dances. Bursars could still wander the streets and admire the prettiest girls leaving their jobs in the stocking mills or milliners' shops. If other boys hired the man they all called Squinting Sandy to clean their shoes, Ogilvie could save six shillings by cleaning his own. Even just buying tea and sugar once a week or supplementing the college's simple dinners with some smoked haddock could add up to a guinea or more. No wonder he didn't buy new clothes.[23]

New clothes would have been prohibitively expensive; even having one's clothes washed cost money. One student estimated that washing alone cost him more than a pound during his year at King's, nearly as much as Ogilvie's full scholarship for the year. When Grant describes Ogilvie living in a "dirty den" (he uses that phrase twice), is he referring to the fact that Ogilvie skimped on this expense? This would not be a surprise, considering that twenty years later Ogilvie would be mocked for wearing distinctively dirty clothes. In an era when no one washed their clothes very often, and when teenaged boys likely had the same capacity to ignore their own stink as they do today, The Ogilviad suggested that Ogilvie stood out. There was nothing he could do about his hand-me-down coat and unfashionable breeches, but perhaps at this point he began to tell himself that, even without wealth, he could distinguish himself among his peers by virtue of his talents instead.

What does an eighteen-year-old do in Scotland with a college degree, a lot of ambition, and few prospects? By the early 1790s, this question felt more urgent than ever because Scotland didn't have much to offer, and opportunities didn't look much better in England. Ogilvie's college rival, Grigor Grant, would enter the church and spend the rest of his days as a clergyman. The poorest and least-educated citizens, particularly from the Highlands, opted to sign contracts to serve as indentured servants: in exchange for the cost of a ticket to America, they promised to provide labor and remain unmarried for a term between four and seven years. Those who could purchase their own passage on a ship often took their chances upon arrival in an American port.[24]

For more than half a century, Scots had emigrated out of the country in favor of the British Caribbean and the American and Canadian mainland. These migrations increased sharply as a result of specific events that made it nearly impossible for thousands of ordinary Scots to earn a living in their country. Scotland had lost its independence as a nation when it became an incorporated part of Great Britain in the Act of Union in 1707, but in the decades afterward some parts of the country continued to resist British rule. The British had tried to replace Catholicism with Protestantism as the state religion, resulting in strong resistance in the Highlands, where Catholicism thrived and Scottish clans remained the primary organization for society. Following a failed violent uprising of the clans in 1745 to restore a Scottish and Catholic monarch to the throne, the British government undertook a determined effort to quell future rebellions and remake Highland society. The government prohibited traditional dress, broke apart landownership and stewardship, and sent Protestant missionaries and English schoolteachers to the hinterlands to assimilate Highlanders to the new regime. The new landowners had often received these lands as a reward for their loyalty to the British crown and began converting large swathes of land from tenant farms to sheep grazing, raising rents precipitously and thus making it harder for poor Scots to earn a living. Desperate, grinding poverty and starvation drove thousands of Highlanders out of the country. One contemporary called it a "rage for emigration." Between 1771 and 1773 alone, more than 28,600 Scots left for the British colonies in America, creating large Scottish settlements in the Carolinas, Pennsylvania, Virginia, and several parts of British Canada. By the turn of the nineteenth century, the out-migration of Scots would increase so much that it provoked a large number of commentators to publish treatises diagnosing the problem and (sometimes) proposing solutions.[25]

As a Lowlander and the son of a long-standing Protestant family, James Ogilvie would have seen little resemblance between himself and the Highland *teuchters* (hicks) who made up about 60 percent of these emigrants, even though his reasons for migrating to the United States resembled theirs. After a couple of years of working as an assistant to a more experienced teacher in England, Ogilvie saw better prospects in the new United States.[26]

He might not have known exactly what he would find when he decided to emigrate to Virginia, but like many other Scots emigrants he had long heard about the experience from relatives who had already made the move. Many chose specific regions because of the encouragement of family members and neighbors who had sent favorable reports home. Ogilvie's uncle James, his father's youngest brother, had immigrated to Virginia in the 1760s and served as an Anglican minister there. Likewise, his cousin Thomas Strachan had moved to the countryside outside Richmond and married into a prominent family, helping to build a mercantile firm there. Both men established connections with a wide range of Virginia elites, including Thomas Jefferson and members of the Randolph family; both married and started families.[27]

Despite those helpful social connections with influential Virginians, uncle James Ogilvie's experience soured during the imperial crisis that led to the start of the American Revolution. By the time the war began, uncle James found himself compelled by his dedication to the Church of England to remain loyal to the crown—a deeply objectionable position in a state that supported independence. Patriots in his Westover Parish on the banks of the James River removed him from his position and kicked him out of the house provided to him by the church. As he remembered it later, "To be deprived of a comfortable residence, and to become in one hour destitute, was a trying and a heavy calamity" made worse by charges of treason against the United States. He returned to Great Britain in 1778, leaving behind his wife and three children. Despite the humiliation and separation from his family, Uncle James insisted that "enduring these distresses" was far preferable "to the sacrifice of his civil and religious principles." Quite a statement, considering that his wife would die on her journey, years later, from Virginia to England. They never saw each other again.[28]

If his uncle had lamented American independence in the 1770s, by the early 1790s James Ogilvie felt very differently about the United States. During his final years in college, Ogilvie had begun to read the inspiring ideas circulated by political radicals on both sides of the Atlantic. With the outbreak of the French Revolution in 1789, those writings had increased and had led many young men of modest backgrounds to imagine profound social and political transformation, and some romanticized the United States as a place of great possibility. What kind of "more perfect Union" would result from the Americans' 1789 ratification of their new constitution, and would it really "secure the Blessings of Liberty" for ordinary people as well as the wealthy? If the actions of some of the poorest people in France could overthrow serfdom and by 1791 establish their own written constitution, what kind of country of, by, and for the people might emerge? From the perspective of an idealistic young Scot, the United States seemed more open than the strongly hierarchical and monarchical society in Great Britain.[29]

Drawn to Virginia by his relatives' reports, Ogilvie had one more reason to try his luck there: Virginia planters loved to hire Scottish schoolteachers and tutors for their children. Even more than in other regions, elites customarily "have all their Tutors, and Schoolmasters from Scotland," as one American-born tutor grumbled, "tho' they begin to be willing to employ their own Countrymen." This preference reflected the Scots' reputation for being adept at Latin, better educated than average English immigrants and American citizens, and familiar with the educational reforms innovated within Scottish colleges. When Ogilvie departed the port of Liverpool for Fredericksburg, Virginia, in 1793, he knew he would find his cousins there well connected enough to assist him in finding work.[30]

Virginia offered an unusually friendly climate to new arrivals. By the 1790s, the state harbored the largest proportion of Scottish immigrants in the nation. The state was exploding with Scottish place-names: Midlothian, Fincastle, Glenmore, Caledonia. The state's governor and Revolutionary hero, Patrick Henry, had named his plantation Scotchtown in honor of his father's Aberdonian youth. Walking down the streets in Alexandria, Richmond, or Fredericksburg, one heard Scottish accents from laborers, artisans, shopkeepers, and elected officeholders. New immigrants to Virginia rarely found success immediately, but prospects for young Scots to find work were as good in this state as anywhere outside British Canada.[31]

After a long passage—transatlantic trips on sailing ships took at least six weeks, and bad weather could stretch them out to three months or more— Ogilvie arrived on the coast of Virginia, but the trip wasn't over yet. Entering the mouth of the Rappahannock River, the ship crept its way another hundred miles upriver to Fredericksburg through brackish water. Along this river voyage, he saw planters' estates perched on the bluffs overlooking the river: grand houses that announced the owners' wealth and standing, circled by tobacco and wheat fields where enslaved women and men of African descent labored. The town of Fredericksburg had a population of less than fifteen hundred, and most of its two hundred houses sat on a single street that paralleled the river. He had left the dynamic port city of Aberdeen for a village about one-thirteenth the size.[32]

Fredericksburg was small, but it offered one key attraction for an idealistic young Scot: a small number of self-identified radicals who shared Ogilvie's interest in democratic politics. To compete with the town's long-standing Federalist-leaning *Virginia Herald* newspaper, an enterprising journalist named Lancelot Mullin established the more radical *Republican Citizen*, which sounded alarms about more conservative political leaders who might be "a friend of monarchic and aristocratic government" and thereby an "enemy to republicanism." "The question is no less than whether monarchy or republicanism shall obtain among us," the author warned. Ogilvie won an attractive position as a teacher at the prestigious Fredericksburg Academy, where he would teach the sons of wealthy planters.[33]

At the age of twenty, James Ogilvie had begun an odyssey, setting aside his days of being the butt of Grigor Grant's jokes and driven forward by his eagerness to make his talent seen. Just a few years after arriving, he would write in a flood of enthusiastic self-promotion that his "mind . . . is uncommonly active: My imagination is restless and ardent and poetical and my passions which turn principally upon a desire to acquire and display talent and information and to become instrumental in promoting the progress of society [is] eager and insatiable." Teaching boys whose families' wealth rivaled that of the wealthiest libertines back at King's College, he roomed in a boardinghouse with a few of his out-of-town students. In his spare time, he read widely to feed his imagination. And, along the way, he found that his ambition became more acute. He didn't yet know what would distinguish him, but he knew that having a talent for public speech could help heighten attention to both his facility for teaching and his interest in American politics. And the more chances he got to speak, the more he liked it.[34]

{ CHAPTER 2 }

"Restless and Ardent and Poetical"

An Ambitious Scottish Schoolteacher in Virginia,

1793–1803

Even at a time when many people in the United States expressed great optimism about education, James Ogilvie's stood out. "There is no pursuit within the reach of man more attractive, no employment of liberty, talents and leisure, better fitted to inspire," he wrote for a newspaper in 1803, "than that of collecting and shedding the concentrated lights of science, on the ingenuous and unprejudiced minds of youth." In concert with others, he believed improving education was crucial to the United States' future. "In a society so auspiciously organized, for the introduction of every useful innovation, the exhibition of every liberal accomplishment, and the practice of every public and private virtue, and at an era too, when every department of science, extensively improved and advancing to farther improvement with [illegible] celerity, furnishes the most abundant and admirable materials for the improvement of juvenile minds." He was not alone in believing that education was vital to the success of the Republic. At the same time that national leaders argued about reforming the nation's financial system, the rise of political parties, and foreign relations with allies and enemies, they also sought means of educating American citizens.[1]

A broad consensus of Americans agreed that the nation required knowledgeable and educated citizens to sustain the nation—to act for the public good rather than private interests. But what did such an education look like? And how to enact it? Ogilvie believed he had solutions. Moreover, he believed his ideas about creating schools suited to a republic might raise him to another level of influence and position, if not wealth. Long before he decided to make his name as an orator, he built a reputation as an exceptional educator by teaching polished speaking skills to his students, tying together self-presentation, ambition, and educational advancement.[2]

Ogilvie's enthusiasm for teaching was inseparable from his own ambition. Both were bound up with his unorthodox political and religious views, which led him to trust simultaneously in the enormous promise of the United States and that it required eager, progressive-minded young men like him. He published frequent, lengthy essays about education in newspapers and pamphlets during these years, making this the most prolific period in his life as a published author. Those writings consistently reflected his trust that his innovative teaching methods and the talented students who graduated from his schools would buttress his reputation and help to transform the United States into a truly modern nation worthy of assuming the mantle of a republic, a republic that improved on the models provided by classical Greece and Rome. He saw the country as an auspicious place for a young man of promise and did what he could to get himself noticed.

Ogilvie arrived in Virginia at the age of twenty as a tall, thin young man, only a year or two older than some of his students. He had embraced the job of teaching despite its notoriously bad pay and low social status; many teachers left the job after a few years to do something—anything—else that promised a better salary or social position. Ogilvie, however, saw it as more than a job. What it lacked in rewards it made up for in the sense of historic and political consequence. Education in America promised to bring about a new and more promising future, for his students and himself.

A typical day of teaching lasted as long as a farmer's. It began at seven in the morning, listening to the younger and less experienced boys (usually from the ages of eight to eleven) recite lessons in geography, grammar, geometry, and other subjects. After a pause for breakfast, as Ogilvie recalled in his memoir, he delivered a lecture to the advanced students (aged about eleven to fifteen, although some were as old as twenty) on subjects that included ethics, rhetoric, natural philosophy, and political economy. He then listened to the younger boys translate from the Greek and Latin classics. Even just in those hours, he remembered, "his voice, temper, faculties and feelings, were exercised intensely and often painfully, and without intermission." He might take a short break before lunch, but, immediately afterward, he reassembled the students and during the course of the afternoon oversaw their studies in an impressive range of topics: Egyptian, Greek, and Roman theology and mythology; Latin and Greek languages; logic, philosophy, poetry, elocution, mathematics, philology, metaphysics, government, criticism, and "the principles of Literature and Taste." He taught all subjects at all levels, from introductory to advanced. After a light supper, he advised some of the students for "an hour or two" of exercises in rhetoric and elocution lasting until at least six or seven at night.[3]

He usually served as his school's only teacher. There were exceptions: he briefly ran a school in Tappahannock with a talented recent graduate as a co-teacher, and on occasion he hired tutors to teach specialty subjects like advanced mathematics and French. But most of the time he juggled between thirty and fifty boys of all ages, often to prepare them for college, finding ways to keep all of them moving forward, trying to squelch the fights and the pranks, the yawns and the grumbles. Throughout, he had to please the school's elite board of overseers, as well as the parents who paid tuition.[4]

His efforts paid off. From the outset, he received high praise for his unusual ability to inspire his students. After less than a year in his first job in Fredericksburg, the academy's president commended him in the local paper for the "extraordinary progress of the students," who displayed more "fervent zeal" under Ogilvie's supervision than they had shown before. In their reminiscences about him, former students often referred to his infectious enthusiasm for ideas. "As a teacher, he was in many respects unrivalled," one wrote. "He wished to serve them by arousing and enlightening their minds." Another recalled that "he managed with consummate skill to fashion the minds" of his students. "Before I entered the Academy I was an idle, listless boy, fonder of every thing by far than mental labor.... Ogilvie inspired me with new desires. He touched some sympathetic chord which instantly responded, and from that moment I felt that there was a divine spark in the human mind, at least in mine, which might be fanned into a flame." Ogilvie had a knack for one of the trickiest elements of teaching: his students learned to find delight in ideas. He inspired them to want to learn and to raise themselves to his high standards, perhaps akin to the ways his father had inspired his parishioners from the pulpit to strengthen and renew their faith.[5]

In some teachers' hands, the Greek and Roman classics could be tedious, but Ogilvie transformed those subjects into vivid models for ambition and intellectual enthusiasm. Contemporaries viewed those languages and literatures as a fundamental grounding for all education and especially vital for a boy's advanced education, as that literature instilled the values of civic responsibility and the importance of leadership. Classical humanism formed a foundation for all education in this period and infused the American imagination and landscape at the turn of the eighteenth century. Americans quite simply thought "of, through, and with the classics," as one commentator described it. Alongside teaching the core texts of Christianity, classicism represented the most important part of an education beyond the most rudimentary basics of learning to read, write, and cipher. Considering how thoroughly American education shed this preoccupation during the twentieth century makes it all the more difficult to recapture a world in which such large numbers of people regularly recognized turns of phrase or arguments from classical orations or lines from Virgil or Cicero quoted in a magazine article. When James Madison, Alexander Hamilton, and John Jay wrote newspaper essays called "The Federalist" under the collective pseudonym "Publius" to defend the new Federal Constitution during the ratification period in 1787–1788, readers with even a smattering of education would have understood that they used that Latinate name to proclaim their dedication to the public. To help his students prepare for college and for life beyond as educated citizens, Ogilvie taught classical subjects extensively.[6]

But he also began to broadcast new teaching innovations after two years of highly praised work in the classroom, changes that made the classics only one part of the advanced education he provided his male students. He explained that these improvements marked his school as uniquely suited to the United States and taught lessons that would make them exemplary citizens in a modern republic. Overemphasizing classical texts, he suggested, distracted students from the needs of the present world. "Those necromantic delusions of grandeur and power, those refined descriptions of sensual fruition and indulgence" dating from a culture with different values might make for thrilling reading, but they failed to motivate boys to become virtuous leaders willing to fight for the rights of Americans as a whole. To abandon a classical education would have been unthinkable. Still, Ogilvie's schools always focused on a larger goal: directing students to develop ideas of their own about everything they read and teaching them to express those ideas with utmost effectiveness.[7]

He was most proud of his innovation in shifting the onus from memorization to urging students to polish the reasoning behind their ideas. He delivered lectures oriented around a series of eight to twelve questions, after which he left the room so students could set about answering each question. After gathering back together to explore their answers, "and any doubts, difficulties or objections which may have occurred are attentively and impartially considered," he directed each student to summarize the most significant parts of the lecture in essays that Ogilvie marked extensively to eliminate "improprieties, inaccuracies or inelegancies."[8]

All American schools shared the core mission of teaching American girls and boys the elocutionary skills they required to speak well: the Young Ladies' Academy of Philadelphia, the New York African Free School, dame and reading schools that taught elementary skills, the Cherokee mission school in Creek Path, Alabama, and every place in between. In each, students memorized and recited passages from their schoolbooks and practiced delivering them with the proper combination of good pronunciation, self-control, expressive physical gesture, and spoken inflection that conveyed the ideas and emotions of the passage at hand. These lessons in recitation achieved two goals at once: by memorizing the material, children absorbed information on the topics they studied; and, by having to recite aloud what they'd learned, they learned to modulate their voices, expressions, and physical bearing. Teachers bore a responsibility not just for the subjects they taught but also for instilling habits of refined self-presentation in their students. And, if daily classroom practice wasn't enough, students also displayed those skills at least twice a year at school exhibitions, which brought large public audiences to observe them deliver speeches, poetry, compositions, and short theatrical scenes. By the time Ogilvie arrived in the United States in 1793, elocution had become ubiquitous.[9]

Elocution played an even more prominent role in Ogilvie's teaching than it did in other American classrooms because he believed experience in effective public speaking would prepare his wealthy boys for leadership positions. Learning to hold themselves in a manner that conveyed authority and to speak in ways that might command attention appeared necessary components of the education of elite men in Virginia. In addition to studying oratory and rhetoric and performing daily recitations, his students composed their own speeches on subjects of their choice, thus displaying their grasp of a subject, their talent for composition, and erudition. To give them ample opportunities to display their talents, Ogilvie placed advertisements in local newspapers to drum up large audiences for their performances, often listing each orator's name and the title of the speech. One boy might deliver a speech "deducing from the nature of mind, and illustrating, from the history of man, the necessary connection that subsists between knowledge and happiness, ignorance and misery," while a classmate spoke on "how far the study of the Greek and Latin languages is necessary." These performances gave boys an opportunity for oratorical glory, a chance to stand before their fellow townspeople as men-in-the-making, with original ideas and gentlemanly bearing that demonstrated their talent and promise. He also urged his students to form debating societies to further practice their "habits of clear reasoning, distinct and graceful elocution, and persuasive eloquence," talents that would propel them into leadership professions like the law and elected office. For him, eloquence was inextricable from the acquisition of knowledge, a strong memory, and reason—and he felt he had a unique facility for teaching it to youth.[10]

Ogilvie believed he had developed significant improvements to a typical intermediate education and didn't hesitate to proclaim it. During his first teaching job in Fredericksburg in the mid-1790s, he wrote lengthy accounts of his ideas for the local papers and sent a letter to Thomas Jefferson, one of the state's most important eminences. "I flatter myself that I am in the right road" to reforming education, he explained, inviting Jefferson to come witness those innovations in his students' performances. (Jefferson politely declined.) When Ogilvie started a new school in Tappahannock a few years later, he sent descriptions of its rigorous academic standards to newspapers as far away as Philadelphia. He published a learned pamphlet describing his philosophy of education in 1801. And his enthusiasm spread to his students' fathers and mothers. "I have just received an invitation from Mr. Ogilvie to attend the exhibition of the 4th of July" at which "orations will be delivered by fourteen of the students," one mother wrote to another about their sons, expressing her hope that they would shine as "con-

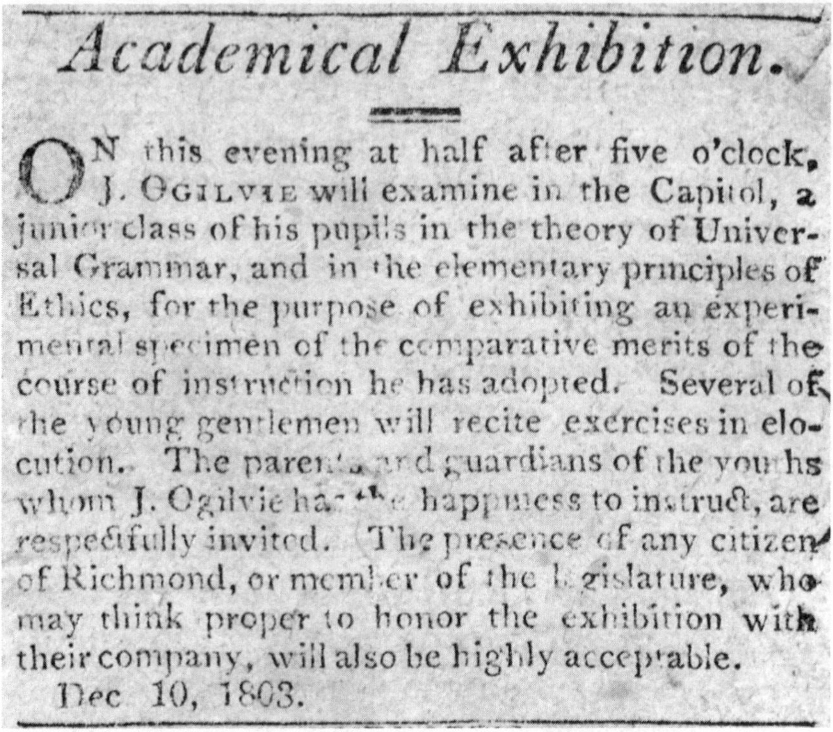

Academical Exhibition.

ON this evening at half after five o'clock, J. OGILVIE will examine in the Capitol, a junior class of his pupils in the theory of Universal Grammar, and in the elementary principles of Ethics, for the purpose of exhibiting an experimental specimen of the comparative merits of the course of instruction he has adopted. Several of the young gentlemen will recite exercises in elocution. The parents and guardians of the youths whom J. Ogilvie has the happiness to instruct, are respectfully invited. The presence of any citizen of Richmond, or member of the Legislature, who may think proper to honor the exhibition with their company, will also be highly acceptable.
Dec 10, 1803.

Figure 8. "Academical Exhibition." From Virginia Argus (Richmond), Dec. 10, 1803, [2]. An advertisement for one of Ogilvie's student exhibitions before the public, which took place in the magnificent State Capitol, designed to evoke a classical Roman temple. What better place to display his students' talents in public speech and their promise for the future? Courtesy of the Special Collections Research Center, William & Mary Libraries, Williamsburg, Va.

spicuous figure[s]." Throughout, Ogilvie urged members of the public—as well as members of the state legislature—to attend his school's quarterly exhibitions, where they could witness the impressive progress his students had made using his methods. In at least one case, a student left the College of William and Mary to attend Ogilvie's school instead.[11]

Publishing frequent self-promotions worked. Ogilvie became known as an exceptional educator in Virginia, the kind of teacher recommended to young men with ambitions. One such young man eager to become a lawyer agonized to his uncle in a letter about his father's refusal to pay the tuition necessary to send him to Ogilvie's school. "The time at which it would have been proper for me to have gone to Mr. Ogilvie has now elapsed," he lamented. "It would now be out of my power to join any of his classes, and they are too far advanced to admit a hope that I should be enabled to overtake them." This boy couldn't imagine finding a less expensive school so well suited to provide him the academic training he needed. His cousin had thrived under Ogilvie's tutelage, writing ecstatic letters home about the training in public speaking he received. "The method of instruction hear is so compendious, facilitated and attractive" that for the first time he truly experienced the thrill of knowledge. Being expected to deliver regular lectures demonstrating what he was learning "not only imprints them deeper but are imparting to me a facility and fluency of language which I am sensible I could not otherwise attain." Moreover, the pressure to compete with his fellow students taught him that it was "a point of honor" to display greater "self command" while speaking. With letters like these circulating among elite Virginia families, Ogilvie solidified his reputation.[12]

At the same time, however, he also became known for harboring unconventional political opinions, views that periodically got him into trouble. Few argued with his central aim of adapting education to produce better American citizens for a republic. But it's one thing to want to raise a generation of good citizens and something else entirely to suggest that the nation's future might require a completely new vision of politics and society.

Ogilvie joined a large group of thinkers around the country in arguing that the United States required education suited to its unique politics. Considering the new "form of government we have assumed," wrote Benjamin Rush, the renowned Philadelphia doctor, signer of the Declaration of Independence, and social reformer, "it becomes us ... to adapt our modes of teaching to the peculiar form of our government." In Virginia, Thomas Jefferson proposed extensive programs for public education as early as 1779. Those proposals languished unrealized, in part because no one wanted to foot the bill and in part because no one could find a way to create viable neighborhood schools in a rural state like Virginia where most residents lived far away from one another. Political and economic obstacles to the realization of such programs didn't stop people from insisting on the importance of education.[13]

But in order to lay out such plans, one needed to reveal one's own views of what the future of the nation might look like, views that might clash with competing political or partisan visions. In his enthusiasm to opine on that subject, Ogilvie didn't hold back in revealing radical political ideas—and, at times, obnoxious disdain for people who disagreed with him.

His strong opinions about the ties between education and politics linked him to other idealists at the radical republican end of the political spectrum. He believed "that light and liberty ought to go together; and that to support our fine form of government, as well as to adorn human nature itself in the best manner, it was necessary to disseminate a taste for knowledge," as one student recalled from his days at Ogilvie's school in the 1790s. Like other republican idealists of the era, he held several key beliefs—beliefs that stemmed from a deep hopefulness about political and social change made possible by the political upheavals of the era and that offered new opportunities for ordinary people to shape their society. If most Americans rejected monarchy as an antiquated political form, the populace diverged over the question of elite power in society. Enthusiastic republicans like Ogilvie condemned it as aristocracy. "Republicanism," Ogilvie wrote in a gush of enthusiasm, "disentangles man from that labyrinth of . . . entrenchments of rank that inoculate and dissever society in countrys where monarchy prevails and opens a free channel to that stream of intercourse and communion from which so much of the improvement and felicity of mankind springs." He believed that the democratic ideals of equality and liberty held incredible potential to benefit humanity. And, finally, like a standard-bearer for the Enlightenment, he believed that citizens should cultivate their capacity for reason not only to understand the world but also to scrutinize the actions of their elected representatives, weigh carefully the various options for political action, and serve their communities.[14]

If none of these ideas sound particularly alarming today, in the 1790s his emphasis on the centrality of ordinary people posed an implicit challenge to elites who had long enjoyed a relatively unquestioned control to shape politics and society. Radicals challenged class power and argued that it was unsuited to an age of reason and a new era of political possibility. Along the way, Ogilvie used the term citizen liberally. He was a citizen in the literal sense, thanks to a Virginia law that permitted new immigrants to declare an oath of fidelity and become naturalized quickly after arrival; but his radical politics also led him to embrace a more figurative use of the word. "Citizen implies the right to think, and the right to think implies an analysis of governmental doctrines and measures," one republican newspaper explained. Thus, when Ogilvie published articles in the newspaper addressed to "Fellow-Citizens," signed his letters "Your affectionate fellow Citizen," or described himself as both a foreigner and an American citizen, he avowed not just a form of American patriotism but also a dedication to political ideals that linked him to a wider transatlantic radical politics. Small towns throughout the country like Fredericksburg increasingly featured newspapers like Lancelot Mullin's Republican Citizen that competed with more conservative Federalist papers and helped to forge communities of like-minded souls. Radicals like Ogilvie and Mullin formed one part of a spectrum of people who gravitated toward the new Republican political party and complained that Federalists like John Adams and Alexander Hamilton enacted policies designed to benefit the wealthy rather than all Americans.[15]

In fact, the very word *citizen* took on new meaning in the United States with the efflorescence of the French Revolution, which ended feudalism, declared all citizens to be equal, and abolished monarchical rule starting in 1789. As the French Revolution continued into the early 1790s, it grew in popularity among many Americans, who celebrated Bastille Day on July 14 in larger numbers than they did the Fourth of July in part because they felt that the French were continuing a tradition of progressive political transformation that the American Revolution had started. One of Ogilvie's Virginia contemporaries, William Wirt, recalled thirty years later how thrilling he had found those celebrations. "Even at this moment my blood runs cold, my breast swells, my temples throb, and I find myself catching my breath, when I recall the ecstasy with which I used to join in that glorious apostrophe to Liberty in the Marseilles Hymn, 'O Liberty! Can man resign thee, once having felt thy gen'rous flame!'" Wirt and other citizens of a wider democratic movement in the early 1790s found the changes in France a hopeful sign of human progress. "O, how we used to hang over them, to devour them, to weep and sing, and pray over these more than human exertions and victories! And how were the names of those heroes of Liberty, 'in our flowing cups, freshly remembered,' and celebrated almost to idolatry!" Wirt continued. Especially during its early years, the French Revolution seemed a harbinger of a new future for liberty and equality.[16]

If young men like Wirt and Ogilvie dreamed of such a future, others decidedly did not, particularly as the French Revolution became increasingly radical and news began to circulate of the Terror in late 1793, the start of a long period of violence most famous for the executions of aristocrats and the royal family. Many Americans began to wonder whether anti-aristocratic rhetoric might pose dangers to the young United States as well. Francophiles and self-described republicans thus grew more defensive over time as they found themselves caught between their optimistic views of the future and news from France that made their political views appear suspicious in America.[17]

Ogilvie and most other self-described radicals of the era did not extend their politics to include enslaved people. In fact, Ogilvie's writings barely acknowledge the presence of black women and men who made up about 40 percent of the Virginia population—96 percent of whom remained enslaved—even though their prevalence in Virginia marked such a striking contrast to the Scotland of Ogilvie's youth. Instead, he advocated for the rights of white men, writing about "the most important duties of a freeman" and "the rights of a freeman" in a republic. He also became an advocate of female education, though he did not teach classes of girls until much later. In these respects, Ogilvie resembled the majority of Britons and Americans who could argue so passionately for equal rights, citizenship, and democracy, yet refrain from inveighing against slavery or racism. They included the British writer William Godwin, Ogilvie's hero and the husband of women's rights pioneer Mary Wollstonecraft. Godwin's writings about the drastic contrast between liberty and slavery included the statement, "It is perhaps right to suffer the negroes in the West Indies to continue in slavery, till they can be gradually prepared for a state of liberty."[18]

Indeed, for the young Ogilvie, now in his early twenties, nothing proved more influential than reading Godwin's *Enquiry concerning Political Justice* (1793), a book that had inspired radicals and romantics throughout the wider Atlantic world. This expansive text brought together a wide range of topics into a single political vision. Godwin believed in human perfectibility: looking at moral and intellectual progress over the long span of human history, "the political, as well as the intellectual state of man, may be presumed to be in a course of progressive improvement." He brought together ideas about literature, government, education, luxury, the rights of man, the duties and rights of citizens, and many other subjects in a tour de force of philosophical inquiry. Ogilvie was riveted by the possibilities it suggested for improving the new United States and wrote Godwin to describe his philosophy of teaching. When Godwin replied, Ogilvie published the letter in a Washington, D.C., newspaper. He sought to bring the principles of *Political Justice* into his teaching methods and used parts of the book itself in his classroom. Godwin was an atheist, however, which made Ogilvie's use of the book with his students worrisome to parents and other observers.[19]

Even worse: Ogilvie himself had begun to confess in conversations with students and friends that, as a man dedicated to reason, he could not believe in God. Atheism placed Ogilvie and Godwin in the same group of anti-Christians as the decade's most notorious political radical, Thomas Paine. Paine had become a hero during the early years of the American Revolution with his bold, clear argument for independence in *Common Sense* (1776). During the 1790s, however, his advocacy of the French Revolution in *Rights of Man* (1791) and his growing attacks on Christianity had made him a champion of radicals but a pariah among moderate Americans. In particular, his assertion that Christianity was simply irrational led many Americans to condemn him. "Of all the systems of religion that ever were invented, there is none more derogatory to the Almighty, more unedifying to man, more repugnant to reason, and more contradictory in itself, than this thing called Christianity," Paine wrote in his *Age of Reason* (1794–1795). If that book seemed outrageous to Christians in Virginia, it was altogether worse to have an atheist and proponent of Paineite-style politics installed as the professor of humanity at the Fredericksburg Academy. Even years later, Virginians recalled Ogilvie's use of *Political Justice* in the classroom with horror.[20]

Paine advocated for deism, not atheism, but, for most Christians, the distinction between those two positions was less important than the divide between them and Christianity. Yes, deists adhered to an understanding of a creator while atheists rejected it, but the deists' God bore little resemblance to the God of the Bible—and especially not the New Testament. Deism was not a version of Christianity; it was an outright rejection of it.

Eighteenth-century deists and atheists both denounced Christianity because they thought it asked believers to abandon their sense of reason. Deists felt that God had created human reason so that humans would use it. To them, the Bible's many tales of miracles—the parting of the waters of the Red Sea, the virgin birth, transforming water into wine, rising from the dead—all were akin to fairy stories asking Christians to believe in magic. Thomas Jefferson believed so fervently that the Bible could be purged of its reliance on supernatural stories that he took a pair of scissors to his copy: he excised every passage that referred to the miraculous, even cutting some verses mid-sentence. Taking the (edited) gospels of Matthew, Mark, Luke, and John, Jefferson reorganized their tales into a single chronological narrative that he glued to the page. This new narrative portrayed Jesus of Nazareth as a transformative moral leader, not a faith healer, and certainly not the virgin-born son of God. Deists like Jefferson admired Jesus's ideas but rejected the notion that he was divine—and therefore they opposed the very foundation of Christianity. No wonder their parents expressed such alarm when Ogilvie told his students that he regretted not being able to believe in God.[21]

Back in college, Ogilvie had fought a duel in poetry to defend his honor. As an adult, when he found his beliefs challenged, he lashed out in print against his critics. In 1795, an anonymous letter writer for Fredericksburg's *Virginia Herald* criticized him for immodestly proclaiming to have invented a new system of education and dismissed those writings as "the pedantic puffings of a simple individual, gaping at popularity, and fondly hoping to immortalize his name." Ogilvie responded with a counteraccusation, accusing this writer of an "incurable and abortive malignity which for the sake of momentary gratification forfeits, without hesitation, every claim to integrity and truth." The conflict between the two men in the pages of the newspaper grew so heated, with Ogilvie accusing him of "mental imbecility," that eventually the newspaper's editor had to intervene to prevent a literal duel with pistols between the two men—with the editor issuing a pronouncement that the two men had publicly resolved their affair of honor.[22]

This behavior won him no fans among Fredericksburg Academy's benefactors, who ultimately fired him. Ogilvie admitted a few years later that he had displayed "improprietys and imprudence" in the affair and that "the political opinions which I have expressed" and "the ardour with which I vindicate and propagate my opinions," as well as "my well-known and implacable abhorrence of all sorts of superstition from the most solemn down to the most light," had all contributed to a damaged public reputation. Still, he insisted that he had been "betray'd at Fredericksburg" by political enemies.[23]

His acknowledgment of his own imprudence didn't stop him from lashing out again a few years later when a different anonymous letter writer complained about his giving lectures in the Virginia State Capitol building in Richmond on Sundays, calling those performances a "gross and open . . . profanation of the Sabbath day." Ogilvie responded by submitting two separate responses to local newspapers. The first, a polite, signed letter appearing in the Federalist *Virginia Gazette*, promised that if his critic "will assign any good reason why it is improper to deliver lectures on morality on Sunday afternoon, I will cheerfully alter the day." Ogilvie's second, anonymous letter appeared in one of the city's Republican papers and accused the critic of self-righteous hypocrisy. "When a stranger comes into the city, whose mental accomplishments [assign?] him a distinguished place in society, there are not wanting *soothsayers* in abundance, to foretell to a tittle, his incapacity to promote moral or intellectual happiness," he ranted in a long letter to the editor. Accusing this critic of fearmongering in response to his effort to "promote good sense and information," he also charged him with digging up old gossip that "Mr. Ogilvie was an Atheist, a reviler of the Christian doctrine, and the climax of every species of infidelity!" Fellow deists and atheists might have enjoyed his screed, but for those who guessed Ogilvie had authored it the letter confirmed his reputation for being bombastic.[24]

The sense of alarm at Ogilvie's atheism haunted him. When he later traveled the country as a celebrity orator, rumors about his early days in Virginia would circulate alongside his advertisements, raising questions about his character even when he studiously avoided the topic of religion. One friend would report more than a decade later about "a general, unspecific ki[nd of?] rumour operating against him, about the bad tendency of his principles; what is meant, I could never ascertain; but I suspect he must have been, in the warmth of youthful research, too unguarded in his religious expressions."[25]

Why didn't his atheism destroy his teaching career from the outset, especially after he was fired in Fredericksburg? His ability to bounce back from that experience suggests that his success as a teacher, particularly with the sons of some of Virginia's elites, simply outweighed objections from the most fastidious Christians. It might also indicate that, however vocal the religious opposition, those critics never represented a meaningful majority. Whatever the reason, it set a pattern in his life, for this would not be the last time Ogilvie faced controversy and potential humiliation only to outlast it and continue to thrive.[26]

Ogilvie's political and religious positions were inextricable from his ambitious teaching. When he inculcated reason, logic, and science and rejected what he saw as blind adherence to the dogma of older generations and institutions, he tied his educational innovations to a political vision of the future of the nation and its citizens. And when he moved to the burgeoning city of Richmond to take charge of a brand-new academy in the state capital, he found new opportunities to showcase other talents, too.

If you were an ambitious young man in Virginia in 1803, you would have wanted to move to Richmond. Compared to the tiny villages of Fredericksburg, Tappahannock, and Stevensburg, where his first three schools had been located, Richmond was a metropolis, with six thousand residents—soon to be the biggest city in the state. It had served as the state capital since the middle of the Revolutionary War, when Williamsburg seemed far too close to the ocean to remain safe from British attack. By the time Ogilvie got there to take the prestigious job as the head of the new Richmond Academy, the city had exploded from its colonial days as a tobacco trading center of only three hundred residents. As a result, nearly all of its buildings were new—and the city had doubled in population in the previous ten years alone. It was full of young men just like Ogilvie: lawyers, merchants, and political figures eager to make a name for themselves. It was a young man's town.[27]

The city advertised itself from the moment visitors approached as they followed the road along the James River. You couldn't miss the "grandeur of the scenery": "its immense Capitol, towering above the Town on a lofty eminence, with its antique appearance," and a view of the penitentiary under construction, just upriver from downtown. Thomas Jefferson's grand Capitol building, which imitated the design of a Roman temple in France, declared the state's post-Revolutionary faith in a new form of American leadership akin to the noblest republicans of the classical world. The penitentiary likewise sought to inspire rather than terrify. Its design and execution were intended, at least during its earliest years, to reflect enlightened new ideas about criminals' repentance rather than warn outsiders of the punishments taking place within.[28]

Richmond was also full of urban pleasures, even as much of the city was still under construction. It had a library, a Masonic hall, and four newspapers; Haymarket Gardens hosted Fourth of July dinners, dances, masquerade parties, and circuses. One could buy hot chocolate at Mrs. Gilbert's Coffee House and apples from Fat Nancy and have one's rotten teeth pulled by a free man named

Figure 9. View of the City of Richmond from the Bank of the James River. By Benjamin Henry Latrobe. Watercolor, 1798. Courtesy of the Maryland Historical Society, 1960-108-1-3-34

Peter Hawkins, the "Tooth-Drawer," "a tall, raw-boned, very black negro, who rode a raw-boned, black horse; for his practice was too extensive to be managed on foot," as one resident recalled. The new downtown rising up around the neoclassical Capitol building featured a smattering of grand new Federal style homes, taverns for out-of-town legislators, countinghouses, and mercantile businesses—all appearing on streets that remained unpaved, many of them unnamed. (It would take decades before the city assigned street addresses to buildings.) Meanwhile, one ambitious entrepreneur had set to work building a toll bridge across the James River—nearly a third of a mile long—to connect the city with the village of Manchester on the other side. When the state legislature was in session, the city's inns and taverns swelled so much with legislators and visitors that their owners crammed as many beds as possible into their few rooms. One traveler described his uncomfortable Richmond tavern as nevertheless offering a mixture of society he hadn't seen elsewhere in the United States. "Generals, Colonels, Captains, Senators, Assemblymen, Judges, Doctors, Clerks, and crowds of Gentlemen, of every weight and calibre and every hue of dress, sat all together about the fire, drinking, smoking, singing, and talking ribaldry." It was a boom town—full of men with ideas and young men who wanted to prove themselves.[29]

Figure 10. View of Richmond from South Side of James River, Showing Capitol, from Bushrod Washington's Island. By Benjamin Henry Latrobe. Watercolor, 1798. Courtesy of the Maryland Historical Society, 1960-108-1-1-36

Here Ogilvie found a cohort of like-minded friends eager to demonstrate their talents on the page. Some of these were former students. Thomas Ritchie ran a bookstore and was on the cusp of taking over publication of the city's Republican newspaper; others served in the state government or worked as lawyers and businessmen in town. Within six months of moving to the city, he accepted a request to deliver that year's Fourth of July address to the city's Republicans, a speech that called on its listeners to "cultivate independence of mind, the love of truth, scepticism and incessant enquiry, for unless these qualities are cultivated, the reign of error must be eternal." (The speech also called on listeners to consider many other things: judging by its length as published in the paper, it must have taken more than an hour and a half to deliver.) By the following year, Ogilvie had established a group of men who called themselves the Rainbow Association, who joined "a whole mass of talents in Virginia" writing for Ritchie's new *Enquirer*, which "contains more original matter than any other publication of the sort I have ever seen." The members of the Rainbow Association published "essays after the manner of the Spectator," essays they also issued as a standalone pamphlet they titled *The Rainbow* (1804).[30]

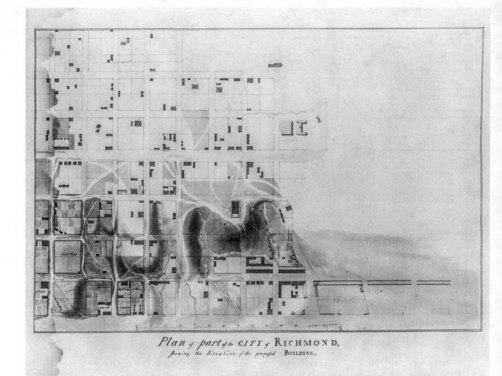

Plan of part of the CITY of RICHMOND,
showing the Situation of the proposed BUILDING.

Figure 11. Plan of Richmond on Shockoe Hill near the Capitol Building. By Benjamin Henry
Latrobe. 1798. This drawing shows the sparse number of buildings yet erected in what would
eventually become the city's bustling downtown. Courtesy of the Library of Congress

Looking at his literary activity during these years in Richmond—all achieved
at the same time that he continued teaching for twelve hours every day—Ogilvie
seems to have felt a manic energy. Most ambitious of all was his plan, only two
months after his move to Richmond, to establish a lecture series to encourage
discussion of civic issues important to society. In a grandiose announcement in
the local papers, Ogilvie explained that "there is probably no source of amusement and instruction more rational and attractive than public discourses on
interesting subjects, when composed and pronounced with tolerable ability and
eloquence." Every other Saturday he delivered lectures in the State Capitol building on "moral, political and literary" subjects, including happiness, education,
dueling, the progress of society, and freedom of the press. He sold subscription
tickets for the first twelve projected lectures for half a guinea and tickets to occasional visitors for two shillings per talk.[31]

Within a couple of weeks of his initial announcement, Ogilvie was delivering
talks to eager audiences. "Too much cannot be said in praise of a plan till now

unattempted in this country; a plan which promises the highest improvement in elocution, the science of all others most desirable in popular governments," his friend at the Richmond *Examiner* effused. By the end of October 1803 he had delivered the first twelve talks, and by the following March he concluded the series with a speech commemorating the anniversary of Thomas Jefferson's inauguration as president. "Mr. Ogilvie acquitted himself in a masterly manner, in enumerating the historic events, on this subject, and in a style unusually nervous, candid, and eloquent," explained a report that circulated as far away as Washington, D.C. He even obtained letters of support from Jefferson and James Madison when he applied for the presidency of the brand-new South Carolina College being built in Columbia, which would later be renamed the University of South Carolina. He did not get the job—it went to an experienced educator who had already served as president of two prominent American colleges—but Ogilvie's application indicates the kinds of ambitions he harbored.[32]

When Ogilvie arrived in Richmond, his long days of teaching were beginning to catch up with him. Only after twelve hours in the classroom could he return to his room in the school's boardinghouse and have the chance to "'think for himself'"—to write orations and essays for the paper. Those writings fed his "restless and ardent and poetical" imagination and polished his talents in ways that would raise his reputation and help him, as he put it, "become instrumental in promoting the progress of society."[33]

How does one survive those long, difficult days giving out to others? Ogilvie explained quite frankly that two things allowed him to survive this period of his life, and one of them was opium.

CHAPTER 3

Ogilvie and Opium, a Love Story,

1803–1809

Long days of teaching, continual efforts to enhance his reputation, periodic opposition to his political ideas and his atheism—it was hard to sustain this work over the years. By the time he arrived in Richmond, he had been teaching for twelve years (in Virginia for ten) and had arrived at the age of thirty. "There is a disheartening and monotonous drudgery" in teaching, James Ogilvie wrote in his memoir, that "fatally saps his constitution, benumbs his faculties, and converts the fuel of enthusiasm, into the cold ashes of apathy, or into the lurid smoke of life-loathing melancholy." How did he survive those difficult days, when he spent all his time giving out to others? Two things: first, a "heart-felt and elevating consciousness" of the "dignity and usefulness" of teaching and, second, "excessive use of opium." The very fact that he confessed so openly to his "excessive" habit illuminates a world that saw all the health benefits of opium and rarely dwelled on the worrying side effects. Only later in life would Ogilvie come to lament its allure.[1]

He admitted to his use of opium so freely because the society in which he lived had only the slightest idea about its addictive qualities. Sources almost never used the word *addiction* in this manner; it doesn't appear at all in Samuel Johnson's definitive eighteenth-century dictionary, nor in most American dictionaries before 1820. Instead, when he alluded to the trouble he ultimately developed with the drug, Ogilvie described it as an "infatuation." He was not the only one; the physician Benjamin Rush referred to one of his patients having an "*Attachment to Laudanum.*" It's worth pausing to think about the ways these words liken a habitual relationship to opium to a love story, for we might say that Americans had fallen in love with opium, which seemed to be a wonder drug integral to treatment for pain and conditions associated with tuberculosis, dysentery, and other dangerous diseases. Ogilvie would ultimately have to confront on his own the darker side of his habitual use. During this brief honeymoon with opium, Americans encountered almost no public discussion of chronic use, as if it did not exist.[2]

Seeing Ogilvie and the early United States in which he lived through their shared preoccupation with opium reveals only the slightest glimmers of the concerns that would gradually emerge about the drug's habit-forming qualities. It's not merely that opium was cheap and available over the counter to anyone.

Opium answered specific needs for a wide range of Americans during the early Republic. Not until the 1860s would physicians begin to collect data on heavy use. Even in 1888, when the renowned physician Oliver Wendell Holmes railed against the overuse of certain drugs, he made an exception for opium, which "the Creator himself seems to prescribe." Understanding Ogilvie's infatuation with the drug requires setting aside stereotypes about opioid use and stepping into a world that saw opium as a medical godsend—and where it was not always used for medical reasons alone.[3]

When Ogilvie took opium, he drank it. Contemporaries referred to habitual users as "opium eaters," but it's more accurate to think of them as opium drinkers, for they usually imbibed it as a tincture, made liquid with wine or other substances. That mix of opium and alcohol differed in both power and effect from the opiates used later in the century, for people at the time used raw opium, the gummy, partially dried juice of white poppy flower seed heads. Raw opium was rolled into balls in Turkey and India, where it was grown, and wrapped in leaves for shipping overseas. Although scientists had already isolated the active ingredient in opium—morphine—they had not yet transformed it into highly effective and more habit-forming drugs; raw opium became the basis for all opiates.[4]

It would be decades before other forms of opium became available. Smoking opium, so famous from portrayals of seedy dens and moral decay in Victorian novels, would not come to the United States until perhaps the 1840s. Intravenous injection was almost unheard-of, not least because the hollow syringe was not invented until the 1850s (and heroin in the 1890s). Instead, Ogilvie purchased vials of a product called laudanum, made by carving an ounce or two off a ball of raw opium and simmering it with wine and spices like cinnamon, nutmeg, and cloves until it became condensed and viscous. He administered it by droplets into a glass of water or wine, which diluted and disguised the opium's bitter taste. Laudanum's seventeenth-century inventor gave it a name that derives from the same Latin root as the word *laudable*: praiseworthy or admirable, which indicates how much contemporaries loved it for its unique medical abilities to cure pain and ease some of the symptoms associated with the era's most common diseases.[5]

Imagine a world that otherwise lacked pain relief. Migraine? Suffer. Need to have a tooth removed? Have some whiskey. A broken bone or dislocated shoulder? Bite down on a wooden spoon while the doctor resets it. Perhaps nothing more thoroughly transformed the experience of everyday life than the advent of cheap and mostly safe means of pain relief in the twentieth century, such that it has become almost impossible for us to conjure what it must have been like to live without them. To discover that opium might ease the often slow, miserable march toward death for the elderly, relax the anxiety of a child recovering from an animal bite, or give someone with back pain the ability to sleep at night—these all seemed miraculous in the eighteenth century. One household medical guide explained that "opium is the most wonderful and divine medicine known to mankind; no irritation, no spasm, no pain, it will not relieve; it cheers the spirits, procures sleep, and promotes perspiration and sweat." Ogilvie probably started taking the drug to combat the pain he still suffered from the rheumatic fever he experienced as a child. This disease, which often began with a throat infection that contemporaries called scarlet fever, could lead to chronic conditions: painful joints and irreparable damage to the heart. Opium eased the rheumatic joint pain Ogilvie felt throughout his life. And he wasn't alone. The vast majority of nineteenth-century Americans would have taken laudanum for one reason or another in their lifetimes. Opium was the most widely used drug in the United States.[6]

In addition to relieving pain, laudanum had an exceptional ability to suppress coughing and diarrhea, two problems that made serious illnesses worse. Lung diseases, especially consumption (tuberculosis), ravaged populations. In the early nineteenth century, doctors in France and England blamed consumption for a quarter of the deaths in their countries. Opium couldn't cure it, but it helped to control the persistent cough of sufferers, which could break ribs, damage throat tissue, rupture the diaphragm, cause hernia, and, most commonly, provoke blood from the lungs. Discovering a medicine that suppressed the cough seemed to represent the first stage in finding a cure for the underlying disease. In the same manner, opium helped with dysentery, cholera, and other gastrointestinal diseases that caused frequent diarrhea, for it hardened the feces. Laudanum could not cure dysentery any more than it could cure tuberculosis, but by resolving diarrhea it could help the sick retain enough liquids and nutrients from their food to stay alive. Dealing with persistent constipation, one of opium's most notorious side effects, was a trade-off many users were willing to accept.

Beyond opium's established medical uses, popular medical writing went further in touting its possible applications, raising it to the level of a cure-all. In everything from home health guides to newspaper articles, a wide range of writers claimed that laudanum could cure everything from sore eyes to the bites of rabid dogs. Mothers learned from these guides to treat colicky or teething babies with laudanum; they also used it themselves for menstrual and postpartum pain. In some cases, writers recommended that laudanum be applied to the skin in topical salves or as a suppository. Owners of horses might find that they could cure the bots (an equine disease) by mixing laudanum into their animals' feed; British farmers regularly fed it to cattle as well. Household medical

To prevent the fatal Effects *of* drinking cold Water, *or* cold Liquors *of any Kind* in warm Weather.

1st. Avoid drinking whilst you are warm, or,

2d. Drink only a small quantity at once, and let it remain a short time in your mouth before you swallow it; or,

3d. Wash your hands and face, and rinse your mouth with cold water before you drink. If these precautions have been neglected, and the disorder incident to drinking cold water hath been produced, the first, and in most instances, the only remedy to be administered, is sixty drops of liquid laudanum in spirit and water, or warm drink of any kind.

If this should fail of giving relief, the same quantity may be given twenty minutes afterwards.

When laudanum cannot be obtained, rum and water, or warm water should be given. Vomits and bleeding should not be used without consulting a physician.

Figure 12. "To prevent the *fatal Effects* . . ." From Poulson's American Daily Advertiser (Philadelphia), Aug. 8, 1805, [2]. This newspaper story explained that opium could treat the dangerous condition of drinking too much cold water. Courtesy of the American Antiquarian Society, Worcester, Mass.

guidebooks recommended it as a crucial part of a family's medicine chest, and local druggists recorded selling laudanum specifically to customers seeking to stock their home cabinets.[7]

Between the proven and more fantastical applications of the drug, it's easy to see why Americans became so enamored. Even more so because it was so easily procured. Like all other medicines at the time, opium went utterly unregulated during the early Republic. One might buy laudanum from a grocer or merchant often as easily as from a doctor or druggist. Sometimes local printers sold it from their offices at the same time that they printed the newspapers or household medical guides that advised people how to use it. In Richmond, Ogilvie could buy it from his landlord, a druggist who supplemented his income by investing in a growing list of rental properties in the city.[8]

When Ogilvie bought a vial of laudanum, he would have had no way of knowing the strength of the blend. The morphine content of raw opium varied widely. Turkish traders graded opium in carats, just as one measured the quality of gold and diamonds; twenty-four carats was pure, which meant the smallest percentage of particulates and other impurities. Anecdotally, Americans found Turkish opium significantly stronger than that from India (and correspondingly more expensive). But by the time the product came through the British merchants who controlled the trade, arrived in American markets, and was processed into laudanum, few consumers would have known the quality of the opium used nor the intensity of the brew. When a newspaper advertisement claimed that a merchant provided pure opium, did this mean sixteen carats, twenty, or twenty-four? Sellers might not have known. In addition, recipes for laudanum varied widely on both the amount of opium added and the degree to which the brew should be condensed. Variations between recipes and the quality of the opium turned dosage into guesswork.[9]

Compounding the problem of its unpredictable strength was the fact that doctors used the vaguest imaginable recommendations for dosages. One medical guide suggested "from ten to fifty drops" but also noted that "it may be given to very great quantities: I have given it to the number of four hundred drops, and much more in two or three hours, and never found it do harm." Moreover, patients accustomed to using laudanum found they needed more to achieve the desired effects. Someone who took it periodically for headaches or as a sleep aid might find it shocking to realize how little should be given to someone unused to the drug. Consumers simply increased the dosage until they felt relief.[10]

With such ambiguity in dosing recommendations, it's unsurprising to find the subject of overdose rising as a public concern. As one writer put it, only a "small quantity of Opium" was "sufficient to produce death in those unaccus-

CHEAP DRUG STORE.

THE subscriber having purchased of Oliver Goodwin his share in the stock of Drugs and Medicines in the store of Goodwin and Clarke, informs the public that he will continue the Druggist Business, by wholesale and retail, at their former stand, no. 143 Pearl-street, where he will sell cheap for cash, and on the usual credit.

5ooo lb Cream Tartar	5oo lb Ivory Black
6ooo lb Red Bark	1oo lb Gum Ammonia
5ooo lb Pale Bark	2oo lb Isinglass
25 lb Ipecacuanna	5oo lb Lapis Calamanati
2oo lb Cantharides	6o doz. Castor Oil
6oo lb Opium Turkey	1oo lb Oil Lavender
1ooo lb Manna Flake	1oo lb Ess. Bergamot
1ooo lb Manna Com	1oo lb Ess. Lemons
5oo lb Liquorice Ball	5oo lb Gentian Root
?ooo lb Liquorice Root	1ooo lb Verdigrease
2oo lb Myrrh	1oo lb Russian Blue
2oo lb Asafoetida	5oo lb Patent Yellow
25oo lb Aloes	1oo lb Sugar of Lead
1oo lb Gambouge	2oo lb White Vitriol

And shop Furniture, with a general assortment of Genuine and Patent Medicines, Surgeon's Instruments, &c. &c.

The greatest attention will be paid to putting up Family Prescriptions. Medicine Chests for Shipping, with directions for their use, containing the method of cure for the usual disorders of seamen, and the treatment of gun shot wounds. The utmost attention will be paid to sell none but Genuine Medicine of the first quality, and on the lowest terms.

march 17   PETER CLARK.

Figure 13. "Cheap Drug Store." From Commercial Advertiser (New York), Jan. 1, 1803, [4]. Note that this druggist has six hundred pounds of Turkish opium available. Many commentators believed that Turkish opium was superior in quality and purity to Indian opium. Courtesy of the American Antiquarian Society, Worcester, Mass.

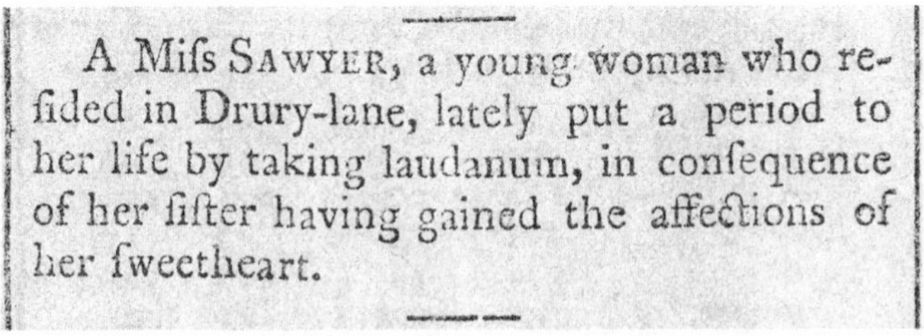

> A Mifs SAWYER, a young woman who re-
> fided in Drury-lane, lately put a period to
> her life by taking laudanum, in confequence
> of her fifter having gained the affections of
> her fweetheart.

Figure 14. "A Miss SAWYER . . ." From Eastern Argus (Portland), Apr. 13, 1804, [4].
*A representative account of a suicide by laudanum, which emphasizes that blame be placed on
the faithless lover. Courtesy of the American Antiquarian Society, Worcester, Mass.*

tomed to its use." Someone suffering from extreme pain might start with a small
dose but double it before feeling the drug's effects. Untreated, an overdose could
slow one's breathing and heart rate to dangerously low levels. Doctors experi-
mented with antidotes to overdose and published their results, recommending
the ingestion of coffee or lime juice to induce vomiting and raise one's heartbeat
back to normal. Even as these experts acknowledged that opium was poisonous
in large quantities, no one suggested its availability should be regulated.[11]

Nor did frequent newspaper stories about suicides via laudanum overdose
lead to calls for regulation—stories almost as frequent as tales about its wonderful curative qualities. Some of these stories were so dramatic that newspapers
up and down the East Coast reprinted them. When a "lady of *amiable qualifications*"
killed herself in New York via overdose, the story circulated throughout the nation. No one suggested that opium itself was the problem. Instead, writers emphasized that she had been deceived by her sweetheart. "May the wretch who was
the cause of the above deed suffer all the tortures of a *guilty conscience*," one paper
admonished. Writers were no more likely to blame laudanum for these deaths
than they were to blame rope for suicides by hanging. Instead, they sought to
place blame where it was due: the unfaithful lover. In 1819, when the British Parliament considered a bill to label all laudanum as poison, the news circulated
widely in the United States, perhaps in part because Congress had made no similar efforts.[12]

Opium's ability to relieve pain and calm some of the symptoms of the era's
worst diseases made it vital to early American medicine. To appreciate the way
Americans fell in love with it as a panacea requires seeing how much it stood
alone as a pain reliever. But it had other uses as well. Some of the same medical
writing that touted the drug often also sang its praises as a stimulant superior to
alcohol and tobacco. In other words, when Ogilvie explained that it had helped
him survive his hardest years of teaching, he didn't mean that he had used it as

an escape. Rather, he found that laudanum sharpened his mind and energized his intellect.

If later opiates tended to sedate their users, laudanum seemed to medical experts of the day to have more complex effects, both stimulating and sedative. As a sedative, it produced a luxurious sense of languor, relieving anxiety and allowing its users to sleep. But others used it rather as a stimulant, the kind of substance one might take in small doses before attending a party to ensure that one had color in one's cheeks, a sparkle in one's eyes, and a facility for charming conversation. "Its first and most common effect is to excite the intellect, stimulate the imagination, and exalt the feelings into a state of great activity and buoyancy, producing unusual vivacity and brilliancy in conversation," one doctor wrote. Medical professionals discussed this duality of stimulation and sedation as varying by user and in different doses. One medical school thesis likened opium to alcohol and tobacco. "Do they produce vigour of body, and chearfulness of mind?—So does opium. Do they excite passion and emotion?—So does opium. Do they induce watchfulness, dissipate sadness, and inspire resolution?—So does opium. Do they, under certain circumstances, induce sleep?—So does opium." This writer went on to offer anecdotal evidence of a surgeon dosing himself with laudanum before "performing an operation of any importance." Another thesis described a doctor taking thirty drops of laudanum to energize himself for studying late at night. Ogilvie explained that it allowed him to spend "four or five hours, in examining and comparing the speculations of the deepest thinkers, on the most important subjects" rather than simply collapsing at the end of a twelve-hour day of teaching. Laudanum's energizing effects on some people seemed to make it appear directly comparable to alcohol and tobacco, and this likewise confounded an easy distinction between sedative and stimulant.[13]

Nor did laudanum provide unfocused, nervous energy akin to too much caffeine. For individuals like Ogilvie who put great stock in their intellectual capacities, it had special appeal for providing mental clarity. Its ability to produce intellectual transcendence drew a wide range of writers and poets gradually into heavy use. The British writer and habitué Thomas De Quincey argued that the pleasure of opium was wholly superior to that of alcohol, which "disorders the mental faculties" and "unsettles and clouds the judgement." In contrast, opium brought "the most exquisite order, legislation, and harmony" to the mind and "communicates serenity and equipoise to all the faculties, active or passive." Laudanum permitted the user to believe "that the divine part of his nature is paramount; that is, the moral affections are in a state of cloudless serenity, and over all is the great light of the majestic intellect." Another habitual user told Benjamin Rush that, although he wanted to curb his use of the drug, it had a wide range of wonderful effects: "his intellects were more brilliant, his language more eloquent, and his talent for writing more easy." No wonder it became so popular with Romantic poets such as Lord Byron and Samuel Taylor Coleridge, with surgeons and medical students, as well as with Ogilvie: it gave them a sense of control over thoughts that otherwise ran rampant and disappeared, like smoke, into the air.[14]

Perhaps the most famous effect of the drug on figures like Byron and Coleridge was its tendency to produce light sleep with fantastic, euphoric dreams. Coleridge's vivid, phantasmagoric poems *Kubla Khan* (1797) and *Rime of the Ancient Mariner* (1797–1798) emerged in part from the opium dreams of their author. But not all users found themselves dreaming in poetry. De Quincey believed opium merely accentuated one's usual thoughts. "If a man 'whose talk is of oxen' should become an opium-eater, the probability is that (if he is not too dull to dream at all) he will dream about oxen," he wrote with undisguised arrogance. In De Quincey's own case, "the Opium-eater boasteth himself to be a philosopher."[15]

Ogilvie never described his opium dreams, but, like De Quincey, he wrote repeatedly of his desire to achieve fame as a philosopher. Many passages in his writing contain the elaborate, rhetorical curlicues and description that appear in laudanum-influenced literature of the day, such that it's impossible to know whether his inspiration came from the juice of the poppy or the writings of the laudanum-taking Romantics he admired. Almost immediately after discussing his use of opium in his 1816 memoir, for example, he waxes eloquent in a romantic vein about his simmering ambition. "Vainly indeed would he attempt to paint, (in the liveliest and most brilliant colours which language can supply,) the delightful prospects that opened, (burst! let him rather say,) on the view of sanguine enthusiasm and generous ambition." Ambition, verbal dexterity, the ability to revive after a long day of teaching, and the promise of mental clarity and philosophic order: laudanum must have appeared an ideal ally. Where did Ogilvie's need for pain relief end and his reliance on it as an effective stimulant begin?[16]

Opium's most common use lay in its ability to relieve pain. Most of those who formed an "attachment" to it did so after using it for medical reasons. But suggestive evidence indicates that some used it socially or as the nineteenth-century equivalent of a study drug. With its capacity to energize and crystallize one's thoughts, it could be an ideal partner for an ambitious young man. At the turn of the nineteenth century, some three decades before Henry Clay would coin the phrase "self-made man," men like Ogilvie lacking money or family status saw opportunities to advance themselves if only they made their talents known. In doing so, they emulated Benjamin Franklin's rags-to-riches story that had begun circulating in the United States: the story of a savvy, ambitious man who knew both how to work hard and to ensure that people *saw* him hard at it. James

Ogilvie believed his chances lay in his writing, public speaking, and other intellectual work; laudanum gave him the ability to do it.[17]

As he later explained hyperbolically, the drug helped him escape the drudgery
of teaching, as well as "insanity and suicide: He survived." But along the way,
"health, equanimity, and steady intellectual energy, were irretrievably sacri-
ficed." Ogilvie was not the only one to find that his "infatuation" with opium
had a dark side. It's tempting to wonder how he and his contemporaries could
have failed to notice its habit-forming qualities or fret about the agonies some
users experienced trying to wean themselves off it. Yet few Americans worried
about compulsive consumption of alcohol either. The parallels between how they
viewed the two substances and the effects of habitual use make a useful gauge
for understanding an early American Republic before the spread of the idea of
addiction.[18]

Contemporaneous discussions about the abuse of alcohol offer a useful comparison, for virtually no one at the time could have imagined calling for regulating
or restricting alcohol. Even more than opium, alcohol was considered by most
women and men to be fundamental to daily life. "Liquor at that time was used
as commonly as the food we ate," one man explained plainly of his youth. Their
preference for alcohol partly reflected the fact that the water in many regions was
foul; only by transforming it into alcohol could the water be made safe to drink.[19]

Americans of all ages usually began their day at breakfast with low-alcohol
small beer (usually between 0.8 and 2.8 percent alcohol by volume); adults
moved on to drams of much higher-proof rum or whiskey (closer to 40 percent)
as the day progressed. Meanwhile, a healthy market for beverages imported from
Europe included wine (12–15 percent), fortified wines like sherry and port (these
added a distilled alcohol like brandy as a preservative; approximately 16–20 percent), and brandy (made by distilling wine; 35–40 percent). Alcohol was served
at every meal, and laborers expected their employers to provide it on their breaks
between meals as well.[20]

If consumption of small beer and wine had a long history, the availability of
cheap, high-proof distilled liquors had radically ratcheted up alcohol intake during the eighteenth century. Britons and Americans had started drinking increasing amounts of rum as the expanding sugar plantations in the Caribbean sought
a use for their excess of molasses, a thick, syrupy by-product from the process
of making sugar. Distilling molasses into rum transformed that by-product into
highly marketable merchandise. Later on, grain farmers in the western regions
of Pennsylvania and Virginia found it more profitable to distill their crops into
whiskey than to pay exorbitant transportation expenses to move their crops
to market. By the early nineteenth century, Americans consumed nearly seven

times the amount of alcohol common a century earlier. They drank more alcohol than at any other point in their history, before or since.[21]

Within such an environment, of course, some noticed the effects on behavior, yet they usually limited their discussions to the problem of drunkenness in public rather than seeing it as a problem resulting inherently from alcohol itself, much less a chronic condition that plagued certain individuals. Rowdy drunken behavior, leaders insisted, ran counter to the ideals of virtuous citizenship. Some states began to levy fines and even jail time on those who disturbed the peace owing to drunkenness. Along the way, some advocated for temperance or abstinence from alcohol as an important practice of self-control. Of these advocates, none was more important than Benjamin Franklin, whose 1791 autobiography described his youthful revulsion against the heavy drinking common to the workplace. "I thought it a detestable Custom," he wrote, and proudly described his decision to drink only water on the job. He also underlined the fact that he persuaded his employer to pay him the money that otherwise would have gone toward his drink, an anecdote that became a part of a larger theme in the *Autobiography* about how much self-control and pecuniary caution contributed to Franklin's later success. His account of his abstinence from alcohol as a young man wasn't necessarily intended as a diatribe against alcohol; rather, it was meant to tout his own exceptional self-discipline and to offer his life as a model to his readers. (Indeed, the older Franklin not only drank alcohol liberally but developed a dependence on laudanum.)[22]

Because temperance advocates demonized overindulgence as a lack of personal control rather than a problem inherent in alcohol itself, contemporaries didn't advance a serious conversation about widespread societal solutions to drink. The same was true for opium, especially because it was less fundamental to daily life for most Americans than alcohol. Thus, comparing the histories of alcohol and opium reveals striking parallels in thinking about how Americans weighed the problem of overindulgence against the perceived social values of these substances. In both cases, they determined that overuse usually represented a personal failing by specific individuals.

People who began taking opium for pain likely had no idea that it could be habit-forming, for even the medical literature offered only glancing information about its addictive qualities. After all, most medical experimentation focused on the drug's effects on specific conditions rather than on long-term use. (Likewise, scientists did not discover delirium tremens—the frightening physical symptoms some experience when withdrawing from drinking alcohol—until 1813.) Yet, when Ogilvie and others took opium for chronic pain, they found that they received diminishing returns from the drug over time, requiring increasing amounts to achieve relief. They also found that, when they tried to scale back their use of laudanum, they experienced excruciating physical pain that could only be relieved by taking more of the drug. To find that one's use of a painkiller could cause as much pain as one's initial condition must have felt like adding insult to injury. Ultimately, it was this quality that led Ogilvie to write regretfully of his "infatuation" with the drug, as if it were a faithless lover.[23]

Printed sources on opium, both scholarly and popular, very occasionally raised the topic of habitual use. When they did, they provided anecdotes about the Turks. According to such anecdotes, the Ottomans saw more opium eaters than elsewhere. One of these rare acknowledgments appeared in an 1803 volume. "Among those who have been in the habit of eating Opium, if they are at any time deprived of the usual dose, they are rendered miserable," the writer explained. To illustrate this problem, he launched into a story about a number of "Turkish, Persian, and Arabian captives" aboard a ship without sufficient opium to satisfy their cravings. One of these captives told the ship's doctor that, "unless you give me and my companions opium, we cannot outlive two days." When the doctor denied him, the captive explained that "the only remedy . . . is, to give each of us a draught of pure wine every morning. Though this is very hard and uneasy to us," for under religious law Muslims abstained from alcohol. This solution worked; by the conclusion of their trip a month later, the doctor reported, they all "neither needed nor desired Opium" and could now safely refuse the wine as well. The anecdote illuminated how much medical writers downgraded the problem of habitual use. When they acknowledged it at all, they suggested that one could kick that habit by simply replacing the opium with wine. If Muslim Turks could quit, this anecdote implied, surely anyone in Christendom could, too.[24]

If print culture generally avoided the topic, rare archival evidence illustrates how some individuals sought to free themselves from chronic use. When George Washington's niece developed a problem in 1812, her husband wrote to Benjamin Rush, the nation's foremost physician, for advice. "Lessen the dose of it gradually until she ceases to take it altogether," Rush suggested. Knowing that the decrease in "the Stimulus of Laudanum upon her System" could result in "weakness" and pain, the doctor recommended that she consume a wide range of tonics, foods, and "sound old wine, or half a pint of porter" to stimulate her heart. Rush concluded his letter with a warning. "Habitual use of opium is often attended with the most serious and distressing consequences. It not only weakens and disorders the body, but it sometimes induces in the mind idiotism and madness." De Quincey, whose heavy use paralleled Ogilvie's almost exactly in time, also gradually decreased his daily use of the drug over time, and notably did not quit entirely. When he published his *Confessions of an English Opium-Eater* in 1821, De Quincey provided the only firsthand account of compulsive and recreational use of the drug, describing "the pains of opium" experienced by those who tried to wean themselves off: insufferable stomach pains "accompanied by intense perspirations" and utter "dejection" of spirits. "Opium had long ceased to found its empire on spells of pleasure," he wrote. "It was solely by the tortures connected with the attempt to abjure it that it kept its hold." If Ogilvie had an infatuation with opium and Rush referred to it as an attachment, De Quincey called it a "fascinating enthrallment."[25]

Ogilvie's infatuation with opium would be similarly double-edged. He believed his love affair with laudanum staved off insanity and the doldrums of teaching, but it would also bring its own unique pains.

While he taught school in Richmond, however, those problems were far in the future. For now, opium helped Ogilvie with the other activities he loved: reading extensively, writing essays and orations, preparing to deliver lectures. Those activities bolstered his confidence and helped him gain repute beyond the classroom. Whether performing at the State Capitol building or writing for the *Enquirer*, these activities brought him into contact with new acquaintances, one of whom was a young woman named Sally.

Opium, you see, was not the only lover competing for the attentions of this young Richmond schoolteacher. He also began romancing a woman. And nothing could more effectively display opium's ubiquity during the early Republic than the fact that we know far more about Ogilvie's use of the drug than his relationship with his wife, their courtship, and their marriage.

In 1803, James Ogilvie was delivering weekly orations to the public, publishing his Fourth of July speech in the paper, beginning to write essays with the other young male members of the Rainbow Association, and teaching for twelve hours a day, often six days a week. This period of his life is exceptionally well documented except for one element: his courtship and marriage. Only about a year after coming to Richmond, Ogilvie married Sally Wilkinson from nearby New Kent, Virginia. We know nothing about how they met, how quickly he proposed, or her educational or family background. Not a single letter survives to display her signature or her handwriting. We can assume they fell in love only because, as we will see, her father disapproved so strongly of the match. To be sure, an exceptional percentage of the documents from this era have been lost. In addition to the usual reasons for the loss of historic documents—building fires, water damage, and later generations who saw old papers as trash—the many Civil War battles and skirmishes that took place in Virginia resulted in widespread damage. Still, the dearth of information about their marriage stands in marked contrast to the number of Ogilvie's writings that do survive, and even the degree to which we know about his opium habit.[26]

Extant documents tell us about the financial struggles that resulted from the marriage. After marrying, Ogilvie moved out of his room in the Richmond Academy's boardinghouse and rented a "large and commodious" home "sufficient for the accommodation of a genteel and numerous family"—a house he could not afford. Almost immediately, he began campaigning for higher pay from his school to meet the couple's expenses. "Until instructors shall receive a pecuniary compensation proportioned to their talents, attainments and services, the education of youth must be abandoned to sciolists [people who pretend to be well informed], pretenders and pedants," he argued in the *Virginia Gazette* about two weeks after the marriage. This article reminded readers of his high standards and excellent results and explained that he had suffered physically and emotionally from years of inadequate compensation. He succeeded: he received permission to raise tuition and boarding fees by about 30 percent each. And, when parents complained about the expense, he defended it vigorously in the local papers. The increased income does not appear to have made up the difference, however, between his income and the young couple's financial needs.[27]

If we know little about Sally and their courtship, we can nevertheless understand this marriage as an important step in the life of an ambitious man. Marriage was the final symbol of adult manhood in this era: a marker that a man had truly arrived, that he had become the head of a household. Husbands bore the responsibility of the household's finances and order, which signaled their maturity and respectability to the rest of the world. Those responsibilities had a basis in law as well as in society. Getting married would have granted him a new degree of social acceptance among his peers, a cachet that would have increased further had he become a father.[28]

Instead, Sally Wilkinson Ogilvie died early in 1805, only about a year after their marriage—and all we know about her death is that it resulted from "sickness." Was it a common illness, like tuberculosis, or complications from pregnancy or childbirth? Something more unusual, like cancer? Not a single letter survives to tell us, except the tantalizing information that her decline was abrupt enough that she and her two doctors had assured Ogilvie that it was safe for him to take a brief trip out of town; she died while he was away. Even more striking: after publishing a long, heartsick eulogy to her in the local paper, Ogilvie never spoke of her again in any of the hundreds of documents that survive today, including his 1816 memoir. Nor did he remarry. Not a single record remaining today indicates that he ever courted another woman.[29]

Rumors circulated after her death that her father had disapproved of the marriage and refused to help them financially. Why he disapproved remains elusive, for all Wilkinson family papers have been lost. Perhaps it came down to familiar-sounding reasons: he simply disliked Ogilvie or believed his low salary and meager job prospects made him a poor match. Or maybe Wilkinson found his political and religious beliefs insufferable, dangerous, and anti-Christian and his behavior unguarded, impulsive. Whatever the reason, within a year of Sally's death Ogilvie found himself with staggering debts amounting to twelve hundred dollars, equivalent to tens of thousands of dollars today—and no way to pay those bills. He escaped debtors' prison only because a group of wealthy friends each donated about one hundred dollars to pay off the full amount without expecting reimbursement.[30]

Was part of the debt the cost of his laudanum? Although none of his specific bills have survived, it's clear that the habit could get expensive. A half-ounce vial cost only twelve or thirteen cents (whereas a day laborer might earn about a dollar per day), but it might only last days for heavy users. One Philadelphia merchant sold it in small amounts several times per week to regular customers, one of whom returned every few days for another half-ounce supply. After five months of frequent laudanum use during the winter of 1800–1801, that customer's total bill had ballooned to $27.54½, or roughly a day laborer's monthly income. If Ogilvie's use continued over the course of several years, those expenses would have compounded his high rent, the cost of hiring a servant, the doctors' bills, and the cost of the funeral.[31]

Relieved of his debts, Ogilvie got more assistance from Thomas Jefferson to escape "the catastrophe of his sufferings" when he offered to establish a school for Ogilvie in 1806 in Milton, only a few miles from Monticello near the village of Charlottesville (which would gain a university in the 1820s). This arrangement proved mutually beneficial for Ogilvie and the president. Long aware of Ogilvie's reputation for unparalleled teaching (and their shared republican politics), Jefferson now gave him charge of the education of his own grandson and namesake, Thomas Jefferson Randolph. Jefferson appears to have relied on him in other respects as well. When his son-in-law got himself into an affair of honor so serious that the two men appeared on the verge of a duel, Jefferson asked Ogilvie—of all people—to persuade Thomas Mann Randolph to resolve the matter with words rather than guns. Ogilvie gained as well. Elite families in the region placed their sons in his school, which revived his reputation and allowed him to recover from his grief. Best of all, Jefferson trusted Ogilvie to borrow books from his splendid library at Monticello, albeit with elaborate instructions for returning each one to its proper place. (Jefferson's generosity might have been unwise. Contemporary letters from others grouse about Ogilvie's habit of borrowing books and being "equally free in lending to every one—and sometimes even to give away Books which were not his own.")[32]

He also resumed giving lectures, this time at Monticello at the request of "the most respectable citizens in its vicinity," who paid by subscription for the pleasure. He and his deistic attendees saw these moral and philosophical talks as a fitting replacement for attending church on Sunday mornings. One visitor marveled at the performance. "He seems to step with as much ease from the Earth to the Clouds, and from thence to stumble about amongst the stars, with the same facility as most other men stump their toes against the common clods of the Earth—My Heavens! he is something, a most luminous body of science and general intelligence," Dr. Charles Everette explained in a letter. "He also has times of visions and of Fancy which peep through the soul of his audience and transports and delights beyond measure." After a particularly skillful performance one weekend when the president was home from Washington visiting his family, Jefferson gave him a gift of a "complete and elegant edition in quarto, of the works of Cicero!" as Ogilvie remembered with effusive appreciation.[33]

After two years of teaching in Milton, Ogilvie found himself at a crossroad by the early months of 1808. On the one hand, his teaching career continued successfully, with students like the president's grandson and other wealthy, well-connected sons of Virginia's elite. "Never, (*surely never!*) was any instructor blessed with pupils, more capable of intellectual improvement, ... or more tractable to affectionate admonition," he later reminisced. On the other hand, nothing much had changed since he had begun teaching fifteen years earlier. His days remained long and enervating, and now his remote, rural location in Albemarle County made him feel farther away from more dynamic politics taking place in the nation's urban centers. His salary was sufficient for a widower, but not enough to amass savings for the future. And then there was the perpetual draw of the laudanum vial, which brought fewer of the clarifying, energizing effects than before. Meanwhile, his "passion for the cultivation and exhibition of oratory, gained strength," as he explained in his memoir.[34]

But to jettison the security of his teaching career in favor of a career as an orator seemed ludicrous. Ogilvie's lectures on subjects like dueling, happiness, and the progress of society looked little like other orations of the day, which tended to be ceremonial (Fourth of July speeches, funeral orations), legal or political (speeches in Congress, in court, or offering ideas for reform), or religious (sermons), all of which people could attend free of charge. Only a few educational lecturers had traveled through the United States' largest cities selling tickets to their presentations, which were often oriented around the discussion of science and natural wonders. Their careers had usually been brief. Audiences had no particular reason to buy tickets to a talk given by a man as unknown as James Ogilvie. When he finally discussed openly the possibility of such a lecture tour, his friends expressed "incredulity and astonishment" to the point that Ogilvie "read in their faces a suspicion, that his mind was deranged." On whether he was deranged, the jury was out.[35]

But Ogilvie had other ideas about a possible lecture tour. Now thirty-five years

old, he had taught school ever since graduating from college at the age of eighteen — nearly half his life — and his essential ambitions remained unfulfilled. He
had come to feel that his talent for public speech matched his skills in the classroom. He might fail, but perhaps it was worth the gamble. Laudanum had allowed him to stay awake late into the night composing and memorizing lectures.
He had already tried out a number of these lectures on his students and Virginia
audiences and believed he had weeded them of controversial material — radical
politics and religious skepticism — that might turn possible auditors away. As a
widower and without dependents, he had a freedom to take risks that husbands
and fathers did not have. Thus, in the spring of 1808, he decided to abandon his
job, leaving behind virtually everyone he knew and what little he owned, in order
to become a traveling orator.

CHAPTER 4

A "Romantic Excursion" to Deliver Oratory,

1808

Years later, when James Ogilvie recalled his decision to become an itinerant lecturer, he employed dramatic flair. With "a prophetic glance," he claimed, he envisioned "all the difficulties to be surmounted; all the good to be done, all the trophies to be won, in the successful execution of so novel and so noble an enterprise." With the benefit of hindsight, he told readers that "from the moment when this idea [of a lecture tour] first crossed his imagination, he felt an assurance not only of ultimate, but of speedy and splendid success" that helped him withstand the cynicism of his friends.[1]

In truth, however, it was a stuttering beginning. When the sixteen-year-old Anne Cary Randolph sent Monticello neighborhood news to her grandfather, Thomas Jefferson, she reported that Ogilvie remained undecided. "Mr. Ogilvie has broken up his school in Milton and does not mean to keep one any where this year but to devote himself to public speaking," she wrote, but in a postscript added that he had changed his mind. Her brother had just returned from visiting his teacher, who had "made a *fresh* determination to continue his school." Two weeks later, her sister reported that Ogilvie had left after all. "He is very much ashamed of the indecision he has shown concerning the breaking up of his school. He first said he would not then that he would then he was uncertain but at last he has gone away." Considering all that Jefferson had done for him, Ogilvie owed him an explanation.[2]

When he wrote to Jefferson several months later, Ogilvie called his tour a "romantic excursion." That distinctive phrase signaled his own mixed feelings, for by that point he could see why such a tour might end with a whimper: his audiences remained small. Calling it "romantic" could encompass both hopes and fears: optimism that his lectures might catch fire in the public's imagination and the awareness of the tour's impracticality. Failure would send him back to the classroom, to obscurity.[3]

Ogilvie faced a series of daunting tasks, none of which was romantic. He had to persuade people to buy his tickets, which weren't cheap, in towns and cities where he was a stranger. He had to compete for audiences with other entertainers who offered less expensive performances that were often more broadly entertaining, such as acrobats, ventriloquists, and exotic animal acts.

His most essential hurdle, however, was convincing people that his form of oratory mattered enough to buy tickets. At their most fundamental, his lectures demonstrated how to think intelligently about important public matters. But he also went further to make a dramatic argument: that Americans needed this style of public speech and public assembly, particularly during an era when the nation felt divided by so many of the issues he explored in his talks. They might not ultimately agree, but they could gather to think together about Ogilvie's topics. In the process, he provided a compelling vision of what oratory could offer the United States: not unity, but community nevertheless.

If Ogilvie had begun his tour fifty years later, improved logistics would have made it easier and more profitable. He likely would have worked with a speaker's bureau that booked his performances, made travel and advertising arrangements, and contracted with local theaters to guarantee his pay whether his tickets sold or not. No booking agents existed in 1808, however. As he traveled from place to place, he rarely possessed information about his next destination until he arrived there. Once he found lodging and stabled his horse, he set out to find an appropriate room for his lectures. Even the largest American cities simply did not have lecture halls, and when a town boasted a theater it was usually booked with formal productions that made it unavailable to an occasional lecturer. Instead, he spoke in other buildings: lodge rooms or ballrooms in taverns, courthouses, college chapels, schoolrooms, and state capitol buildings. Very few of these featured a permanent stage, much less upholstered seats, private boxes tucked around the room, curtains, or acoustics designed to allow everyone to hear what was said. Most of the time his auditors sat on benches, easily removed when the room was used for dances, Fourth of July parties, or courtroom hearings. It was Ogilvie's responsibility to outfit the room as he required: to buy candles to light the room and to hire someone to construct and decorate a rostrum, the raised platform that he used as a stage, about two feet off the floor, covered with a carpet to muffle the sound of his shoes. In Philadelphia, building and decorating the rostrum alone cost him $30 (a month's wages for a laborer); add to that the cost of renting the room and finding lodging, and the total ballooned to $120. He advertised his talks by purchasing ad space in the local newspaper or by printing single-sheet handbills that he handed out or posted on notice boards. Sometimes he sold tickets from his lodging or in bookstores as well as at the door of his venue. These efforts often took at least two weeks, all before he'd earned a penny. You can see why his friends called the plan foolhardy: with small audiences, he could never hope to break even.[4]

He began his tour by heading west from Milton for Staunton, Virginia, perhaps with the intention of starting with what we might call a soft opening rather than going northeast to Washington, D.C. By trying out his lectures in a series of smaller towns comparatively remote from large coastal cities, he exercised a degree of caution. If he stumbled, these towns were far enough away from dense urban populations that reports of failure wouldn't ruin his reputation. Staunton appeared a good first stop. With fewer than twenty-five hundred residents and lying close to the mineral springs where elite Virginians came to improve their health in the summer months, Staunton was "neat, flourishing, and increasing" and noted for "the excellence of the taverns, and their moderate charges," as one visitor wrote approvingly. There he could perfect his speaking style before small but respectable audiences and learn to negotiate unfamiliar social circles.[5]

He found himself in good company among other itinerant entrepreneurs, performers, craftsmen, and teachers—the "hawkers and walkers"—who crowded the American landscape during these years. Artists traveled the countryside painting portraits; peddlers sold clocks, furniture, books, and other goods. Itinerant dancing masters offered classes in how to master the most fashionable and complex dances and often booked private appointments with wealthy families. At least 179 full-time teachers of penmanship offered classes to those who believed that good handwriting might lead to personal advancement (and perhaps conceal other gaps in one's education); itinerant language teachers did the same. Occasionally a scientific lecturer traveled through displaying dramatic experiments with electricity, magnetism, or chemistry; others offered exhibitions of public portraits, waxworks, or enormous panoramas painted on fabric that seemed to move across the stage as they unspooled from one giant scroll to another. And alongside an array of circuses, exotic animals, trapeze artists, and theater troupes, one traveler exhibited a "learned pig" that (allegedly) could count, spell, and performed "feats with cards." Taken together, this swarm of itinerants helped to forge an early American popular culture that swirled around a constellation of novelty performances, artistic display, and education.[6]

Ogilvie certainly drew on those popular elements but portrayed his performances as "literary amusements" more refined and cerebral than the entertainment offered by other itinerants. He assured his attendees that he avoided controversy like partisan politics and religion but rather spoke on moral and philosophical subjects. Spread over the course of two to four weeks, the talks each tackled a new topic: one night he spoke on the benefits of female education or "the progress and prospects of society," and the following week he might analyze suicide, dueling, or gambling. Far from being a miscellaneous selection, this series of subjects would have appeared highly relevant to his early national audience members, each matter deserving public discussion. Female education— how it ought to differ from the education of boys, what kind of women it ought to produce, whether cultivating their intellects allowed girls to become better wives and mothers—was such a hotly debated subject during these years that it appeared not just in tracts and essays but also in novels, newspaper articles, and poetry. When Ogilvie analyzed any given subject over the course of a ninety-minute talk, he sought to enrich and encourage public conversation.[7]

His talks drew on a range of oratorical styles. Most Americans were familiar with the exhortation of their ministers in church, the ceremonial oratory of Fourth of July speeches or funeral services, and the give-and-take of legal argument on court days as neighbors engaged in land disputes or when lawyers debated cases of theft or assault. Some might have attended debates in their state legislatures or even in Congress. Those with slightly more education would have had to memorize speeches by the greats of ancient Greece and Rome in school. They might even have been familiar with the conventional ways that their schoolbooks divided oratory into categories, drawing on Cicero's three branches: forensic or judicial oratory, intended to arbitrate justice; deliberative or legislative oratory, intended to persuade an audience of the proper course of action; and epideictic or demonstrative oratory, often used at ceremonies or in religious sermons intended to discuss goodness, excellence, nobility, dishonor, or vice. Ogilvie's lectures mixed aspects of all three categories.[8]

He especially merged deliberative and ceremonial styles, moving back and forth between persuasion and praise, emotional appeals and an insistence on reason. One admirer told a Philadelphia newspaper how successfully Ogilvie had satisfied a wide range of listeners. "Those who have only eyes, and ears, must be pleased; those whose fancy and taste are their own active powers must be gratified; those who are beings of pure intellect, must be delighted with the Orator," whose lectures "contain so refined a chain of reasoning." Rather than deliver a close argument on each evening's subject, he transformed seemingly straightforward questions into complex ones. He spoke with such passion and care on both the pros and cons of dueling, for example, that some of his listeners wondered whether he would ultimately try to convince them that it was socially acceptable—an increasingly unpopular opinion. Only after considering the topic from all sides, bringing in "the moral, social, political and religious evils" as well as "private sentiment or individual fears," did he ultimately reject dueling as a means of settling affairs of honor. Some even noted "that he said more in favour than against it." He asked listeners to follow him through a close examination of a subject in ways that might challenge their preconceptions. In other words, he modeled intelligent deliberation on these topics for his audiences, showing how one might give the matter complete consideration.[9]

This was not a purely intellectual exercise. He insisted that his listeners consider seriously the emotional aspects of civic questions. His tour de force lecture on suicide demonstrated this at length. As with his consideration of dueling, attendees might well have been surprised by his similarly evenhanded treatment of suicide. Christians had long condemned the act as usurping the power of God to grant life or death and refused to bury suicides in consecrated ground. The subject resonated more than ever in the new United States, for many believed that suicide had nearly reached epidemic levels and that it threatened the nation. Newspaper reports describing "self-murder" by laudanum overdose and other means appeared frequently, enhancing the sense of panic. To many, this flood of deaths represented a breach in the social contract: a rejection of one's social responsibility to the larger republic in favor of selfish personal liberty, threatening the integrity of the country. To suggest that suicide might be justifiable demanded rhetorical finesse to avoid alienating his audiences. Ogilvie appealed to their emotions.[10]

He stepped out of the more familiar religious, intellectual, and political debates and begged his listeners to sympathize with one who suffered unbearable melancholy and suicidal thoughts. In a relentless series of questions and descriptions, Ogilvie enacted the torment of existence for one who could feel no joy. "Have they not a right to shorten their own lifes when overwhelmed with misery and bereft of the means or hope of happiness?" he asked. "May I not cut a nerve that thrills with agony, or open an artery that throbs with anguish, stay the palpitations of an agitated heart and launch a hopeless afflicted soul on the ocean of futurity in search of another and a better world?" He relentlessly continued through a series of depictions of melancholy and desolation that sought to show why suicide could be justifiable to "common sense, to the uniform practice of mankind in all times and places and to the spirit and principle of whatever deserves the name of philosophy." His manuscript orations that survive today display vivid empathy for sufferers like these, and his material on the opposite side—suicide as unjustifiable—amounts to only half the length, doubtless again leading listeners to wonder whether Ogilvie had only a halfhearted interest in denouncing suicide.[11]

He did not speak on the subject of slavery, a decision that appears more striking from our perspective than from that of his nineteenth-century listeners. Thirty years later, with a much more vigorous national debate about the abolition of slavery during the 1830s, many towns would prohibit public lectures on the topic because they found it too divisive within their communities. No such prohibition existed in 1808. To be sure, the antislavery movement of the early part of the century portrayed the matter as considerably less urgent than it would later appear. Still, important changes to the law of slavery were under way. By this time, every northern state had set limits on slavery either by prohibiting it outright or by establishing gradual emancipation laws intended to eliminate enslavement, albeit slowly. In addition, Congress had banned the international trade in enslaved women and men, a law that reflected growing opposition to "the barter of *human flesh*" but also far less noble motivations, for the new law worked to the economic advantage of slaveholders. Ogilvie likely had no passion for the subject; his writings suggest that he largely took the institution of slavery for granted, saying little on the topic. He was hardly alone. And considering that he needed to sell tickets to his performances, his avoidance of slavery reflected a widespread ambivalence among a majority of white Americans.[12]

No matter what subject he selected on any given evening, the appeal of Ogilvie's performances rested only in part on the words he spoke aloud or the arguments he elaborated during the course of a lecture. Just as significant was how he said them. "It would be difficult to determine whether, as to *matter* or *manner*, [his speeches] were entitled to the highest approbation," one enthusiastic report from Baltimore proclaimed. Orators had to master a battery of talents. One writer listed these as "Correctness of composition, elegance of language, gracefulness of attitude, propriety of gesture, and strength of argument." Add to that a voice capable of dramatic modulation, a wide range of apt facial expressions and physical postures, and a crack talent for memorization, and we can see why so many commented on the "peculiar powers of Mr. Ogilvie" for bringing words, movement, and expression into a harmonious whole.[13]

Someone who met James Ogilvie in the weeks before a talk might not expect him to be effective as a performer onstage. "He is tall, lean, and badly formed," described a friend, capturing a physical appearance hobbled by years of suffering from rheumatism and the laudanum habit. "His cheek bones high and prominent, his shoulders narrow and round; indeed his whole figure is rather ungraceful; but when he speaks you forget his personal defects. His eye, which is bright and quick, bespeaks the energy of his mind. It is the Orator then only that claims your attention and leads captive your every feeling." Another friend, Washington Irving, painted a similar picture when he created a fictionalized version of Ogilvie for a short story. "He was a pale, melancholy-looking man" with a "meagre, pallid countenance" and "an awkward and embarrassed manner," Irving wrote. "But we soon discovered that under this unpromising exterior existed the kindest urbanity of temper; the warmest sympathies; the most enthusiastic benevolence," and, best of all, a mind "crowded" with information about philosophy and literature. When excited by ideas, "The change in the whole man was wonderful. His meagre form would acquire a dignity and grace; his long, pale visage would flash with a hectic glow; his eyes would beam with intense speculation; and there would be pathetic tones and deep modulations in his voice, that delighted the ear, and spoke movingly to the heart." That "meagre" appearance made his performative dynamism all the more transfixing.[14]

The idea that good speech required an elegant integration of words and action was ingrained in elocutionary education. Schools even defined the word *reading* as encompassing gesture and vocal inflection threaded together. "Every thing necessary to [teach] children to read" involved "*cadence, emphasis, [and] suitable modulations of the voice*," as one schoolbook explained. Books like this taught even the youngest children simple movements of the feet and gestures to accompany their recitations. As they progressed, the instructions became more detailed, as displayed in *Chironomia; or, A Treatise on Rhetorical Delivery* (1806), an influential book designed for all who might become public speakers. The minister who wrote the book directed his advice equally to orators, actors, ministers, and lawyers and offered dozens of illustrations demonstrating the postures and gestures needed to accompany the expression of various emotions. "Horror, which is aversion or astonishment mingled with terror, is seldom capable of retreating but remains petrified in one attitude, with the eyes rivetted on its object, and the arm held forwards to guard the person, the hands vertical, and the whole frame trembling," its author explained, whereas "Veneration crosses both hands on the breast, casts down the eyes slowly, and bows the head." For audience members during the early Republic, physical expressions like these enhanced the spoken word in powerful, meaningful ways. "A slight movement of the head, a look of the eye, a turn of hand, a judicious pause or interruption of gesture, or a change of position in the feet often illuminates the meaning of a passage, and sends it full of light and warmth into the understanding." Of course, an awkward public speaker could bungle these movements or make them appear hackneyed, inauthentic. But having seen poor performers made the movements of a polished orator all the more breathtaking to an early American audience. Such physical grace conveyed both masterful self-control and the capacity for fine feeling— a ideal combination for public figures in a republic.[15]

If he wanted the members of his audiences to witness his perfect integration of the spoken word and physical expression, Ogilvie had to buy enough candles for his venues. Following one of his first performances in Philadelphia, one letter to the editor of *Poulson's American Daily Advertiser* complained about poor lighting. "Owing to the partial illumination of the Hall, the features and countenance of the Orator, were but very imperfectly discernible," the letter writer complained. "Everyone knows how essential it is when estimating the abilities of a publick speaker, to witness that expression of soul depicted, in the countenance, without which eloquence has not half its effect." That "everyone" knew such a fact helps to explain how observers might rave about a speaker's eloquence even when, as with the case of listening to some Native American orators, they could not understand a word of the language being spoken. In short, far from finding elocutionary postures and facial expressions exaggerated or inauthentic, contemporaries viewed gesture as essential to the performance of the spoken word. Elo-

Plate. 10.

Complex Significant Gestures.

Figure 15. "Complex Significant Gestures." From Gilbert Austin, Chironomia;
or, A Treatise on Rhetorical Delivery . . . (London, 1806), a guidebook for ministers,
orators, and actors. These gestures include horror (103), veneration (105), and deprecation (106).
Courtesy of the Southern Illinois University Press, Carbondale, Ill.

quence could be conveyed through bodily performance even when its words were lost in translation.[16]

To emphasize the close connection between his orations and the styles of elocution taught in schools, he concluded each evening's performance with recitations of poetry that further demonstrated graceful oratorical action. "If not too much exhausted by the delivery of this discourse, Mr. O. will recite a few exquisitely pathetick effusions from the pens of modern Poets," his advertisements promised. Including these recitations proved a winning combination in an era when listening to poetry read aloud was a major form of entertainment, from

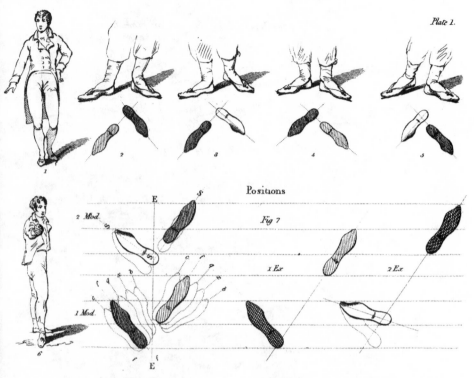

Figure 16. *Positions of the Feet.* From Gilbert Austin, Chironomia;
or, A Treatise on Rhetorical Delivery . . . (London, 1806). *Austin's Chironomia
demonstrates precise positioning of the feet and their movements to accompany changing postures.
Courtesy of the Southern Illinois University Press, Carbondale, Ill.*

small social gatherings to theatrical performances. Most of his listeners would know at least some of these by heart. Ogilvie included passages from some of the classics, like Milton's *Paradise Lost* or soliloquies from Shakespeare; poetry going back to the mid-eighteenth century (James Thomson, Thomas Gray); and selections from the most current popular poems from Walter Scott (*Marmion* and *The Lady of the Lake*). He particularly favored contemporary Scottish poets, many of whom cultivated romantic views of Highlands life or history, such as the "Battle of Flodden" from Scott's *Marmion* and the works of Thomas Campbell, but he also liked to throw in the occasional "highly humorous effusion." In doing so, he combined reason, pathos, grace, and drama together in one performance, displaying a full range of what oratory might achieve as a medium for communication.[17]

As his unique gifts for eloquence began earning compliments, Ogilvie started to suggest that the goals of his lecture tour went beyond considering civic prob-

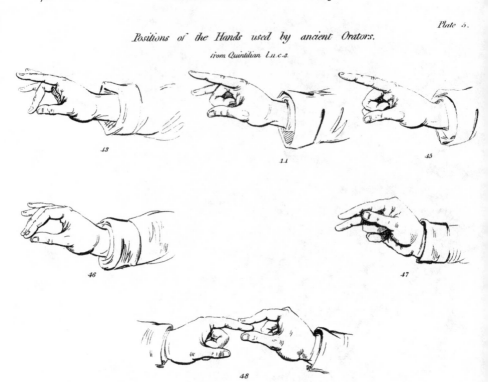

Figure 17. "*Positions of the Hands Used by Ancient Orators.*" From Gilbert Austin, Chironomia;
or, A Treatise on Rhetorical Delivery . . . (London, 1806). Austin quotes the classical writer
Quintilian at length in discussing them. About the pointing gesture (45), the book explains that Cicero
admired another orator's use of this hand position, "used in reproach" unless the hand was raised, in
which case "it affirms by a small inclination. When turned toward the earth," the book continues,
"it is urgent" (328). Courtesy of the Southern Illinois University Press, Carbondale, Ill.

lems. He began to state that oratory itself was his goal: to "restore the Rostrum
to that station from which so many causes have combined to degrade it" and
to advocate for eloquence as "the advocate of virtue and the adversary of vice
. . . especially at this time, and in this country." He believed that his own style of
public speech opened up new possibilities for communication that other more
common forms—sermons, political speechifying, courtroom argumentation—
could achieve only "*partially and incidentally.*" His unique mixture of argument,
emotional appeal, and demonstration of elocutionary panache, he suggested,
had the capacity to raise the place of oratory in the American Republic and give
speech a central role in preserving the democratic process. Only by expanding
this form of oratory, he explained with a flourish, could Americans give eloquence "her *altar;* her *chosen* ministers; her *exclusive* votaries; her *fairest* ornaments;

Figure 18. Detail from "The Miser and Plutus." From Gilbert Austin, Chironomia; or, A Treatise on Rhetorical Delivery . . . (London, 1806). Austin illustrates how one might perform the recitation of a poem by John Gay, even to the point of annotating the images with arrows to indicate the motions of the arms. Courtesy of the Rare Book Division, Special Collections, Princeton University Library

her most *formidable* weapons; and her *proudest* trophies." All of this would allow them to realize oratory's true "dignity, grandeur, and usefulness." His performances demonstrated that public speech offered occasions and guidance for a community to gather and think together about matters important to their future, just as in churches eloquence encouraged religious reflection and fostered communities of faith.[18]

If expanding the scope of oratory was Ogilvie's first major aim, his second goal was to demonstrate its political significance to a republic. This should not be confused with political partisanship, for he studiously avoided anything divisive. Rather, he worked "to revive the Republican eloquence of the ancient rostrum . . . in this, the only Republic now remaining in the world." The very nature of oratory was important to the nation, he argued. One journalist found himself persuaded. "Eloquence in a free state is power, and it is power of the noblest kind, because it rules the minds of men by the force of reason, and allures their hearts by the attractions of virtue. Before the accomplished orator, the miser turns pale, the tyrant trembles, and drops his sceptre."[19]

Oratory had such potential for American civic life because it heightened auditors' senses and emotions by means of an almost mystical electric "energy or force," as Increase Cooke explained in a schoolbook. The electricity of oratory operated at an individual level as each member of an audience visually and aurally witnessed the performance; it also functioned collectively as all the auditors together experienced the orator's charismatic energy en masse. The spoken word dynamically clarified the feelings and articulated the necessary actions of a group of auditors. Indeed, early nineteenth-century print culture frequently likened it to a force of nature. "Tones, looks and gestures, are natural interpreters of the sentiments of the mind," Cooke continued. "They remove ambiguities; they enforce impression; they operate on us by means of sympathy, which is one of the most powerful instruments of persuasion. Our sympathy is always awakened more by hearing the speaker, than by reading his works in our closet." The orator's performance and the audience's breathless attention bound them together in an emotional and sympathetic relationship. Fine oratory generated an electrical current among listeners and helped to bind them together as a community.[20]

Ogilvie had that rare capacity to electrify rooms and galvanize publics, as a self-described "Admirer of Eloquence" explained in a letter to a Philadelphia paper. "Eloquence inveigles both our eyes and ears, and it is only from the operation of this mysterious power on both senses, that its [w]hole and undivided energy can be felt," the letter noted. "The mind is lost in a variety of delightful reveries, and when the spell breaks up, we regret that we are incompetent to give to the same sentiment, the fervor, the pathos and energy, that the orator exhibits." This profound effect resulted from the dynamism between speaker and listeners. "The Poetry of PINDAR and the Histories of HERODOTUS, owe their existence to the ambition infused and encouraged by these public exhibitions," opined a Charleston correspondent. "So should it be in REPUBLICAN AMERICA." Ogilvie's American lecture tour gradually evolved to advocate for oratory as a democratic mode of communication, a merger of wonder and reason in a harmonious whole. If religious speakers sought to enchant their listeners with the glories of faith, Ogilvie sought to entrance his auditors with the magic of public assembly in a republic and the thrill of secular deliberation.[21]

The wonder and delight that he cultivated around the discussion of secular topics offered a compelling vision of public assembly for oratory. It proposed that the Republic required not just an active and critical press but also a parallel institution for the oral discussion and elaboration of ideas that allowed citizens to encounter one another in person. Such an ideal of public assembly privileged the notion that audience and speaker would engage in dynamic, embodied exchanges, encounters that were rare in Ogilvie's America and would only proliferate later with the rise of the lyceum system in the late 1820s and 1830s. Some of those orators would later theorize about the importance of public assembly. In his 1836–1837 series, "The Philosophy of History," Ralph Waldo Emerson—who saw Ogilvie perform in 1817—idealized a society "of minds (eloquence)." "Eloquence is the power which one man in an age possesses of piercing the superficial crusts of condition which discriminate man from man and addressing the common soul of them all." Thirty years earlier, Ogilvie initiated a conversation about the role of spoken-word performances in confirming and enacting national publics, discussing civic action and public ideas, and providing sites for self-definition, a conversation that would accelerate in decades to come.[22]

Yet even with grandiose ideas about the power of oratory in a republic, at the beginning of his tour Ogilvie still faced the most daunting obstacle of all: no one knew him. During his earlier lectures in Richmond and at Monticello, he had known many of the attendees. He had been their neighbor and their children's teacher, and, in Milton, he had benefited from the patronage of the president of the United States. In places where he was a stranger, however, how could the locals determine whether he deserved the money they spent on his tickets?

Ogilvie was hardly the only stranger making his way across the American landscape during an era when anxieties about strangers was on the rise—and, as a result, he struggled to sell tickets during his earliest months. Print media had fueled those fears. Newspapers often contained accounts of charming swindlers, counterfeiters, and cheats who might pretend to be a town's new schoolmaster or minister but eventually disappeared, taking with them valuable goods or church funds and leaving behind pregnant girls and heavy debts. That some of these charlatans went on to publish eminently entertaining autobiographies of their exploits only enhanced the cultural preoccupation with deception by strangers. Tales like these made Americans jittery about whom to trust. As a result, Ogilvie learned the hard way how small one's audiences could be.[23]

During his earliest months of lecturing, he found audiences of only about "twenty or thirty persons in number; accidentally and spontaneously assembled." When he arrived in Washington, D.C., during the summer months, Thomas Jefferson reported that Ogilvie spoke before "very unequal audiences of from 15. to 50." Numbers this low simply could not keep his career afloat. With a ticket price of $.50 (about half the amount a laborer might earn in a day, and a price that only those with a disposable income could afford), he might make between $7.50 and $15 per lecture. Because he usually presented between three and six talks in any given town, depending on the population, his gross proceeds might amount to between $22.50 and $90. Those totals might cover his expenses, but they failed to give him a financial cushion to start over again in the next town.[24]

His most disappointing night came in Frederick, Maryland, in May 1808, about two months after starting his tour, when he stepped onto the stage to find only four men in the audience. He started the oration anyway but was quickly "and very politely" interrupted by one of them "whose appearance and deportment bespoke urbanity and intelligence," as he remembered later. "You do not, sir, I hope, think of delivering your discourse in the presence of four persons," the man asked, incredulous. He explained that the handbill Ogilvie had commissioned to advertise the talk had not yet circulated in town and promised that, if he postponed the talk, he would certainly find a larger audience. But Ogilvie insisted on continuing, modestly saying "that he was a stranger in Fredericktown: That his exhibition was of a nature somewhat novel: that he had no sort of ground to expect in the first instance a numerous audience," and, most important, that he "*wished to draw* attention, solely by means of the favourable impression" he might leave on the minds of his auditors. The men settled back into their seats, and Ogilvie completed his lecture on dueling "with as much earnestness and energy" as he could muster. His performance proved winning. As his four audience members stood to leave, they assured him, "If our exertions, sir, can fill your room to-morrow evening, it shall not be *full* merely, it shall overflow." In Ogilvie's triumphal retelling, the following night's talk was crowded—a fitting outcome for a deserving performer who had displayed both talent and humility.[25]

This night in Frederick taught him the importance of the patronage of gentlemen: word-of-mouth publicity from men like these was more effective than any other form of advertising. The value of their good words rested not just in what they said but in that men of "urbanity and intelligence" were saying it. When they attested to Ogilvie's talents as well as his respectability, the integrity of his material, and the value of listening to talks on his proposed subjects, their opinions held weight. Gentlemen of high social rank and influence made ideal patrons.

Deputizing such self-consciously influential residents did more than fill his halls and buttress his reputation. It gave him a way to tap into existing social networks. By doing so, Ogilvie could take more control over the many logistical and geographical obstacles he faced and slowly generate more sustained success.

Learning this lesson about the value of influential locals led him to ask his friends to provide letters of introduction to their acquaintances in neighboring towns and cities. "In the progress of the romantic excursion I have undertaken," he explained to Thomas Jefferson as he requested a letter, "I was not [initially] so fully aware of the utility of such letters as I have since become." When he arrived to speak in Washington, D.C., and nearby Alexandria, he met with Jefferson, then in the final year of his presidency, and procured letters addressed to Jefferson's friends in the cities he planned to visit next—Baltimore, Philadelphia, and New York. One of Jefferson's letters indicates the kind of work required of such a document. First, it reminded the recipient of Jefferson's "friendly attachment and high respect" for the recipient, before entering into detailed advocacy of Ogilvie and his talks. "Having myself been occasionally one of his hearers, I am safe in assuring you that no one, however learned, will hear him without instruction. None, however moral, will leave him without better impressions," Jefferson told a Baltimore minister. "The correctness of his morals, the purity of his views and his high degree of understanding and cultivation, will not fail to impress you. In short, those who attend him once, will not fail to attend afterwards as often as occasion shall be offered." Shared between two men of high stature, letters of introduction boosted Ogilvie's reputation. They conferred patronage at the same time that they confirmed the friendship between letter writer and recipient. And when a letter arrived from someone of higher status, the recipient felt all the more compelled to assist. "My respect for the writer of the letter would have induced me to avail myself of the honor it offered me," one recipient explained to the older, wealthy man who asked him to help, conveying a powerful sense of the webs of status and obligation that such letters wove. For his own part, Ogilvie usually carried a stack of them when he arrived in new places, sometimes two or three addressed to the same person.[26]

His letter writers could be quite specific and insistent in asking their friends to assist Ogilvie. When the middle-aged statesman Alexander Dallas wrote to a twenty-five-year-old state representative in Lancaster, Pennsylvania, he left nothing to chance. "I have the pleasure of introducing him to you, because I know you will have taste to enjoy his literary displays, and because I believe you will have some gratification in obliging me, by shewing every attention in your power to him," he wrote. "Pray, assist him in obtaining accommodations, to deliver his Orations, and in reccommending him to the distinction of the best and fullest audience, our Capitol can afford." However heavy-handed it might sound ("you will have some gratification in obliging me"), consider how valuable it must have been to find appropriate accommodations and a venue in a mid-sized city of fifty-four hundred residents. With guidance, Ogilvie could avoid raising eyebrows with an overly showy, expensive apartment or a decrepit room at a disreputable tavern, thereby sending the right signals to the rest of the town's residents about his status and character.[27]

Ogilvie's second tactic was to engage the influential social networks in the towns he visited, a procedure he called "courting." Starting with one or two friends of friends, he sought acquaintance with other members of their circles, using his charm and conversation to cement his value as a companion at social events. One might invite him to dinner, arrive at his performances with an elegant wife and daughter in tow, or offer to escort him to cultural events in the city. The son of a minister himself, Ogilvie especially courted religious men whose unparalleled reputations and connections might guarantee him entry into local society. When he arrived in Salem, Massachusetts, he enjoyed several dinners with the Reverend William Bentley, who immediately approved of the orator. "Mr. O's powers in conversation are quite equal to his talents as an Orator," Bentley wrote with satisfaction in his diary. "His abundance of Anecdotes furnishes much entertainment." To win their approval, Ogilvie often mentioned his minister-poet father and alluded to family connections with that other James Ogilvie, the earl of Findlater, who had once given Ogilvie his scholarship to King's College. The endorsement of local ministers almost always expanded his networks.[28]

If his courting was successful, elites in the area took turns passing him around with invitations, thereby conferring on him the benefits of their social imprimatur and conveying a sense that Ogilvie enjoyed a friendly intimacy with them. In Boston, Col. David Humphreys brought him to hear John Quincy Adams lecture on rhetoric at Harvard, which resulted only a few days later in an invitation to a dinner with "a small party of Gentlemen." Two weeks later, Ogilvie earned an invitation to Adams's home. He "pass'd the Evening and Supp'd with us — We Sat conversing upon poetry, criticism and philosophy untill after midnight," Adams wrote in his diary. He ultimately attended four of Ogilvie's lectures and would have heard a fifth "but could not get a place" in the packed room. When Adams arrived at one of the talks with his cosmopolitan wife and sister-in-law, he signaled to all the value of Ogilvie's performances for both sexes. Gaining such approval would smooth Ogilvie's path for weeks to come, particularly if those individuals provided him with letters of introduction for his appearances further down the road. These social connections solved logistical problems by helping him move from one town to the next without having to start networking from scratch; they also granted the lectures the aura of exclusivity.[29]

As he built these social connections, Ogilvie apparently set aside the partisanship of his younger days to welcome supporters of all political stripes. Notwithstanding the vigor with which he had once advocated for the political ideas of William Godwin and the ethos of Jeffersonian Republicanism — even to the point of alienating those on the other side — he now benefited from the patronage of New England Federalists like Adams and Humphreys as frequently as from Pennsylvania Republicans like Alexander Dallas. Playing the role of a disinterested nonpartisan helped to sell tickets and evade controversy, of course, but Ogilvie likely had other motives. In developing a style of oratory that sought to examine civic matters from all sides, he insisted that it must remain above the partisan fray. Having supporters as varied as Dallas and Adams was not merely instrumental. It signaled to all that his eloquence had hit its mark.

When he sought out patrons from among society women — his third tactic for success — he revealed how much women's support mattered as much as a wide range of partisans. Martha Laurens Ramsay of Charleston wrote to her niece in 1811 explaining that "Mr. Ogilvie called, in *propria persona* [himself, in person], yesterday morning, to request I would hear his oration this evening. Can I do less than accept the invitation of Mr. Ogilvie, especially as he assures me it is what he thinks his best oration, and will feel himself honoured by my presence[?]" In Boston he used parlor visits to issue invitations directly to Louisa Catherine Adams, who attended at least three of his talks, and not always with her husband, John Quincy Adams. In Washington, D.C., he visited influential women and talked to them of poetry and literature. One of these, Margaret Bayard Smith, wrote to her sister that he had arrived on a Tuesday morning and sat with the women of the home while they were "busied with [their] needles." Ogilvie gave them a gift of Lord Byron's new book of poetry, *The Bride of Abydos*; "in return" they set about "hemming him some new cravats." Their wide-ranging conversation touched on Byron's gifts as a poet as well as his notorious personal life (Byron's sexual indiscretions were legion), and, as a group, they collectively agreed to disapprove of his "principles, sentiments, misanthropy, and morbid sensibility." Smith did not miss the way Ogilvie used such visits with respectable matrons to mark a contrast between his own behavior and Byron's. "Whatever his own opinions are, respecting religion I know not, but I have never heard him in public or private, utter a sentiment that could wound or offend the most pious," she reported. He was, she declared, a man of "highly cultivated taste" and "great research." And she doubtless repeated that testimony in letters to friends and relations, encouraging them to welcome Ogilvie into their parlors and thus confer on him their public approval.[30]

He also went out of his way to ensure a strong female presence at his talks, for he believed that he would never succeed without approval of "ladies of intelligence and taste." Having equal numbers of women in attendance was "essential . . . to give dignity and attraction to the rostrum; to animate the attention of his auditors, and the exertions of the orator; to impart efficacy to every effort that is intended, or has a tendency, to 'raise the genius and to mend the heart,'" he wrote. Ogilvie believed that oratory in America could only achieve its true potential if it passed muster with such women and inspired them as much as it did their husbands.[31]

All of this networking required an extensive outlay of time and effort—an exhausting procession of parlor visits with relative strangers, visits to hear children declaim in local schools, and trips to church. Dinner invitations might provide him with numerous benefits (and a free meal), but his hosts often expected him to sing for his supper. One memoirist remembered a Boston dinner party after which Ogilvie delivered some "very effective recitations from Scott, Campbell, and Moore" to the great delight of the guests. Years later, perhaps buttressed by an increasing sense of social prominence, he declined to recite poetry at social gatherings, seemingly wearied by needing to stand and perform not just on the nights of his own lectures but all the time. That work could be draining. Offering gratitude for the assistance of his social superiors might have become progressively more onerous considering that his brief one- to two-month visits in each place inhibited his ability to develop more lasting friendships with the people whose parlor visits and dinner gatherings he enjoyed. Because they were seldom his friends or social equals according to contemporary views of status, he had to maintain a constant vigilance regarding his behavior lest he risk losing their support.[32]

Step back and consider these different ways that Ogilvie built his reputation as a speaker by means of social networks. All those elite family and business connections gradually permitted him to move from one city to the next and find patrons who might help him move from city to city across the nineteenth-century United States. These networks operated by word of mouth and via handwritten letters that traversed the U.S. mail, all outside print media. Slowly, reports from influential patrons began to make appearances in local papers when Ogilvie came to town. When he arrived in Baltimore in August 1808 after procuring letters of introduction from Jefferson and others, the local papers ran testimonials from friendly sources, as from "a friend, on whose judgment and correctness we have entire reliance," who had nothing but praise for the orator. "Of Mr. O.'s manner of performing this task, the specimens I have witnessed have certainly been of a very superior order." In detailing "the rich embellishments of imagery, the glow and pathos of sentiment, and the elegance and splendour of diction, which characterize his exhibition," this friend transmitted not just approval but also a clear sense of the writer's own learning and discernment. Several days later, the paper described Ogilvie's successful first lecture and pronounced him "a man of genius" who "gave universal satisfaction and excited applause." Other self-consciously learned patrons offered letters to the editors of local papers. "Philopatris" told a newspaper that "the native force and beauty of Ogilvie's genius ought certainly to be considered as the beginning of a new aera in the annals of modern eloquence." Such letters amounted to more than compliments. They reminded readers that the orator's friends included educated elites who used Latinate pseudonyms when writing to the paper.[33]

Ogilvie's own use of print media paled in comparison to the time he dedicated to courting prominent citizens, particularly considering the ways that later celebrities would artfully manipulate the press to benefit their careers. The contrast is illustrative. Sure, he did his best to blanket local newspapers with advertisements, making it a significant part of his expenses when he arrived in town. Ads might help to drum up interest, but they achieved little more than keeping his name before the eyes of a reading public. He expended far more of his time visiting ladies' parlors and gentlemen's dinner tables. He could exercise a much greater degree of control over social forms of networking than he could over the press. If he had tried to submit an anonymous letter to the editor praising his own gifts, the editor might recognize the handwriting and spread that information around via gossip as an unforgivable example of self-promotion and immodesty. He gained far more from the patronage of influential friends than from attempts to manipulate newspapers to his advantage.[34]

After traveling and speaking for six months, Ogilvie arrived in Philadelphia in late September 1808, carrying an armload of letters of introduction to some of the city's most important men. Those introductions would be important in such a large and culturally significant place. The metropolitan region was so large that the U.S. census delineated the city of Philadelphia, the Northern Liberties township, and the Southwark district as three distinct places, each of which ranked in the nation's top eight most populous urban areas. Altogether, nearly eighty-seven thousand residents lived there, and the city housed the country's most influential publishers and a formidable population of literary and scientific figures. It might have had a population only a tenth the size of London's, but in America Philadelphia's reputation as a metropolis that brought together culture, politics, economics, and intellectual life remained peerless.[35]

The city's residents enjoyed a steady stream of visiting lecturers and entertainers of all sorts. A series of scientific lecturers had dramatized their presentations by displaying the effects of nitrous oxide by gassing audience members, projecting images onto a screen by use of a magic lantern, and unveiling a geared model that demonstrated the movement of the planets. Ogilvie's lectures overlapped with those by a Mr. Woodhouse who illustrated his talks with "a very curious and extensive apparatus" that revealed nature's "most brilliant phenomena, many of her most valuable arcana to the enquiring mind." In addition to these educational presentations, a wide variety of entertainments also competed for the Philadelphia public's discretionary income. "The Theatre is open now, which will furnish the young people with amusement," Esther Cox wrote to her friend Mary Chesnut in November 1808, "and there are several other places of resort, such as Lectures, in which the greatest display of Oratory, and Elocution are exhibited by a Mr. Ogilvie, and the highest degree of deception, or slight of hand, by a Mr. Martin—a circus is building so that the heavy may have many ways of lightening themselves." Meanwhile, the Antipodean Whirligig "performed a wonderful feat by standing on his head, and whirling around in that position like a top in its quickest motion," sometimes adding "fireworks attached to his heels and other parts of his person." For Ogilvie to offer only the spoken word as competition placed an enormous amount of faith in his audiences.[36]

At first, his success appeared so promising that he decided to remain a second month to repeat his most popular lectures and add a few more to his roster. Extending his stay certainly offered him financial benefits: having already spent the money to build and decorate his stage, every additional lecture cost him only the expense of renting the hall and buying candles. Best of all, his new acquaintances helped by writing letters to the editor. One wrote, "I sincerely hope he may be induced to repeat this particular [talk] a second time," in a letter that appeared simultaneously in three of the city's fourteen newspapers. The prospect of postponing his trek to the next city, with the stresses and uncertainty of starting over, must have held terrific appeal. He had begun to realize the benefits of his hard work—socializing in parlors, performing recitations at dinner, playing the grateful subordinate. James Ogilvie had begun to flourish as a recognized talent.[37]

But perhaps he had become too comfortable in Philadelphia, for at this point he nearly destroyed his reputation. His blunder remained so vivid that years later he tried to describe it in a rambling, disjointed six-page footnote in his memoir. His mistake? He hinted publicly that he was an atheist.

CHAPTER 5

Navigating the Shoals of Belief and Skepticism,
October–November

1808

Everything had been going so well. Upon arrival in Philadelphia after a successful series in Baltimore, James Ogilvie had noted in his advertisements that his talks had "been pronounced in the presence of Ladies and Gentlemen of the first distinction and accomplishments, in Virginia and Maryland, with flattering tokens of approbation." He rented a hall belonging to the University of Pennsylvania on Fourth Street and began his usual round of courting the men and women for whom he had letters of introduction—people who might buy tickets, introduce him to their friends, and offer public praise of his performances. And, indeed, he saw an increase in attendance each evening and more enthusiastic accounts appearing in the newspapers. A writer signing himself "Philologus" (lover of learning) praised Ogilvie's "superior stile of eloquence in which his sentiments are expressed, the graceful and impressive manner with which they are enforced, and the pure precepts of morality which they inculcate." This letter insisted that the orations were "as interesting and instructive to the youthful Belles Lettres student, as they are to the man of confirmed taste, and the liberal and accomplished scholar." These reports and others in the papers never failed to notice the "persons of the highest reputation and influence in the city" who decorated the audience.[1]

After delivering six of his most polished lectures in the city, his tour had grown so successful that he received permission from the university to continue in the same room with a combination of several new lectures as well as repeats of his two most popular talks. Throughout, he had presented a persona that won the approval of the right people. "The truly modest and unassuming manner in which Mr. OGILVIE has presented himself to the public, begins now to experience the just reward of genuine merit," explained one letter to the newspapers. He enjoyed evenings engaging with the elite social salon of Caspar Wister, a renowned professor of anatomy at the university, and the painter and museum creator Charles Willson Peale. Ogilvie's new friend Charles Brockden Brown, a novelist and journalist who wrote for local papers, puffed his oratorical talent. "A more eloquent and powerful dissuasive from gaming was surely never before delivered to a public assembly," Brown raved after the talk on gambling. "It

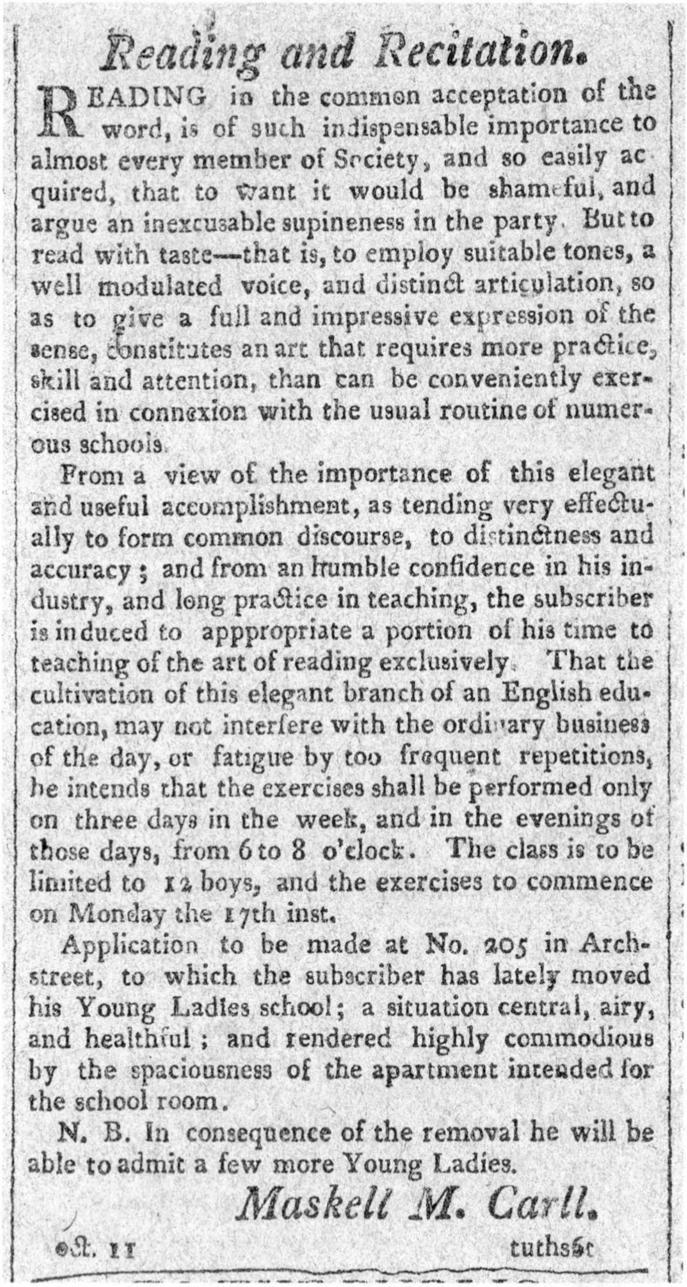

Reading and Recitation.

READING in the common acceptation of the word, is of such indispensable importance to almost every member of Society, and so easily acquired, that to want it would be shameful, and argue an inexcusable supineness in the party. But to read with taste—that is, to employ suitable tones, a well modulated voice, and distinct articulation, so as to give a full and impressive expression of the sense, constitutes an art that requires more practice, skill and attention, than can be conveniently exercised in connexion with the usual routine of numerous schools.

From a view of the importance of this elegant and useful accomplishment, as tending very effectually to form common discourse, to distinctness and accuracy ; and from an humble confidence in his industry, and long practice in teaching, the subscriber is induced to apppropriate a portion of his time to teaching of the art of reading exclusively. That the cultivation of this elegant branch of an English education, may not interfere with the ordinary business of the day, or fatigue by too frequent repetitions, he intends that the exercises shall be performed only on three days in the week, and in the evenings of those days, from 6 to 8 o'clock. The class is to be limited to 12 boys, and the exercises to commence on Monday the 17th inst.

Application to be made at No. 205 in Arch-street, to which the subscriber has lately moved his Young Ladies school; a situation central, airy, and healthful ; and rendered highly commodious by the spaciousness of the apartment intended for the school room.

N. B. In consequence of the removal he will be able to admit a few more Young Ladies.

Maskell M. Carll.

oct. 11   tuths5t

Figure 19. "Reading and Recitation." From Poulson's American Daily Advertiser (Philadelphia), Oct. 18, 1808, [4]. At the peak of Ogilvie's popularity as an eloquent speaker in Philadelphia, this teacher began advertising lessons in elocutionary skills. Courtesy of the American Antiquarian Society, Worcester, Mass.

is so rare a thing to see eloquence enlisted on the side of morality." One entre-preneurial teacher in the city began offering classes in reading and oral recita-tion—"to read with taste . . . to employ suitable tones, a well modulated voice, and distinct articulation, so as to give a full and impressive expression of the sense"—perhaps banking on increased attention to "this elegant and useful ac-complishment." Clearly, Ogilvie's efforts had truly begun to pay off.[2]

All of this momentum screeched to a halt when, in the middle of a talk on the night of Saturday, October 30, a slip in his performance led his audience to turn on him. When he'd delivered this talk ten days before, the audience had loved it. He would continue to perform this speech throughout his career, never again with this reaction. But this time, somewhere in the middle, the audience went silent—a silence that "was deep and dead: His auditors seemed even to hold their breath, and to stare at each other with 'stony eyes.'" Charles Brock-den Brown reported a current of horror among his fellow attendees. The physi-cian Benjamin Rush told Ogilvie the next day, "Well, sir, you have thrown away an empire of fame and emolument!" and predicted that all respectable society would now shun him. This time, Brown and Rush told him, he had seemed to advocate for atheism. His youthful reputation as an atheist and political radical from his days as a schoolteacher in Virginia now seemed to catch up with him, and his Philadelphia audience believed they had witnessed a particular moment in the talk when Ogilvie revealed not only his own unbelief but perhaps a desire to spread irreligion to his audiences.[3]

That gaffe occurred at a time when anxieties about religion and radicalism were already high. The danger that atheists and deists seemed to pose to Ameri-can Protestants far outweighed the small numbers of American atheists and sig-naled worries about the country's future. But the underlying tensions cannot be characterized simply as a clash between atheists and believers, between differ-ent styles of Christian worship, or the ways that some tied their religious beliefs to their political views. The drama that unfolded in Philadelphia also illustrates that eloquence itself might appear dangerous. Eloquence could delight and in-spire, but it could also provoke unease. If an orator possessed an extraordinary ability to touch public emotions, was it unreasonable to fret that he might use those skills to undermine social stability and perhaps even democracy itself?[4]

Ogilvie spent a lot of time promising that he would not discuss religion in public. From the outset of his tour six months earlier, he had taken care in his advertise-ments to assure newspaper readers that "all questions connected with theology or domestic politics, will be carefully avoided." In requesting letters of introduc-tion from influential friends, he vowed to "abstain scrupulously from questions" that might "scandalize the faith" of religious believers, allowing his friends to make the same promises in their letters. In fact, he went out of his way to insist that the very nature of his oratory demanded that he appeal to members of all faiths and sects. He explained in his memoir that "the pulpit is the proper and appointed place for the exposition and inculcation of religious doctrines." Further, because "liberal amusement is one of the primary objects" of his own style of rostrum oratory, to opine about religion would destroy the tenor of edutainment he sought to strike in his talks. "The illustration of such subjects [as religion] demands a temper and tone of feeling, far too serious and solemn" for his lectures. Above all, he wanted his talks to appeal to intelligent people "of all classes and denominations"; to transgress into religious topics, he insisted, would destroy his goal.[5]

Those passages made him sound as if he protested too much—and in doing so they revealed how much the topic of religion touched a nerve. His reputation as an atheist and follower of the radical politics of William Godwin stretched back fifteen years to his teaching days in Fredericksburg in the mid-1790s, at a moment when Americans associated those views with the most radical and violent excesses of the French Revolution. And news about that early radicalism had spread. In fact, an 1801 letter to the editor of a Philadelphia newspaper had featured an alarmist note about Ogilvie's use of Godwin's *Political Justice* in his Virginia classroom, claiming that he had "zealously inculcated" the book's insidious values and that some of his students "were very apt in imbibing the Godwinian doctrines: they used to carry copies of the book in their pockets, and swear by its dogmas almost on all occasions." Considering that he had lost his job at the time, it should be no surprise that, thirteen years later, he would strenuously avoid the subject.[6]

In fact, Ogilvie had come to lace his talks with the religious language and biblical references that constituted a lingua franca in the early American Republic, especially for public speakers. He might have been a skeptic himself, but he was also the son of a minister in a family full of ministers. He felt the cadences of homiletics and the language of the King James Bible running in his veins. The popular poetry he quoted was rife with references to faith and God. More important, he knew that using those rhythms and words could make his talks both persuasive and gratifying to his listeners. No matter how ardently he addressed the problems of this world and avoided doctrinal controversy, his talks lifted liberally from the syntax, if not the substance, of faith.

He no longer sounded like an atheist, nor did he behave like someone who sought to overturn the religious beliefs of his audiences. But Ogilvie had a more serious hurdle to overcome: whispers had started to circulate alongside his appearances. This chatter alluded to the atheism and political radicalism of his younger days that had so scandalized his students' parents. Earlier that summer, the editor of the *Washington Federalist* invoked those whispers when he told his readers, "We acknowledge, from some rumours that had reached us, we attended [his talk] with some prepossessions against the speaker; but they soon yielded, and we have very rarely spent an evening so much to our satisfaction." Similar rumors reached Philadelphia as well such that, when the University of Pennsylvania agreed to rent a hall to him that was used on Sundays for religious services, they did so on the condition that he guarantee his talks would "contain no sentiments, which could be offensive to persons of any religious persuasion." Ogilvie's years in Virginia had taught him to tread lightly when it came to matters of religion, so he readily consented to the university's restrictions.[7]

By the time he repeated his talk on "The Progress and Prospects of Society" at the end of October, he had insisted that he felt it was his very best. He even went so far as to advertise that it was "far superior to any of the course, with respect to brilliancy of diction, variety of representation, cogency of argument, and energy of thought and action," and that this was the talk "on which he wishes to rest his merit, as a writer and an orator, having bestowed upon its execution the utmost exertion of various talents." It displayed his most ambitious aims for oratory, his penchant for narrative and emotional drama, and his most expansive breadth as a thinker.[8]

At its heart, "Progress and Prospects" sought to remind audiences that the progress of civilization ultimately relied on human action and sought to inspire them to act to bring about continued moral progress. He combined a grand discussion of world history that spanned centuries, a dramatic reminder that human progress could be reversed by corrupt and power-hungry leaders, and a climactic conclusion that urged the public to show vigilance against such corruptions. His narrative encompassed the long history of Christianity in improving civilization, the historic revival of classical literature during the Renaissance, and the invention of printing. All of these signaled propitious progress for mankind, he told his auditors, and each had played an important role in setting the stage for revolutions in America and France. To this point, his talk engaged common narratives of the day that emphasized providential improvement and the United States' exceptional place in a Christian vision of history—narratives so familiar that they regularly appeared in everything from Fourth of July orations to working men's toasts in taverns.[9]

But after weaving together that reassuring and familiar history, Ogilvie pivoted to a more ominous narrative. He raised the question of the French nation's postrevolutionary turn toward despotism and militarism and, summoning his most portentous tones, asked his auditors to consider what such events might mean for the United States. He reminded them that, whereas the French Revolution had begun with great optimism, it had descended into chaos from which

Napoleon had risen as an emperor. What did the specter of Napoleon Bonaparte's French Empire signal for the future of humanity? Would democracies inevitably create authoritarian leaders? Would we, he asked, continue to witness steady progress for mankind—or would those historic improvements get reversed? For American audiences who regularly encountered alarming news in the papers about the Napoleonic Wars in Europe, such discussions had particular significance.

His narrative became even darker when he touched on the United States' recent trade embargo against "the potent interference of Great Britain." Philadelphians had been hard hit by the embargo, which shut down American overseas trade in an attempt to force the warring nations of Britain and France to respect American neutrality in their war. The British navy had committed the most objectionable offenses by capturing ships and impressing American sailors into service, which the United States saw as a form of kidnapping. In barring its ships from engaging in trade with foreign nations, Philadelphia's vibrant shipping trade had shrunk radically as ships remained in port, sometimes rotting at the docks. Even at our remove, we can understand why Ogilvie's evocation of such potent economic and political uncertainties would produce tension among his listeners. No more dramatic evidence would challenge his auditors' faith in continued improvement for the future or heighten their emotional response at this dark point in the lecture.[10]

In the midst of this dramatic, stark turn, he quoted from a popular poem to underline his point, but he altered the wording just enough to startle the audience and amplify the anxiety in the room. Many members of his audience would have known *The Hermit* by the Aberdonian poet and philosopher James Beattie for its ecstatic confirmation of Christian faith. Beattie—the same professor who had taught his Aberdeen college students to eliminate all traces of Scots words from their conversation—had his hermit speak directly to God in the poem. As he witnessed the beautiful world around him, the hermit roundly rejected religious doubt in favor of trust in providential goodness. "From doubt and from darkness thou only canst free," the hermit says, before exclaiming:

> And darkness and doubt are now flying away.
> No longer I roam in conjecture forlorn.
> So breaks on the traveller, faint and astray,
> The bright and the balmy effulgence of morn.
> See Truth, Love, and Mercy, in triumph descending,
> And Nature all glowing in Eden's first bloom!

But Ogilvie changed it, reversing the poem's joyful trust in God. He had the hermit cry out in fear from a soul troubled by doubt: "But darkness and doubt are not flying away, / Alas, I still roam, in conjecture forlorn," Ogilvie recited instead. By shifting those famous lines to convey doubt and fear instead of faith, he sought to underline the existential anxiety of the moment. He wanted his auditors to experience the terror of uncertainty intellectually as well as emotionally.[11]

He presumably intended the recitation of these lines to be a dramatic, desperate moment in the lecture's structure that he would resolve with a final series of points restoring his audience's trust in the notion of progress—to puncture the audience's optimism in the middle of a lecture that would ultimately offer a much more hopeful conclusion. Such drama set the stage all the more for the talk's final passages, which provided an inspiring vision of the power of human morality to guarantee progress rather than regression. As he explained later, he found that clothing his sentiments "in that hyperbolical and bombastic jargon, and deliver[ing it] with that impassioned vehemence, and unaffected enthusiasm" usually worked. This time, it did not.[12]

These dramatic and contradictory passages had won exuberant praise two weeks earlier. That evening in late October, however, he could feel a shift in his audience's response. Charles Brockden Brown told him afterward that the palpable horror of the audience made "an aera in his sensations." From his rostrum he could not tell what this meant—were they responding as he had planned? Or did their silence indicate a different kind of reaction? Ogilvie continued with his talk, which "drew a picture" of the "*speedy* and *inevitable downfal*, the penal and irretrievable perdition, of that most despicable and detestable usurper" Napoleon Bonaparte. Following a hopeful final section dedicated to restoring the auditors' sense of moral certainty, the applause was "loud, long, and apparently unanimous." He left the hall believing he had triumphed yet again. Only in the course of a raucous dinner conversation afterward with a group of literary Philadelphians did one of them explain to Ogilvie that his talk "had given great offence, not only to one or two clergymen ... but to sundry grave and serious persons, of both sexes." The news got worse the next day, particularly when Benjamin Rush berated him. At the very moment that he might have realized lasting success, Rush insisted, he had threatened his career with a cheap effort to inject more drama into the performance.[13]

What went wrong?

Rush believed that Ogilvie had seemed to open the question of whether Christianity had been created by human beings rather than God. In fact, Ogilvie had delivered a line that could be confusing. In the midst of discussing the possibility that human history might not always reflect forward progress, he had issued a caveat intended to reassure his listeners that his talk would avoid theological matters: he stated that he would "forbear to examine" the "awful and mysterious question, in relation to [Christianity's] divine origin." With this line, he sought to inoculate himself against the charge of dabbling in religious doctrine. But on this night, Rush believed, the line had the opposite effect: Ogilvie had appeared to suggest that Christianity's origin was up for question, not a settled truth. This implication on its own seemed to mark him as an atheist.[14]

To question the divine establishment of the institution of Christianity and insinuate that mere mortals had developed this religion was to say that Christianity was invented and thus necessarily flawed. When deists and atheists made such claims in the early nineteenth century, they often attacked Christianity as an institution that might actually operate against the will of God. Could human beings be capable of ethical action without God or religion? Without them, could societies enjoy a functioning social contract? Should humans follow a Bible that had been written by men, even if those authors had been inspired by God? To question Christianity's divine origin and suggest it had been created by humans was to question the very ground on which most Americans stood. Rush expressed his exasperation at Ogilvie's misstep. "It had been whispered, soon after your arrival here, that your orthodoxy was doubtful; but no one even suspected, that you would have the audacity and *imprudence* to avow scepticism," Rush told him in a dressing-down that Ogilvie recounted vividly in his memoir. Moreover, Rush warned him to expect "a sudden and considerable reduction in the number and respectability of your auditors" as well as "an abrupt cessation of intercourse with respectable persons, who have hitherto sought your society." Rush believed no apology would suffice to repair such a devastating evening.[15]

Rush chalked up the public reaction to Ogilvie's words alone. But perhaps a more complex penumbra of words, emphasis, performance, and the scenario of the room all contributed to Ogilvie's problem. The large room he rented from the university stood on the upper floor of what they called the Old Academy Building—and nearly all the documents referring to it emphasized the word *old*, giving the general sense that it had seen better days. Built in 1749, the building featured four classrooms on the bottom floor and an "old fashioned" staircase leading up to the big upper-floor meeting room, which by 1808 was primarily used for Sunday services. The large number of arch-topped windows circling the room allowed enough daylight to stream in to reveal the "much worn" pine floors and "very old" paint on the walls. (Nine years later, when the university applied for insurance coverage for the building, it would be declined.) Still, with a space of about thirty-five hundred square feet, it could seat hundreds. On the late October evening when Ogilvie performed there, the room's scuffed paint would disappear in the glow of candles and lamps, with the audience distracted by the buzz of anticipation.[16]

Rather than stand at the pulpit established at one end of the room, Ogilvie had arranged for his two-foot-high rostrum to be built in front of it, thereby relegat-

THE OLD ACADEMY, ERECTED 1749

West side of Fourth St. below Arch

"THE COLLEGE of PHILAD" 1753

"THE UNIVERSITY" 1779

Figure 20. The Old Academy, Erected 1749. By Benjamin Evans. Watercolor, 1882, from a circa 1780 sketch by Pierre Eugéne Du Simitiére. The Old Academy building (left) at the University of Pennsylvania was at Fourth and Arch Streets; the second floor was an open room used for church services during the early nineteenth century. The New Building (right) provided dormitory rooms and hosted the university's Charity School on the bottom floor. Courtesy of the Library Company of Philadelphia

ing the pulpit to the status of a backdrop. Standing on a stage constructed on that spot, "in a place appropriated to the worship of God," meant that Ogilvie stood *before* the pulpit—thus seeming to place himself metaphorically in front of the church, with the power to pronounce upon it. Words that could appear innocuous on paper or when pronounced in a different setting now potentially suggested that he was snubbing the authority that the pulpit signified.[17]

What proceeded differently on this night as opposed to his previous performances of "Progress and Prospects"? Did he deliver his caveat about Christianity's origin with a different intonation that undermined his words? Did he recite the poem in an overly enthusiastic way that showed his inclination for religious doubt? Or was it a gesture? We can imagine that as he paced the rostrum and enacted the agony of doubt onstage, he might have made a careless gesture that seemed dismissive of the pulpit behind him. A minor tweak to his perfor-

Figure 21. Detail of "Complex Significant Gestures." From Gilbert Austin,
Chironomia; or, A Treatise on Rhetorical Delivery . . . (London, 1806). In his
guidebook for public speakers (ministers, orators, and actors), Austin included a series of
illustrations, including this image of how to perform the emotion of aversion. Did Ogilvie
inadvertently display such distaste for the pulpit behind him during the course of his lecture?
Courtesy of the Southern Illinois University Press, Carbondale, Ill.

mance could suddenly undermine his efforts to be uncontroversial. For an audience already aware of whispers about his atheism, such a scenario might have seemed to challenge Christianity.

Having now committed an unforgivable sin, Ogilvie scrambled to recover. Rush told him that "no acknowledgment, however contrite, no apology, however ample and explicit, would expiate the offense" because these auditors "*conceived that they had a right to be offended.*" Likewise, a learned and sympathetic Episcopalian minister sternly chastised him: "Whatever, sir, may have been your intention, you have done mischief. . . . By avowing these impressions on the Rostrum, you not only excite or encourage doubts, in immature and uninformed minds; but indispose such minds, to examine this all-important question." Ogilvie apologized anyway at the beginning of his next talk, but the die was cast: he received a formal letter from university trustees revoking his permission to use the hall. When he sat down to write an autobiographical narrative of his career almost a decade later, at the height of his American celebrity, he included the full text of their letter as a way to culminate the retelling of the story of this failure in Philadelphia.[18]

Rejected by the somber men who directed the university, Ogilvie continued with his lectures nevertheless. He gave a lecture at the Universalist Church to benefit the Female Association at which he raised his ticket price from fifty cents to a dollar, donating all of the proceeds to the charity; but this was the last time he spoke in a Philadelphia church. Nothing signified his drop in social status more than when he moved the location of his talks to the much smaller ballroom at Sicard's Tavern near the (very quiet) docks—a room that ordinarily hosted meetings and dances. Declining attendance led his friends to try to resuscitate his reputation by issuing a public request in *Poulson's American Daily Advertiser* that he deliver "Progress and Prospects" one more time, this time "omitting any par[t] which may have been heretofore deeme[d] exceptionable." This talk, the newspaper editor promised, "is beyond comparison" his best and provided "a most splendid exhibition of the powers of genius and eloquence" that had earlier led so many to admire his oratory. Ogilvie politely declined. He rounded up all the letters of introduction he could muster from his Philadelphia supporters and departed for New York to start again.[19]

Two hundred years later, many still feel that atheism represents a dangerous rejection of religious faith. Some still associate it with a more general threat to national institutions. But as the passages above suggest, early nineteenth-century concerns about the infidelity of atheism and deism were unique to this place and time. Philadelphia Christians at the time had seen the threat of infidelity on a much more immediate level. They saw themselves embattled by anti-Christian forces with grand designs on the United States. For them, the conundrum that Ogilvie had outlined in "Progress and Prospects" between darkness and light and corruption and moral progress illuminated some of the immediate conflicts taking place in their city, state, and nation. Moreover, some Christians worried that their own side might be losing.

When Ogilvie remembered this affair in his memoir, he claimed that he had stumbled into controversy in Philadelphia out of sheer naïveté. "Although thirty-four years of age," he wrote, he had spent most of his adulthood "in a scholastic and contemplative seclusion: that he was as raw, ignorant and inexperienced in the ways of the world, and as little accustomed to the society, notions and manners of men and women of the world, as *any*, and much less informed and disciplined." Such an excuse must have appeared as unpersuasive then as it does today, particularly given Ogilvie's history of provoking controversy. If there was one area where he couldn't have claimed ignorance, it was about a widespread antipathy to atheism—after all, precisely the same kind of scandal had cost him a job in Fredericksburg fifteen years earlier. Nor had tensions about atheism and deism died down. A decade earlier, the subject aroused public anxieties in part because Americans associated it with some of the most disturbing elements of the French Revolution, including its executions and imprisonments of priests and nuns. By 1808, many American Christians saw the problem of atheism as more diffuse, but no less alarming. Unwittingly or not, Ogilvie had opened a Pandora's box. Concerns about atheism and deism now focused less on a pernicious

French influence on society and more on a domestic enemy rising up from within American culture. In all, the anxiety over infidelity reflected conflicting visions of an American future.[20]

For their part, deists expressed great optimism about the potential for enlightened religion to bring about an age of reason in the United States. Deists believed that in a republic, citizens especially required human reason to make wise choices at the ballot box rather than merely placing blind faith in their elected leaders. Groups of deists formed Societies of Theophilanthropists (lovers of God and Man) in several American towns and cities in the early 1800s, including Baltimore, Philadelphia, and New York. Inspired by a French movement of the same name, these societies took on particularly American forms in the fractious political culture of the early nineteenth century. French Theophilanthropists had idealistically hoped their movement would curtail some of the terrifying violence of the Revolution by providing replacements for the calming rituals of Christian worship. In the United States, the societies focused more intently on educating their fellow citizens. In 1800, a Philadelphian named Denis Driscol formed a deist newspaper entitled *Temple of Reason* whose masthead proclaimed triumphantly, "GREAT IS TRUTH, AND IT SHALL PREVAIL." It continued to deliver feisty denunciations of conventional Christianity on a weekly basis for two years, with support coming almost entirely from its hefty annual three-dollar subscriptions rather than its thin stream of advertisements.[21]

Philadelphia's deists thus sought to protect democracy against what they saw as the anti-intellectualist strain within Christianity, which taught adherents to believe rather than to question—a pattern that, they believed, would have dire effects on the new American Republic. Driscol wanted citizens to ask whether we are "the mere passive engines of men, who may chance to be in power; or, on every occasion, determine our conduct by the dictates of sound reason and the good of mankind." For the Republic to survive, deists believed, it required a populace that had the will and the capacity to think for itself—an argument that might have gained a stronger foothold among like-minded citizens had deists not also insisted on displacing religion.[22]

They also sought to legitimize the movement by establishing institutions that competed with the church in educating the public. During 1801 and 1802, Philadelphia's Theophilanthropists sought funds to construct a Temple of Reason to provide a gathering place where citizens might "rally round the same standard of Reason" and where their children could receive a deist education to prepare them for citizenship in a new republic. When one woman heard about these efforts to raise funds, she fretted in her diary, "Poor Philadelphia how art thou alt[e]red!— and where will all this end?"[23]

Hearing the anguish in that diary entry points to the heart of the matter.

Christians and deists held two things in common. First, they shared the hopeful vision that their own faith would progressively spread to become universal, a vision perpetually compromised by the fear that they were instead losing ground. And second, they saw one another as enemies. Learning about the Theophilanthropists' plans to establish a full-fledged institution and school in the city forced this diarist to imagine that the deists were winning. Which path would the United States follow?

The deists and atheists were in fact not winning. The Theophilanthropists never raised enough funds to build a Temple of Reason, so the effort quietly disappeared from the Philadelphia news. Because the movement's popularity suffered from an increasing public backlash against its perceived political radicalism during the early nineteenth century, fewer people identified with or joined it. Almost everyone who commented on the threat of infidelity acknowledged that they knew of very few actual deists or atheists even as they warned of the ongoing menace. Those who led the charge against infidelity didn't allow the lack of evidence to get in their way; their histrionics on the subject would last decades.[24]

If public tensions about the Temple of Reason had died down by the time Ogilvie got to town, other atheist/deist controversies kept the issue alive. In fact, Ogilvie was not the only alleged atheist to face controversy in Philadelphia that month. The Federalist candidate for governor of Pennsylvania, James Ross, had long held a reputation for irreligion, but the rumors during the 1808 election became particularly bizarre. One rumor had it that his scorn for religion was so extreme that it had led him to administer the sacrament to his dogs. Ross's friends scorned such ludicrous claims. One of them told a Philadelphia newspaper in September that only those who "live by Scandal" would "tell you that he is an atheist, a cheat, and given to all the other vices which can enter into the most depraved imagination." They maintained that Ross's "conduct through life" revealed his "belief not only in a *Supreme Being* but ... in the doctrines of the *Christian* Religion." Despite their protests, nothing could overcome the sense of danger fomented by the tales. By the time the votes were counted, Ross's Republican opponent had triumphed and Ross had gone home to western Pennsylvania, never to seek office again. The fact that Ogilvie's lectures in Philadelphia overlapped with Ross's scandal-ridden election likely made his audiences all the more vigilant for evidence of infidelity. By that time, they had seen themselves in a high-stakes battle against atheism for more than a decade.[25]

When Ogilvie appeared to throw open the origins of Christianity as a "question" in the middle of his "Progress and Prospects" lecture, some of his Christian listeners heard him give credence to the possibility that the deists were right and that human progress might indeed require turning one's back on Christianity and the fantastic, supernatural tales it asked its adherents to believe. Suddenly, a talk that focused on moral progress would seem, to some people in the room, to call for an anti-Christian vision of the future.

It's tempting to scoff at Ogilvie's professions of naïveté, but there may be one good reason to listen to him this time. An outsider like Ogilvie might have felt inclined to attribute election-season tales of James Ross's atheism—charges of delivering the sacrament to dogs, for heaven's sake—to the provincial corners of the state, not the cosmopolitan city of Philadelphia. After living for fifteen years in Virginia villages and the small city of Richmond (about a tenth of Philadelphia's size), Ogilvie might well have overestimated the sophistication of a city that boasted educated and worldly citizens, scientists, literary figures, and salon gatherings of women and men. Having attended some of the social gatherings of Philadelphia's beau monde (the fashionable set), he might have relaxed his vigilance regarding his self-presentation.

For those most interested in these matters, the battle between Christianity and atheism was ultimately a battle for the future. Which direction would the United States take? Ogilvie's error in Philadelphia illustrates the divisions in American society that continued to complicate a sense of national unity or common purpose.

On the surface, James Ogilvie's gaffe in Philadelphia had everything to do with Protestant concerns about atheism. But that might not have been the only thing that made Philadelphians nervous that night. If the perceived threat of infidelity came from urban centers positioned around the Atlantic—cities like London, Dublin, and Paris, where radicals and deists gathered together and produced tracts designed to bring others to their cause—another threat to mainstream Christianity seemed to loom from the western frontier: the evangelical camp meetings and raucous religious revivals that had migrated from the frontier areas of Tennessee and Kentucky toward the East Coast and that increasingly threatened the religious orthodoxy of denominational Protestantism.

Since the turn of the century, Philadelphians had read in the newspapers about the revivals that took place in the West. Spearheaded by charismatic preachers, those meetings stretched out over the course of several days and often drew thousands of attendees. Philadelphia's mainstream Protestants did not oppose advocacy of the Christian faith, of course. Rather, they worried about the rapid spread of unruly, ecstatic forms of faith led by exhorters who might have had extraordinary gifts for contrasting hellfire with heaven but who often lacked formal theological education and the respectability that went along with it. These lay preachers could rouse the emotions of their listeners to a fever pitch such that attendees could, quite simply, lose control of their bodies.[26]

Alarming reports of these meetings described disturbing bodily agitations by converts. In what was called the falling exercise, converts collapsed to the ground as the preacher described the horrors of hell. Others spoke in tongues, cried uncontrollably, danced, or barked like dogs. In some cases they experienced "the jerks," violent convulsions that looked like seizures. To believers, letting loose their bodies to these seemingly involuntary movements represented releasing their souls to God. But to newspaper readers, these extreme behaviors seemed to describe an alarming, unseemly, and irrational new trend. "What real worth or goodness can be imagined in the bodily agitations, the noise, hallooing, jumping and falling, . . . which the Preachers are at so much pains to excite and encourage, which are so highly commended and gloried in?" asked a writer in the Carlisle, Pennsylvania, paper about a month before Ogilvie appeared in Philadelphia. "Are they consistent with the exercise of sober judgment?" This writer ultimately doubted "whether such meetings are entitled to the countenance of the lovers of religion[,] decency, and order."[27]

At one end of the spectrum, atheists and deists privileged reason above the institutions of the Christian church. At the other end, the evangelists privileged religious frenzy above "decency, and order" and certainly above rationality. Members of long-standing Protestant denominations found themselves agreeing with atheists in one respect: such ecstatic forms of Christianity seduced the weak-minded by weaving webs of mystification rather than undergirding their faith with reason.

By the fall of 1808, when Ogilvie appeared in Philadelphia, reports of camp meetings flanked his advertisements in the papers. One meeting, held on a farmer's property about eleven miles outside Baltimore, drew an estimated twelve thousand people. Another in Salem County, New Jersey, featured eleven traveling preachers, seventeen local Methodist preachers, and twelve exhorters and attracted six thousand to seven thousand women and men; the newspaper article that described its success reported upcoming meetings on Staten Island and in Burlington County, New Jersey, just across the river from Philadelphia. Writers alternated between listing impressive numbers of how many souls were brought to God during these meetings and bemoaning the "fanaticism" that prevailed there. They also described another kind of chaos. In addition to earnest believers, rabble-rousers came to wreak "wrath and malice" and disrupt the meeting. One account of a meeting in Weathersfield, Vermont, described "the wicked" going so far as to "seize a falling woman, and undertook to whip a preacher; dressed themselves in women's cloathing; and employed black and drunken men to pray in derision; hooting like owls and howling like wolves and in the woods imitating savages." Whether camp revivals produced good or ill was precisely the question newspaper editors sought to leave in the minds of their readers. After the long description of chaos at the Weathersfield meeting, the writer con-

Religious Intelligence.

Carlisle, Sep. 2.

The religious Camp Meeting by the people denominated Methodists which took place near Shippensburgh on Thursday the 18th of August continued until Tuesday evening following—we are informed that twenty preachers belonging to that society attended—and upwards of 3000 people attended at the camp—from the very orderly and decent behaviour of the people who attended much benefit it is presumed will flow from the meeting—we also understand that several of the clergymen of other religious denominations attended the camp—The Methodist clergymen have expressed a grateful satisfaction for the very prudent and good conduct which they experienced from the people of the town of Shippensburgh and its neighbourhood.

Figure 22. "Religious Intelligence." From True American (Trenton, N.J.), Oct. 10, 1808, [3]. At the same time that Ogilvie's atheism scandal rocked the city of Philadelphia, regional papers recorded the growing popularity of camp meetings and revivals. This one featured twenty preachers and more than three thousand attendees. The writer's careful attention to the participants' "very orderly and decent behaviour" reflected the fact that religious camp meetings had become increasingly respectable, yet still reminded newspaper readers of the revivals' reputation for disorder. Courtesy of the American Antiquarian Society, Worcester, Mass.

cluded, "We leave the account without any remarks, before the public." Revivals were now popular enough that editors no longer felt comfortable attacking them outright; instead, newspapers told readers: You decide.[28]

Despite the many differences between Ogilvie's lectures and camp revivals, they both raised concerns for similar reasons: the possibility that eloquent leaders might sway their listeners to irrational beliefs or anti-republican behavior. To be sure, the disparities were considerable. From the price of his tickets to his desire to have his audiences think together about matters of civic importance, he sought to create a far different kind of experience, for a decidedly respectable, fashionable audience. His emphasis on education alone placed him at odds with some of the most visionary religious movements, which spurned worldly knowledge and sometimes even literacy itself. Indeed, no one at the time drew direct parallels between Ogilvie's oratory and that offered up by ecstatic revivalists. Yet widening the lens shows nevertheless that he shared common elements with the "mystagogues" who used their gifts for speech to influence members of the public. The very fact that he tried to thread the needle between reason and powerful emotional appeal itself could have raised hackles. Even though he put primary stress on rational discussion, he also engaged the audience's emotions in potent ways that mirrored a preacher's exhortation. Consider the magical, swirling tendrils of Ogilvie's intonation, his quotation of sentimental poetry, his performance onstage of a skeptic's dark worries about the future or the melancholic's anguished suicidal thoughts—all intended to bring listeners to the same unsettled state, to entrance them with the sheer force of his eloquence rather than persuade them via a strictly rational argument. Even if he ultimately insisted that civic-minded men and women could, by force of reason, keep civilization on course for human progress, one might see a similarity between his dramatic enactment of concern about Napoleon's march across Europe and a preacher's characterization of hell. Both forced listeners to worry about the future and to correct their ways to bring about a more desirable outcome.[29]

After being tarred with the brush of atheism in Philadelphia, it's unsurprising that no one would draw a direct parallel between Ogilvie and camp meeting preachers. But to worry about a religious huckster and a political or atheistical demagogue amounted to two sides of the same coin in the early Republic. Some might have found his sheer eloquence disturbing, as if the gift for speech automatically raised doubt for its capacity to sway weaker-minded followers. In contrast to less talented speakers or those who emphasized plain, direct address, orators like Ogilvie who conjured evocative tangles of rhetorical excess and entrancing physical performance might well draw forth resistance from some. In fact, they might resist his appeal for the same reasons they worried about evangelical exhorters: because he might also be a fanatic with a dangerous power to wield language and hold a room rapt before him.[30]

There was one final link between Ogilvie and the ecstatic religious exhorters of the Second Great Awakening: they, too, were often Scottish, and their enthusiastic preaching style had been born in Scotland.[31]

The conflict over Ogilvie's gaffe thus reveals broader divisions in American society over religion, the future of the American Republic, and the possibility that public speakers of many stripes might not necessarily have the best interests of the nation at heart. Ogilvie thought his "Progress and Prospects" lecture was his best because it so vividly acknowledged real world problems while also encouraging listeners to work together for the continued progress of society. He felt that this progressive vision of the future, in which Americans did their best to prevent traumatic political upheaval as in France, would have obvious appeal to his audiences. Instead, on this night in Philadelphia, his listeners believed they had witnessed something quite different: they heard him suggest that they jettison their Christian faith. Such a call evoked anxieties that touched on a variety of other social pressures, including the increasing ubiquity of alarmingly animated preachers with their thousands of shaking, jerking converts.

As Ogilvie delivered his final performances in Philadelphia to pitifully small houses, he prepared to decamp for New York—where, he hoped, any news of his gaffe would matter less. He also began to acknowledge that his "romantic excursion" might not be long-lived. Writing to a Virginia patron to request more letters of introduction, he alluded vaguely to the "frivolous circumstances that have successively combined to promote and obstruct" his lectures and suggested that the tour might end quickly. "Twelve or eighteen months hence" when "I shall have finished my excursions," he wrote, "I shall have the pleasure of seeing you in Virginia, where I propose to return and reorganize an academy." No matter how romantic his dreams, by the end of November 1808 his terrible mistake had even led him to consider returning to teaching.[32]

What he found in New York defied his expectations. On one hand, most of his new acquaintances were unfazed by the atheism scandal in Philadelphia. On the other hand, Ogilvie discovered that he had the capacity to rouse deep and angry hatred from one of them. And, unlike the offended Philadelphians who simply shunned him, this new opponent displayed a wicked gift for satire.

{ CHAPTER 6 }
How to Hate Mr. O,
1809–1814

In the spring of 1809, just after James Ogilvie finished lecturing in New York and had left the city for New England, an anonymously authored pamphlet appeared that mocked him relentlessly. *Fragment of a Journal of a Sentimental Philosopher* purported to be his secret diary in which he confessed the many ways he had snookered New York society into thinking him a genius. "Easiest thing in the world to shine in conversation—steal a little from different authors, alter here and there a word, and no danger of detection—played off a good thing, which they all took for the eccentricity of genius," read one passage. "Astonished 'em all with bright sayings I had purloined, studied, and repeated before," it continued. The true author, a shopkeeper named John Rodman, had come to hate the orator after a short acquaintance and sought to render "a very important service to the community" by exposing him as a fraud. The pamphlet never used Ogilvie's name, but no one at the time would have missed the object of Rodman's acrimony. And, because it didn't appear until after Ogilvie left town, its author tried to get in the last word on the orator's performances using satire that still retains a bite. *Fragment of a Journal* remains terrific reading today.[1]

Rodman mocked elements of Ogilvie's character that made sense to him and his readers and left aside what looked to later generations like low-hanging fruit. Although *Fragment of a Journal* portrayed Ogilvie sipping all too regularly at a vial of laudanum, it didn't ridicule that habit—a habit Ogilvie did not conceal, for he had no reason to. Instead, Rodman characterized the opium use as an eccentricity rather than as a flaw in his character. He did not target Ogilvie's intellectual pretensions or his project to reinvigorate oratory in the early Republic. Nor did he mock Ogilvie's Scottishness or complain about his accent, neither of which would have been true if Ogilvie had been Irish. In an era when Irish immigrants were widely scorned for being poor, Catholic, marginally literate, and desperate enough to take on some of the nastiest laboring jobs available, Americans generally held Scottish immigrants in high regard, particularly the Protestant Lowlanders. Although they were not quite as numerous as in Virginia, Scots had risen in New York mercantile, banking, and shipping trades for more than a generation, and the most respected American doctors, including Benjamin Rush and many of the medical professors at Columbia University, had received their medical training at Scottish universities. Educated Scots, in particular, commanded respect, and it had become common to find them and second-generation Scottish Americans in significant leadership positions at American colleges. Instead, Rodman directed his criticism at what he saw as the orator's treacherous politics and at his fellow New Yorkers for being too naive to notice.[2]

Coming only a few months after the scandal over religion in Philadelphia, one might expect that Rodman's pamphlet unmasking Ogilvie's allegedly sinister motivations would have terminated his hopes for success. Certainly, for a performer of a later era to receive such criticism in the nation's two largest cities might have posed an insurmountable problem, making it less likely he could muster admirers elsewhere. But it would be a mistake to make such assumptions about the cultural influence of a metropolis over other parts of the country during the early Republic, when far different dynamics came into play. The furor over *Fragment of a Journal* revealed those dynamics and illustrated the specific reasons Ogilvie could not only survive the scandal but thrive, despite Rodman's deliciously vicious humor and the no-holds-barred attack on what he saw as Ogilvie's dangerous ideas.

Ogilvie arrived in New York in December 1808, shortly after the fracas over religion in Philadelphia that had tarnished his final weeks. Armed with piles of letters of introduction, he set to work courting elite New Yorkers and local ministers, trying to persuade them to attend his talks. The courting paid off. Local newspapers published friendly pieces that downplayed any religious objections. "Far from clashing with religion or its principles," one writer explained in the *Public Advertiser*, Ogilvie "inspires the mind with awful gratitude to the Almighty for the superiority of our existence." Letters from Joseph Cabell of Virginia allowed Ogilvie to meet the twenty-five-year-old Washington Irving (whose father was a Scottish immigrant and successful merchant), James Kirke Paulding, and their circle of literary friends, who smoothed his entrance into New York society. In addition to their social connections, Irving and Paulding had already won reputations as writers with their satirical literary magazine *Salmagundi* as well as other publications in magazines and newspapers. With this warm welcome, Ogilvie extended what he had initially planned to be a short stay. Although he had intended to deliver only four talks in the city, by early January 1809 he announced that he would repeat several of his orations "in compliance with the wishes of ma[n]y respectable persons." He ultimately remained in town more than three months before continuing north and east to Hartford, Providence, and Boston. New York newspapers conveyed nothing but delight. "Mr. Ogilvie's celebrity has already invited the attention of the great body of the most refined and respectable persons in our city," effused one letter to the *American Citizen*.[3]

But not everyone agreed. Only a few weeks after his departure in late March,

Fragment of a Journal appeared. About eight inches tall, the pamphlet's thirty-eight pages were stitched together, making it a cheap purchase. It featured on its title page a quote in Latin from the Roman writer Horace, signaling the pamphlet's satirical intent—at least to those who read Latin. But satire was not its only goal. Taken as a whole, the pamphlet careened between lampoon and fearmongering, warning the public about "the pernicious tendency of the opinions and sentiments expressed in conversation by popular characters, who gain an admittance into our families," as the pamphlet's preface explained. Should we laugh at Ogilvie, or should we beware of him? Both, the pamphlet seemed to indicate— and above all it begged readers to stop attending his performances and to shun him from their homes.[4]

The fake journal delighted in gutting Ogilvie's reputation and attacked those members of New York's society who admired him most. The Ogilvie who appeared here was a flim-flam man, a narcissist with a knack for memorizing passages from other writers and passing them off as his own, and an accomplished actor who carefully adjusted his self-presentation and conversation to suit his company. All the while he affected a sentimental and philosophical persona because he believed it attracted the weak-minded. The fake journal traced his daily social life as he flitted from parlor to parlor seeking to impress socialites with his knowledge and fine feeling. Not that maintaining this guise was easy. Pretending to be respectable, as well as a genius, remained such a constant struggle that this so-called philosopher needed to dose himself liberally with laudanum and spend hours memorizing other writers' words and perfecting his gestures and facial expressions in front of the mirror. "A good deal of practice [is] necessary to make 'em easy," he told his diary wryly.[5]

Much of the Journal displayed with mock seriousness Ogilvie's extreme dedication to gesture and oratorical action, which it portrayed him practicing daily. At one point, he became so exercised in that practice that he broke a mirror. "In whirling suddenly round, and making a violent plunge, with my hand clinched above my head, reciting that d——d German tale," he rammed into the large looking glass and shattered it. "Feel stiff yet in my arms and shoulders in consequence of practising some new gestures," he sulked afterward. At the end of the pamphlet appeared a "Discourse upon Eloquence," also supposedly written by Ogilvie, which argued that gesticulation was the true key to eloquence. "The power of gesticulation collects, fixes, and embodies the sublimest flights of genius—the most laboured researches of learning—the deepest investigations of science—the beauties of diction, and the elegancies of style. It infuses a soul into the inert mass of words," the pamphlet read, revealing razor-sharp mimicry of Ogilvie's hyperbole. "Here the whole art of oratory lies." Mastery of dramatic gestures allowed a speaker to cover up all manner of errors—intellectual sloppi-

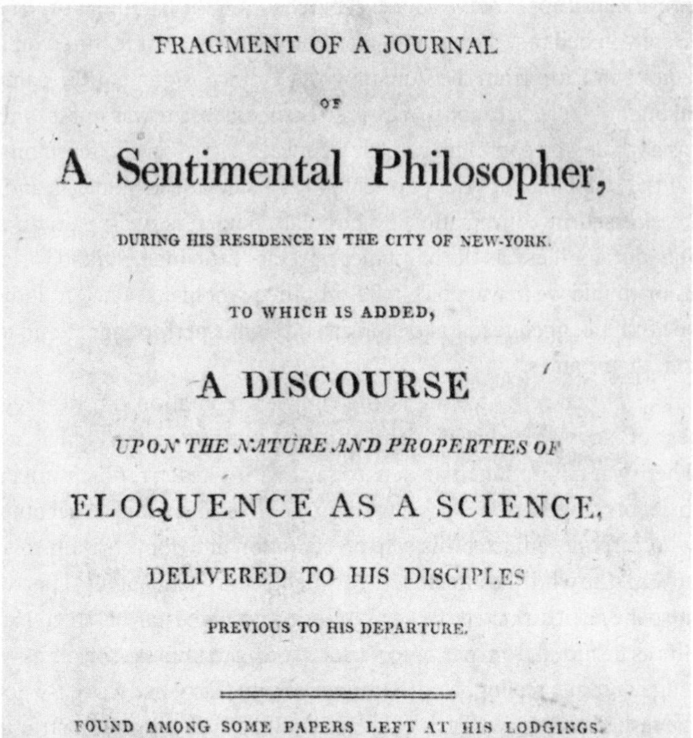

FRAGMENT OF A JOURNAL

OF

A Sentimental Philosopher,

DURING HIS RESIDENCE IN THE CITY OF NEW-YORK.

TO WHICH IS ADDED,

A DISCOURSE

UPON THE NATURE AND PROPERTIES OF

ELOQUENCE AS A SCIENCE,

DELIVERED TO HIS DISCIPLES

PREVIOUS TO HIS DEPARTURE.

FOUND AMONG SOME PAPERS LEFT AT HIS LODGINGS.

———Ego si risi quod ineptus
Pastillos Rufillus olet—lividus et mordax videar?
HORACE.

By John Rodman

NEW-YORK:
PUBLISHED BY E. SARGEANT,
NO. 39 WALL-STREET.

1809.

Figure 23. Title Page of [John Rodman], Fragment of a Journal of a Sentimental
Philosopher . . . (New York, 1809). Rodman's pamphlet includes a quote in Latin from Horace,
the Roman lyric poet, that translates as, "If I laugh because silly Rufillus smells of perfumes, do I seem
sarcastic?" The quote would have signaled to Rodman's readers not only the pamphlet's satirical tone but
also would have foreshadowed Rodman's complaints about Ogilvie's hygiene. Translation courtesy
of Jennifer Eastman. Image courtesy of Rare Books and Manuscripts, Boston Public Library

ness, moral ambiguity, and even outright plagiarism—and the pamphlet assured readers that he was guilty of all three.[6]

Like a con man, the Ogilvie of the *Journal* spoke of his acquaintances as "marks" and the art of conning them as "the game." When he noticed that the many Scottish residents of New York were "mighty proud of me" and "run me down with invitations," he dismissed them as "not the game for me—too steady, industrious and religious a race—not fashionable." His real targets? Women and pretentious would-be intellectuals who imagined themselves part of the beau monde, or the fashionable world. According to the pamphlet's logic, both groups lacked the critical capability to see through Ogilvie's disguise. The pamphlet showed young men hanging upon his words, believing them to reflect original genius rather than carefully plagiarized tidbits from the philosophical greats. Likewise, "The ladies all listened to me with the greatest attention—clung around me—hung upon my words, as if from an angel—swallowed all the jargon of the Godwinian school." Lines like this implied that Ogilvie himself didn't really believe the subversive ideas he spread to the gullible.[7]

The pamphlet especially fretted that women responded to him—in part because they fell like fools for his "*soft blue eyes*" and in part because they became so disarmed by his affectations of eccentricity. Those affectations were, of course, carefully chosen. When he found that "the ladies languish for novelty," he decided that they must be "tired of the manners and dress of a gentleman." Thus, he insisted on wearing dirty clothes. "The more filthy my dress and person—the more sentimental and interesting—cleanliness a real obstacle to gaining their favour," he wrote. When one of his friends politely suggested that he "wash my hands and put on a clean shirt" before going out to a party, he declined. "Would have ruined me with the ladies," he confessed to the diary. "Any body can be clean—no merit in that—they think me above such trifles." (One cannot help but remember that back in college, Grigor Grant had derided him in *The Ogilviad* for living in a "dirty den.")[8]

But even as this material was manifestly entertaining, the pamphlet harbored an earnest desire to warn readers of the dangers the orator represented. Characters like Ogilvie posed serious problems because, the pamphlet suggested, once welcomed into polite society, they instilled "the poison of their principles into the very bosom of domestic life." "They vitiate and corrupt every tender, every amiable, every noble sentiment of the heart," as Rodman warned in his anonymous preface to the pamphlet. The real problem? Ogilvie's atheism and political radicalism.[9]

All of the pamphlet's jests at his dirty clothing, eccentric mannerisms, and overly elaborate oratorical gestures made the text funny, but its true goal was to alarm the public, to spread concerns about the potential contamination of dangerous ideas, and to characterize him as a transgressor of all the values Americans held most dear. "As long as I can keep up the infatuation that now prevails in my favour—I do not despair of producing a complete revolution in domestic society—a total change in the principles, sentiments, feelings, taste, and conduct of women," wrote the Ogilvie of the secret diary in one of the most sinister, moustache-twirling passages. He targeted women not merely because he saw them as more easily duped but also because he knew they were crucial to his plan. Previous crusading atheists had failed to gain traction owing to flaws in their tactics, he mused in the journal, because they focused their efforts primarily on persuading men. Instead, Ogilvie concocted for his lectures a heady mixture of eloquent quotations, timely subject material, and a dose of sentimentalism, for "'tis sentiment touches the women, and *they rule the men*." The *Journal* showed Ogilvie carefully manipulating his acquaintances while keeping his abhorrent views of religion under wraps. "Must, however, proceed with caution on this subject—people are cursed religious in this city—yet don't despair of correcting that evil—must avoid the rock I split upon in Philadelphia," he wrote in a staccato, fragmented tone. "Be careful not to speak publicly against christianity, nor to enter into any argument about it—on the contrary praise it, as *an excellent institution*—good system of morals; but lament *my misfortune* in not believing in its *divine origin*." He flattered his acquaintances at the same time that he slipped into their conversation references to the authors most associated with atheism and deism: William Godwin and Thomas Paine. And, sure enough, by the end of the pamphlet, it appeared that he had succeeded: he referred to his young male visitors as his "disciples, (as I call them)," and he hoped that after he left the city they would "use their best endeavours to forward the great work of reformation" of society.[10]

The pamphlet's author never named the New York society figures taken in by him, but it did provide easily decipherable pseudonyms in the form of initials, such as Mrs. Y. and Dr. MacN. When it described a young Mr. T. who "has genius," "wrote a book," and was friends with Thomas Jefferson's neighbor Mr. C., many readers could have guessed that this was the writer Washington Irving, who had helped Ogilvie navigate the city during his three months there. Several years earlier Irving had traveled in Europe with Joseph Cabell, a neighbor of Jefferson's and patron of Ogilvie's; Cabell and Irving had reconnected in Richmond in 1807 to observe the treason trial of Aaron Burr. Other major New York figures it lampooned included Joseph Dennie, editor of the *Port Folio*, and the novelist and journalist Charles Brockden Brown, who had supported Ogilvie in Philadelphia through the scandal there. Nor was the pamphlet's author, John Rodman, seriously concerned with concealing their identities. He ultimately felt so pleased with his production that one surviving copy of the pamphlet that found its way

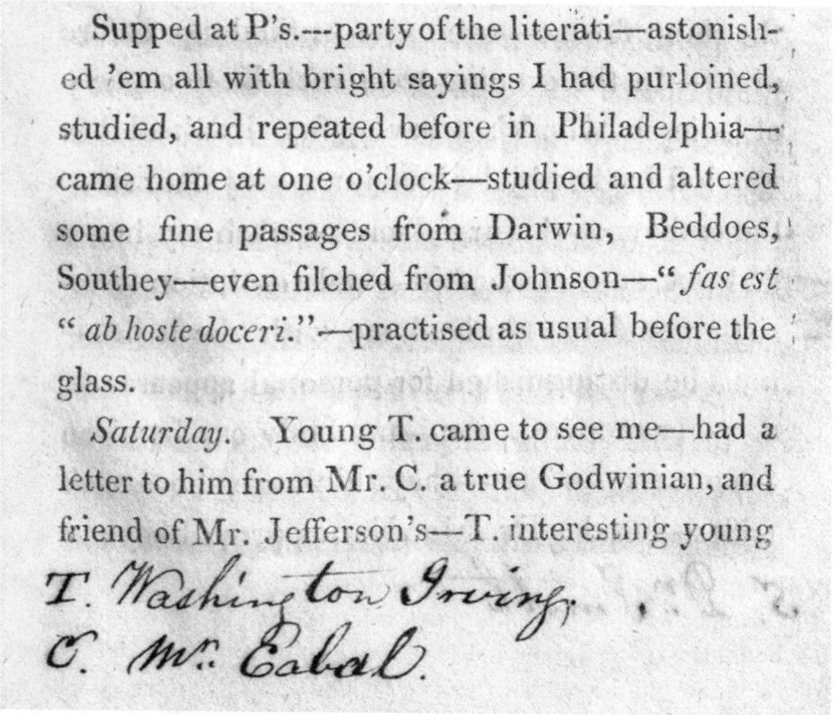

> Supped at P's.---party of the literati—astonish-
> ed 'em all with bright sayings I had purloined,
> studied, and repeated before in Philadelphia—
> came home at one o'clock—studied and altered
> some fine passages from Darwin, Beddoes,
> Southey—even filched from Johnson—" *fas est*
> " *ab hoste doceri.*"—practised as usual before the
> glass.
>
> *Saturday.* Young T. came to see me—had a
> letter to him from Mr. C. a true Godwinian, and
> friend of Mr. Jefferson's—T. interesting young

T. Washington Irving.
C. Mr. Cabal.

Figure 24. Entry from [John Rodman], Fragment of a Journal of a Sentimental Philosopher . . . (New York, 1809), 11. Rodman identified his targets, who appear only with capital letters in the pamphlet. Courtesy of Rare Books and Manuscripts, Boston Public Library

into the Boston Public Library included the notation that the author himself provided identifications for each of his targets.[11]

If Rodman had wanted to maintain his own anonymity as the pamphlet's author, he failed—in part because he was simply too closely connected to many of the New Yorkers whose gullibility he mocked. It would have been difficult for anyone to remain anonymous after publishing a piece like *Fragment of a Journal*, so clearly penned by someone intimate to the very society that he rebuked. Rodman had married into the Fenno family, a prominent two-generation publishing family that included some of Irving's closest friends. In fact, Irving and his friends—a proto-Knickerbocker group—met regularly for discussion at the bookshop of Ezra Sargeant, who had purchased the Fenno bookshop and had continued to foster Federalist-leaning readership and publications that the Fennos had helped establish. Rodman also had family ties to Matilda Hoffman, a woman Irving had hoped to marry before her untimely death from consumption earlier that winter, and whom he would mourn for years. As with the barely dis-

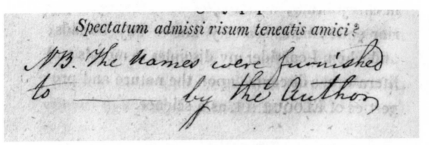

Figure 25. Notation from [John Rodman], Fragment of a Journal of a Sentimental
Philosopher . . . (New York, 1809). The notation, "The names were furnished to —— by the
Author," appears at the end of the Boston Public Library's copy of Rodman's pamphlet. The quotation
above it (also from Horace) reads, "If you saw such a thing, friends, could you restrain your laughter?"
Courtesy of Rare Books and Manuscripts, Boston Public Library

guised portrait of Irving himself, the Journal's depictions of parlor conversations
and evening parties clearly reflected real events and identifiable people — many
of whom knew Rodman and his opinions well.[12]

One might wonder whether Rodman was motivated by partisanship, given
that he affiliated more with Republicans, unlike his in-laws and many of Irving's
friends mocked in the pamphlet. But those lines are not clear, especially considering that both Ogilvie and Irving leaned toward Republicanism as well.
Rodman's warnings about Ogilvie's dangerous political and religious inclinations sounded more like Federalist anxieties about the threat of democratic radicalism. It appears more likely that Rodman set aside partisan concerns as he
sought to warn readers and that he ultimately mustered an argument that skirted
politics to focus on Ogilvie as a danger to civil society.[13]

Shortly after the pamphlet's publication, when a group of those very men
gathered at Sargeant's bookshop to discuss it, they quickly deduced that Rodman
had written it. One of them later reported their collective outrage at the way
Rodman had "very injudiciously ridiculed Mr. Paulding, Mr. Irving, and some
others of the New York literati." When Rodman himself arrived that evening,
the group criticized the pamphlet with such vitriol that he realized his mask was
off and stormed out. In an anonymous letter to the editor of a local newspaper a
few days later, Rodman redoubled his insults, briefly reiterating his complaints
about Ogilvie but mostly condemning the Irving group and mocking their criticisms of *Fragment of a Journal*. "One of these lynx-eyed geniuses discovered several
words *spelled wrong*; and ran triumphantly with the book to some *ladies* to show
them," he ridiculed, "rejoicing to find so strong an evidence of the *stupidity* of the
work." Another, he wrote, had held forth on the misuse of the word *upon* in one
sentence. Rodman expressed disdain for these self-satisfied "profound critics,"

proclaiming that they "deserved the satiric thong full as much as their friend, the philosopher." In an era when one did not insult someone by name in the paper, Rodman came as close as possible to identifying these men, writing sarcastically that they "constantly revolve[d] round the *resplendent* orbs of Salmagundi," and calling out Irving in particular as "a gentleman already distinguished in the literary world, having written several *neat things* which appeared in the Port Folio." No one in their social compass would have failed to miss the fact that Rodman intended to insult several very identifiable men, Washington Irving most of all.[14]

Rodman had wanted the pamphlet to articulate broad concerns about Ogilvie's effect on American culture and New York society, but the subsequent infighting between him and the Irving crowd revealed a petty skirmish among New Yorkers who simply didn't like each other. Rodman spent more time in the paper throwing barbs at Irving and Paulding than at Ogilvie—and for their part, insulted twice in print, Irving and his friends struck back. They first submitted sharp responses in the *Evening Post*, offering full-throated defenses of Ogilvie. They expressed particular outrage that Rodman should offer such public attacks only after Ogilvie had left the city and could no longer defend himself. They expressed offense that Rodman had "made it his particular business to hunt up all the anecdotes" about "private if not confidential conversations" and to "reproach the conduct of those gentlemen who were the particular intimates of Mr. O." Over the course of five letters to the editor, Rodman and the Irving group exchanged attacks, with Rodman usually publishing the more aggressive and insulting abuses. With Rodman showing no sign of backing down, they retaliated by publishing a nineteen-page pamphlet in the guise of a book review from a nonexistent magazine called the *New-York Review; or Critical Journal*.[15]

If Irving and his circle had resisted ad hominem attacks on Rodman in the *Evening Post*, they didn't hold back in this faux review. "Among our painful duties" as reviewers, they began, sharpening their knives, was "that we have occasionally to toil through the muddy volumes of blundering stupidity, or to skim over the frothy pages of conceited impertinence." They insulted Rodman's language, his tendency to borrow all his ideas from the same source, and even his short stature, often depicting him as a particularly annoying little dog "in full yelp at the heels of the Philosopher." Just as Rodman had made Irving's identity transparent to anyone in their social circle, so the *New-York Review* described Rodman as a "certain brisk, dapper little Ironmonger; who has long been beating the bushes of literature, without starting any game, and rapping at the door of several professions, without gaining admittance into any," and derided the shopkeeper's delusions of wit. In the end, they accused him of being nothing more than an envious man who "darts his venom at the object of his ill humor" and hid his jealousy behind "religious zeal." Their insults were funny, but mostly mean.[16]

Irving and Paulding dedicated most of their pamphlet to dismantling Rodman's character, but they also backed away from the strong support they had previously shown for Ogilvie. They insisted that his lectures together with "the whole tenor of his conversation, as far as it reached our ears, were free from harm or reproach." But they also described him as simply too earnest and naive to harbor Machiavellian plans. "We consider him, in fact, a mere amusing, philosophical Quixote; who had not wickedness to devise, nor artfulness enough to execute, the mischiefs our windy alarmist has asserted—and whose harmless eccentricities and visionary speculations, might have excited the smile of the gay, or the compassion of the charitable; but could never deserve the unfeeling and personal lash of the censorious." Most of all, they demanded evidence of any malevolent effects. "Multitudes of our fellow citizens, of all descriptions thronged to hear him, yet we do not find that our churches are the less attended, the order of society subverted, or infidelity more prevalent than formerly." In other words, "If Mr. O——'s opinions were really as pernicious and as insidiously instilled, as our journalist would fain have us believe, why were they not attacked before? why was he suffered to remain several weeks in this city, and no assault made until his back was turned, and his power of doing injury had ceased?" They then addressed Rodman directly, "We advise him to abstain from pen, ink, and paper," and concluded with a threat. "But if, notwithstanding this friendly hint, we ever catch him" in the act of literary satire again, "we will most certainly straddle him over a rail, and ride him round the premises, to the great amusement and laughter of the muses, and the eternal terror of all interlopers." Threatening to force Rodman to ride the rail amounted to more than public humiliation. Like tarring and feathering, another form of mob violence during the long Revolutionary era, riding the rail could cause severe pain and lasting damage to the groin. Townspeople forced their victim to straddle a fence rail carried on the shoulders of two strong men, who jostled and violently bounced the victim up and down. Even if Irving and his friends meant it metaphorically—not a literal rail but rather more embarrassment—they invoked a vicious form of bullying.[17]

The battle of words and threats between Rodman and the Irving circle thus became an internecine fight between New Yorkers who knew each other too well. As a result, they took heat off Ogilvie himself. When Irving and his friends unveiled Rodman's true identity to the public as he had theirs, and when the two sets of men began taking turns insulting one another's intellects and social standing in earnest, the story transformed. By the end, the story focused less on Ogilvie than on whose opinion should be trusted: that of a shopkeeper with an ax to grind or a well-connected group of writers eager to defend a friend from defamation.

Rodman apparently never again set foot in the realm of literature and social satire, but we can't know whether this was owing to embarrassment, his opponents' threats, or circumstance. He departed New York shortly after the publication of the Irving-Paulding *New-York Review* and remained away for a stint in the military during the War of 1812. One could understand if he had felt humiliated. After all, his invective had ricocheted around to smack him in the face, his anonymity unmasked, and some of his own friends and in-laws now bullied and mocked him. Worse, he saw no measurable change in Ogilvie's reputation.[18]

Indeed, when Ogilvie returned to New York a year later, he went out of his way to reassure the public of the purity of his motives and his aversion to deception by publishing an odd, rambling broadside. "He has scrupulously and even fastidiously avoided any expression that could exhibit the semblance of artifice or ostentation," he wrote in an awkward third-person style, and in the tiny font required to get all eighteen hundred words onto a single newspaper-sized page. If at any point he had misspoken, he promised, it was more because of his naïveté or the "sudden vicissitudes of energy and apathy" that made up his "temperament and habit." Most of all, he maintained that his central aim was as straightforward as he had always promised: to combine education and entertainment in the "revival and cultivation of the noble art" of oratory.[19]

In the end, the conflict over *Fragment of a Journal* revolved around a series of contradictory elements. Rodman believed that Ogilvie represented a real danger to society. Cloaked behind all his affected eccentricities lay a conniver eager to turn a Christian nation into unbelievers. His most easily mocked qualities paled next to his potential to corrupt society, and especially women, with dangerous aims. But amid the controversy over the pamphlet, Rodman revealed far less public-minded goals, instead showing his personal animus toward some of Ogilvie's friends and raising questions about his own character and judgment. Rather than turn the public away from Ogilvie's performances, the pamphlet appears to have led New Yorkers to decide for themselves whether Ogilvie deserved censure or celebration.

Had Ogilvie simply stretched the limits of his welcome?

It's easy to understand why he stayed so long in New York, and in Philadelphia before that. The hardest part of his lecture tour consisted of the long days or weeks of traveling, getting settled in a new place, working out the logistics of his performance venue, and knocking on the doors of people to whom he held letters of introduction. He earned no income during these stretches, and so he might have anticipated each new round of lectures with apprehension. No wonder he stayed more than three months in each of these two major American metropolises. Extending his visit delayed the inevitable stresses of living, at least temporarily, without an income.

For contrast, consider that when Washington Irving offered career advice to the young itinerant actor John Howard Payne in 1809, the kernel was: never stay more than a week. "Leave Baltimore as soon as possible," Irving wrote. "I know you are much caressed there and are surrounded by friends, but that is the reason why you should decamp—You cannot excite more attention—You cannot gain greater notoriety and applause; but you may cease to be a novelty . . . and the public becoming familiar with you in private as well as in public, will not have the same eagerness to see you perform, on future occasions." Irving assured his friend that if the Angel Gabriel were to "come down from heaven," even he would enjoy only a brief window of public interest. "Do you recollect the comet that made its appearance about two years ago? how much we stared at it the first week—how little the second?—had it remained a third I warrant we would not have thought a whit more of it," Irving declared in warning. Whether or not the "comet" was a veiled reference to Ogilvie, Irving's letter illuminated the difficulties in staying too long in any one place.[20]

To be sure, an itinerant actor shouldered far less financial risk than a sole performer like Ogilvie. Payne could contract with theater managers in the range of American cities that featured permanent companies. A weeklong visit was possible because the theater manager handled all the logistics of bringing a play to life and selling tickets; Payne simply had to memorize the lines for his roles, cultivate the curiosity of the public, and, in Irving's words, "fill your pockets from their curiosity." In contrast, before Ogilvie could even begin a series of performances, he needed to invest significant amounts of time and money. Only if he sold an exceptional number of tickets or managed to repeat his lectures could he amass the savings that might see him through an illness or a break from performing. Staying only a week in any given city might have kept Ogilvie from overstaying his welcome, but it was logistically impossible.[21]

If any region of the country offered better opportunities for shorter stays, it was the more densely populated New England states where Ogilvie arrived in March 1809. At a moment when the United States had only forty-six cities larger than twenty-five hundred people, twenty of them lay within an easy distance of the New England coastline, the majority of which were in Massachusetts. This region also featured comparatively good roads. When Ogilvie effused to a friend about the "comfortable and even delightful apartments" in Boston's Coffee Exchange building, he did so because this new hotel marked such a decided improvement over his usual lodgings. Over the course of the ensuing year, he ricocheted around these four states and the District of Maine delivering dozens of lectures. He rarely stayed more than a month in any single place but performed in Boston, Salem, and Providence twice, and three times each in Portsmouth and Newburyport. From each he made short day trips to smaller villages nearby, as when he traveled fourteen miles from the coastal city of Portsmouth to the hamlet of Exeter for a performance. It left little time for rest.[22]

Along the way, he encountered more criticism—often on his second or third visit to a city. At times this criticism displayed forms of intimate warfare akin to what happened in New York with John Rodman—a battle between local individuals or groups that ultimately had less to do with Ogilvie himself. At other points the criticism suggested something broader: larger disagreements over the shape and future of American society. Sometimes disparaging his performances could provide these writers with opportunities to try out the role of cultural critic or to offer fine-tuned complaints about aspects of his performances.[23]

As a younger man back in Virginia, Ogilvie had responded to criticism with scathing letters to the editors of local papers. Now he restrained himself. He might have begun to realize that the whiff of controversy didn't necessarily hurt him.

If some New Englanders had gotten wind of Ogilvie's atheism controversies in Philadelphia or from Rodman's pamphlet, they left little trace that it mattered to them—in the public press, anyway. The rumor mills, however, were another matter entirely.

Gossip in Salem, Massachusetts, the nation's ninth largest city with a population of more than twelve thousand, made Ogilvie's second visit there in the fall of 1809 a mixed bag. The fragmentary evidence provides only the most general outlines of the affair. The minister William Bentley expressed disgust in his diary over the rumors circulating about Ogilvie, with whom he had frequently socialized and whose lectures Bentley enjoyed. He blamed the "lazy interference" of two local men, including a local Baptist preacher, who stirred up gossip about the orator. Worst of all, those rumors had tainted one of Ogilvie's benefit lectures. When he sought to raise funds for the Salem Female Asylum, a charitable organization dedicated to educating orphaned girls and preparing them for work in domestic service, his critics fostered such misgivings via the local gossip mill that "not one of the Clergy was present and not a third of the Company was of Gentlemen." Despite the fact that Ogilvie's talk raised $120 in much-needed funds for the charity (akin to four months of a laborer's earnings), his critics' suggestions of impropriety and especially Ogilvie's irreligion ended up casting censure on the ladies at the helm of the Female Asylum who had asked him to speak. Bentley was repulsed by the entire affair. "Such is the influence of the ignorant upon sincere and good minds," he groused in his diary. "The best [people], sure of good intentions and little able to bear the censure of the world are thus deeply wounded." Were these rumors about Ogilvie entirely based on his reputation as an atheist? Were other issues at play, comparable to the simmering dislike between John Rodman and Washington Irving that had turned Ogilvie into a convenient opportunity for a skirmish? The scanty evidence that survives does not say.[24]

What is clear is that none of those concerns became fierce enough to appear in regional newspapers. The vast majority of newspaper content praised the orations and promoted the events during the spring and summer of 1809, as Ogilvie made numerous stops in the many cities between Boston and Portland in the District of Maine. But starting in late September, several critics began publishing pieces that cycled through the Portsmouth, Salem, and Newburyport papers, sometimes getting reprinted in all of them. These writers didn't follow Rodman's example by fearmongering about Ogilvie's contaminating influence on women, his hygiene, personal transgressions, or alleged plagiarism of other people's ideas. Nor did they deploy sarcasm or satire. These northern New England critics took care to reveal no sense of animus and instead criticized Ogilvie as an orator—his style, his choice of subject matter, the content of his talks, and his skill as a speaker. Rather than fan fears of ideological contagion, these writers complained more modestly that Ogilvie did not deserve his celebrity as a public speaker. In other words, they took him seriously as an orator even as they found fault.

Virtually all critics acknowledged his talents, but they often suggested he ought to scale back on his enthusiastic delivery in order to offer a more moderate performance. Criticisms like this often implied that Ogilvie's oratory was less polished than reports had suggested—and that the critic himself knew better how such performances should look. "His virtues are carried to an extreme: his fancy is too luxuriant; his language is studded with epithets; and his description is overcharged," one writer suggested in the Portsmouth Oracle. "He soars aloft, and appears to disdain to come down to the level of common understanding." Critics advised that his performances ought to be "pruned, chastened and corrected." Another writer in the same paper agreed, suggesting that Ogilvie's effusions ran the risk of becoming "all smoke and no fire" because the showiness of his elocution seemed intended to cover up the fact that none of his talks "evinced solid or original thoughts." This criticism resembled that reported by a Boston schoolgirl, who told her diary that she had heard Ogilvie's orations described as "like a whip sillybub in an eggshell" (a whipped syllabub was a frothy drink made with wine and whipped egg whites) for speaking "too much to the passions and not enough to the reason." This writer expressed bafflement as to what cultural role Ogilvie's form of oratory might play, considering how much it differed from the usual forms of public speech in classrooms, courtrooms, and churches. Bentley, who admired Ogilvie's lectures as well as his company, ranted in his diary that "there is nothing appropriate and nothing true" contained in the anonymous letters to the editor of the local paper. Some of Bentley's friends guessed that the real author was "some book girl" (an epithet especially cutting because it suggested the letter had been written by a bookish, overeager girl), but he speculated that they were "more probably" written by a youth, "some sophimore."[25]

Bentley guessed well. That specific essay by "some sophimore" had been written by John Gallison, a twenty-one-year-old studying to enter the law in Salem. Since Gallison spent many of his evenings in impromptu debates with his friends—debates intended to teach them verbal agility and eloquence for use in the courtroom—he believed he had grown particularly adept in assessing the oratory of others. In his diary, Gallison offered a full paragraph of praise for Ogilvie's performances. "He directed all his powers of language and action to excite in the breasts of his hearers, the zeal for reformation," he marveled. "In description he excels, and never neglects an opportunity to exhibit that talent. He has fancy, imagination, and a powerful command of language. His action is spirited and graceful. His voice has great compass and is ever well modulated." Still, he ultimately deemed Ogilvie "an actor rather than an orator." Gallison told his diary that, whereas the goal of "a real orator" emphasized argument rather than performance, "to carry his words with greater force to the understanding and hearts of his audience," Ogilvie's "ultimate object is to please." "He does not speak like one warmed with the vehement desire to impress some opinion upon the minds of his hearers, or to persuade them to some action," he complained. These passages in Gallison's diary actually sounded sharper than his anonymous critique of Ogilvie in the local paper, which was more generous. "Those who deny to Mr. O the ability powerfully to awake the feelings of his audience, and to set in motion the whole machinery of fancy, have surely never listened to his eloquence. But it may be asked, is not the orator admired while his words are forgotten? do not his powers astonish rather than impress us? does he persuade us to love virtue, or to praise her advocate?" Of all the published criticisms during his New England tour, Gallison's was the most even-handed—but, like the rest, he focused, not on whether Ogilvie represented a danger, but whether one could truly deem him an orator.[26]

In each case, Ogilvie's defenders rushed to counter those criticisms in print, arguing that to quibble about the orator's skills detracted from the larger point that his lectures represented something new and important. One writer in the *Newburyport Herald* expressed exasperation at the overly "generalizing manner of condemnation," which provided no specific details and could thus "be applied to every Orator or Actor, who has appeared since the English language was spoken." This writer denounced such vague criticisms. "Let not his attainments be derided, for they are great, nor his talents ridiculed for they are brilliant." He dismissed the implication that Ogilvie's supporters and fans lacked discernment.

Their support emerged "not from indiscriminating admiration, or stupid wonder; not from any belief in his infallibility, or blindness to his errors; but in perfect confidence" that any criticism would sit alongside the "unbiassed opinions of the judicious" and allow Ogilvie's listeners to judge for themselves. Another defender claimed that some priggish New Englanders despised "public amusements of every kind, even those which are innocent in themselves, and whose influence on society is beneficial and salutary." No one who had heard Ogilvie's lecture could "recollect a finer effusion of chaste, manly, dignified, and impressive eloquence," he declared. Gallison's anonymous essay also concluded with lavish praise for the larger project. "How glorious an enterprise! to restore to Eloquence that dignified station, which antiquity assigned her among the liberal arts! to make her once more the able advocate of virtue and morality, of wise policy, of philosophic truth!" These writers insisted that any criticism focus on that project, keeping their eyes on the prize of invigorating oratory in the American Republic.[27]

Self-consciously serious letters like these (and those in other city newspapers sporadically over the course of Ogilvie's tour) contained relatively modest critiques. They picked at the details of Ogilvie's lectures and his performance, complaining that his talks weren't quite original enough, or his oratorical action too theatrical. But these letter writers ultimately agreed with Ogilvie that the United States needed better oratory, even if they might disagree about what it ought to look like. In other words, Ogilvie's performances provided a useful opportunity for them to step forward onto their own (printed) stage: to demonstrate fine discernment and learning and to act as model citizens who engaged in refined debate about the pros and cons of public figures.[28]

Ogilvie held back from responding to his New England critics, but John Rodman's vicious criticism rankled for a long time. Five years after the publication of *Fragment of a Journal of a Sentimental Philosopher*, Ogilvie returned to New York to find Rodman, also back in the city after many years away. Ludicrous as it might seem, Ogilvie went so far as to challenge him to a duel. "I lost no time in demanding redress," Ogilvie reported in a letter to a friend. After exchanging a series of angry letters, the two men resolved their animosity without resorting to pistols at dawn, likely because of the intervention of friends. But Ogilvie insisted on having the last word. He instructed his friend Pierre Van Wyck, a former member of city government (serving as Ogilvie's second, in the language of affairs of honor), to approach Rodman and read aloud a final letter that concluded their exchange with a final volley of insults. "Mr. Ogilvie takes no pleasure in degrading or stigmatising any one, and is sorry to assure John Rodman, that he considers him as an infamous calumniator and an abject coward, and will at all times and on all occasions whenever he condescends to speak of him, couple these ignominious epithets with his name as the qualities they express are indelibly stamped on his character." In other situations, calling someone a coward made pistols necessary. In this case, Rodman proved the more even-tempered, permitting Ogilvie to vent his spleen to end the conflict.[29]

Since part of his regular rotation of lectures included a critique of dueling, for Ogilvie to have come so close to the dueling ground himself appears baffling—and not least because it took place five years after the initial insult. In fact, Ogilvie's reputation suffered virtually no ill effects from the publication of *Fragment of a Journal*, making his 1814 challenge all the more confounding. By that time his reputation as an exemplar of eloquence had grown and the pamphlet had faded to obscurity. The pamphlet had perversely enhanced Ogilvie's appeal, prompting people to attend his performances.

To Rodman, Ogilvie represented a radical danger to the public: his atheism in tandem with his eccentric appeal to society women and men seemed to escalate into an outsized problem requiring a caustic pen. But Rodman could not separate his scorn for Ogilvie from his frustration with his acquaintances, in-laws, and members of his social circle who did the most to boost Ogilvie's career. The resulting fight between New Yorkers undermined his plan to use *Fragment of a Journal* as a battering ram against Ogilvie's pernicious effects. Hints of similar local fights appeared in Salem as well, with ministers using Ogilvie's presence in town to face off over matters that have largely been lost to the historical record. Meanwhile, letters to the editors of local papers, by far the most common form of criticism, displayed how self-consciously discerning individuals might reinforce the importance of Ogilvie's project to enhance oratory in the Republic, even if they complained that his specific performances weren't quite good enough.

Why didn't the scandals over atheism in Philadelphia and the appearance of the satirical *Fragment of a Journal of a Sentimental Philosopher* in New York, both within the first year of his lecturing, cause lasting damage to Ogilvie's career, particularly as these were the two largest cities in the United States? These scandals reveal how profoundly insular even these two cities could be at this point in American history. Ogilvie's Philadelphia friends had assured him that he had destroyed his career by seeming to advocate for atheism, yet he found that scandal largely inconsequential to his New York acquaintances. Likewise, John Rodman's memorable caricature of Ogilvie in filthy clothes, swigging at his laudanum vial and profiting from the gullibility of his fashionable admirers, appeared to outsiders as a local affair unique to a particular segment of New York society, as if Ogilvie had merely been a lightning rod for battles that had little to do with the orator and his performances. At no point later in Ogilvie's career did any of

Rodman's best insults reappear; they simply didn't stick. Only by grasping how deeply localized the United States was, even to the point that an entertaining satire like Rodman's gained no traction, can we begin to see how Ogilvie might not just survive a scandal but thrive in the next city down the road.

In fact, a parallel phenomenon began to emerge that also reflected the relative cultural isolation of different parts of the country. The same sense of regionalism played a large role in accelerating the prodigious praise he began receiving from newspapers. To comprehend it requires recognizing how rare it was for Ogilvie to encounter much criticism at all. Instead, the overwhelming response to his performances was to offer effusive, extravagant tributes to his talents—tributes that almost seemed to have each town newspaper vying to outdo the next in its acclaim for the orator's eloquence.[30]

That praise did more than testify to public approval. His appearances seemed to shine a particularly bright light on the towns he visited, such that local newspapers spent almost as much time commenting on their own citizens as they did applauding Ogilvie's skills. The reviews revealed a deep self-consciousness that emerged when a cosmopolitan figure like Ogilvie came to town. In other words, the same regionalism that stymied criticism like John Rodman's ultimately helped to fuel James Ogilvie's celebrity.

CHAPTER 7

A Cosmopolitan Celebrity in a Provincial Republic

During the nine years James Ogilvie spent lecturing in America, he traveled to seventeen states, two territories, and parts of Lower Canada. The only two states he didn't visit were Louisiana and Vermont. Even today, with comparatively comfortable and speedy cars, trains, and planes, the average American has visited only twelve of the fifty United States; two hundred years ago, the average American hadn't been further than a hundred miles from home. (An example of such relative regional isolation: one memoirist remembered that they didn't eat with forks during his youth in the inland town of Columbia, South Carolina, though they had heard tell of what they called "split spoons.") To many of his audience members, Ogilvie was a cosmopolitan. That combination—having traveled widely and being well known for it—helped to transform him into a celebrity.[1]

Knowing that he had already spoken in large cities and diverse regions of the country and that he had been embraced there by eminent citizens shaped the views of his listeners. When he got to Boston in 1809, the papers described him as having performed "in the various capital cities of the United States" to audiences who found him "eminently distinguished for his rhetorick and elocution." When he arrived in Charleston, the newspapers described his lectures as "delivered, to numerous and respectable audiences, in Philadelphia, New-York, Boston, etc." Reports like these seemed to take his cosmopolitanism for granted.[2]

Ogilvie's arrival could be thrilling, for it allowed locals to witness the same talks as the denizens of more glamorous urban places, suggesting that his appearance might elevate their town to the same level as "Philadelphia, New-York, Boston, etc." But not all reacted in this manner. Some expressed nagging feelings that their town might not measure up to the orator's standards or that they would appear hopelessly backward, unfashionable. Ogilvie's aura of cosmopolitan celebrity could provoke a contrasting sense of provincialism that appeared in reviews of the orator's performances. At the same time that Ogilvie's celebrity grew, it held up a mirror, making some observers aware of their own limitations.[3]

Patriotic boosters liked to sing about the American populace's mobility during the early Republic, though we should view their boosterism with a grain of salt. "There is more travelling [in the United States] than in any part of the world," proclaimed one newspaper article. "Here, the whole population is in motion; whereas, in old countries, there are millions who have never been beyond the sound of the parish bell." To be sure, the roads could be busy. Itinerant peddlers' wagons and mail coaches trundled past laborers in search of farms offering work, students walking to school, or merchants on horseback traveling to the nearest trade center or a more distant port city. In most of these cases, *traveling* might be too strong a word for the movement on the roads; locals simply traversed the same carriageways on a daily or weekly basis. Moreover, in most areas, a road meant a single-tracked bridle path that had, perhaps, been widened to accommodate carts and wagons but remained best suited for travel by horse or on foot—the latter being by far the most common form of transportation. Only gradually did new turnpike corporations begin to transform some of those roads—the routes connecting major trade centers—into graded roads paved with packed rocks, gravel, or logs and lined with drainage ditches designed to prevent erosion, which one traversed for a fee. To emphasize how unusual these turnpikes were, contemporaries called them "artificial roads."[4]

"Of the roads I can say nothing in favor of them," fumed one diarist, describing his travels in Virginia. "They are by far the worst I have seen in any of the Northern States, very little attention is paid to them the Stones and roots etc. not being removed makes them very rough and unpleasant to the travellers." When this diarist's mail stage left Alexandria at one o'clock in the morning, it took fourteen hours to travel the fifty miles from Alexandria to Fredericksburg, with an hour's stop for a meal. Coaches took their time on such roads, keeping their horses at a walk, because they risked serious damage otherwise. For travelers prone to exasperation, such as British diplomat Henry Unwin Addington, the frequent sight of "the wreck of a coach or wagon, sticking in picturesque attitudes in some hole in the log road," served as a reminder of the need for patience. While traveling in New York state, Addington summarized his experience as "an uninterrupted series of plunges from one hole to another." In addition to the holes, rocks, and stumps, roads were slippery in icy weather, muddy in wet weather, and during dry periods they were dusty and rutted by the wheels of teamsters' wagons. This was the nature of travel in the early American Republic: erratic, uncomfortable, and excruciatingly slow—and travelers found colorful ways to express their irritation.[5]

The United States' roads did not help tie the nation together; in some cases, they emphasized regionalism and even aggressive opposition to outsiders. If Americans liked to see themselves as highly mobile, particularly in contrast to the "old countries," we should not underestimate the extent to which the nation largely remained regionally divided and provincial, sometimes out of sheer pigheadedness. Traveling south from Boston into Rhode Island, one Scottish writer "learned that the people of Massachusetts had offered to extend the turnpike to Providence, but the people of this state would not agree to it, and thus the road remained almost impassable." Meanwhile, Connecticut residents "seem to take pleasure in insulting travellers whose equipage they may deem aristocratic, or above the mediocrity of their own state by making it as inconvenient as possible to pass them on the road." This traveler encountered two men who took such umbrage at his "aristocratic" carriage that they rammed their ox-driven cart against it with such violence that it shattered a wheel. Most didn't have to worry about resentful Connecticut farmers, however, because the decrepit state of the roads demanded that travelers abandon their expensive carriages in favor of riding on horseback. Once travelers left the more carefully maintained streets of the nation's cities, poor roads forced the wealthy to abandon the very vehicles that displayed their social rank to passersby and compelled them to proceed on horseback like everyone else. The United States' busy roads exaggerated the already considerable regional divisions as well as the divide between urban and rural.[6]

In choosing to spend his life as an itinerant, Ogilvie committed to long hours navigating these routes. He reported in 1809 that, when impassable roads prevented him from traveling the seventy-five miles from Hartford to Providence, he had to cancel all the plans he'd made for speaking in that city; wasted were the letters of introduction, inquiries, and planned parlor visits with influential patrons. Instead he took the turnpike directly to Boston and started over. Beyond the great port cities of the Eastern Seaboard, traveling got slower and more expensive. To traverse the state of Pennsylvania from Philadelphia to Pittsburgh took six days on the stage and cost twenty-seven dollars, roughly a laborer's monthly earnings; it was cheaper if you rode in a wagon, but the trip lengthened to about twenty days. Ogilvie also witnessed firsthand some of the transportation improvements that began to transform the American landscape. On his first trip between Baltimore and Philadelphia in 1808, the coach moved slowly, requiring two twelve-hour days of travel. When he revisited that route five years later, the pilot stage flew up the newly improved hundred-mile road in only sixteen hours, "which was great dispatch"—in other words, drivers could take their horses from a walk to a trot without risking damage to their carriages. Nearly doubling one's speed seemed a profound improvement in this era even if it only meant going from a walk to a trot.[7]

Improvement projects like the Baltimore-Philadelphia turnpike appeared intermittently throughout the American landscape during the early Republic, often spearheaded by private enterprise rather than via state or federal initiatives. Progress on these projects could be excruciatingly slow. Starting in 1785, some of the most prominent men in Virginia had invested financially and politically in the James River and Kanawha Canal Company, intended to stretch hundreds of miles upriver from Richmond toward western parts of the state to grant those residents easier access to markets. After five years' labor, however, the canal had extended only seven miles. The Erie Canal, which ultimately spanned hundreds of miles between Buffalo and the Hudson River just north of Albany, began in 1817 and reached its goal eight years later. When Secretary of the Treasury Albert Gallatin proposed a massive, federally supported series of construction projects to advance the nation's transportation routes in 1808, Congress's partisan and regional bickering was so intense that almost nothing was achieved until more than ten years later. It took seven years to complete the first 140-mile leg of the famous National Road, a project to build an "artificial road" through the Appalachians to the West, after beginning work in the remote town of Cumberland, Maryland, in 1811. In many regions, turnpike proposals led to strong opposition from locals who objected to paying tolls on heretofore free roads that had received only nominal improvements. In some regions, brand-new steamboats made it possible to move along the coast or navigable rivers with relative dispatch. The real revolutions in transportation came later, with canals and especially railroads, but these took time, too. As a result, when Ogilvie spent a decade on the nation's roads and waterways during the 1810s, he witnessed less a revolution in transportation than gradual improvements that made travel a little less excruciating, and only some of the time.[8]

These portrayals of the nation's roads have important implications for how we understand Ogilvie's experiences, for they reflect the people he encountered as well as the United States they inhabited. Residents of areas as disparate as Augusta, Georgia, and Springfield, Massachusetts, as well as the port cities of Baltimore and Providence, had just begun to realize some of the social changes that might result from better transportation networks — most prominently the dissemination of communications and easier inland trade. And when these residents described being awestruck by Ogilvie's performances, they revealed what regional divisions meant for the American populace.

One thing that managed to travel with surprising effectiveness was the news. Because the 1792 U.S. Postal Act had made it possible for newspaper editors to exchange their papers with one another via the U.S. Mail free of postage charges, any given newspaper might include reprinted stories from its associates all over the country. The rationale behind this law, of course, was to guarantee that the American people would be well informed about the workings of government and world events — to cast sunlight on legislation and one's elected representatives. But in the case of news about James Ogilvie's lectures, what seemed to spread most effectively was a prevailing mystification about his talents. That mystification provides important insights into the people who wrote those accounts.[9]

Among the hundreds of pages of reviews and accounts of his performances, few offered much descriptive detail. Reports most often described his performances as inexplicable. "Of his elocution it is most difficult to speak," the *Port-*

land Gazette wrote in 1809. A Salem paper sang the praises of his genius by saying he "must be heard to be conceived" and that his "effect cannot be described." Instead, they focused on the effect of his eloquence, as when a Charleston paper wrote that "every mind was left in that ineffable state of luminous enjoyment, when man forgets this little world and communes with the spirits of another." The upshot was that he was a "genius" capable of working "magic" on his audiences.[10]

One might suspect Ogilvie of submitting these reviews anonymously, but such a move entailed far too much risk. Newspaper editors often recognized the handwriting of individuals who submitted letters and reviews, and they would have known Ogilvie's from the advertisements he purchased. Editors and readers alike shared a deep aversion to naked self-promotion and immodesty, which would have produced withering gossip. Ogilvie might have suggested language to the elites he befriended, hoping they might submit letters to the editor, but he almost certainly would not have composed one himself.[11]

Reviewers threw themselves into the task of verbose reportage, often providing a jumble of popular elocutionary terms in a crescendo of description that only seemed to obscure the performance. The Middlesex Gazette praised "the gracefulness of his manner, the variations of his tones, the elegance of his language, the profundity of his literature, and depth of his knowledge." A Philadelphia paper praised "his powers of bold, descriptive, and impassioned eloquence" that "obtained the mastery of the mind. Every ear was intent, every eye was fixed upon him. The former was charmed by his modulated and harmonious voice. The latter by his spirited and graceful action." Readers would have seen those sentiments about the importance of gracefulness in manner and elegance of language used many times, for they appeared not just in newspapers but in schoolbooks, which were cheap and almost as ubiquitous in early Republican homes as Bibles and psalters and which provided extensive guidelines for public speaking and recitation. Yet ultimately such descriptions remain generic. Were his gestures deemed proper because they seemed to adhere so closely to schoolbooks' instructions, or did he innovate in ways that surprised his auditors? How, specifically, did his audience members find his combination of language, literary references and quotations, and argument to be so compelling? Only a fog of gushing praise exists in the printed reviews.[12]

But shift your attention to a different question, and that praise takes on a new cast. Instead of asking what it can tell us about Ogilvie's performances, ask instead: What can it tell us about his audiences? What can their awe—their inability to describe his oratory, and their eagerness to convey their own delight in the performances—tell us about them?

The sources themselves draw our attention to Ogilvie's audiences. Accounts of his speeches often dedicated the most detailed descriptions not to the orator but to the reactions of the attendees. The *Portland Gazette* marveled at his capacity to "fix a spell on the spirits of his hearers, of irresistible influence. The young listen in mute surprize, and the old man places his withered finger on his lip, lest suspiration should dissolve the charm." A Pennsylvania observer depicted with even more power the orator's effect on staid Lancaster society. "I had thought that our immovable Germans, would not readily enjoy an entertainment where there was neither stale decoration nor broad merriment—and that the members would turn pale at the name of a fresh oration after those they are condemned to hear during the day. But such is the magic of genius that Mr. O. has completely overcome these difficulties, and carries away from Lancaster the most flattering success," he wrote. "The good people seem to enter perfectly into the spirit of the orator and are so ready to yield to his impressions that to use the phrase of some of them at the oration on duelling 'before they knew where they were, they found their hands up to their eyes.'" Describing rapt attendees who held their breath or dabbed at their eyes would have heightened interest in Ogilvie's performances. These depictions flattered the orator's skills by turning attention to the dumbstruck responses of Ogilvie's listeners.[13]

Americans usually had quite a lot to say about the orators they heard. To be rendered uncritical, if not speechless, by a public speaker was not common. Diaries and letters abound in strongly worded opinions about local speakers. Describing the oration by a minister visiting from seventy miles up the coast of Maine, a Kennebunk physician explained wryly in a letter that "it was a very elegant thing, highly poetical and flowery, but much too long for the occasion." Moreover, this writer added, "His publick performances and private conversations go far to convince me that he is a *small man*." Elsewhere, a Quaker clerk reported in his diary feeling unimpressed by a Methodist preacher. "He sang several Psalms alone with much elegance, but I did not admire his manner of preaching, being too theatrical, and an appearance of a want of sincerity to please my taste." When they were impressed, these observers still had something to say about the talk and its delivery. Listening to a speech on "the defeat and downfall of Bonepart," a young Connecticut woman wrote approvingly in an 1814 letter to her cousin that "it was written in fine stile, deliver'd with much dignity." In other cases, diarists also noted details about a speech's argument, content, and structure, a recording tradition particularly common among New Englanders. In general, auditors attended these performances with their critical faculties on high alert: eager to gauge speakers' talents, declare success or failure, and display their own facility for discernment along the way. Their accounts suggest that they felt fully equipped to assess the oratory they usually heard.[14]

But consider the limited range of people heard in a typical lifetime, during an era when more than 92 percent of the American public lived in rural areas of fewer than twenty-five hundred people. The overwhelming majority of what they heard were sermons, giving them a sense of proficiency in judging those discourses. And, indeed, many communities witnessed a broad range of pulpit performance conducted by long-familiar ministers, ministers in training, visiting ministers, ministers from competing congregations or denominations, and some of the new exhorters who felt called to preach in the highly emotional, antiauthoritarian styles of camp meetings and revivals. In addition, men and women heard legal debates on court days, Fourth of July speeches, exhibition and commencement speeches by local schoolchildren, and the occasional partisan political speech. In almost all of those cases, the speakers themselves would have hailed from the town or the region and would have reflected standards of public speech that emerged locally.[15]

The United States was made up of vernacular communities of listeners in the early nineteenth century—communities defined by their provincial, regionally distinct patterns of public speech and habits of listening. Though distinctive, these communities were not hermetic. Every summer, college students fanned out across the regional landscape to teach common schools, thus disseminating to some extent the forms of speech and comportment they learned at Dartmouth, William and Mary, Princeton, or Aberdeen. When those college students graduated, they might land back in a small town to apprentice as a minister, lawyer, merchant, or physician and eventually become a likely choice for a future Fourth of July speaker or political candidate. The most privileged in any region might have opportunities to travel to hear legislative debates taking place in the statehouse or in Congress, perhaps even theater in Philadelphia or London. Still, for the most part, neighborhoods remained defined by continuities. Towns established and monitored locally defined standards of public speech through gossip, disapproval, or dismissal of schoolteachers and ministers who didn't conform—not because they aggressively sought to maintain the status quo or reject outsiders, but because they had come to judge public speech by the range of speakers they had heard in their lifetimes. It was through that lens that they interpreted the great eloquence they had read about in the pages of schoolbooks, magazines, and history books—for, in most cases, they would have only read about the powerful civic oratory that had stirred citizens to action in the past. The oratory they had actually heard invariably paled in comparison to what they could imagine from other orators, in other settings. After all, imagination usually trumps reality.[16]

If we understand that American men and women were positioned between these two poles—guidelines for rhetorical delivery that were interpreted within regions with vernacular experience and expectations, and an appreciation for true eloquence based almost entirely on the imagination—we can begin to glimpse why they might have been rendered speechless by Ogilvie's performances. It wasn't because these auditors had little experience listening to and criticizing oratory. Rather, the nature of their reactions suggest that they now found themselves self-conscious—all too aware that their responses to this speaker might be seen by a larger public and that their own performance as an audience would be compared to more sophisticated audiences elsewhere.

Indeed, as his tour continued during 1809 and news spread of his talent, newspaper accounts lavished profuse detail on describing local audiences. These articles uniformly emphasized the respectability and glamour of the attendees as well as the size of the audience, accounts that were as common in the metropolis as in smaller burgs. In one case, news spread from New York to a Philadelphia newspaper and was reprinted in Rhode Island that Ogilvie "is honoured by the presence of persons of the first respectability for taste and intelligence." The Baltimore papers declared that "Mr. OGILVIE could not be more flattered by the number, taste and intelligence of his spectators, than they were instructed and delighted by his oration and other performances." When he appeared in the town of Lexington, Kentucky (population 4,500), the local paper congratulated the members of the audience for their "degree of delicacy, refinement and intelligence, that but rarely characterizes a miscellaneous audience," a fact that "must, we are sure, have been peculiarly gratifying to the Orator." From one region to the next, newspapers provided an undeviating sense that he always found a "highly respectable and numerous auditory" no matter how small the town.[17]

Maybe it was true. After all, when he raised his admission fee from fifty cents per lecture to one dollar in 1810—an amount he described as the absolute maximum he could charge—he ruled out attendance by all but those with the most "respectable" incomes who could afford this kind of discretionary spending. He filled his lecture halls with auditors eager to show off their town's appreciation for literature and eloquence—and perhaps also their finest clothes, as when a New York newspaper reprinted news about "persons of unquestionable partiality, intelligence, and taste" offering their full approval of his lecture in Boston. After all, his appearances represented a rare opportunity to experience high culture. Joining a room filled with a town's wealthy, powerful, and well-dressed citizens must have generated a curious sense of identity, as if they collectively performed a form of local pride for the benefit of their guest.[18]

But on closer scrutiny, many of these accounts reveal anxieties about the ability of local towns to meet the expectations of an orator who had visited larger and more glamorous cities with more polished auditors. There was no secret about his prior appearances. In case their readers had missed the information about his prior successes, reviews never failed to mention that he had appeared in "the most polished cities of America, where the perception of taste, and the

discriminations of judgment, are exercised to a degree, at once elegant and refined." This editor of the Charleston Times noted explicitly something that usually
went unsaid: that Ogilvie's seemingly universal success put certain pressures on
their city to "throw another ray of light upon the illuminations of his fame." To
fail to offer identical praise would reveal Charleston's "insensibility of Letters."
American towns did not just perform for Ogilvie but also for each other.[19]

Newspaper accounts reveal that they feared Ogilvie would be disappointed
by their city's lack of cultured listeners. When he appeared in Portland in the
District of Maine, listed as the eighteenth-largest city on the 1810 census with
a population just over seventy-one hundred, one of the local papers expressed
"lament that this town could not give audiences like New-York and Boston, but
we are glad for the honor of the place that it has fully turned out its quota." Other
notices expressed in the same breath that they regretted that his lecture room
was "less crowded" than in New York but were still "honoured by the presence
of persons of the first respectability for taste and intelligence." The embarrassment of offering Ogilvie a smaller or less fashionable audience got worse when
one could only imagine how large and glamorous his New York audience had
truly been. By the time he arrived in Savannah in May 1811, he recognized and responded to their anxieties and announced to his assembled crowd that "he had
the satisfaction of addressing a more numerous audience, in proportion to the population of the place, than any of his Orations had before attracted, in any of the cities
through which he had passed." The Savannah newspaper expressed delight with
the comment, "a fact remarkable enough not only to attract editorial notice, but
perhaps of sufficient magnitude and interest to deserve a place in the annals of
Georgia." Size mattered.[20]

Just as ubiquitous were the insistent notices that his local audiences were
worthy of the intellectual repasts Ogilvie offered up in his lectures. No matter
how brief the review, it invariably contained a variant on "an uncommonly intelligent and polite audience were present on the occasion." In Newport, Rhode
Island—a town of nearly eight thousand people in 1810—the newspaper bragged
that "it is complimentary to our public taste to say, that Mr. OGILVIE's orations
are highly approved and fully attended." The variations on this theme from town
to town appear so inconsequential as to suggest a kind of boilerplate language,
as if picked up from other newspapers and repurposed with minor changes. Yet,
even if such expressions gave editors easy ways to fill space in a column, they
also reveal a constant sense of comparison or even competition between towns.
Was the crowd "large"—as large as at his last stop in Pittsburgh? Were they
"polite" and "respectable"—and would their appearance compare with Charleston's wealthy patrons? And a more oblique question: Did they have the "intelligence" and "discernment" to appreciate the argument and the performance the

way the audience had in Philadelphia or Boston? That newspaper editors uniformly sought to answer those questions suggests that more was on their minds than paraphrasing someone else's text.[21]

Newspaper notices like these could be so repetitive that they raise questions about their sincerity. One might ask whether such sentiments reflected the modesty of citizens in small cities such as Savannah or Portland rather than a deeper-seated anxiety—or even whether such statements were merely formulaic. But other writers moved away from the script to offer more detail. A writer in Charleston offered the clearest statement. "Wherever his powers have been witnessed, he has walked in a blaze of admiration," the paper commented. "Should this gentleman meet with limited success in this city, we fear the reproach will rest among ourselves," for it would reveal that the Charleston public lacked the "discernment" to appreciate his eloquence. Even if such reports could sound as if they'd been reprinted from one paper to the next, this Charleston writer and others indicated a self-consciousness that drove both positive reviews and reports of sizable audiences.[22]

Newspaper editors' florid yet oddly vague passages about his performances illustrate one final aspect of Ogilvie's effect on audiences. Take, for example, a grandiloquent account in Raleigh's *Star* celebrating his "manly eloquence, which breaking forth from a mind luminous with science and a heart strong in virtue, moves on like an heavenly vision, in its lofty course, and sheds its glory on every object; that eloquence which is pure, correct and sublime, at once eliciting the force of truth, the charms of wisdom and the light of genius." Certainly we should read such a passage with a grain of salt. But after reading a number of such passages, one begins to notice distinctive phrasing—indicative of Ogilvie's own excessive, belletristic style. This newspaper article appeared to imitate his propensity for long compound sentences, poetic flights of fancy, and a liberal use of adjectives. In other words, this was not a review or an assessment (or plagiarism) but a remediation of Ogilvie's particular form of eloquence. Following the adage that imitation is the sincerest form of flattery, accounts like this copied his style, recycling his prolix, emotional performances into their reviews, spinning upward with their hyperbole, aspiring to mimic that rhetorical grandiosity. His spoken-word verbosity was so infectious that editors offered not criticism or even descriptions of his performances but settled instead for impersonations.[23]

As they impersonated his rhetoric, editors also increasingly used a distinctive term to describe Ogilvie's success: *celebrity*. And, in doing so, they fueled that celebrity.

In the early nineteenth century, Americans were still comparatively new to the term *celebrity* and used the word in distinctive ways with increasing frequency.

Most often, they applied it to uniquely exemplary figures, including writers, scientists, explorers, military leaders, and ministers known for their genius or achievements. A newspaper advertisement might announce a book of sermons for sale, announcing that they had earned their author "a celebrity as a learned and evangelical Divine to which few writers have attained," while a nearby column might discuss "an Athenian philosopher of celebrity" who had studied under Socrates. They rarely used the word for people who were simply fashionable or popular without known talents or whose names merely appeared "in a newspaper," which granted "a certain species of consequential celebrity," as one author sniffed disapprovingly. An exhibition of waxworks advertised that these included models of "figures, of established character for celebrity," which might include women known for their beauty. Each used the term *celebrity* in a manner unique to the time: they would not have said that a person could be a celebrity, but rather that a person possessed it. Celebrity was a quality of being well known, an attribute, a degree of popularity and fame—the state of being celebrated by others. Not until the 1840s would Americans use it as a strong noun, as when one character in the 1849 novel *The Ogilvies* (no relation) says to another, "Did you see any of those 'celebrities,' as you call them . . . ?" revealing a use of the term that was just then becoming familiar to the ear.[24]

Writers frequently applied the term to Ogilvie. "Mr. Ogilvie's celebrity has already invited the attention of the great body of the most refined and respectable persons in our city," wrote a letter writer calling himself "Humanitas" in an 1809 New York paper. An Albany editor described Ogilvie as having "already acquired so high a degree of celebrity," while a Charleston writer referred to his "well merited celebrity." Others referred to "the celebrated orator," "this celebrated man," or "a man celebrated for his eloquence." Ogilvie himself took to using the term, as when he wrote about his desire for "permanent and extended celebrity." He also admired this quality in others. In a letter referring to the English intellectual Samuel Johnson, a figure made even more famous by James Boswell's 1791 biography, Ogilvie described "Johnson[']s claims to preeminent and permanent celebrity:—His claims to much celebrity have been admitted by so many persons more illustrious than himself, that it becomes almost presumptuous to question their validity." (Johnson himself had invoked the word back in the 1750s, once complaining wryly that he "did not find myself yet enriched in proportion to my celebrity.")[25]

If Americans saw the term *celebrity* frequently in their public prints, they did not experience the same degree of intense *celebrity culture* as had emerged overseas. The British and French had grown far more familiar with celebrity over the course of a generation or more. There, London- and Paris-based media trades had saturated the public with print and visual materials that cultivated intense interest in the lives, fashionable clothing, and personal peccadillos of certain figures like the British actress Sarah Siddons, the French actor François-Joseph Talma, and members of the aristocracy or royalty. People with leisure and discretionary income on their hands could buy any number of prints displaying Talma's dark, brooding good looks, Siddons enacting one of her most famous "breeches" roles (in which she took a male role like Hamlet), and gossip rags detailing the sexual affairs of aristocrats. Even more recently, a cult of celebrity had grown up around the British poet Lord Byron by playing up a potent mix of his Romantic poetry, aristocratic title, handsome face, and sexual transgressions. Meanwhile, entrepreneurs and traffickers in gossip helped to accelerate public interest. Celebrity culture brought together this complex set of economic actors, institutions, and media technologies that heightened the public's fascination with individuals identified as being talented, attractive, influential, and fashionable. Although Americans imported some of these prints, images, and other vestiges of British celebrity culture, the United States had not yet realized the unique density of media, mass public audiences, and behind-the-scenes agents. At no point in Ogilvie's American career, for example, did an engraver produce an admiring print for sale. In contrast to much larger European cities, the United States at the turn of the nineteenth century did not yet have a celebrity culture (though it would several decades later). Yet a few American celebrities had begun to appear.[26]

American newspapers took the lead in emphasizing Ogilvie's celebrity. They particularly underlined the fact that he had won popularity among the most fashionable crowds, explaining that he was "attended by the whole throng of fashion, chased by sympathetic murmurs, or loud thunders of applause," as one New York paper wrote. Boston papers, too, remarked on "the avidity with which the society of Mr. Ogilvie has been sought in private circles of the first respectability." By creating an aura of glamour, applause, and fashion around him, editors distinguished him from the usual body of traveling performers and theater folk who visited the country's cities and towns during the same years.[27]

Within two years of beginning his tour, Ogilvie found himself discussed even when he wasn't performing locally and when he wasn't anticipated soon. In fact, any information about his progress became seen as news. Magazines and newspapers repeated tidbits of his clever conversation. One gave him credit for the invention of the term *gerrymander*. Another claimed he had authored a popular song, "The Battle of Tippecanoe." These claims and similar ones were almost certainly inaccurate, but their appearance signals how quickly he catapulted into celebrity and how eagerly the press granted him a reputation for genius.[28]

From these beginnings, writers began to employ exaggeration and even poetry

Muneret, Pinx.   P.C. Augrand, Sculp.

F. J. TALMA,   DANS NÉRON

Figure 26. F. J. Talma, dans Neron. *Talma as Nero in* Brittanicus, *a play by
playwright Jean Racine that had enjoyed more than a century of popularity by the time Talma
appeared in the role. This print by Muneret & P. Augrand guarantees that viewers notice the
actor's muscular arm, distinctive hand gesture, and piercing gaze. Courtesy of the Rare
Book & Manuscript Library, University of Illinois at Urbana-Champaign*

to praise him, almost as if to one-up each other. The *Utica Patriot* in upstate New York published a poem that circulated in regional papers, and which effused:

> In the expression of every passion by *words*, SHAKESPEARE was nature's masterpiece. In the display of passion by action, GARRICK [a British celebrity actor] was her son.
> The force of nature could no farther go,
> To make a third she join'd the former two —
> That THIRD is — OGILVIE.

Eloquence and action, genius and performance; to be described as nature's ultimate triumph as an orator was so hyperbolic a compliment that it marked a new attainment in Ogilvie's career. Another writer characterized him as an extraordinary polymath whose genius crackled and sparked, describing "evenings when his genius was like the electricity which coruscating on the summer cloud scarcely intermits its flashes long enough for you to pause and admire." That magical brilliance had an ineffable effect on listeners, the writer continued. "His cultivated mind is familiar with every subject, and whether he chooses to place you at Rome or at Athens, illustrate the mysteries of science, or survey the columns of the *Parthenon*, whether like the delicate spirit of Shakespeare his genius sports on a cloud, or reposes on a sunbeam, *with him conversing you forget all time*." This author was hardly alone in characterizing an evening with Ogilvie as a transformative experience.[29]

Along the way, writers came to use his name as a ready referent for all things eloquent. Within two years of beginning his tour, Ogilvie had become a household name, referred to whenever the topic of oratory came to mind. Washington Irving reported on the young son of a friend who "is studying an Ogilvian oration to be delivered before the Washington Society on the fourth of July." In Boston, one article teased a member of a local debating society by describing his style as overly imitative. "He pours forth a torrent of words, accompanied with gestures since Mr. Ogilvie was here, with metaphors and figures in imitation of Mr. Ogilvie — and at last overpowers his audience by the mere force of rhetorick." An Albany magazine speculated that a prominent young actor had modeled his stage style on "Ogilvie, whose oratory has nearly set every body crazy." Yet another publication praised a youthful orator by calling him "a young Mr. Ogilvie." Offhand references like these illuminate an important side of his growing celebrity: each one magnified his reputation and solidified the ready association of his name with eloquence. Ogilvie = oratory.[30]

The barrage of frequent, gratuitous, and effusive accolades raised him from being merely famous into a new category of celebrity. To be sure, his celebrity looked different from that enjoyed by his British contemporaries like Byron;

without gossip magazines and engravings of Ogilvie's visage for sale, the American phenomenon of celebrity appeared significantly less elaborate. Yet by American standards, Ogilvie had come to enjoy a swirl of attention and praise in the American press that went unchallenged even when his performances weren't perfect.[31]

Nothing better captures the self-consciousness of provincial audiences in the face of celebrity than when an audience member misbehaved, or when Ogilvie's eloquence failed him. Ogilvie's recollections of his career show what many newspaper reports avoided: he, like other performers at the time, was subject to rude disruptions that would later be called heckling. His serious and lofty goals for public deliberation made him all the more exasperated when he found his lectures "exposed to irritating, vexatious and mortifying interruption" by the occasional belligerent attendee. His memoir recalls incidents like these in such detail that they reveal how much they rankled in his memory, even years later. At one point in Charleston, a group of young boys seated themselves on his rostrum and refused to move. Sometimes the problem could be explained in one word: alcohol. In Paris, "one of the smallest towns in Kentucky," a man arrived so drunk that he "repeatedly disturbed the audience" with "epithets brutal, savage or barbarous" before passing out on one of the front benches. No one, Ogilvie believed, "could have so shamelessly sunk below the instinctive dignity of human nature." Beholding this sight from his stage, he descended from the platform and stood silent for a few moments, arms folded, in front of the man's unconscious body. In an attempt to regain the audience's attention and his own equanimity, he proclaimed, "Declamation may well be dumb" before behavior like this; the audience breathed a sigh of relief. In those moments, he believed, orators needed to pause to acknowledge examples of human debauchery that served as a lesson to everyone else.[32]

If Ogilvie fretted about how to respond to interruptions, local communities could be vindictive. Following an interruption during one of his early talks in New York, local newspapers decided to blame a usual suspect: not just an Irishman—for who was more likely to be drunk and disruptive than the Irish, according to nineteenth-century national stereotypes—but one tied to the United Irishmen cause that sought to end British rule of Ireland. "Impudence," the papers hissed at the offender. "We trust Mr. Ogilvie will once more, at least, gratify every lover of his country, every admirer of genius and talent, by repeating this wonderful performance with his wonderful powers, to a delighted and electrified audience." A few years later in the remote town of Washington, Pennsylvania, south of Pittsburgh, the papers reported that some "worthless vagabonds" broke the windows of the Lodge Room while Ogilvie "was entertaining a respectable audience." That event was so mortifying to the town's residents that they banded together to raise one hundred dollars as a reward for the identification of the criminals, an extraordinary sum.[33]

It was one thing to face belligerence from the audience and another to disrupt one's own talk because of exhaustion or faulty memory. Yet even when the papers reported on Ogilvie's lapses on stage, their tone was so generous that it rarely sounded like criticism. In Boston in the winter of 1810, he found himself so disturbed by accidentally omitting "some of the finest passages" of his oration on dueling that he returned to the stage afterward and told his audience that he would repeat the lecture the following night for no charge. "We were perfectly satisfied with the first delivery," one magazine confessed, "till we were told by the orator himself that he had mangled it; and we think that our optics would be less acute in discerning Mr. Ogilvie's foibles, if he did not himself tell us he has so many."[34]

Not long after his failure of memory in Boston, he struggled again in Providence—this time, the papers explained, because of the "delicate state of the Orator's health," which was "incapable of bearing out the energy which the occasion demanded, and seemed to hang like a dead weight on his exertions." Still, the paper insisted, his powers of eloquence remained strong enough "to arouse and awaken admiration and delight," and the review mainly discussed the talk's varied "pleasures." About a month later, the same paper included a notice: "We rejoice to find that the Orator's health and spirits were so far confirmed, that he was capable of *appearing like himself.* The audience felt the magnetick versatility of the Orator's powers, which was capable of attracting smiles or tears at his command."[35]

Those lapses onstage came at a point in Ogilvie's life at which he had been touring nonstop for nearly two years. The papers never provided details about his malady, but Ogilvie's letters reveal a slew of problems affecting his "health and spirits": periods of melancholy, painful rheumatism, and an increasing reliance on laudanum. That public reports generally remained so positive even when he forgot his material further confirms the pattern: to criticize such a man might make your town seem less capable of recognizing genius when it arrived.[36]

Reports like these—anxious to please, eager to mimic Ogilvie's style—revealed the concerns of a United States at a time when the arrival of a cosmopolitan celebrity held up a mirror to the country's provincial towns and cities. Ogilvie's transformation from a Virginia schoolteacher into a famous personage was complete by June 1809, just over a year after starting his tour, and only increased during the next few years. This transformation had been amplified initially by his successful engagement of social elites as his patrons; the press quickened the process, circulating news of his triumphs throughout the nation. With elite networks and the public prints fanning the flame, his fame began to transform into celebrity. Having traveled nearly a thousand miles on those excruciating American roads, and having earned seemingly universal applause, his appearances made local audiences all the more aware that they might appear inferior compared with more sophisticated cities or more sizable audiences. Understanding the phenomenon of celebrity doesn't just require scrutinizing those beguiling figures who rise and gain our attention. Celebrity is also about the fans. It's about who we are, and who we think we are.

Having someone as celebrated as Ogilvie arrive in town produced mixed feelings. The honor of hosting such a figure or witnessing his performative magic could not make up for nagging worries about inadequacy. Exploring the origin of responses like these permit us to understand better why the 1808 atheism scandal seemed to cast so few ripples beyond the city of Philadelphia, and why the hubbub started by John Rodman's 1809 pamphlet *Fragment of a Journal of a Sentimental Philosopher* only seemed to bother a small circle of New Yorkers. Despite occurring within the first year of James Ogilvie's lecture tour, neither restricted his growing fame. Both ultimately appeared as local, short-lived affairs, unique to the peculiarities of limited social circles. Ogilvie did more than merely survive two scandals; he found in the aftermath that they did not tarnish his star. Just when he seemed to have fallen in the eyes of his listeners in Philadelphia or New York, he found it easy to rise again elsewhere. Nor was he the only one to benefit from the early Republic's uniquely forgiving environment.[37]

If his early setbacks failed to matter much in the long run, the media scrum of flattery that began emerging during the summer of 1809 continued unabated for years. That growing chorus of praise from so many print outlets propelled Ogilvie's reputation in a way the scandals did not and made it increasingly difficult to voice criticism. Seeing American towns and cities as vernacular communities of listeners helps to illuminate a United States in the midst of construction. Americans' poor roads helped to divide the country in the same way that citizens were divided by region, political affiliation, religious beliefs, and culture. But Ogilvie's rising celebrity gave them something to share. Even occasional criticism helped to turn attention toward the same star.[38]

Nothing illustrates his emerging celebrity more than the fact that not a single critic mocked the singular costume Ogilvie used while performing. One of the most distinctive things about James Ogilvie almost never got mentioned by the very audiences who donned their most fashionable clothes to attend his lectures. When onstage, he wore a Roman toga. A *toga*.

{ CHAPTER 8 }

Forging Celebrity and Manliness in a Toga,

1810–1815

To observers unfamiliar with the dynamics of the early nineteenth-century United States, nothing might appear more preposterous about Ogilvie's lecture tour than that he wore a toga on stage. Yet, in all of their enthusiastic accounts, only a handful of commentators mentioned it—and they usually did so obliquely. "His delivery derived a peculiar charm from a classical and highly appropriate costume," a London paper explained. One of the very few explicit mentions of the toga appeared after Ogilvie's death, when an imitator advertised that he would "appear in the Roman Toga, after the manner of the late James Ogilvie, Esq." Though the toga would convey very different connotations in the centuries that followed, Ogilvie's contemporaries saw it in a particular light because of the ways the toga appeared in popular culture. In fact, if you speculate that his admirers declined to draw attention to it because they found it embarrassing, you would be hard-pressed to imagine why his severest critics—those most likely to mock his pretensions—did not mention the toga at all.[1]

Commentators might not have discussed it, but Ogilvie's toga became crucial to his public persona as a celebrity orator. This costume was invested with potent meaning for the new nation. The toga had been the dress of Roman orators and champions of civic and moral virtue, who exemplified self-controlled, noble, public-minded manliness. To Americans, it represented the highest of human achievements and the Republic's most idealistic hopes. Moreover, the toga was just one of a range of classical symbols adopted and deployed during these decades, when embracing such emblems invested one's cause with the imprimatur of authority and wisdom. Cicero's and Seneca's reputations for noble republican virtue had remained intact for nearly eighteen hundred years; when nineteenth-century men and women adopted symbols lifted from the ancient republics, they claimed to be the true inheritors of that legacy.[2]

The toga also symbolized manliness. The Romans instructed that the toga be worn in a way that was *splendidus et virilis* (distinguished and manly) and insisted that the orator convey masculine authority in his bodily performance. Ogilvie's use of the toga as his signature costume thus reveals not just how he undergirded his celebrity with a visual emblem but also how he invested his self-presentation with the gendered qualities of self-control and restrained male power prized during this era. For a performer like Ogilvie, who so explicitly sought to attract equal numbers of women and men to his orations, such a presentation of masculinity required walking a fine line lest he draw criticism like that in John Rodman's *Fragment of a Journal of a Sentimental Philosopher*, which fretted about Ogilvie's effects on his female fans. Wearing a toga thus conveyed a wide range of manly ideals, from civic virtue to the embodiment of authority. If you start looking, you find togas everywhere during the early Republic.

Any discussion of togas must begin with one important clarification: early Americans had no use for bare chests. In fact, when in 1840 the renowned American sculptor Horatio Greenough unveiled a statue of George Washington that portrayed him shirtless, seated, and in a vaguely classical robe that draped over one raised arm and waist, Americans were disgusted. Congress, which had commissioned the statue, quickly banished it from the rotunda of the Capitol building. Some joked that it showed Washington preparing for a bath. Americans in the early nineteenth century simply did not want to see the skin of their leaders, and the togas that appeared in that era always concealed the man's torso.[3]

Aside from its coverage of men's chests, however, togas appeared in such a wide range of forms that it seems no one was certain about exactly what this garment was supposed to look like. Classical sources instructed that the draping robe of the toga was worn over a tunic that concealed the body from the collarbone and upper arms down to at least the knee. Quintilian's *Institutio Oratoria* (*Institutes of Oratory*, circa 95 CE), a Roman guide to public speaking, offered details about the circular cut, appropriate size, and elegant folds of the orator's toga. This author insisted that the toga should fall from the wearer's left shoulder, leaving the right arm open to gesture. He acknowledged that Cicero had stretched those rules and allowed his toga to fall quite low (out of vanity: to conceal his varicose veins), but in general Quintilian recommended that the drapes reveal more of the leg.[4]

But beyond these instructions, even well-educated Americans would have had little ability to distinguish a proper Roman toga from an inauthentic one. Images of classical statues of togate men were rare, largely limited to expensive books containing engravings of antiquities throughout the Mediterranean. Because visual information was so difficult to obtain, artists and sculptors took considerable license when portraying their subjects in togas.[5]

Three prominent examples of public art in the early Republic placed contemporary figures in classical dress that contemporaries called togas. In 1768, the young American artist Charles Willson Peale received a commission from a group of Virginians to paint a portrait of William Pitt, who as a member of Parliament had offered eloquent opposition to the Stamp Act on behalf of American colonists. Peale's painting cast Pitt as an oratorical hero. Holding the Magna

Figure 27. George Washington. By Horatio Greenough. In 1840, Greenough unveiled his statue of Washington in a toga. Americans hated the shirtless portrayal, and Congress removed the statue from its original prestigious spot in the Rotunda of the Capitol. Courtesy of the Library of Congress

Carta in his left hand, Pitt gestured emphatically with his right toward the figure of British liberty. Pitt's toga appeared disheveled, slumping off his shoulders in a sloppy manner that would have offended Quintilian, yet Peale's painting subsequently appeared in mezzotint prints for sale to Americans, permitting the image to circulate for at least thirty years after its original appearance, never raising questions. Quintilian would have been even more perplexed by the strange mix of classical and modern clothing on the statue of Benjamin Franklin donated to the Library Company of Philadelphia in 1792. The celebratory description of the statue, which circulated in newspapers up and down the East Coast, proclaimed this a Roman toga despite the fact that the awkward robe was draped over an eighteenth-century man's shirt and cravat.[6]

Yet another so-called toga appeared in the sculpture of George Washington commissioned for the North Carolina State Capitol building in 1815. The artist followed Thomas Jefferson's advice that Washington appear in what the newspapers called a toga, even though this tunic yet again departed from the styles offered in the Pitt image and the Franklin sculpture. It portrayed Washington writing the opening lines of his Farewell Address, which by 1815 was a beloved text in large part because it allowed Americans to hail Washington as a modern Cincinnatus, the Roman who resigned his leadership and returned to his farm after leading the Republic through crisis. Ironically, however, the statue used a Roman dress unique to imperators, those Roman commanders who loyally served the empire—not men dedicated to the virtuous Republic.[7]

American women and men would have had more familiarity with the togas worn by actors in classically themed plays, which displayed even less concern with accuracy. Productions of eternally popular plays like Shakespeare's *Julius Caesar* (1599) and Joseph Addison's *Cato: A Tragedy* (1712), as well as more recent ones like James Sheridan Knowles's *Caius Gracchus* (1815) and *Virginius* (1820), dressed their stars in garments that would not become unwieldy in the course of the play's dramatic action. After all, early nineteenth-century guides to public speaking for orators, ministers, and actors indicated that a performer's power emerged as much from the physical and even athletic expression of emotion as the delivery of lines. To lose the visibility of one arm underneath the toga's folds, hide the actor's legs under a bulky robe, or burden an actor with elaborate drapery that would lose its elegance once the actor began to move might diminish the power of the performance. Theatrical prints that featured star actors in classical roles thus displayed a wide range of interpretations of the toga. Although the sources tell us little about what James Ogilvie's toga looked like— What color was it? Did it cover his skinny legs, like Cicero sought to conceal his varicose veins? What did he wear on his feet?—they confirm that he manipulated his robe in the course of each performance in a manner that permitted

Figure 28. William Pitt. By Charles Willson Peale. 1768, mezzotint and burin.
An engraving of Peale's portrait of William Pitt in the artist's conception of a Roman toga,
nobly fighting on behalf of American colonists against British parliamentary taxes.
Courtesy of the Davis Museum at Wellesley College, Welleseley, Mass.

Figure 29. Benjamin Franklin. A togate statue of Franklin was presented to the
Library Company of Philadelphia in 1792, shortly after his death. This reproduction of
the now-damaged original still appears in front of the American Philosophical Society.
Courtesy of the American Philosophical Society, Philadelphia

Figure 30. George Washington. By Antonio Canova. 1815–1821. Canova's statue of Washington, completed for the state of North Carolina, again portrayed Washington in a variant of classical dress that Americans called a toga. Photo by the North Carolina Museum of History, Raleigh

Wageman

Wageman

Mr. Wallack as Alcibiades

"Must it be so? it must not be:
My Lords, I do beseech you, know me".
Timon of Athens Act 3 Scene 3.

Engraved for the Theatrical Inquisitor.

London Published Aug.st 1 1817 by C Chapple. Pall Mall.

Figure 31. M. Wallack as Alcibiades. By Thomas Charles Wageman. 1817.
The actor James Wallack sports a perfectly composed toga over his tunic in the role of
Alcibiades in the play Timon of Athens, as portrayed in this theatrical print. Wageman
depicted Wallack in an authoritative posture and exaggerated the actor's muscularity.
Courtesy of the Rare Book & Manuscript Library, University of Illinois at Urbana-Champaign

him to display a full range of postures and gestures so that even the attendees at the back of the room could witness the emotional power behind his delivery. We don't know exactly what Ogilvie's toga looked like. But looking at the odd assortment of early nineteenth-century "togas" suggests it simply didn't matter to his audiences.

If costumes like these contributed to a pervasive fuzziness in American notions of what a toga ought to look like, taken together they demonstrated a preoccupation with a very specific historical time: the Roman Republic. Plays and statuary comprised only two elements of an American culture engrossed with classicism. It is impossible to overstate the crucial importance of classicism to education in this era. The striking absence of classicism in our own culture today makes it difficult for us to appreciate the extent to which classical humanism infused the early American imagination and landscape, matched only by Christianity's core texts in its position at the center of American educational and cultural life. Reconstructing this culture, we can begin to understand why donning a toga to deliver oratory might have received so few comments in the press.

Until at least late in the nineteenth century, as one commentator observed, Americans quite simply thought "of, through, and with the classics." Even American women and men with little formal education imbibed from the world around them that eloquence was a form of heroism and that oratory was more than mere talk. They learned early on that Cicero and the other classical greats had galvanized and mobilized their publics through virtuous speech, articulating pathways through the morass of difficult political choices. Schoolbooks of the era and inexpensive anthologies available in stores even in the most hardscrabble regions of the country likewise gave classical writing and oratory a prominent place. These books reproduced the great speeches of figures like Demosthenes and Cicero and almost always included instructions for oral delivery by Quintilian or his eighteenth-century popularizers. They taught that eloquence represented moral action by righteous leaders eager to promote and protect the public good. To behold a man on stage in a toga delivering spoken eloquence was to be reminded of the greatest oratory known in human history.[8]

Referring to the classics while discussing Ogilvie's performances seemed natural, automatic to his reviewers. Few notices mentioned Ogilvie's toga, but no one missed its significance. Rather than refer to his robe directly, newspaper reports were replete with comparisons to the classical greats. "Whatever we have conceived of the genius of Tully or fierce fire of Demosthenes—whatever opinion we have entertain'd of the bold nervous sentences of the latter, on the full, smooth swelling periods of the former, we find verified in this modern Orator," the *Middlesex Gazette* wrote admiringly. To Baltimore's *Federal Republican*, "he seems to have formed himself on the model of *Caius Gracchus*. Like him he delights in the vehemence of protracted periods, and the pathos of animated zeal." The *Montréal Gazette* featured a long letter from a correspondent who saw Ogilvie's eloquence as a harbinger of human progress. "If his efforts continue to receive support; if deserved applause continue to reward his labours, what well grounded hopes may we not entertain of the restoration, not to say the improvement of that bold, independent and hitherto inimitable eloquence, which distinguished the best ages of Greece and Rome?" To underline the link between the orator and the classical past, reviews often inserted a line or two in the original Latin. "*Ille regit dictis animos,*" one paper quoted from Virgil's *Aeneid:* "He guides [or governs] their spirits with his words." By drawing connections between Ogilvie and classical oratory, reviewers pronounced him the heir to the ancients.[9]

Ogilvie's toga became an established visual emblem of his celebrity: it seemed to confirm his talent for true eloquence and assure commentators of the significance of his mission. They might not have mentioned the toga in their reviews, but it loomed large in reviewers' comments nevertheless. To wit: the *Albany Register* termed him a "modern Cicero." The toga helped his celebrity reach new heights, establishing a public identity distinct from any given night's performance. His eloquence and his toga became interlinked in a powerful public persona. Thus, when he appeared in a new city and local newspapers began to publicize his upcoming lectures, his name prompted commentators to draw connections to the classics. "His whole attention," Annapolis's *Maryland Gazette* explained upon his arrival there, "has been directed to the revival of Oratory, an art which has slumbered with but few intermissions since the proud days of Greek and Roman greatness." In this early incarnation of American celebrity, drawing such a close connection between one's public identity and classical oratory made that persona all the more instantly legible as he made his way from place to place, greeting new audiences along the way. His toga helped to affiliate his name closely with classical erudition; that swirl of associations catapulted his celebrity and name recognition. It might also have protected him against damning criticism, for Americans associated classical oratory with good men eager to protect and defend the public good.[10]

Ogilvie's goal to revive the eloquence of the ancient republics amounted to more than just encouraging public interest in oratory as a form of communication. It reminded his contemporaries of the ties between public speech, moral leadership, and admirable character that appeared in classical texts. The classics taught early Americans that knowledge was inert on its own; it required rhetorical persuasion from real people to make knowledge meaningful in the realm of human affairs. The embodied performance of ideas permitted listeners to judge not only the relative merits of the argument or to compare the eloquence of the debaters but also to gauge their manly character. "Above all," Quintilian had posited about the orator, "he must be a good man," a sentiment that appeared repeatedly (or was paraphrased) in American schoolbooks. This line of thinking held that leaders inspired by the will to do good would ultimately prove more persuasive than others with motives less pure, for their auditors would perceive the difference. Even the most talented deceiver could not outperform a leader whose righteous rhetorical power revealed his sterling character. Americans idealized this public performance of leadership, as shown by their canonization of George Washington's oratory, particularly his Farewell Address (an address that, ironically, Washington never delivered orally). Hence, when a young orator from the College of William and Mary was portrayed in a toga by a portrait painter, his noble gaze and oratorical hand gesture anticipated the young man's future as a moral leader.[11]

The toga's semiotics were not limited to its association with classical oratory. When Dr. James Warren delivered his commemorative Boston Massacre oration in a toga in March 1775 to a powder keg tense Boston audience, he evoked the classical opposition to tyranny. But by the early nineteenth century, the toga was just as important for what it wasn't: it symbolized the social stability of a culture that would not succumb to extralegal violence, as had the French Revolution. In the years after the 1793 Terror, classically inspired plays like *Cato: A Tragedy* accrued powerful political meaning for Americans and Britons alike. John Philip Kemble, the British actor so famous for his portrayals of Cato and Coriolanus throughout the late eighteenth and early nineteenth century, specialized in deliberate, thoughtful delivery and the stoical self-possession that audiences expected from the noble Roman republicans they witnessed onstage. His performances exemplified felicitous leadership: dignity, reason, and conviction in the face of tyranny or demagoguery, even to the point of conservative political caution, and a rejection of the rash political upheavals of the French Revolution. Thus, Ogilvie's toga epitomized the gravity and rationality that placed him in fundamental opposition to mob rule. It also destabilized his own reputation for political radicalism and atheism. The toga constituted a visual symbol so potent that it could undercut the toga's origins among a people who rejected Christianity. It signified erudition and principled heroism vital to the defense of the Republic.[12]

If early Americans associated good speech with good men and good leadership, they also associated the toga with manliness. The toga "should, therefore, be distinguished and manly [*splendidus et virilis*], as, indeed, it ought to be with all men

Figure 32. Samuel Myers. Unknown artist. Circa 1810, oil on canvas. William and Mary graduate Samuel Myers performed oratory as a student and went on to become a leading lawyer in Norfolk. Courtesy of the Chrysler Museum of Art, Nofolk, Va.

of position," Quintilian explained. It was the orator's behavior that made the toga *virilis*; it exemplified male power. Wearing it was an art that required practice, and thus how the orator manipulated the toga with apparent effortlessness in the course of a speech exemplified character and experience. Ogilvie disguised his gaunt frame with a robe that emphasized breadth of chest and, therefore, offered an illusion of authority and physical power long associated with manly oratory.

Cruikshank del.   Murray sc.

Mr. KEMBLE as CATO,

It must be so — Plato, thou reason'st well —
Else why this pleasing hope.

Publish'd by J. Roach, Russell Court, Drury Lane, May. 15. 1799.

Figure 33. Mr. Kemble as Cato. 1799. John Kemble in the title role as Cato,
showing the dramatic scene in which the play's noble republican hero commits suicide rather
than submit to the tyranny of Julius Caesar. Courtesy of the Rare Book & Manuscript
Library, University of Illinois at Urbana-Champaign

Figure 34. *Orator in a Toga. From Gilbert Austin,* Chironomia; or,
A Treatise on Rhetorical Delivery . . . *(London, 1806). Alongside figures wearing
regular men's dress, Austin's guidebook for public speaking includes the occasional man in a toga
or other theatrical costume. Courtesy of Southern Illinois University Press, Carbondale, Ill.*

Analyzing his embodied performance thus raises larger questions about his relationships with his fans, the women and men he socialized with, and his insistence on the importance of women in American culture—all of which marked
clear distinctions between the male-only world of classical oratory and the particular social and gender dynamics of the early American Republic.[13]

Quintilian specifically addressed the bodily and manly elements of powerful speech as he explained how good speakers might maneuver the toga in the
midst of a passionate display. He insisted that it was vital to keep the throat
and chest open, allowing one's listeners to appreciate "the impressive effect produced by breadth at the chest." The drapes of the toga disguised thin, habitually
sickly men's frames like Ogilvie's, creating an illusion of broad-chested robust-
ness and masculine dominance early in a performance. Once the orator began
to perform, however, his own energy on the rostrum replaced the visual illusion
of vigor. At that point, as it became more difficult to maintain the elegant folds
of the toga, Quintilian advised handling it in ways that freed the speaker from
being confined by the garment. "Throw back the toga from the left shoulder," he
advised, for, above all, the orator needed to maintain "an air of vigour and freedom." In fact, to throw the drape "over the right shoulder"—thus covering up the
speaker's tunic-clad breast and open throat—"would be a foppish and effeminate gesture." These details about the speaker's manipulation of the toga to convey energy and physical presence reveal how explicit and long-standing were the
connections between masculinity and public speech. Ogilvie followed those instructions, according to a Baltimore paper: "He moves from one end of the *rostra*
to the other, throws back his robe, smites himself with his hands, and leaves un-
practised no look or gesture that can assist the imagination of his hearers." Con-

MR KEMBLE.

AS CATO.

Engraved by T. WOOLNOTH from a drawing by WAGEMAN.

Published 1823 by Simpkin & Marshall Stationers Ct & Chapple Pall Mall.

Figure 35. Mr. Kemble as Cato. 1823. Note John Kemble's open throat, framed by the elegant folds of the toga, setting off his firm gaze and muscular grip of the blade. Courtesy of the Rare Book & Manuscript Library, University of Illinois at Urbana-Champaign

veying a manly presence was so important that one engraver used a well-known muscular boxer as the model for the actor John Kemble's body rather than faithfully reproduce Kemble's less appealing frame.[14]

And, indeed, Americans in the early Republic associated oratory with manliness. Hundreds of newspaper accounts of legislative and political speakers invoked variations of the phrase *manly eloquence* in ways that they never needed to explain, repeating it over the course of decades. "The free states of antiquity have passed away, and with them have perished their liberal and elegant arts— their masculine oratory," explained the *National Advocate* upon witnessing one of Ogilvie's performances. "But if lost to the old, we trust it may be transplanted to, and flourish in the *new* world." Even if its users never explained the phrase, they heralded *manly eloquence* and complimented speakers for their *masculine delivery* in ways that indicated both physical and intellectual qualities—and marked distinctions between admirable speech and its opposite. Manly eloquence emerged from the embodied speaker: the man's physical appearance, speaking talents, and energetic yet controlled delivery all contributed to his power and authority as an orator. The performative dimension of a speech conveyed the man's physicality as well as the enactment of self-possession and forceful intellect.[15]

Manly eloquence also reflected the intended effects of the oration on an audience. To deliver masculine oratory was to call forth thoughtful deliberation from one's listeners, not mere emotion. If a demagogue sowed fear or used cheap emotionalism to move his audience, the true orator called for his listeners to consider the issues rationally. Contemporaries never used the term *feminine eloquence*, nor is it clear that they would have characterized the opposite of manly eloquence as feminine or effeminate. Rather, the opposite of manly eloquence was disingenuous, emotional, or overly forceful speech that sought to subvert reason. The phrase *manly eloquence* allowed a critic to mark distinctions between virtuous leaders and deceptive ones, and to insist that listeners who noticed the rhetorical strategies and the characters of those men could tell the difference.

They might not have viewed deceptive speech as feminine, but early Americans commonly believed that women were more prone to emotional responses than men, who were seen as possessing more capacity for reason. No wonder Rodman's scathing *Fragments of a Journal of a Sentimental Philosopher* dedicated so much verbiage to imagining Ogilvie's dangerous eagerness to acquire female acolytes. For Rodman and others, Ogilvie's appeal to women raised questions about the manliness of his oratory.[16]

Ogilvie roundly rejected the Romans' views of oratory being appropriate only for male audiences. His own faith in women's intellectual and civic significance reflected a far more contemporary source: Scottish Enlightenment thinkers, who held that any society that claimed to be civilized ought to be scrutinized not merely for its politics, arts, ideas, and economy but also for the condition of its women and domestic society. Only barbaric nations kept their women ignorant or subservient, these writers believed. While such a viewpoint of women's role in civil society wasn't universal in the early United States, Scottish moral philosophy had become de rigueur in college education and circulated widely in membership libraries, women's magazines, and conduct manuals. Moreover, this viewpoint was associated with a progressive, forward-looking vision of national identity. The same people who advocated for substantial girls' education (which, to be clear, was not equivalent to boys') often tied it to the United States' position among nations. Thus, when Ogilvie advertised so publicly his eagerness to earn the approval of women and to ensure that his audiences remained equally divided between male and female attendees, he sustained this Enlightenment perspective of women's importance in civilized society.[17]

His writing about his style of rostrum oratory revealed these views with clarity. Its very nature, he proclaimed, ought "to attract the attention of ladies of intelligence and taste," for they grant "dignity and attraction to the rostrum." These were not empty words or false compliments, he insisted. Rather, they captured his conviction that the opinions of such women were fundamental to public opinion. If his performances onstage should be praised by men but "call down the matrons' indignant frown, or avert the virgins' eye with shame and scorn," his efforts to foster a new age of eloquence would be doomed. His newspaper advertisements frequently requested the attendance of women at his talks.[18]

Not all men felt comfortable with Ogilvie's effects on his female attendees, particularly because women proved to be so enthusiastic. When he visited the small towns along New Hampshire's seacoast, one man commented on the responses by women in his own family. "Their expectations were raised to the highest pitch, and as usual with enthusiastic Girls their ideas were somewhat extravagant," Robert Means, Jr., wrote to a friend. "Lucretia was delighted and Dolly praised Ogilvie without bounds." That Ogilvie's talk was delivered to benefit the Portsmouth Female Asylum, a female-run organization designed to raise, educate, and train orphaned girls, might have enhanced their appreciation. After attending a second lecture in the village of Exeter, Means mused, "What impressions he left on the minds of the better informed Gentlemen, I know not; but it is very certain that the Ladies were highly delighted." For Means, the women's enthusiasm seemed to have heightened his skepticism about Ogilvie's performances. Without offering any specific criticisms, he cast himself into the category of "better informed Gentlemen"—men less likely to be swept away by the emotional fervor of a celebrity sighting. Means's letter offers evidence of Ogilvie's impact on female auditors as well as the corresponding distrust it might arouse from men.[19]

It is precisely Means's distrust of his rhetorical power over the women in his family that made Ogilvie's other associations with women—his friendships and frequent visits to their parlors—so striking. If men like Means felt that their wives or daughters might become overly entranced by the orator's performances, why didn't they appear to feel nervous when he socialized with the same women? We have good reason to believe that evidence of any such nervousness might appear in men's letters. After all, those same letters reveal the extent to which critics gossiped throughout his career about his atheism and political radicalism. No matter how often he sought to undermine those rumors by incorporating religious imagery and biblical verse into his lectures, rumors continued to raise questions about his beliefs. In contrast, Ogilvie's eagerness to cultivate the friendships and patronage of society women, especially matrons, appears to have remained above board: both platonic and respectable. The absolute lack of evidence of gossip about his possible flirtations with women suggests that he avoided it and, perhaps, had little inclination in that direction. Considering that some of the known side effects of heavy opiate use are diminished libido and impaired sexual performance, Ogilvie's drug habit might have eliminated flirtatious or unguarded sexual frissons from his interactions.

The approval of women was foundational to his career and depended upon maintaining scrupulously respectable behavior. At the same time that a contemporaneous British celebrity like Lord Byron found that his sexual transgressions and scandals actually piqued his fans' interest and compounded his celebrity, Ogilvie's situation looked quite different. Lacking Byron's youth, striking good looks, and the social and financial protections of his aristocratic title, Ogilvie relied on his continued favor among the United States' wealthy social circles to guarantee his fortunes. Condemnation or social ostracization because of unguarded behavior with women could destroy his career, brand him a rake, and threaten the women's reputations. Provided that he walked the line of respectability, those women's patronage bolstered his career. It assured a strong female presence at his talks and allowed him to benefit from their social networks.[20]

Yet his letters and memoirs indicate that he believed that some of these women had truly become his friends, not merely strategic alliances. Recalling his youth in Virginia, he particularly spoke of the high character of one "matron" who made him "happy, by having access to the society and friendship of a truly accomplished woman: A modern Cornelia" whom he professed always to "admire, revere, and love." By likening her to the Cornelia commemorated in Plutarch's *Lives*—a woman revered for her virtue and her dedication to her children—Ogilvie ensured that his friend would enjoy an unblemished reputation and, by extension, so would he. (This line also, of course, reminded readers yet again of his close association with classical virtue.) In Philadelphia, he befriended a

Mrs. Hopkinson. "He visits her frequently and she is one of his best friends, and also one of the most witty agreeable smart, tidy little women I ever met," wrote a female acquaintance. "He gives us an oration to morrow, and under Mrs. Hopkinsons patronage I shall go to hear him." To the novelist Charles Brockden Brown, Ogilvie waxed eloquent about a Mrs. Ellis, who had provided valued friendship; in Boston he enjoyed the company of "one of the dearest of my friends[,] Mrs. Humphreys," who helped introduce him to figures of note; and in London he took public walks with a Mrs. Hamilton and called on mutual friends with a Mrs. Dixon. Their friendships might have been socially acceptable because of the class differences between them. Then, again, perhaps age differences mitigated against gossip. It's also tempting to wonder whether the women likewise saw Ogilvie as a friend or instead primarily as a client for their patronage. No matter how they mutually upheld the strict respectability of these relationships, these friendships became a distinctive feature of Ogilvie's public persona. Matrons provided him with social access and the stamp of social approval as well as companionship, and he provided charming, learned conversation that expressed his core belief in women's intellectual and civic significance.[21]

He went out of his way to cultivate those relationships and to advertise his progressive views of women in two ways. First, for his oft-repeated speech on "the radical importance of female education," as he advertised it in the newspapers, he provided free admission to female attendees and spoke at length on the social good that resulted from giving women substantial foundations in education. Like the Scottish theorists on whom he drew, he tied female education to the progress of civilization. Women should not be reduced to "the slave of savage life, or the effeminate victim of licentious indulgence," one Charleston commentator summarized after hearing this speech. Ogilvie painted those two extremes as equally dire for women's character. He painted in histrionic terms the ways that a society that failed to educate its women doomed them to "wretchedness" and crippled marriages, giving children the terrible disadvantage of having ignorant mothers and thereby impeding national progress. Instead, women should be educated to become "the rational companion of man; the sentimental associate of all his joys." If this vision appears less radical than his advertisements seemed to promise—certainly less so than Mary Wollstonecraft's *Vindication of the Rights of Woman* of twenty years earlier—we should remember that, by the early 1810s, Wollstonecraft's posthumous reputation remained so damaged that many discussions of female education took a conservative bent, as authors hastened to insist that women did not require the more extensive aspects of men's education because they would never rise to take on professions that demanded it.[22]

Female education varied radically by region and especially by race and the wealth of one's family—so much so that it is difficult to generalize. Girls from prosperous families could attend rigorous academies that provided educations rich in humanistic and scientific knowledge. Viewed more widely, however, education for girls remained more limited than that for boys, especially in the South. As a result, Ogilvie's oration on female education could arouse a public conversation among local attendees. After his oration on the subject in Charleston in 1811, a correspondent to the Charleston *Times* contributed a lengthy, four-part essay on the topic that repackaged many of Ogilvie's views about female education, albeit with fewer rhetorical flourishes and more references to the Bible. To be sure, this writer acknowledged, women "are not designed to govern the state, or to command armies; to plead at the bar, or to preach in the Church," and thus could skip certain subjects. Still, women required "no small degree of knowledge" for their many roles and responsibilities. Although the author highlighted their duties as wives, mothers, and Christians, he also discussed women's economic contributions to the household and society at large and suggested that the education of impoverished girls would help them become virtuous household servants rather than streetwalkers.[23]

The second way Ogilvie demonstrated his respect for and gratitude to elite women was by offering benefit evenings—performances he delivered for charitable purposes. Several times each year he offered special lectures on the subject of beneficence, after which he donated the night's ticket sales to a local charity or library. More than half of these organizations were headed by women: orphan asylums, humane societies, and charitable associations to benefit poor widows, among others. He often initiated those arrangements with a stately letter to the overseers offering his services. To the female managers of the Charleston Orphan House he explained in his best hand that these evenings gave him "the most solid and unalloy'd pleasures I have enjoyed" and went out of his way to guarantee their approval by refusing to accept reimbursement even for his own costs of renting the hall, lighting the room with candles, and supplying the door-keeper's wages. These formal, elegantly worded letters back and forth allowed both Ogilvie and his lady correspondents to demonstrate the right degree of feeling and mutual gratitude. Like a dance performed on a stage, the arrangements between them demonstrated their mutual respect and public-mindedness. These performances benefited Ogilvie the most, for what he lost in revenue on those evenings he gained in social access to elite families and public expressions of thanks that often circulated throughout the nation's newspapers.[24]

News about his donations also spurred attendance. When just a month after his Charleston benefit he began planning a lecture benefiting Savannah's orphan asylum, he advertised the amounts he had donated elsewhere: in Boston, "550 dollars; in New-York, 340 dollars; in Charleston, 250 dollars; in Salem, 120 dollars; and in most of the smaller towns to the eastward, to betwixt 70 and 100

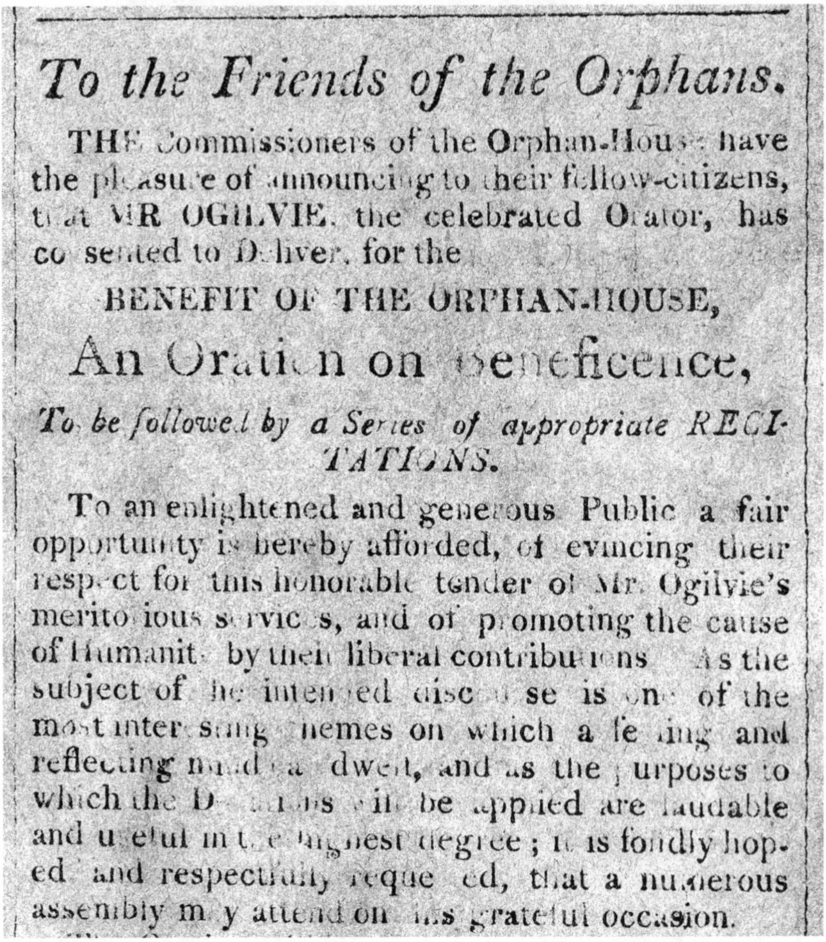

To the Friends of the Orphans.

THE Commissioners of the Orphan-House have the pleasure of announcing to their fellow-citizens, that MR OGILVIE, the celebrated Orator, has consented to Deliver, for the

BENEFIT OF THE ORPHAN-HOUSE,

An Oration on beneficence,

To be followed by a Series of appropriate RECI-TATIONS.

To an enlightened and generous Public a fair opportunity is hereby afforded, of evincing their respect for this honorable tender of Mr. Ogilvie's meritorious services, and of promoting the cause of Humanity by their liberal contributions. As the subject of the intended discourse is one of the most interesting themes on which a feeling and reflecting mind can dwell, and as the purposes to which the Donations will be applied are laudable and useful in the highest degree; it is fondly hoped and respectfully requested, that a numerous assembly may attend on this grateful occasion.

Figure 36. "To the Friends of the Orphans." From Charleston Courier, Apr. 19, 1811, [2].
An advertisement for one of Ogilvie's benefits on behalf of a women's organization to help orphans,
benefits that often helped him establish close ties with prominent, public-minded women.
Courtesy of the American Antiquarian Society, Worcester, Mass.

dollars." Denoting precise dollar amounts was probably a canny move. Considering the petty sense of competition among cities, not to mention the provincial anxieties that made small cities like Savannah want to prove themselves equal or superior to others, the inclusion of a list like this might have spurred Savannah's residents to get out their pocketbooks. Imagine their pride when Ogilvie's lecture raised $250 for the Savannah Female Asylum—the same amount that his Charleston benefit had raised, although Savannah's population was only a fifth the size. They wasted no time in announcing that fact in the newspapers, and then saw it reprinted as far away as Kentucky and Massachusetts.[25]

Viewing Ogilvie's advocacy of women's education alongside his wearing of the toga onstage allows us to see twinned ways that he called forth fantasies of American progress. His advocacy, his benefit evenings dedicated to the success of female-run charities, and his widely recognized friendships with women all signaled an optimistic sense of national improvement. For, according to the Scottish writers read by virtually all educated people in the early nineteenth century, truly civilized nations could be measured by the respect and civic position they accorded to women. Meanwhile, the toga helped to anchor Ogilvie's oratory to both past and future. It marked a connection to the classical republics and great leader-orators like Cicero while also suggesting that oratory had an important role to play in bringing about a bright and virtuous future for the United States. His toga helped to popularize the idea that, as in the classical past, their new republic would produce noble leaders who governed by persuasion and reason rather than coercion or emotional manipulation. It was an infectiously optimistic view of the nation's future.

After spending the spring of 1811 in Charleston and Savannah, James Ogilvie concluded a series of lectures in the village of Columbia in the chapel of the South Carolina College (later the University of South Carolina). "Eloquence in a free state is power, and it is power of the noblest kind, because it rules the minds of men by the force of reason," the *Columbia State Gazette* wrote, caught up in the exhilaration of the moment. Ogilvie's "manly eloquence, which breaking forth from a mind luminous with science and a heart strong in virtue, moves on like an heavenly vision, in its lofty course, and sheds its glory on every object." When the attendees walked out of the chapel, they found the college and the president's house "brilliantly illuminated" on this early summer night. "Over the front door of each was displayed the American Eagle soaring aloft with the name of Ogilvie." Clearly, Ogilvie had a knack for inspiring optimistic views of national progress.[26]

But the hard work of performing in ways that invoked those inspiring views had begun to take its toll on Ogilvie's health and spirits, such that he had decided to take a break from lecturing. He planned to embark on a five-hundred-mile horseback ride from Columbia to Lexington, Kentucky. "In a few weeks I shall retire to a solitary room in a little healthy rural village in Kentucky," he announced. To President James Madison, he described this trip to Kentucky grandiosely as "moral seclusion and solitary study" where he would be "stimulated by every motive to strenuous exertion that the love of glory, the love of good, or the love of gold can awaken." In letter after letter, Ogilvie romanticized this seclusion in a "healthy" state, where he planned to rest and write new lectures. His letters did not reveal a second motive: to address the problem of his considerable opium habit.[27]

When he got to Kentucky during the summer of 1811, however, he found something besides a romantic, secluded spot for rest and rehabilitation. Oh, he would rest. But he also discovered an unexpected source of inspiration for his own future. The toga-wearing celebrity who spoke so movingly about American progress would join with other Kentuckians in beating the drum for war.

{ CHAPTER 9 }

Fighting Indians in a Masculine Kentucky Landscape,
1811–1813

In later years, James Ogilvie often repeated an anecdote about his travels in Kentucky: a night when, after a long day's ride, he stopped at a lonely one-room cabin with the hope of finding a place to sleep. The old woman there offered him "a supper of comfortable, but homely fare." He had just gotten into bed when he heard the cabin's door latch rattle. "There entered a dark looking man of gigantic stature and form, with stiff black hair, eyebrows, and beard," "dressed in a brown hunting shirt, which partly concealed a pair of dirty buckskin overalls, and he wore moccasins of the same material." When Ogilvie told this tale, he insisted "he had never seen any thing half so ferocious." The man and his mother sat by the fire whispering inaudibly while Ogilvie pretended to sleep. Hearing them ask one another, "Don't you think he's asleep now[?]" he began to fear for his life.

When they decided he had fallen asleep, the hunter rose to his full height, took down from the rack an enormous greasy knife, and walked with a "noiseless step" toward Ogilvie's bed. But "at the moment that Mr. O. was about to implore his pity" and beg for his life, the man reached above the bed toward the rafters to cut down a venison ham, returned to his stool near the fire, and began to slice off pieces for his supper. "The hungry hunter, who had eaten nothing since the morning, had forbore making a noise, lest they should interrupt the slumbers of their way-worn guest," Ogilvie realized. He repeated the story often, "which furnished him with a favorite occasion of exercising his powers of declamation to great advantage," declaring "that he had never taken a more refreshing night's rest, or made a more grateful repast than he had done in this humble cottage."[1]

Like a lot of good anecdotes, this one played on easterners' stereotypes about Kentucky as a wilderness, a place where ferocious men sliced meat off enormous venison hams for their suppers. The contrast between that figure and the scrawny Ogilvie, cowering underneath his covers, couldn't have been more delightful. It characterized the state as a place caught out of time in contrast to easterners' concerns with business, fashion, and improvements; it was a place still linked to an ancient way of life. But the Kentucky he actually encountered in 1811 was far more diverse and socially complex than his tale might suggest. The easy stereotype in his tale about a fierce frontiersman belies how surprised Ogilvie was by his experience there and how much the events of the moment—especially the growing tensions with Britain—would change him.

His plan: after settling in Kentucky, he would revive his health and spirits, rid himself of his reliance on opium, and write new orations, all of which would allow him to resume his national lecture tour with renewed strength and improved material. Along the way, however, he found his new neighbors caught up in war fever against the British and the Native Americans nearby, and he ended up throwing his celebrity to support the American cause. He even went so far as to enlist in the Kentucky militia during the War of 1812, a conflict that would last for years and end inconclusively. During his two years there, Ogilvie vanquished his addiction. And, along the way, caught up in the uniquely pro-war rhetoric of this western region, he tried to vanquish Indians as well.

Fifteen years earlier, visitors had considered Kentucky a frontier. One traveler to the region in 1797 had noted with disparagement that houses in Lexington were constructed of "hewn logs, with the chimneys *outside*." But by the 1810s "the log cabins had disappeared, and in their places stood costly brick mansions, well painted and enclosed by fine yards, bespeaking the taste and wealth of their possessors." Lexington, the largest city in the state's "garden spot," had doubled in size since the 1790s to forty-five hundred residents and now featured a university, a public library, a range of small manufacturers, and three schools offering advanced education to girls. Travelers liked to admire Lexington for its "excessive fertility, pre-eminent beauty, and abundant advantages"; they described it as "flourishing." One British visitor noted that "a small party of rich citizens are endeavouring to withdraw themselves from the multitude," to "draw a line of distinction between themselves as *gens comme il faut* and the *canaille*" (people who are proper versus the vulgar, a slur made more pointed by use of French). That distinction was striking, according to this man, considering that "the prevailing individual amusements of Lexington are drinking, and gambling at billiards and cards." Eighty miles west at the falls of the Ohio River, Louisville would nearly overtake Lexington in size within the next decade. Eighty miles north, Cincinnati grew faster than both cities during the same years. The state's most vigorous boosters used the language of progress to describe it. "No State has excelled us in Agriculture and Manufactures — and happy am I to say that Republicanism keeps pace," the Lexington postmaster wrote to Thomas Jefferson in 1811.[2]

The five-hundred-mile horseback trek from Columbia, South Carolina, to Lexington through the Appalachian Mountains and Tennessee took about a month during the summer of 1811. Before leaving, Ogilvie had suffered a crippling bout of melancholy, which made his desire for rest and solitude all the more pointed. "You know," he wrote to a young friend, "the truly terrible visitations of motiveless apathy and life-sick despondence to which I am periodically liable." This one he described as "among the most painful and protracted

I have ever endured." Notwithstanding those complaints, however, Ogilvie arrived energized. His early months in Kentucky looked surprisingly busy—no different from his chockablock schedule of the previous three years. He lectured, courted members of influential families, and traveled. Local newspapers advertised the appearance of "the celebrated Orator" by borrowing from effusive accounts in eastern and southern papers. Within a week of arriving in Lexington, he had booked the ballroom at Mr. Postlethwait's hotel and begun advertising his talks. After his second lecture in early July, he donated one hundred dollars to the Lexington Library—a significant proportion of his earnings in the city. "I must say you have furnished, what was not wanted, an additional evidence of that devotion to literature, and that disinterested liberality, which you have invariably so eminently displayed," Henry Clay wrote in thanks on behalf of the library. Almost immediately Ogilvie began to make plans to continue to Frankfort, the state capital and the nearest large town. By the end of September he had hit the road again. He rode 250 miles southwest to Nashville, carrying letters of introduction to Andrew Jackson, a man whose triumphs in the War of 1812 would make him a national hero within a few years. "You cannot but be pleased with him," one of these letters promised Jackson, asking that he give Ogilvie "all your civility and attention which you so well know how to make acceptable, to a stranger."[3]

Perhaps the delay of Ogilvie's long-anticipated rest and relaxation resulted from the enthusiasm for oratory he encountered during these early months. Local bookstores advertised the availability of Thomas Browne's three-volume *The British Cicero; or, a Selection of the Most Admired Speeches in the English Language*, a collection that also offered "an introduction to the study and practice of eloquence." The Frankfort *Palladium* inserted a long "Essay on Eloquence Philosophically Considered" amid its breathless accounts of political tensions with Great Britain. Transylvania University students displayed their oratory during periodic examination days and with impressive commencement-day speeches, while members of the Logical Society and the Investigating Society, two young men's debating clubs, met weekly to help one another hone their talents for public address. Annual Fourth of July speeches were elaborate events, often combined with barbecues at the homes of wealthy political figures and described in detail afterward in local papers. Meanwhile, Henry Clay had already begun to build his reputation as a political speaker, having been elected to the U.S. House of Representatives. As part of a coalition of hawks who advocated going to war with Great Britain, Clay was elected Speaker of the House.[4]

Ogilvie found eager listeners. One of these, a twenty-three-year-old law student named William Little Brown, another aficionado of William Godwin's writings, kept a diary dedicated to recording his efforts at self-improvement and the cultivation of noble feelings. In between solemnly promising not to engage in the "unnatural and unmanly" act of masturbation and describing his attempts to improve in public speaking, Brown paid close attention to the orators he observed. "My maxim at present is 'Study law, cultivate feeling,'" he wrote, discussing his views of good oratory. "By culture I am convinced a man may give flexibility to his feelings, which will make him eloquent on every subject of interest. This is one of the greatest springs of forcible speech. 'Feel right and you will speak right,' is the aphorism of a great man." Along the way he especially made note of the flow of language and persuasion, so when he attended one of Ogilvie's Lexington speeches, Brown dedicated a long entry to discussing it. "It was a splendid discourse and not devoid of logical accuracy and deduction. His style is Mr. Godwin's decorated with many beautiful poetic images."[5]

One demonstration of Kentuckians' appreciation for Ogilvie's oratory must have taken him aback when it first occurred. Upon the conclusion of one of his lectures, the audience remained completely silent. "*There was no clapping of hands, neither during the delivery nor at the close of the Orations, nor even after the recitation of a variety of exquisite poetical effusions, although pronounced with an elocution in the highest degree impassioned and electrifying,*" the *Kentucky Gazette* wrote. "The feelings of the audience were expressed only by a profound respectful and solemn silence," the writer continued, hastening to assure Ogilvie that in Kentucky, at least, this silence reflected the audience's highest regard. "Mr. Ogilvie could not be insensible to so decided a token of respect for the dignity of the Rostrum." Indeed, this writer insisted, such behavior must be the pinnacle of "delicacy, refinement and intelligence, that but rarely characterizes a miscellaneous audience and must, we are sure, have been peculiarly gratifying to the Orator." None of Ogilvie's performances elsewhere had been received in this way. His audience's silence must have reminded him of the "deep and dead" silence in the middle of his scandalous Philadelphia lecture that had nearly destroyed his career. Had his new patrons warned him beforehand of this odd practice, unique to Kentucky? Or did they need to explain it to him afterward? The very length of this article in the *Gazette* suggested a sudden self-consciousness about how easily this practice might have been misunderstood by the very celebrity they sought to praise with their lack of applause.[6]

After four months of speaking, socializing, and traveling, in November 1811 Ogilvie finally took his long-anticipated break. He rented a cabin he had found on his trek to Nashville, located in a remote part of the state some 150 miles southeast of Lexington and about 30 miles into the countryside from the tiny town of Bowling Green on the Nashville Road. He painted a romantic picture of its location in a letter to Thomas Jefferson. "There exists not a human being within several miles of this place: I reside in a log-house situated in a deep glen and encircled by hills, which I climb twice a day for exercise—Here I am determined to remain until I can accomplish the purpose of my temporary seclusion": regaining his health and revising his lectures. Later in the century, a traveler to the same spot used similarly romantic language, describing it as "situated away from the 'hurly burly' down amid verdant hills resting their feet on rocky bases whose old gray sides are carpeted with mosses, ferns and intersected by caverns from whose unexplored depths gush forth streams of cold spring water." The location: Chameleon Springs, Kentucky.[7]

Chameleon Springs's attraction was the mineral water, which Ogilvie believed would help restore his health and spirits. Having access to pure spring water—a rare luxury in the nineteenth century—would permit him to drink enough to return natural balance to his health. Restoring a patient's body to a systemic balance was the primary aim of medical treatment in this era and reflected views of health and medicine that stretched back to Greek and Roman writers. Those theorists had laid out the notion that the body's health required equilibrium between four main humors—four major bodily fluids (blood, yellow bile, phlegm, and black bile) that caused pain and illness when one or more grew out of proportion to the others. Because they viewed the body as a mechanism that required action when one of the humors overwhelmed the others, doctors stepped in with techniques to restore a balance of those fluids—methods that could be invasive. They used bloodletting, emetics (which induced vomiting), purgatives (diarrhea), diaphoretics (sweating), diuretics (urinating), and other interventions that required scalpels or harsh drugs like mercury and tartar emetics, all to release the excess fluids that had brought on illness. And because everyone at the time saw the physical and mental aspects of health as intertwined, Ogilvie would have viewed his three predominant health complaints—his reliance on opium, his melancholy, and his rheumatic pain—as intertwined.[8]

A sufferer might also attempt to restore balance to one's health without a doctor's assistance by finding less extreme means of expelling bodily fluids, like drinking large amounts of untainted water or submerging oneself in a hot spring bath to induce sweating. And in an era when most water was unsafe to drink, a pure mountain spring offered a rare opportunity to use this natural cure. In 1808, a Charlottesville doctor recommended to a patient that the hot spring waters at Virginia's White Sulphur Springs would produce a health-restoring sweat, "with the additional advantage of clearing out various other impurities." Growing numbers of wealthy residents had recently begun to seek out mountain springs during long southern summers for medical reasons, and entrepreneurs had developed increasingly elaborate lodgings to accommodate them. Over the course of the nineteenth century, those spa destinations would seek to draw paying guests by promising that they could socialize with other elites, merging together the restoration of health with exclusive vacation spots dedicated to leisure. Similar entrepreneurial enterprises had just begun to appear in areas of Kentucky not far from Lexington and Frankfort.[9]

Chameleon Springs was too far away for its reputation for healthful waters to spread (or to attract elites eager to socialize with one another), but within a generation that would change. By 1844, a doctor in nearby Bowling Green would promise a patient: "We have some fine medical waters in the neighborhood. We have fine sulphur waters as well as calibeate [springs containing iron salts], suited to almost all diseases. Infirmities have been greatly benefited. Persons laboring under afflictions of the liver, bowels, and all diseases of this kind. All diseases of Females have been greatly benefited by the use of our medical waters." Ogilvie's experience among Virginia elites would have acquainted him with the curative powers of mineral springs. In resolving to climb the hills near his cabin daily, he indicated familiarity with the view that regular exercise would help him sweat out his body's humoral imbalance. His daily hikes also provided an energizing way for him to withstand the longing for opium.[10]

The exercise, the restorative spring water, and sheer willpower helped him triumph over his opium habit. It was not easy. "Before I changed my place of residence," he wrote to a friend, "physicians told me death would be the certain consequence" of quitting laudanum abruptly. He tried it anyway. He survived the first night owing to sheer fatigue, but the second night was "horrible": "Every individual fibre appeared to have its peculiar pang; every sense brought agony. I suffered the tortures of the damned. Twice I rose and put the vial of laudanum to my lips—twice I put it away untasted. I was in most excruciating pain." Finally, acknowledging how powerful was the pull of the drug, he "opened the window with desperate resolution and threw it out on the ground.—When I saw its fragments glitter in the moonlight, I felt a sentiment of triumph—I am regenerated—but it is as resurrection from the grave. Before, I was languid and nerveless as a new born infant—now I have regained health, strength and spirits—and look back on my infatuation with horror."[11]

This letter was the only account that documented his triumph over the drug, and it left open questions about exactly how easy it had been for him to loosen the drug's hold over him. Had he really quit it entirely, as the letter suggested, or did he wean himself gradually with lower doses over the course of months, as most doctors advised? Even Thomas De Quincey, whose 1821 *Confessions of an English Opium-Eater* would provide a riveting account of one man's struggles to overcome the habit, admitted that he had never completely quit the drug but gradually diminished it to a reasonable amount. We might read Ogilvie's triumphal account skeptically, for it probably revealed more about his *desire* for such will-

Medicinal Springs.

I HAVE moved from Springfield to the Medicinal Springs, near Harrodsburg, at which place I have opened a house of

Entertainment,

for the accommodation of those who wish to attend the Springs. A considerable number of buildings have lately been erected for the purpose, among which are about twenty Cabbins for the use of those who may wish to board themselves.

The beneficial effects which have been produced upon those who have used these waters, are the best evidence of their utility.

These Springs are situated in a neighbourhood equal to any in Kentucky for furnishing a market; and the public may rest assured that every exertion will be made by me to render the place not only useful, but pleasurable.

28th June, 1807.   D. JENINGS.

Figure 37. "Medicinal Springs." From Western World (Frankfort, Ky.), Sept. 3, 1807, [4]. Medicinal and therapeutic springs had not yet become big business in Kentucky as they had in Virginia, but entrepreneurs had begun to develop the infrastructure that would attract customers: boardinghouses, individual cabins, and entertainment. Courtesy of the American Antiquarian Society, Worcester, Mass.

power. He also did not mention that opium had become expensive as a result of the United States' embargo against British goods; remaining a habitué of the drug had become burdensome for a variety of reasons.[12]

Whatever the details of his months of recuperating his "health, strength and spirits" in Chameleon Springs, the retreat successfully recharged his enthusiasm for public speaking. By the time he returned to Lexington in May 1812, Ogilvie had developed a grandiose plan. He announced that he had revised old orations and composed new ones "on a plan more systematic, and with an exertion of his faculties more uninterrupted and intense." That plan, he now stated, was "to revive the study of Rhetoric and Elocution in a state of society peculiarly auspicious to the renovation of these noble and long neglected Arts." His new lectures would display this more "systematic," "intense" sense of direction.[13]

By testing this plan in Kentucky, far from the more densely networked areas of the East Coast, Ogilvie had the chance to make any adjustments necessary to satisfy his audiences. Once again, the reviews were ecstatic. "At each successive oration, his hearers were more numerous and crowded. — That they were charmed with the orator was manifest from their continued, profound, and almost breathless attention," effused the *Kentucky Reporter*, which explained that Ogilvie had "the happy talent of marching with a force irresistable, through the feelings to the judgment. Having carried you to the temple of reason, he there dwells until the charm of the orator is lost in the truths he advances." This, the paper proclaimed, was "genuine eloquence." His lectures in Cincinnati and southern Ohio as well as along the Lexington-Frankfort-Louisville corridor during the summer of 1812 allowed Ogilvie to hone his performances. He also reported that he had lost his wallet containing all his money—some $175, equivalent to nearly six months' earnings for a laborer—and that he had failed to borrow enough from his friends to make ends meet, making those performances all the more necessary.[14]

After months of isolation, Ogilvie encountered a new preoccupation among his Kentucky acquaintances: an unequivocal demand for war with Great Britain.

White Kentuckians and their western neighbors in Tennessee, Ohio, and the Indiana Territory had different reasons from other Americans for supporting war. To be sure, they shared some common beliefs. Many people had long felt angered by British attacks on American maritime commerce and the British navy's practice of kidnapping Americans and impressing them into service aboard its ships. They also resented what they saw as Britain's stranglehold over the American economy. But, to a greater degree than any other region, anti-British fervor for war in Kentucky was inextricable from their loathing of the confederacy of Indian tribes living to the north in the Great Lakes region. Ken-

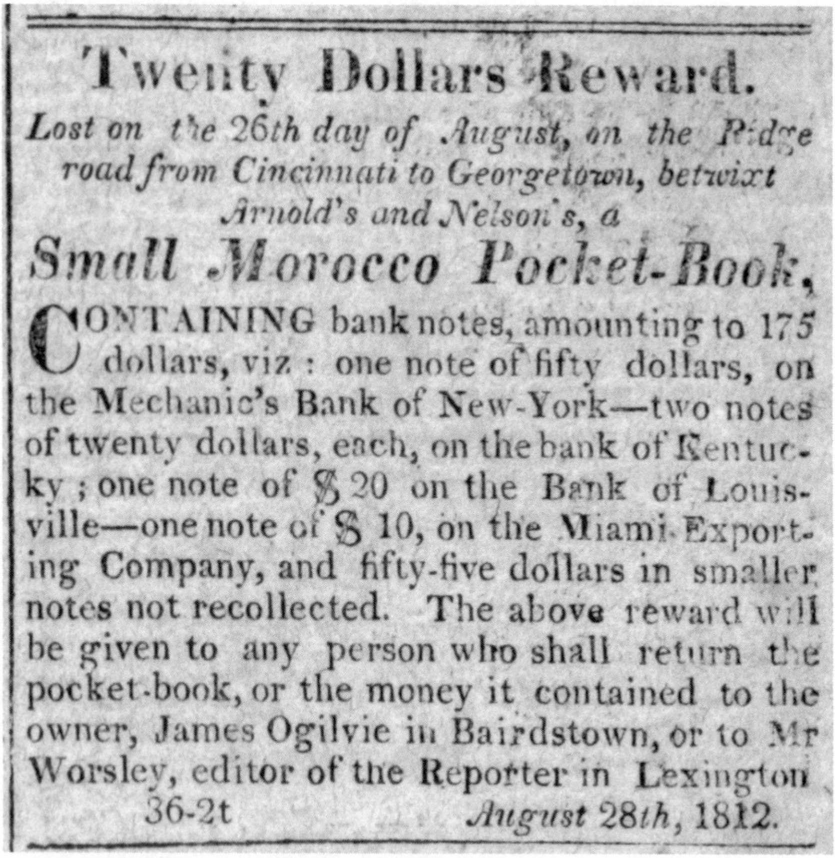

> # Twenty Dollars Reward.
>
> *Lost on the 26th day of August, on the Ridge road from Cincinnati to Georgetown, betwixt Arnold's and Nelson's, a*
>
> ## Small Morocco Pocket-Book,
>
> CONTAINING bank notes, amounting to 175 dollars, viz : one note of fifty dollars, on the Mechanic's Bank of New-York—two notes of twenty dollars, each, on the bank of Kentucky ; one note of $ 20 on the Bank of Louisville—one note of $ 10, on the Miami Exporting Company, and fifty-five dollars in smaller notes not recollected. The above reward will be given to any person who shall return the pocket-book, or the money it contained to the owner, James Ogilvie in Bairdstown, or to Mr Worsley, editor of the Reporter in Lexington
>
> 36-2t   *August 28th*, 1812.

Figure 38. "Twenty Dollars Reward." From Kentucky Gazette (Lexington), Sept. 1, 1812, [3]. Ogilvie lost his wallet during the summer of 1812, and it contained a breathtaking amount of money; $175 was perhaps equivalent to six months' income for an ordinary laborer at the time. In an era before the advent of banks with numerous branches, an itinerant's only financial choice lay in keeping money on him. Courtesy of Special Collections, University of Kentucky Libraries, Lexington

tuckians saw Native Americans as the brutal allies of the British and an immediate threat to their livelihoods. "We are fully convinced that the formation of the combination headed by the Shawanoe Prophet, is a British scheme," proclaimed a resolution of the citizens of Vincennes, Indiana Territory, printed in Kentucky papers during August 1811. And, because their mistrust of Indians predated the more specific tensions with Britain that had emerged since the turn of the nineteenth century, Kentuckians now found a convenient opportunity to merge their hatred of both groups into a potent argument for war.[15]

Surrounded by increasingly histrionic newspaper accounts and passionate oratory on the subject, perhaps it was inevitable that Ogilvie would get drawn into that local war fever and the eagerness to kill Native Americans. Indian hating, conspiratorial thinking about British alliances with various Indian tribes, and anger at British attacks on commerce and free white Americans: all appeared in shifting colors and affecting tones in Kentucky media during the spring and summer of 1812. Unlike much of the rest of the United States, white Kentuckians seemed to speak with one voice in calling for war, perhaps in part because war fit neatly into a long-standing drama they had manufactured that portrayed Native Americans as brutal aggressors and white settlers as their innocent victims.[16]

Ogilvie found white Kentuckians expressing near uniformity in their pro-war fever, a unanimity distinctly absent in other regions of the country. Elsewhere, Americans found themselves divided along many lines about the possibility of war, for the lead-up to the War of 1812 revealed all the ways that the United States was fragmented by political and regional divides. A region's concerns often depended on how much its residents relied on the shipping trade with Britain, how inhabitants of the northern and western borderlands felt about their Native and Canadian neighbors, and how much British impressment of American sailors had affected their communities. New Englanders who depended on the Anglo-Atlantic shipping trade, for example, felt far more sympathetic to the British, on whom their businesses relied. These divisions sometimes also reflected partisan battles between local Republicans and Federalists. In Baltimore, when the newspaper *Federal Republican* denounced the declaration of war, Republicans rioted and beat and tortured Federalists who supported the paper. Republicans in areas less reliant on trade with Britain found New Englanders' British sympathies so abhorrent that they suspected them of conspiring to break up the United States. This was the true story of Americans' responses to the conflicts with Great Britain that led to the War of 1812: views varied widely by region, and many of those regions disagreed so violently on the issues at stake that the conflict ultimately felt like a civil war.[17]

Ogilvie had previously avoided taking a public stance on these matters to maintain friendly relations with people on all sides. But remaining neutral seemed impossible in Kentucky, where white citizens' war fervor reflected the culmination of years of aggression against Native Americans in the region. Things had grown increasingly tense as a result of specific conflicts between Governor William Henry Harrison of the Indiana Territory and the Native American tribes who had sought to keep their lands and cultures in the region. Over the course of several years, Harrison had demanded—and obtained—vast cessions of land from destitute Native Americans, some of whom had acted without the official sanction of their tribes. Meanwhile, the Shawnee leader Tenskwatawa, known as the Prophet, sought to restore strength to the pan-Indian confederacy in the region. The Prophet held up a religious vision of a bright future if his followers rejected white ways and defended their lands in common. Tenskwatawa's half-brother, Tecumseh, merged that vision with a call for greater military resistance to white incursions and attempts to seize their land. Thus, although white Kentuckians wanted to see the Prophet's confederacy as a mere "British scheme," in fact it was a force in its own right, seeking above all to buttress Native sovereignty in the region. In the past, Indigenous groups had successfully played the British, French, and Americans off one another with strategic alliances and mutual support; now their proximity to the British in Canada provided only the stingiest assistance. Yet the Indians and the British now found themselves on the same path to war with the Americans, albeit for separate reasons, such that Tecumseh grudgingly allied with the British. From the perspective of white Kentuckians, the only solution to this increasingly militant Indian resistance was to break up their confederacy and presumably kill Tenskwatawa as well. Hatred of Native Americans thus became fundamental to the calls for war in the region, such that many urged the total destruction of the tribes—and James Ogilvie found this view infectious.[18]

During the fall of 1811, while Ogilvie recuperated in Chameleon Springs, William Henry Harrison assembled an army and marched to Prophet's Town to demand justice for depredations against white settlements. In the ensuing battle, Harrison lost about two hundred men—about twice the number of Indian casualties—but claimed victory nevertheless after the Native Americans abandoned the region. Harrison's troops burned the town and all their food supplies. When many of those displaced Indians reassembled in Canada with the help of British arms and supplies, Americans expressed outrage all over again at the British and suspected conspiracy at every turn. "The SCALPING KNIFE and TOMAHAWK *of British savages, is now, again devastating our frontiers,*" proclaimed the Lexington *Reporter* in a crescendo of all-caps and italics during the spring of 1812. Kentucky's governor, Charles Scott, declared that "the hand of British intrigue is not difficult to be perceived in this thing." Local papers speculated that the British had hired Native Americans to serve as mercenaries, like the Hessians during the Revolution. Fearmongering tales of murder by Indians filled the papers. These accounts painted Native Americans simultaneously as pawns, yet capable of murdering and terrorizing white settlers for their own ends; mere mercenaries, yet somehow a better target for American retaliation than the British themselves. Frontier wars against Native Americans had not always been so overtly racist, but by the time of the War of 1812 that racism had hardened into a race war of conquest.[19]

By June 1812, while Ogilvie trotted out his new lectures, white Kentuckians focused on Congress's declaration of war against the British, spearheaded by Henry Clay and his coalition of war hawks. For Kentuckians, the announcement of war brought together a wide range of associations from martial patriotism to Indian hating to aggressive American expansionism. "The citizens saw their country a SECOND time declared independent," the *Kentucky Gazette* pronounced, an event so joyous that they lit up the towns of Frankfort and Lexington and spent the night firing cannons and muskets into the air. Most of these jubilant citizens celebrated out of a powerful sense of American nationalism. In Mercer County, not far from Lexington, crowds at the Fourth of July celebration toasted to the fact that the "American Eagle roused by the British Lion . . . [had] soared aloft with revenge in her breast." Moreover, this toast continued, the American eagle's "arrows [would] continue to descend, like lightning upon his head, until he crouches at her feet, and respects her nation's rights." The toasts became more visionary in their anticipation of American expansion, toasting that the nation would "never enter the scabbard in peace, until it has victoriously added two more laurels, the Canadas and East Florida, to the United States." When Henry Clay returned from Washington in late July 1812, he wrote to James Monroe about the passionate "evidences of public feeling and sensibility" in favor of war. "Indeed I have almost been alarmed at the ardor that has been displayed, knowing how prone human nature is to extremes." Responses to the outbreak of war might have varied drastically by region, but in Kentucky it prompted passionate nationalistic ardor.[20]

If Clay felt "almost" "alarmed," Ogilvie was inspired by this blend of aggressive patriotism, expansionist visions, and fearmongering about Indians. He attended a large Fourth of July dinner in Lexington alongside honored guests, including Clay, and helped them toast to the American side. The toasts included "War—Energetic war: better than peace purchased with our national honor and independence," and "The people of Canada—May they prefer freedom to slavery, and accept the terms offered them by our government through General Hull." The twenty-fourth of twenty-five toasts reported to the *Kentucky Gazette* was Ogilvie's, who quoted from Godwin's *Political Justice* as he toasted "Our brethren in Europe—May they become 'ripe for the reception and competent for the assertion' of self government." Meanwhile, local newspapers used the occasion to remind readers of the Revolution, printing the Declaration of Independence in full and inserting accounts of the lives of Revolutionary leaders.[21]

Outsiders might have found such warmongering overly dramatic or worrisome, but, within the state, the drumbeat of war proved infectious. Ogilvie's political radicalism had never encompassed the rights of people who weren't white, and that did not change in Kentucky. In fact, his private writings reveal how much that mix of patriotism and racism afforded a common cause for war. He described finding himself "roused by feelings so natural to patriots and freemen" such that he sought to join the cause to "repel the incursions and avenge the barbarities of a savage foe; a foe that give no quarter, spare no victim, butcher, without mercy or remorse, the young and the old, the sick and the wounded; pour forth on the same altar the mingled blood of the mother and her infants." Much of this fervor blossomed during August 1812, when he watched thousands of volunteers sign up for military service. "I beheld company after company composed of individuals at every stage of existence, from vernal youth to hoary age; congregated from all classes of society, farmers, manufacturers, artisans and merchants, practitioners of law and medicine, even ministers of the gospel, marching in arms," he explained at length in a letter. "I reflected that for eighteen years I had exercised ... the glorious rights of an American citizen, and participated freely and fully [in] the blessings of Republican liberty. I reflected, that neither wife nor child, nor personal nor domestic duties, forbade me to encounter the hardships and hazard of war." Several years later, his reminiscences about Kentucky still invoked a view of the progress of civilization as being reserved for whites only. Whereas once it had been a "howling wilderness, ... it had been explored, reclaimed and populated by a portion of the illustrious race of men, who derive their descent from Scotland, England and Ireland." Such thoughts "chased repose from my couch," and he "rose next morning at an early hour, ordered my horse to be saddled, and attached myself to a company of volunteers from the vicinity of Danville." He purchased a musket and a pair of pistols and joined Captain Jeremiah Briscoe's company of the Kentucky Mounted Volunteer Militia on September 1 for the term of one month alongside men who had similarly committed to terms ranging from ten days to six or seven weeks. (Captain Briscoe himself enlisted for ten days.) All anticipated a speedy victory.[22]

Local newspapers fanned the flames of patriotism and fears of Native Americans. Newspapers like Frankfort's *Western Citizen* published broadsides describing Indian murders of families, women, and infants, such that by the end of October 1812 Kentuckians bragged that the state had "at least 10,000 Volunteers under arms," while the remaining "whole Country has been employ'd in furnishing various articles old Ladies kniting socks and Gloves Young ones making up Linsey Coats overalls etc." In December 1813, the Lexington *Reporter* reprinted a story from a Boston paper that claimed Kentuckians "are the most patriotic people I have ever seen or heard of." This Bostonian had expressed astonishment at seeing older men in their forties and fifties enlist as volunteers—often men from prominent families who risked life, limb, and family livelihoods in these campaigns. "These things to a New-Englandman looks like madness," he wrote, but "here it is considered glorious." Those volunteers included the editor of the *Kentucky Gazette* himself, who editorialized eloquently about his decision to leave the security of Lexington. "In becoming a Volunteer, to *serve* my country was my only object: I could not expect distinction by the act, for I sought no commis-

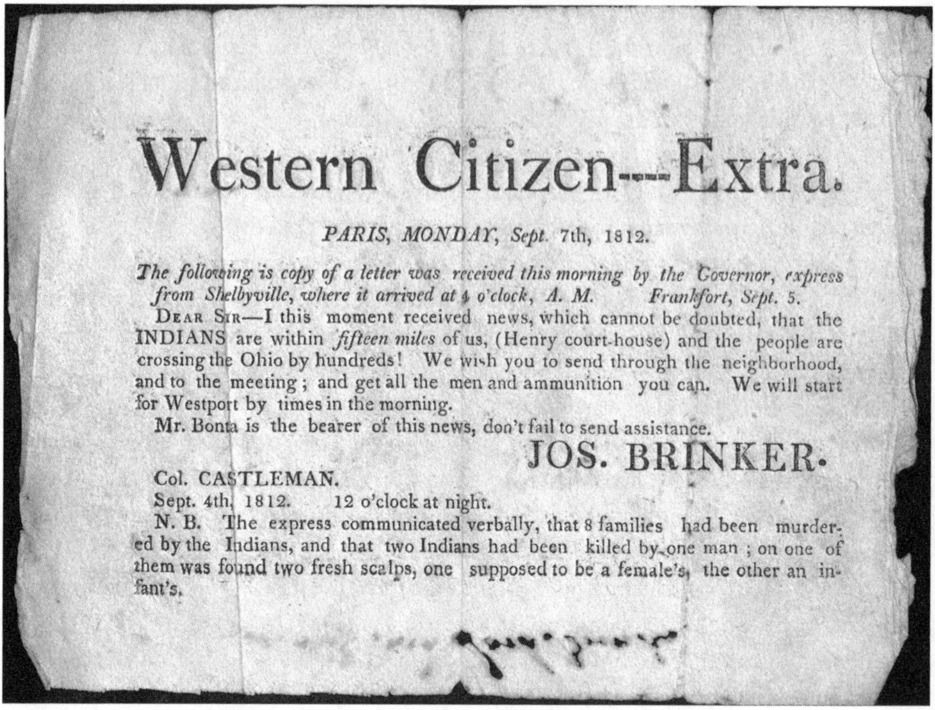

Western Citizen---Extra.

PARIS, MONDAY, Sept. 7th, 1812.

The following is copy of a letter was received this morning by the Governor, express from Shelbyville, where it arrived at 4 o'clock, A. M. *Frankfort, Sept.* 5.

DEAR SIR—I this moment received news, which cannot be doubted, that the INDIANS are within *fifteen miles* of us, (Henry court-house) and the people are crossing the Ohio by hundreds! We wish you to send through the neighborhood, and to the meeting; and get all the men and ammunition you can. We will start for Westport by times in the morning.

Mr. Bonta is the bearer of this news, don't fail to send assistance.

JOS. BRINKER.

Col. CASTLEMAN.

Sept. 4th, 1812. 12 o'clock at night.

N. B. The express communicated verbally, that 8 families had been murdered by the Indians, and that two Indians had been killed by one man; on one of them was found two fresh scalps, one supposed to be a female's, the other an infant's.

Figure 39. Western Citizen—Extra, Sept. 7, 1812. *From Lyle Family Papers, Special Collections, University of Kentucky. This broadside published by Paris's* Western Citizen *describes alleged attacks by Native Americans. The author claims that "8 families had been murdered by the Indians" and goes further to offer details of scalping. Courtesy of Special Collections, University of Kentucky Libraries, Lexington*

sion: I could not expect fame for I occupy the station of a private soldier: I but participated in the feelings of the times, and claim no merit which is not common to all my companions." Four or five of every six men in Kentucky eligible for the military saw some service during the war, including a large percentage of its elected leaders.[23]

The number of volunteers quickly overwhelmed the men in charge of the war effort. An officer at the main camp in Vincennes, Indiana Territory, reported back to Frankfort that "the men have come in so scatteringly and in numbers so far superior to our expectations or our wishes that the greater part of ten days have been employed in Organizing" and inspecting them. The enthusiasm of the volunteers often outstripped their martial abilities. Even men who had previously served in the state's militia knew little about military maneuvers or the discipline required for battle. Militia musters in peacetime had been infrequent, and the volunteers' strikingly short enlistments could not inculcate in them the order needed for a large martial force, which grew to more than eleven thousand men by the end of 1812. In many cases, the men's excitement presented such problems that officers spent much of their time issuing new orders.[24]

The chaos of these camps emerges vividly in official logbooks, replete with comments about failures of discipline. "The Lieut. Col. Cornett in addition positively ferbids the practice of Wrastling and drawing tomahawks or Knives [on] each other even in jest as it very unlike a soldier and might be productive of mischief—Wrastling has absolutely produced some dislocation and ingrous [injuries] to the men and must be discontinued under penalty of confinement and trial of Court Martial," one log entry recorded. Subsequent entries reveal that the men often randomly fired their muskets as they marched, mixed with the Indians in the region, slept while on watch, and permanently damaged their muskets by sticking them nose down into the soil while in camp—all requiring stern new rules and threats of punishment. Clearly, the volunteers' enthusiasm exceeded the officers' ability to exert control and enforce martial regularity. "We started for the war with high Spirits but poor fellows but few if any of us antisapated what awaited us for few of us knew what a Soldier's life was," confessed one private, remembering his experience.[25]

In Vincennes, surrounded by the disarray of new volunteers arriving daily and fretting about the basic question of how to feed and train everyone, officer William Trigg still took a moment in a letter to report back to Frankfort on catching sight of the thirty-nine-year-old Ogilvie. "I just steped into the passage and found Oglivy standing shaving himself dry, a sad change from his fine oritori[c]al robe," Trigg wrote, with tongue in cheek. "He seems however pleased with the prospect of the Campaign and anxious to kill an Indian, but is certainly badly qualified for this kind of life." In reading this line, one cannot help but consider the wide range of unlikely recruits Trigg had encountered over the course of his weeks in Vincennes. The brevity of the vignette suggests that Trigg knew he didn't need to explain all the reasons Ogilvie was unqualified for a soldier's life; the recipient of his letter would enjoy the image all the more without detail. Not that Ogilvie himself harbored any illusions. When invited by Maj. Gen. Samuel Hopkins, the commander-in-chief of the Illinois and Indiana troops, to join his staff, Ogilvie agreed. He saw this as his best opportunity to be useful to the campaign because he was "profoundly conscious however of my ignorance of military affairs, and how actually I was unqualified to perform any military duty," as Ogilvie explained in a letter afterward. He ultimately took the job of judge-advocate to General Jonathan Ramsey's brigade, a position perhaps more suited to his talents and that withdrew him from the rank and file.[26]

Ogilvie also took advantage of the opportunity to deliver two patriotic talks to the troops at Fort Harrison to renew their dedication and anchor his celebrity to the cause. He found the experience exhilarating. "A camp too is a glaring theater for the occasional exhibition of oratory," he explained. Speaking before "auditors who are immediately, personally, and deeply interested in the subject" made for a refreshing change from his usual audiences. "This is the difference between the solar and lunar ray; between the discharge of an electric battery and the momentum of a battering ram; between the agitation of the wave and the convulsions of an earthquake," he wrote enthusiastically. He was preaching to the choir, and he added layers of grandiosity. The moment recalls Shakespeare's rendition of the St. Crispin's Day speech delivered on the eve of battle, from *Henry V*: "Old men forget: yet all shall be forgot, / But he'll remember with advantages / What feats he did that day." Even if Ogilvie had skipped the lines — and he rarely avoided an opportunity for a good quote — his listeners heard the same evocation of heroism and historic significance.[27]

From the perspective of Ogilvie and other volunteers, the sight of those thousands of men produced an inflated sense of imminent success. No matter how frequently their officers fretted about the men's capability or discipline, many volunteers believed they might defeat the Native Americans in the region in a single campaign and return home quickly. After all, leaving home during September and October meant abandoning the harvest of key crops, including tobacco; no one wanted to abandon their financial responsibilities for long. Political leaders shared that optimism. "I have never seen such a body of men in the western country or anywhere else," Kentucky's new war hawk governor, Isaac Shelby, wrote to William Henry Harrison in September 1812, touting the high quality of the troops.[28]

But by early November, Shelby's optimism had turned sour. "It gives me pain to be the messenger of bad news," he wrote to Harrison. "Such I consider the failure of Genl. Hopkins's expedition against Peoria and the Kickapoo Towns on Illinois River." The problems were twofold: their guides had left them "bewildered and lost, not knowing which way to Stere," and they severely lacked supplies. Leaders in Frankfort and Lexington had never managed to develop reliable supply lines to the troops and, making matters worse, Native Americans had burned the prairies, leaving no grass for the troops' horses to eat. "Discouraged and disheartened by their situation," the army returned to Fort Harrison, and most of the volunteers abandoned the cause. Ogilvie claimed to be one of only two volunteers in his unit to reenlist for a second expedition in November — but that, too, proved a failure. "For three months we sought but could not find the enemy; we thought ourselves twice on the eve of a battle but were disappointed," he reported. Ogilvie returned to Lexington by early January 1813 within a few weeks of the news that American forces had lost again in a battle with the British near the River Raisin, just south of Detroit; 397 American troops were killed there, most of whom were Kentuckians. As a result, recruitment of new Kentucky volunteers plummeted and Americans' fantasies of capturing Canada faded quickly. Meanwhile the remaining troops established a new, inglorious routine of building roads and protecting army garrisons. Throughout 1813, Governor Shelby sought to revive Kentuckians' enthusiasm to bolster the state's forces, but by midsummer he was reduced to ordering a conscription of troops. Western newspapers focused their optimism instead on American triumphs at sea in the war's Atlantic theater to boost local spirits.[29]

The War of 1812 had been divisive from the outset amid the various regions in the United States — so much so that in retrospect the war as a whole looked more like a far-ranging series of discrete sectional raids and battles than the tightly organized national efforts that became familiar during twentieth-century wars. Militias like Ogilvie's could be so resolutely dedicated to their individual state rather than the United States as a whole that they refused to cross state borders to help other groups fight. The war proceeded on a variety of fronts and borderlands, including the Niagara region, the Atlantic Ocean, the Mississippi River, and the Gulf of Mexico — each fought by different militias, volunteers, soldiers, and seamen. Those groups might have fought out of patriotic pride in the United States, and might have expressed that nationalism in the form of toasts, songs, and flags, but that pride was likely tempered by a primary dedication to one state or region even to the point of jealousy of others. In short, the pull of patriotism coexisted with the push of different regions, groups, and political partisans fighting against one another.[30]

Ogilvie's experience reflected that push-pull of American nationalism and regionalism. In addition, his inglorious experiences in battle contrasted with his enthusiasm for the effort more broadly. Like many other Kentucky volunteers who abandoned the cause after their enlistments expired, he found his military experience a discouraging letdown after the passions expressed during the summer and early fall of 1812, when so many in the state had confidently predicted speedy victory. After three months of "unsuccessful" militia life, he returned to lecturing. "I have resumed my former pursuits with more awakened enthusiasm," he wrote in a letter to a former student. "From the commencement till the close of our campaign, my health, strength, and spirits experienced a sensible, gradual, and radical renovation, and I can safely affirm, that not one of my companions in the arms endured occasional fatigue, privation, and hardship with more cheerfulness and constancy than myself. There are circumstances in military life peculiarly and unexpectedly attractive." The effect of that patriotic service seemed to thrill him no matter how ignoble the action he witnessed, or how little glory he beheld.[31]

Ogilvie's experience in Kentucky changed him. He had entered the region seeking a romantic, quiet place amid pastoral hills and valleys where he might rid himself of his reliance on opium and recover his health and spirits. He achieved that recovery through a process he described as a strict regimen of exercise, spring water, and willpower. "Constituted as I am, to enjoy any degree of happiness, even to avert intolerable misery, I must be intensely active. This activity can only be exerted and kept alive by powerful motives," he explained in a letter. Reemerging from his retreat from society at Chameleon Springs, he returned to Lexington to find Kentuckians riveted by the possibility of war with Britain and specifically against the Native American tribes living to the north. Intoxicated by the belligerent and nationalistic rhetoric of the region, he became motivated to "kill an Indian" himself and share in what he and his compatriots believed would be the glory of war. That he ultimately saw no action and ended his terms of service disappointed did not diminish his enthusiasm for war. In fact, it energized his sense of patriotism. This experience led Ogilvie increasingly over the ensuing months to refer to himself as an American citizen and make his lectures more nationalistic.[32]

He returned to Lexington in January 1813 to deliver lectures, making sure to reprise his rousing address to the troops and remind his audience of his military service. For the next six months, he performed throughout the region, including a series in Ohio's Senate Chamber in Chillicothe, building up his stamina (and finances) for a return to the East Coast. Along the way, he began to formulate ways of incorporating that patriotic consciousness into his oratory. By midsummer of 1813, he began the slow voyage up the Ohio River toward Pittsburgh, the first stop he would make on the path back east.

As he got closer to the Atlantic, he learned to stop telling stories about his war service in Kentucky lest he incur regional and partisan animosities. Differences concerning the War of 1812 still drove wedges between the populations of various parts of the United States, and many viewed Kentuckians as shameless war hawks. "On my arrival in Boston," he wrote in a February 1814 letter, "I found that a strong prejudice had been excited against me in consequence of my having gone out with the volunteers of Kentucky." "I treated the prejudice with ineffable scorn; I delivered three of my orations and several specimens of philosophical criticism. My audiences were select and numerous; on the third evening the room was crowded and my auditors testified their approbation in a manner the most unequivocal and respectful." He ultimately refrained entirely

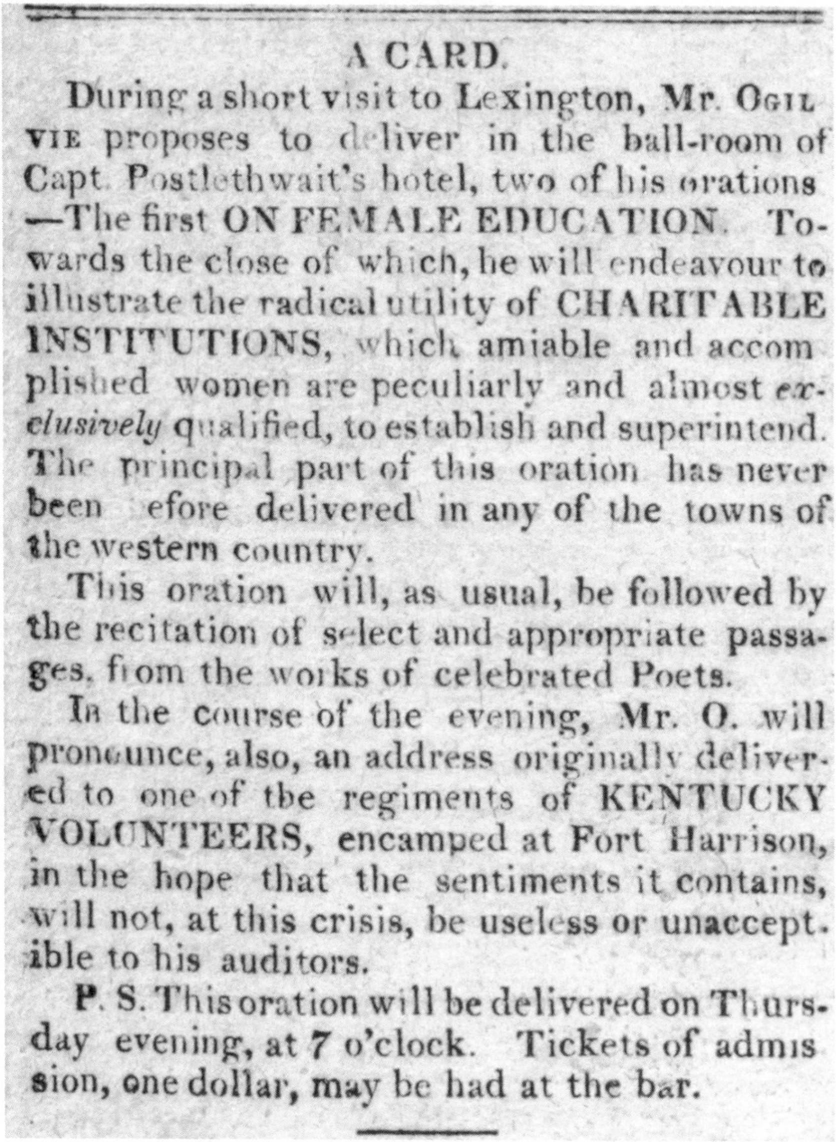

A CARD.

During a short visit to Lexington, Mr. OGIL VIE proposes to deliver in the ball-room of Capt. Postlethwait's hotel, two of his orations —The first ON FEMALE EDUCATION. Towards the close of which, he will endeavour to illustrate the radical utility of CHARITABLE INSTITUTIONS, which amiable and accomplished women are peculiarly and almost *exclusively* qualified, to establish and superintend. The principal part of this oration has never been efore delivered in any of the towns of the western country.

This oration will, as usual, be followed by the recitation of select and appropriate passages, from the works of celebrated Poets.

In the course of the evening, Mr. O. will pronounce, also, an address originally delivered to one of the regiments of KENTUCKY VOLUNTEERS, encamped at Fort Harrison, in the hope that the sentiments it contains, will not, at this crisis, be useless or unacceptible to his auditors.

P. S. This oration will be delivered on Thursday evening, at 7 o'clock. Tickets of admission, one dollar, may be had at the bar.

Figure 40. "A Card." From Kentucky Gazette (Lexington), Jan. 19, 1813, [3].
After delivering inspirational lectures to Kentucky volunteers at Fort Harrison during
the War of 1812, Ogilvie repeated one of them when he had returned to Lexington.
Courtesy of Special Collections, University of Kentucky Libraries, Lexington

from discussing his time in the militia. It appears nowhere in his 1816 memoir, published only a year after the war's end. Instead, he reverted to telling his story about sleeping in the cabin of the enormous bearded frontiersman, reviving old stereotypes rather than summoning Kentucky's more recent history of warmongering and Indian hating.[33]

He also sent off a long essay for publication in the prominent Philadelphia magazine *Port Folio*. "The magnitude of the design," he wrote to a friend, "may possibly startle you, yet it is preparatory merely to a far grander enterprise, of which I meditate, and if I live, and retain my health and intellectual energy, will certainly attempt the execution." Published in September 1813, the essay described formulating a sweeping new plan while being "secluded in the western country" in "a log house beyond the mountains." "In proposing to undertake this delicate office, Mr. Ogilvie is perfectly conscious of the responsibility he incurs and the difficulties he must encounter. From this responsibility he will not shrink, nor have these difficulties any terrors for him. It is his destiny, in the voyage of life, to tug a labouring oar, and stem an adverse current," he wrote in the third-person style he often used in his printed pieces. The plan he proposed aimed to make public speech integral to American democracy.[34]

CHAPTER 10

A Golden Age of American Eloquence,

1814–1817

While in Kentucky, James Ogilvie encountered something new: an imitator.

As he was lecturing in Lexington, the Frankfort newspaper forty miles away featured ads announcing the arrival of a Mr. Huntington, whose performances resembled Ogilvie's in almost all respects. He usually rented the same rooms that Ogilvie had visited earlier, where he delivered "Moral Lectures" followed by "entertaining Recitations" that he listed in his advertisements ahead of time. Like Ogilvie, he made high-profile donations to worthy causes such as public libraries and ladies' benevolent societies. For newspaper commentators, the comparison was obvious. Charleston's *City Gazette* reported of Huntington's talks that "we must say, that with the exception of the eloquent *Ogilvie*, we never were more agreeably entertained." By 1815, newspapers would also comment on the performances of a Mr. Flagg "of the Ogilvie School" of orators, to be followed by Mr. Hazelton, Mr. Walter, and others who similarly found it possible to live as itinerant orators. Hazelton and Walter both adopted the toga as their costume and at different times advertised that they recited from Ogilvie's favorite literature "after the manner" of Mr. O, performing passages from Sir Walter Scott and poet Thomas Campbell's description of the Battle of Culloden. The main difference? The imitators' tickets cost half the price.[1]

Ogilvie's career might well have appeared attractive to men like Huntington, Hazelton, and Flagg for a range of reasons, from the relatively easy means of making a living to the promise of fame and travel. But looking beyond the individual motivations of the imitators, their arrival on the cultural scene heralded a broader pattern. Ogilvie's central message—the importance of eloquence to the American Republic—was spreading. The popularity of public speaking reached new heights as a result of Ogilvie's celebrity. People increasingly came to share his view that oratory could tie the nation together and that it might articulate forms of identity that bridged the gap between local or regional affiliations and a broader sense of American purpose.

Ogilvie's return to Washington, D.C., in 1814 represented a high point in his career, at the confluence of his celebrity and the popularity of oratory in the midst of the War of 1812. The United States did not enjoy any real sense of national unity, nor did a majority of the public have the money or the opportunity to hear Ogilvie deliver his lectures, yet his idea about the importance of this form of communication in the invention of the United States now seemed more popular than ever. Nor was it only the imitators who joined in the chorus. From prominent writers who celebrated American orators to grassroots debating societies, the 1810s saw the emergence of what a later commentator would call the "golden age of American oratory."[2]

Ogilvie's arrival in Washington marked a triumphant return to the capital. At the outset of his lecture tour six years earlier, when he had spoken in local Washington and Alexandria taverns, Thomas Jefferson had reported to his daughter that local audiences had little interest in the performances of an unknown. But this time, Ogilvie's reputation preceded him. Now, local newspapers reprinted ecstatic accounts from neighboring cities of his successes there. More important, Washington society was preoccupied with oratory, particularly as the War of 1812 raged. Attending congressional debates and speeches at the Capitol building was a popular social activity in this ten-thousand-person city. Sitting in the galleries, women and men witnessed the drama of real life: talented men engaged in high-stakes debates in which they conveyed different visions of the nation's future. Ogilvie's performances in Washington, Georgetown, and Alexandria drew crowds of spectators whose experience with eloquence far exceeded that in other places and who were eager to compare his nonpartisan ideas to the politicians they observed regularly, debating policy, law, and the workings of government during wartime.[3]

Women made up a prominent part of the audiences for debates in Congress. This reflected as much the emerging sense of the portentousness of those debates as the general lack of other things to do. Catherine Mitchill, whose husband was a senator from New York, explained to her sister that, "as there are few amusements here, this is quite a fashionable place of resort for the Ladies, and when there is any interesting subject of debate before the House, this is to me, a very agreeable way of spending the morning." But this was not merely a diverting pastime. The anticipation of great debates thrilled the attendees. "Mr. Clay speaks tomorrow on the Land Bill. I can scarcely think of sleep when this prospect is before me," she wrote. For women like Mitchill, the grand exchanges that took place there were "as good as going to a play, but here all the characters are real instead of fictitious." She often stayed for several hours, even returning after dinner in the evening to hear a debate through to its end.[4]

Since the federal government had moved to the new District of Columbia in late 1800, residents of the city had scrambled to construct infrastructure to match the grand design envisioned by the city's urban planners. By 1814, it remained a construction zone. It was one thing to imagine a city with grand avenues crisscrossed with dramatic diagonal streets; it was another to pave those

streets and populate them with homes and businesses. At first overrun by specu-
lators who bought land and began to develop it, the city now revealed the de-
pressing reality of how many of those builders had slowed in their progress and
had merely erected temporary structures on half-heartedly cleared plots. Any
given street might feature a row of uniform new homes flanked by muddy yards
with wooden tenement buildings. Aside from a smattering of services like bar-
bers, grocers, and blacksmiths, the city had virtually no shops or commerce. The
streets, still largely unpaved, were no better. Dignitaries attempting to visit the
White House reported that on rainy days their elegant coaches sank up to the axle
in the red mud of Pennsylvania Avenue—making it impossible to arrive in clean
clothes, and equally impossible to depart.[5]

Visitors sniffed at the mess. "A few scattered hamlets, many miles remote
from each other, compose all that has arisen of the promised metropolis; while
as many vast half-finished piles of building, at great distances apart, from commanding eminences, frown desolate and despairing on the dreary wastes that
separate and environ them," wrote one disgusted visitor. Altogether, "instead of
rising like Carthage," the city's "enormous joints fall asunder before they can be
well knit together." Several decades later, Henry Adams noted the contrast between the neoclassical governmental buildings and the city's general bleakness,
comparing it to "white Greek temples in the abandoned gravel-pits of a deserted
Syrian city." More succinctly, a traveler from Britain simply called the city "grotesque." No wonder that so many women found the Capitol to be the city's most
attractive destination.[6]

If the city remained a work in progress, the spectacle of governmental oratory
illustrated another form of national construction—one that promised better
prospects. Attendees of the eloquence taking place in the Capitol building witnessed the emerging shape of republican government in the new United States
in words, if not materially. Deeply invested with the personalities of the men
who stood to address the assembly, this form of politics placed the performance
of ideas at the center of governmental deliberation. Political figures, moreover,
were not merely performing for one another. When they debated, they were fully
conscious of the attendees in galleries built to draw ordinary Americans to the
spectacle of democracy. Indeed, political figures were wont to alter their performance depending on the makeup of the audiences. Margaret Bayard Smith,
another society matron and wife of a prominent banker, described walking into
the Supreme Court in 1814 with a throng of women during the conclusion of an
argument by Attorney General William Pinkney. Noticing the women's entrance,
Pinkney started his argument all over again, "went over the same ground, using
fewer arguments, but scattering more flowers." "And the day I was there I am
certain he thought more of the female part of his audience than of the court,"

even going so far as to bow low to the ladies and acknowledge them in his finale. This, too, was part of the invention of the United States: the ways that legislators learned to make persuasive cases for policy decisions, conscious of the gaze of the people.[7]

Smith seems to have disapproved of Pinkney's using more rhetorical "flowers" to delight his female audience, but her experience as an attendee taught her the exhilaration of listening to the gladiatorial debates in Congress. In a subsequent work of fiction, she described in detail the titillating anticipation of a favorite orator's delivery and the sheer pleasure of watching and listening to such men, a passage so rich that it's worth quoting at length:

> He rose—and, in that easy and graceful manner, peculiarly his own; in that full and harmonious voice, whose very sound persuades; with that strength of argument, and warmth of eloquence, which convince and charm; he delivered those patriotic sentiments, presented those just views, and expressed those noble resolutions, which fixed the wavering, enlightened the ignorant, and kindled enthusiasm in all who listened. Attention hung upon his accents, conviction followed his reasoning, and unanimity of opinion crowned this most eloquent and powerful speech. For five long hours he spoke; sometimes pausing to rest, taking a glass of water to refresh himself; often changing his position; now gracefully leaning on the back of his chair; now standing erect, with out-stretched arm; now eagerly bending forward, as if the better to reach the hearts of his hearers. His eye now thrown in a general glance round the whole assembly; now bent in inquiry, as if to catch coincidence of opinion from his friends, and now fixed with penetrating force on the face of an opponent, as if he could detect and destroy opposition with an eye-beam! His voice, his gestures, his looks, varied with his varying subjects; soft and persuasive, rapid and energetic, lofty and commanding, as the subject by turns required.

At the same time that Washington's streets remained "grotesque," its women and men had more opportunities to deliberate during debate and oratory than any other city's population in the nation—speech delivered by political stars drawn from across the union. To many this situation echoed the republican virtue of the classical world, where oratory had been paramount. "The Senate chamber," Smith wrote to her sister, "is the present arena and never were the amphitheatres of Rome more crowded by the highest ranks of both sexes." The city had become more than the place where federal laws got debated and passed. Its residents saw it as something special, a site where some of the country's finest intellects gathered to shape the nation's future. Whereas the leading figures of Boston, New York, and Charleston thought primarily about the marketplace, in Washington they were preoccupied with the making of the United States—an ongoing invention made all the more vivid by the contrast of the elegant Capitol building to the rest of the muddy, ramshackle city.[8]

Ogilvie's celebrity as a public speaker—and his appearances in a toga—had helped to build the optimism that the United States might rise to the oratorical glory of the classical republics. "In a free, civilized, and polished country, his is an art that *should*, that *must* flourish," proclaimed New York's *National Advocate* about Ogilvie's 1813 lecture there. "An attempt to revive the Republican eloquence of the ancient rostrum cannot fail of success in this, the only Republic now remaining in the world." If "the free states of antiquity" had long since disappeared along with their noble public speech, "we trust that it may be transplanted to, and flourish in the *new* world," this observer wrote with a hopefulness that mirrored Margaret Smith's.[9]

Ogilvie's trek to Washington, D.C., took him through all the major northeastern port cities, and in each the newspapers catalogued his successes. In Philadelphia, the audience listened to a two-hour oration with "profound and almost unbreathing attention." In Baltimore, where nearly four hundred women and men attended each of his talks, he "riveted, as if by magic, the ears of the audience; affected their hearts; enlightened their understandings; and exhibited the best possible proof, of the truth of the interesting subjects inculcated." By the time he arrived at the nation's capital, he had given a full test to his roster of new and revised orations, so he booked the Assembly Room at Mr. Tomlinson's Hotel for a series of five lectures with the expectation that news of his recent triumphs would help fill seats. He took one more step to guarantee media attention: he wrote to his Kentucky acquaintance Henry Clay, Speaker of the House, for permission to deliver a lecture in the Capitol building—and was granted it. He wasted no time issuing invitations to his talk to President James Madison, the members of both houses of Congress, the justices of the Supreme Court, and all "gentlemen of the Bar now in the city of Washington" and promptly advertised their attendance to the rest of the city. The subject of his talk was oratory itself.[10]

The House chamber where he spoke underlined the grandeur of the occasion and made architectural gestures to the United States' desired ties to classical republics. The neoclassical building was modeled on the ancient Parthenon of Rome, and its design had been overseen by the famously persnickety Thomas Jefferson, who fought hard to add to the top of the room a dome with glass panels to allow light to flood the room dramatically from above—an architectural metaphor for enlightenment if ever there was one. In arguing for the addition of the skylights, Jefferson had insisted that this would become "the handsomest room in the world, without a single exception," even more than Paris's Pantheon building, from which he had borrowed the idea. This elegant, light-

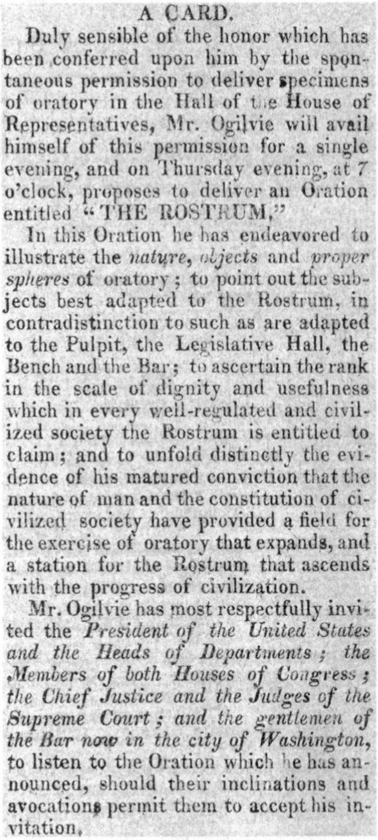

A CARD.

Duly sensible of the honor which has been conferred upon him by the spontaneous permission to deliver specimens of oratory in the Hall of the House of Representatives, Mr. Ogilvie will avail himself of this permission for a single evening, and on Thursday evening, at 7 o'clock, proposes to deliver an Oration entitled " THE ROSTRUM,"

In this Oration he has endeavored to illustrate the *nature, objects* and *proper spheres* of oratory ; to point out the subjects best adapted to the Rostrum, in contradistinction to such as are adapted to the Pulpit, the Legislative Hall, the Bench and the Bar; to ascertain the rank in the scale of dignity and usefulness which in every well-regulated and civilized society the Rostrum is entitled to claim ; and to unfold distinctly the evidence of his matured conviction that the nature of man and the constitution of civilized society have provided a field for the exercise of oratory that expands, and a station for the Rostrum that ascends with the progress of civilization.

Mr. Ogilvie has most respectfully invited the *President of the United States and the Heads of Departments ; the Members of both Houses of Congress ; the Chief Justice and the Judges of the Supreme Court ; and the gentlemen of the Bar now in the city of Washington,* to listen to the Oration which he has announced, should their inclinations and avocations permit them to accept his invitation,

Figure 41. "A Card." From Daily National Intelligencer
(Washington, D.C.), Mar. 9, 1814, [3]. Ogilvie's advertisements for his talk
in the Capitol building issued invitations to the president, congressmen, members of the Supreme
Court, and the city's lawyers. Between this unusually preeminent audience and the classical
setting of the Capitol's Rotunda, the lecture represented a high point during Ogilvie's career.
Courtesy of Special Collections, the Sheridan Libraries, Johns Hopkins University

filled setting would, he hoped, inspire the people's representatives to the highest aims; having sunlight illuminating them from above would call forth model political behavior. In part because of Jefferson's ongoing interferences in the construction process, the room had only been completed in 1811. Even the snootiest of British travelers acknowledged it to be "truly elegant." As Ogilvie began his talk, the last light in Washington's March skies would have shone through the skylights, helping the room's lamps illuminate him in his Roman toga, thus bringing the nation's fantasies of classical republicanism full circle.[11]

When Ogilvie rose to speak in this room, not a seat was vacant, and attendees

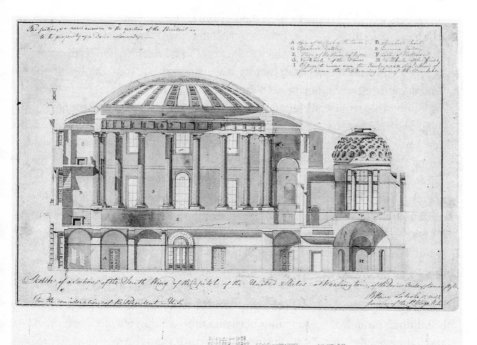

Figure 42. Sketch of a Section of the South Wing of the Capitol of the United States....
By Benjamin Henry Latrobe. Circa 1803–1814. Working with Thomas Jefferson, who supplied endless
suggestions and alterations to the design, Latrobe designed the magnificent Rotunda for the south
wing of the U. S. Capitol building in Washington, D.C. Courtesy of the Library of Congress

were nervous. As one newspaper put it, their tension was "enhanced, perhaps, by the doubt whether we should be gratified by a display of his powers." The perception of Ogilvie's audacity must have been awful. He had booked the most distinctive site for national oratory and filled the room with a greater concentration of public speakers than anywhere else in the country—and then presumed to stand up and tell them about oratory. The speakers who now sat in his audience had good reason to doubt that his performance could live up to the anticipation. After all, explained Washington's *Daily National Intelligencer*, he would stand before an "audience, which, without derogating from the merits of other places, might well inspire him with a degree of hope and fear previously unknown to his breast." Thus, when he finally rose to speak, he graciously acknowledged "the select character of his audience and the magnificent theatre in which they were convened," both of which inspired awe in him. He spoke humbly of his profound emotions on assuming that stage.[12]

By opening his talk with humility and compliments to the audience, he hewed closely to expectations for public speaking—an unusual move for him. Virtually every speech of this era opens with almost boilerplate language that made similarly modest gestures. Ogilvie, however, had long since abandoned such opening lines during his regular performances; his oratorical celebrity rendered words like those implausible, if not transparently insincere. But speaking before the United States' elected officials was a different matter. If ever he needed an opening gambit that requested the indulgence of his listeners, this was the moment.

He also insisted from the outset that he had no interest in telling his auditors how to deliver the legislative oratory and argumentative debate that they employed regularly in Congress. Rather, he used this occasion to advocate for the cultural and institutional expansion of oratory like his own—the oratory of the Rostrum, or an amalgam of rhetorical display and deliberative consideration of contemporary social and moral problems. This argument had been at the heart of his essay in the *Port Folio*: that the nation would benefit from greater investment in oratory. In other words, Ogilvie's lecture called upon his illustrious audience to act—to establish a broader national infrastructure for the advocacy of oratory by building new halls of eloquence and supporting national education in elocution. Newspaper critics loved the idea. "The sphere of useful knowledge would be infinitely extended, the sanctions of virtue enforced, the general taste refined, and happiness diffused, by the inculcation of truth from the rostrum, adorned with the claims of elocution, animated by the enthusiasm of numbers and the almost magical influence of sympathy, instead of exclusively relying on the rigid abstractions and sluggish feelings of the closet," effused the *Daily National Intelligencer*. "Who, indeed, can doubt the mighty influence of such an art, enthusiastically cultivated, in rousing and directing the latent powers of a free people?" The *Maryland Gazette* chimed in with agreement. "His whole aim seems directed to public utility, in enlightening the understanding and amending the heart." To foster such public speech and debate would, Ogilvie declared, provide newly secure footing for the United States' democracy by enhancing public knowledge and bringing more Americans into the conversation.[13]

Considering that the cost of his lectures would have prohibited most people on the lower half of the social spectrum from attending—and that he had self-consciously pushed his ticket price as high as possible—we might view his expansive gestures to inclusivity skeptically. Clearly his audiences did not look like America. Ogilvie knew well that it was the wealthier half of society that bought his tickets and provided the patronage that burnished his reputation. Still, his hopes for an increasingly more educated American populace held wide appeal. The people who attended his talks might not have wanted to sit next to just anyone, but they roundly applauded the passages in which he asked them to imagine national progress in the form of education at all levels of society. This progressive enthusiasm to lift up the people of the United States could coexist with the seemingly contradictory desire to live in a social bubble, surrounded by like-minded people of similar social status.

Ogilvie's triumph at the Capitol was crowned by the elites of Washington society, who made him a part of each evening's entertainments. Here again, the influence of women was strong. Margaret Bayard Smith was one such woman who chronicled in her correspondence the importance of parlor politics and social networking. "The drawing-room, — that centre of attention, — affords opportunity of seeing all these whom fashion, fame, beauty, wealth or talents, have render'd celebrated," she told her sister. It was in these settings, Smith understood, that a visitor's reputation was made; hence, she was impressed that Ogilvie had made himself "quite the Ton here," as in a member of the bon ton, or fashionable world. One evening, she explained, after Ogilvie had dined with the Madisons at the White House, he arrived at the Smiths' drawing room for a gathering that proved so charming that "it was half past twelve, e'er we thought it ten." Nor was it merely his elegance as a conversationalist that impressed her. "I know not whether he can be called a man of original genius, but he is certainly one of highly cultivated taste, a man of great research, not only in classical learning, but in natural history, philosophy, and morals," she wrote with a full-throated vote of approval. "He receives the most flattering attentions and is not a day disengaged." All of Ogilvie's years of courting elite women and men, of providing erudite conversation in exchange for their patronage and influence, now culminated. He was in demand.[14]

By the time his lectures in Washington, Georgetown, and Alexandria had concluded, he had spent almost two months in the city and confirmed his national celebrity. "How much more rational these amusements than our balls or parties," Margaret Smith wrote admiringly. Many attendees made explicit connections between his success and the nation's rising star. If the art of oratory had fallen away since the days of the classical republics of Greece and Rome, "a new era in eloquence seems to have already commenced" in the American Republic, as a Charleston newspaper marveled. "As Homer is called the *Poet* by way of eminence, so has Mr. OGILVIE been called the *Orator*." As if to confirm Ogilvie's success, the imitator Mr. Huntington appeared in Washington a month later to take advantage of the flurry of interest in Rostrum oratory—and, continuing his pattern of hitching his wagon to Ogilvie's star, his advertisements still contained flattering comparisons to "the eloquent Ogilvie."[15]

That imitators like Huntington, Hazelton, and Walter sought to make careers following Ogilvie's model during the 1810s indicates more than the popularity of oratory. It illustrates the pervasive connection of eloquence to a sense of national progress. Ogilvie's lectures offered up a vision of a republic tied together by democratic deliberation—and he enacted that vision for his attendees. As

Ogilvie led his audiences to deliberate on civic questions about dueling, suicide, or female education, they could extrapolate about how such gatherings might enhance democracy on a wider basis. His lectures repackaged a core tenet of republicanism: that democracy required an educated, vigilant public well versed in how to weigh carefully the various arguments from their leaders about civic matters. Oratory like his placed public assembly and republican deliberation on stage, encouraging listeners to imagine the national progress that might ensue if such events were more common and if more members of the public participated as both speakers and listeners.[16]

By the middle of the 1810s, performances by figures like Ogilvie and Huntington were only one component of a wider cultural preoccupation with the spoken word. In a variety of ways, Americans joined in to promote a culture of eloquence.

For several years, Ogilvie's visits to American towns and cities had prompted an efflorescence of interest in oratory, as local newspapers reveal. One of the most common results of one of his visits was the introduction of classes and clubs to teach and cultivate the fine art of public speech. Shortly after Ogilvie departed Philadelphia in 1813, for example, a Dr. Abercrombie began offering classes in elocution for young men, while a Mr. Dennison promised a similar course for young ladies that included "the principles of correct and elegant Reading." Dennison followed up those classes with an Ogilvie-like series of dramatic recitations, for which he charged fifty cents per ticket. Meanwhile, a group of young men and women formed the Philadelphia Literary Association as a "union of effort in the attainment of useful knowledge." Some three hundred people attended the association's first oration in Harmonic Hall in March 1813, a speech that was "received with great applause, both during the delivery and after the conclusion." In New York, a group of young men and women created the Forum, "an attempt to revive the ancient Forum" that sought "to encourage free discussion and to promote the cultivation of eloquence." In each of these cases, many American women and men, especially the young, found ways to improve themselves in public speaking and to foster a broader culture of eloquence.[17]

Ambitious young people drove these grassroots efforts because, for them, strong skills in speech meant something less abstract than national progress: it could advance their careers and even their marriage prospects. Young men training for the law, the pulpit, or business required a gift for speech and persuasion. Young women learned from their schoolbooks that young men of talent and ambition sought out educated, well-spoken wives who would instill those values in their children. The most progressive advocates of female education went even further, insisting that happy marriages required an intellectual sympathy between partners—the kind of mutual understanding and respect that would long outlast youthful infatuation (immortalized in Jane Austen's contemporaneous portrayals of courtship). In each of these ways, young women and men learned that developing their ability to speak well would benefit them personally with advantageous marriages and professional success at the same time that it contributed to the reputation of the United States' citizens.[18]

Alongside these developments, the promotion of American eloquence appeared in another form during the 1810s. Two men Ogilvie had long known from his Virginia teaching days—and who, like Ogilvie, had expressed unusual interest in the medium of the spoken word—now sought to convince the public that the United States had already produced great orators.

Both men had long drawn strong connections between personal ambition and public speech. Ogilvie and William Wirt, only a few months apart in age, had been familiar since their early days in Richmond a decade earlier, when they joined with other ambitious young men in publishing literary and philosophical essays under the heading of "The Rainbow." Wirt, a lawyer, had already won popularity from the publication of a series of newspaper essays under the pseudonym "The British Spy" in 1803 that commented broadly on American life. In one of the earliest, he decried the "scarcity, of genuine and sublime eloquence" in the United States. "What the charm by which the orator binds the senses of his audience; by which he attunes and touches and sweeps the human lyre, with the resistless sway and master hand of a Timotheus?" Wirt marveled at the magical effects of oratory's ability to "awaken and arouse me, like the clangour of the martial trumpet," and to "descend upon me like an angel of light, breathe new energies into my frame, dilate my soul with his own intelligence, exalt me into a new and nobler region of thought, snatch me from the earth at pleasure, and rap me to the seventh heaven." Considering Wirt's capacity to spin out such exultant sentences, it's no wonder that his colleagues called him "the whip syllabub genius" for his overblown rhetoric, a characterization we have also seen applied to Ogilvie, likening both men's speech to the frothy sweet wine drink. When Wirt earned national fame for his attempt to prosecute Aaron Burr for treason in 1807, his speech detailing Burr's crimes lasted four hours—and won praise from all corners of the nation upon its subsequent publication.[19]

Wirt's early writing on the importance of oratory in a republic, together with his experience as a litigator, quickly blossomed into a preoccupation with the eloquence of a single figure: Patrick Henry, who had died in 1799. Wirt never met Henry, but, like many other young Virginians, he had heard tales of Henry's breathtaking speeches before, during, and after the Revolution. Inspired by a plan to develop a biography and record of Henry's most notable speeches, Wirt began corresponding with Virginians who had known Henry and even hired an assistant to conduct oral interviews, asking detailed questions about the orator's skills. Writing this biography would take Wirt twelve years.

He hoped the biography would serve as a didactic tool to provide ambitious young men with a model for personal and professional advancement. Developing one's skills in public speech, he believed from personal experience, could propel them into public service. "Considering what a very powerful engine [oratory] is in a republic," it was surprising to find it "so negligently cultivated in the United States," sparking concern for the nation's future. As he explained in 1810 when he wrote to Thomas Jefferson asking for reminiscences, "Mr. Henry seems to me a good text for a discourse on rhetoric, patriotism and morals: the work might be made useful to young men who are just coming forward into life," he wrote. "Nor do I deem the object a trifling one, since on these young men the care and safety of the republic must soon devolve." When he finally published the biography in 1817, he included a reconstruction of Henry's famous 1775 "Give Me Liberty or Give Me Death!" speech, compiled from the recollections of Henry's contemporaries—the only text of this oration that remains available today.[20]

All along, he mentored his young brother-in-law, Francis Walker Gilmer, in letters that reiterated Wirt's preoccupation with youthful ambition and skills in public speech. These letters were often preachy. Learn to "speak deliberately and articulately" in conversation, Wirt advised the sixteen-year-old Gilmer in 1806. In school, "get a habit, a *passion* for reading—not flying from book to book with the squeamish caprice of a literary epicure." Most of all, he urged Gilmer to cultivate ambition. "If you find your spirits and attention beginning to flag, think of being buried all your life in obscurity—confounded with the gross and ignorant herd around you—crawling in the kennel of filth and trash with the mass of human maggots and reptiles—and then compare with this vile and disgusting condition the state of the man, who has industriously improved the boon of genius—springing from his native fen, on wings of every radiant hue, he rises above the admiring crowd." No wonder Gilmer elected to follow his mentor's advice. The choice that Wirt presented ultimately portrayed ordinary citizens as "gross and ignorant," in contrast with the privileged, educated man with "wings of every radiant hue"; was there really a choice? And considering that Gilmer had begun studying with Ogilvie to prepare for college at William and Mary, he was likely getting a similar message from both men simultaneously.[21]

All three men associated the practice of fine speech with both self-making and the making of American national identity. This had been a vital element of Ogilvie's teaching style over the course of his fifteen-year career and remained fundamental to the lectures he delivered throughout the country. And, during the years that Ogilvie's oratorical celebrity increased, Gilmer and Wirt each wrote books that interlinked the topics of public speech, personal ambition, the character of American political leaders, and national identity—for, at the same time that Wirt was completing his celebratory biography of Patrick Henry, Francis Walker Gilmer published a book that turned six contemporary political figures into oratorical heroes for the new American nation.

Gilmer's slim forty-eight-page *Sketches of American Orators* (1816) didn't offer biographical sketches of these legislators. Rather, it focused entirely on the experience of listening to them. Writing about Chief Justice John Marshall, he described a wondrous cohering of purpose and talent that took place mid-speech. "He begins with reluctance, hesitation, and vacancy of eye; presently his articulation becomes less broken, his eye more fixed, until finally, his voice is full, clear, and rapid, his manner bold, and his whole face lighted up with the mingled fires of genius and passion: and he pours forth the unbroken stream of eloquence, in a current deep, majestic, smooth, and strong," Gilmer wrote, describing in lavish terms the surprisingly powerful speech that Marshall ultimately mustered in the course of an oration. "He reminds one of some great bird, which flounders and flounces on the earth for a while, before it acquires the impetus to sustain its soaring flight. The characteristic of his eloquence is an irresistible cogency, and a luminous simplicity in the order of his reasoning." A transcription of one of Marshall's speeches could never convey the ecstatic experience Gilmer described in listening to the man. This was the book's real goal: to celebrate American eloquence by fostering habits of appreciation in other listeners.[22]

Sketches of American Orators exemplified the ideal of an orator and an audience bound together in an emotional and sympathetic relationship, a bond that amounted to something more powerful than other collective events. The electrical current that ran from speaker to listeners glued them together into a meaningful community, a public. The United States required such galvanizing events that created microcosms of a national public, discussed national purpose, and provided a site for national self-definition. Gilmer reminded his readers that listening was important. To listen well—critically, and with a considered appreciation for the orator's talent—was the job of the good citizen, just as it was the job of the orator to summon all his talents to persuade.

Gilmer opened the pamphlet with a dramatic firsthand account of the pleasures of listening. "The first time I ever felt the spell of eloquence was when standing in the gallery of the capitol in the year 1808. It was on the floor of that house I saw rise a gentleman, who in every quality of his person, his voice, his mind, his character, is a phenomenon amongst men," Gilmer wrote, before identifying this "phenomenon" as John Randolph of Virginia. "In his speech not a breath of air is lost; it is all compressed into round, smooth, liquid sound; and its inflections are so sweet, its emphasis so appropriate and varied, that there is a positive pleasure in hearing him speak any words whatever." Going from one sketch to the next, Gilmer peppered his depictions with references to the full sensory experience of each man's eloquence, encouraging his readers to join in the act of observing and contrasting their qualities. He concluded the anonymously published pamphlet with high praise for his brother-in-law, William Wirt (no wonder Gilmer published it anonymously), in an array of compliments that built to a superlative finale: "His person is dignified and commanding; his countenance open, manly and playful; his voice clear and musical; and his whole appearance truly oratorical. Judgment and imagination hold a divided dominion over his mind, and each is so conspicuous that it is difficult to decide which is ascendant. His diction unites force, purity, variety and splendour more perfectly than that of any speaker I have heard." Inasmuch as *Sketches of American Orators* established a preliminary pantheon of great American leaders, it also served as an instructional manual on how to observe and describe public speech, how to be a talented and critical listener.[23]

James Ogilvie was noticeably absent from Gilmer's pantheon of orators. Even considering Gilmer's focus on men in public office, Ogilvie's absence was striking in 1816, when he remained the most famous orator in the country. Or is there a coy reference to him, after all? The pamphlet opened with a lament that "our countrymen" are "but coarse judges of eloquence." Perhaps because they are distracted by business and unfamiliar with true talent, Gilmer suggested, "they have so few public amusements, and opportunities of acquiring information, that any one who can entertain them with jests, and give a few unsatisfactory hints on the subject of deliberation, is acknowledged to be not only an amusing speaker, but a considerable orator." To write "any one who can entertain them"—was this a condemnation of Ogilvie's performances? If so, Gilmer took a risk in proffering such an insinuation, for gossip swirled about the pamphlet's anonymous author and in some circles his authorship was an open secret. His fellow lawyer Hugh Legaré wrote from Philadelphia asking whether he'd written it. "Indeed, I was not surprised to hear that it was yours—for as soon as I read two pages of it, I told Ogilvie (in whose hands I found it) that it bore your mark. He did not think so—but paid a tribute to the anonymous gentleman." It's difficult to read this passage and not imagine Ogilvie's thoughts at the idea that his former student might have declined to place him in this company.[24]

It was not just Ogilvie's ego on the line; it was that he felt they were friends. They had maintained a correspondence ever since Gilmer had left Ogilvie's tutelage for college at William and Mary. As he had with other former students, Ogilvie wrote letters to Gilmer that blurred the conventional boundaries between teacher and student. If William Wirt had taken on the role of mentor with the younger man, Ogilvie showed little concern for the difference in their ages.

Several years earlier he had sent Gilmer a letter replete with flattery, describing him as "probably without a rival amongst the young men of Virginia, in extent of useful information, in the range of liberal reading, in the variety, solidity and brilliancy of your intellectual accomplishments." At times, Ogilvie's letters turned confessional. In one, he alternated between bragging of his own successes and petulantly reporting feeling "betrayed" and "calumniated" by a critic. In another, he reported his mortification when only 150 people appeared for one of his Philadelphia performances. In each, he begged Gilmer to keep writing and signed himself "your most affectionate friend."[25]

If Ogilvie felt slighted by Gilmer's book—or if he felt insulted by the line about how American audiences were delighted by "any one who can entertain them"—he left no record of it. Perhaps he recognized that the book focused solely on political speech rather than the Rostrum oratory he had popularized. Certainly his own mode, which foreswore partisan debate, stood in stark contrast to the speech of Randolph, Marshall, and Wirt. Perhaps he assured himself that the book had its own role to play in Ogilvie's larger design of promoting oratory in the American Republic and inspiring young people to cultivate their talents in good speech. In combination with William Wirt's oratory-obsessed *Sketches of the Life and Character of Patrick Henry*, Gilmer's *Sketches of American Orators* confirmed in print a moment in the 1810s when Americans made a turn. Whereas before writers had expressed a sense of inferiority about their nation's lack of true eloquence, now they began asserting that American eloquence had blossomed. The writer who later termed this "the golden age of American oratory" proclaimed sententiously that "in the enthusiastic springtime of a nation's kindling youth, and the conscious pride of such a new-born majesty, full-armed with victory from its very birth, the orators of the Republic have trembled with Pythic frenzy under a thousand inspirations." For a nation eager to tie itself to the legacy of the classical republics, Gilmer's and Wirt's books helped Americans imagine that they had already realized a culture of eloquence that bound together good leaders and thoughtful, attentive public assemblies that listened closely as matters of public importance were debated.[26]

For Ogilvie's part, he now saw an opportunity to continue his own role in the national promotion of oratory. Departing Washington, D.C., in May 1814, he continued his tour south through Virginia toward South Carolina, where he hoped to teach at the South Carolina College in Columbia. To do so would allow him to realize one of the central aims he had publicized in his *Port Folio* essay: to urge American colleges to invest in the teaching of elocution and oratory and thereby to bring up a new generation of orators.

In retrospect, his departure from the nation's capital was timely considering the progress of the War of 1812, which made American prospects look increas-

Figure 43. View of the Capitol of the United States, after the Conflagration, in 1814.
From Jesse Torrey, A Portraiture of Domestic Slavery, in the United States ... (Philadelphia, 1817), frontispiece. An image of the destroyed Capitol building in Washington, D.C., after British troops burned it, from Torrey's antislavery text. Courtesy of the Library of Virginia, Richmond

ingly bleak that summer. British forces moved ever closer to the Chesapeake Bay during their attacks on eastern cities, and by August they threatened Washington. Governmental officials including James and Dolley Madison fled the city on the heels of the Americans' defeat in Bladensburg, Maryland, just a few miles northeast of Washington. On August 24, the British entered the capital city and began burning its neoclassical buildings: the White House, the Treasury, the building containing the War and State Departments, and the Capitol building that Jefferson had designed with such pride. To get the Capitol to burn, British soldiers entered the Rotunda where Ogilvie had performed a few months earlier, "made a great pile in the Center of the room" of the desks and furniture, and lit it like a bonfire, as Benjamin Henry Latrobe later reported to Jefferson. "So intense was the flame" shooting up toward Jefferson's beautiful dome with its glass sky-lights "that the Glass of the Lights was melted, and I now have lumps weighing many pounds of Glass, run into Mass." In a city previously described by visitors as "grotesque," this destruction took down those few buildings, like the Capitol, that tourists had described as "elegant." And, while most of Britain celebrated the burning of Washington, some members of Parliament and opposition newspapers publicly bemoaned the scorched-earth policy. It would take years to reconstruct the public buildings destroyed, keeping the city a construction zone for a generation.[27]

Despite this defeat, the war was almost over. Treaty negotiations had begun long before the city was burned. Both the United States and Britain had come to see the war as a stalemate, even as their continued battles helped each side position itself advantageously during the diplomatic process of treaty making, finally concluded on Christmas Eve of 1814. But Americans at the time nevertheless hastened to declare themselves winners. Following Andrew Jackson's triumph in New Orleans—an exceptionally lopsided battle that took place months after the signing of the treaty in Europe and had no effect on those negotiations—newspapers and politicians alike turned Jackson into a celebrity and insisted that his success was exemplary of the Americans' overall victory. "Americans! Rejoice!" cried Washington's *Daily National Intelligencer*. "By the unsurpassed exploits of your Army and Navy, and the consummate wisdom of your statesmen, you have achieved an honorable peace with one of the most powerful nations on the globe." President Madison confirmed the overarching sense of the Americans' "most brilliant successes." In a message delivered to Congress, the president described the war as having been "waged with a success which is the natural result of the legislative counsels, of the patriotism of the people, of the public spirit of the militia, and of the valor of the military and naval forces of the country." Orators and print media alike joined in this full-throated attempt to cast the war's end as an American triumph.[28]

As American boosters reframed the war's ambiguous conclusion and declared it (counterfactually) a national success, Ogilvie moved to South Carolina for his own campaign—to teach ambitious young men and women the art of speaking well. Buoyed by his successes and the balmy South Carolina climate, he also made the worst move of his career. He decided to write a book.

CHAPTER 11

A Fall from Grace; or, Oratory versus Print,

1815–1817

When James Ogilvie made the long, slow overland trip from Thomas Jefferson's Monticello to South Carolina during the fall and winter of 1814, he planned to stay for a while. He'd been there before, he'd liked it, and the feeling had been mutual. Four years earlier, the ecstatic students in Columbia had commemorated his lectures on a warm spring evening by illuminating all the college's windows so that as he exited the building he could see the banner they had hung featuring an American eagle emblazoned with Ogilvie's name. Surely now that his celebrity had reached new heights on the national stage he might receive an even warmer reception.[1]

His aims for this extended trip suggest that he had begun to formulate new plans for his future. Since his first visit in 1811, his mission had grown more elaborate. He now had several items on his agenda. He hoped to mobilize the inhabitants of Charleston to act on his advice to establish a hall for public debate and the display of eloquence. He also hoped, on returning to Columbia, to teach oratory at the South Carolina College for a term. Time in the classroom would augment his reputation as both an orator and a teacher, and he hoped it would lead to future temporary appointments at American colleges. If nothing else, he could use the experience to advertise the need to bring public speech training more vigorously into schools to raise a new generation of Americans who could take up the mantle to maintain American eloquence, as he had discussed in his article in the Port Folio. Finally, he saw this extended stay as a good opportunity to write the book he had long contemplated. Giving lectures in South Carolina and Georgia could provide enough money to step away from the stage entirely during the hot summer, when lecturing became intolerable.[2]

Writing a book and seeking long-term residencies at American colleges were the actions of a man ready to adopt a new style of life. Or, rather, one willing to rethink earlier forms of paying work. Remember how much he used to complain about teaching? The decision to seek teaching positions, even short-term ones, must have resulted from a reconsideration of the rigors of itinerant lecturing, or at least the conviction that teaching at the college level might be less taxing.

The book would get written. The academic career would not materialize. And in between those two things, we would witness yet another permutation of the phenomenon of celebrity: what happens when the public turns against you.

When he arrived in Columbia, Ogilvie persuaded the faculty and trustees of the college to let him teach a course on rhetoric and elocution. The timing was perfect. His strongest support came from the college president, Jonathan Maxcy, who had taught similar subjects but was currently too ill to continue. Maxcy had arrived ten years earlier, in 1805, when the college opened its doors with only two faculty members, and he had felt so strongly about polishing his students' speaking skills that he helped them establish debating societies to promote public speech on campus. Thus, when Ogilvie proposed to teach junior-level and senior-level classes encompassing "rhetoric, and exercises in elocution, criticism, and composition" to a restricted number of students during the spring of 1815, he found himself overrun with applicants. He allowed the classes to swell in size and raved about his students' talents (admitting, however, that there were "one or two *very* melancholy exceptions"). By the end of the semester he arranged a three-evening series of performances by his senior students, each of whom delivered an oration of his own composition before "very crouded and brilliant audiences." The college's president, professors, and trustees raved, too. Maxcy published a letter commending Ogilvie's work in promoting oratory "in a country that presents so many peculiar incentives to the acquisition, and opportunities for the exercise of oratorical skill: in a society where public speaking, next to the press, is the most authentic organ of public opinion, and contributes perhaps more than the press to influence the public mind." Upon the conclusion of the class, his students presented him with a gold medal "'as a token of their esteem and gratitude towards him, for his unremitting attention, in promoting their improvement.'"[3]

Such a triumphal conclusion of the term in June 1815 prompted him to begin pressing hard for his larger goals of establishing professorships of oratory in American colleges and "the erection of spacious and magnificent halls, (exclusively dedicated to the exercise and exhibition of oratory, on the Rostrum)." The first such professorship had been established at Harvard in 1805, with John Quincy Adams installed as the Boylston Professor of Rhetorick and Oratory. After that, many magazine articles had called on religious seminaries to establish professorships of "pulpit eloquence" to teach seminarians how to exhort effectively to compete with eloquent but untrained camp meeting preachers. While in Columbia, Ogilvie tried to persuade the state legislature to establish a professorship of oratory and, as he insisted in his memoir, "on no former occasion, in South Carolina, [had he] spoken so impressively." But, despite support from a cohort of "intelligent and patriotic members of the legislature" and his insistence that he would not accept such a job if offered to him, the state declined to create it. "In vain!" he recalled bitterly. "The feelings of his respectable auditors, after venting themselves in a loud and protracted plaudit, evaporated 'into thin air.'"[4]

With this failure fresh in his mind, he returned to Charleston and by November of 1815 had returned to delivering his usual lectures, albeit this time with the singular determination to encourage Charlestonians to build a hall for the performance of oratory. He particularly sought to appeal to their patriotism. In European cities, he reminded his listeners, one could find remarkable institutions: museums, theaters, colleges, and halls of justice—"glorious monuments these, of the progress of civilization," he explained. But "in Europe, oratory alone, has neither an asylum nor an altar, neither resting place nor refuge!" This offered Americans a unique opportunity to supersede the Old World. "What American citizen can be insensible to the honour of providing an asylum for so glorious an exile; a home for so illustrious a guest! Ever *last* to retreat, and *first* to re-appear, in the train of republican liberty." To build a hall of eloquence would establish something "truly American, worthy of a people who have recently achieved their independence, and established with a deliberation and concert, unparalleled in the annals of history, a republican government," he concluded with a flourish. Such an effort would provide opportunities for civic pride within the city of Charleston such that other cities might follow, and the United States might become known for its noble contributions to the revival of true eloquence. The lectures certainly sold out; one notice circulated around the country noting that his lecture in a room designed to seat eight hundred had been "so full that benches could not be placed for the gentlemen, and many of them were obliged to sit upon the floor, at the *Ladies' feet!*" Six months later another reviewer claimed never to have seen a more numerous and respectable audience.[5]

He might have sold a lot of tickets, but he proved less convincing in persuading Charlestonians to build a hall for the display of eloquence. Many locals liked the idea, including influential elites who promised to throw themselves and their wealth behind the plan. Writers for Charleston's newspapers touted the plan, too. The *Southern Patriot* admitted that local residents were often "too much occupied with the business of commerce" to see the benefits of an oratorical hall. "But is GAIN to take up all our attention? Have we not leisure enough and riches enough, to undertake other enterprises?" If such institutions in the ancient republics of Greece and Rome had fostered eloquent genius, "so should it be with REPUBLICAN AMERICA." Ogilvie felt so strongly about the creation of such halls that in his 1816 memoir he held forth on the topic for twenty-six pages, more than a page of which consisted of a single, effusive, and slightly mad sentence.[6]

Despite the help of these elites and newspaper essayists, and despite Ogilvie's holding forth "at considerable length" on the value of such a building (wearing the gold medal from his South Carolina College students over his toga), his plan to establish a hall of eloquence failed to drum up enough support. That this followed so quickly on the heels of his thwarted attempt to get the South Carolina legislature to create a professorship of eloquence made it more painful. As he explained it, as a man of the world, and "at his time of life, (near forty years of age,)"—actually, he was nearly forty-three—he admitted that it sounded overwrought to "have suffered his mind to be so heated by romantic enthusiasm, as to have experienced keen and enduring anguish, from the frustration of his efforts to accomplish this design, in the metropolis of South Carolina." But he suffered an "agony as exquisite and protracted, as he ever remembers to have endured." In fact, he became so withdrawn and misanthropic that he later felt the need to apologize publicly to Charlestonians for his behavior.[7]

To divert himself from his unhappiness, he set himself a new task: he took on the instruction of girls in Charleston to demonstrate how quickly and effectively he could teach them an extensive range of material on the subjects of reading, grammar, and geography—and thus to advertise the effectiveness of his methods to female academies. Never in his fifteen-year-long teaching career had his schools admitted female students, yet he had built his oratorical reputation in part on his advocacy of female education in the United States—a project that remained controversial, at least for some observers, who continued to debate whether intellectual accomplishments were appropriate for girls.

The contrast between proponents and opponents of advanced female education could be stark. Even before Mary Wollstonecraft's *Vindication of the Rights of Woman* appeared on bookstore shelves in the United States following its 1792 British publication, American writers discussed whether to enhance female education. "Since [women] have the same improveable minds as the male part of the species, why should they not be cultivated by the same method?" asked one popular schoolbook. Writers for newspapers and magazines likewise continued this conversation such that Wollstonecraft's views of female education, written in a bracingly direct style, found eager audiences well prepared to be convinced by her arguments. Female academies designed to offer advanced education to girls grew in popularity among elite American families and spread to middling families by the 1810s and 1820s.[8]

To critics of such forms of education, however, encouraging young women to expand their intellects was a project rife with danger, for it had the potential to undermine their femininity and thus their ability to marry, become dutiful wives and mothers, and remain satisfied with the distinct sphere of life allotted to women. Too much education, such writers suggested, made such women more masculine. "Learned women," just like women who engaged in war or politics, "equally abandon the circle which nature and institutions have traced round their sex; they convert themselves into men," decreed the *Boston Weekly Magazine* in 1804. Others fretted that an emphasis on study made both girls and boys more prone to illness. Especially after the controversial appearance of William Godwin's biography of Mary Wollstonecraft in 1799, which revealed her unconventional sexual life, radical political beliefs, and suicide attempt, the effort to expand women's education encountered renewed opposition at the turn of the century and afterward. By the early nineteenth century, opponents of advanced female education raised Wollstonecraft's name whenever they required an example of how far "learned ladies" might deviate from acceptable female behavior. Even as female education expanded for middling and wealthy girls during the early Republic, a steady stream of opposition continued to question its value.[9]

Ogilvie hoped to skirt possible critiques of female education by placing the heaviest emphasis on his innovative teaching techniques. Following closely on the completion of his term with the boys at South Carolina College, this course for girls allowed him to demonstrate the universal applicability of his methods. When he posted notices about it, he emphasized first and foremost what the girls would learn in his class. They would meet for ninety minutes, three times a week, yet Ogilvie claimed he would teach them as much in only one month as they might typically learn in six months. Perhaps by undertaking this course in Charleston, he believed he might persuade wealthy South Carolinians after all to build a hall of eloquence.[10]

Observers of his students' final exhibition in April 1816 were impressed. "In his method of teaching Geography, Mr. O. has unquestionably been triumphantly successful," one reviewer wrote. "The plan which he has adopted is in the highest degree simple and perspicuous, easily applied, and undoubted in its efficacy. It depends upon the clearest principles of the understanding, and could be completely explained and communicated to an intelligent mind in less than an hour." The students' progress in grammar, "though much beyond expectation, was not so striking as in Geography," but the reviewer explained that this doubtless reflected the difficulty of the subject. After all, "it is questionable whether one in ten of the youths who leave our schools or graduate at our colleges, has acquired a complete knowledge of this important branch of education." Ogilvie abandoned teaching abstract sets of grammatical rules that in other schools "load the memory of the pupil with an accumulation of words [rather] than convey any clear intelligible ideas." Instead, he trained their minds "to habits of reflection and analysis," making the process more active, and taught students "the best possible discipline for the study of logic and metaphysics." In the end, this reviewer felt "no hesitation in declaring that, in his opinion, it is incomparably superior to the common modes of instruction; and that the youth reared under such discipline could scarcely fail of acquiring no ordinary share of mental sagacity." One or two complained that ordinary teachers could glean little about Ogilvie's unique pedagogical methods simply by witnessing the progress of his students at an exhibition, but most agreed it was a terrific success.[11]

After the girls' exhibition, Ogilvie stepped away from the limelight. He had earned enough from his lectures and teaching to stop for several months. He used his time away to complete his *Philosophical Essays* for publication with a Philadelphia printer. He wrote the entire four-hundred-page book—and had it printed—in only four months of working at fever pitch. Rather than transcribe his orations, which he planned to reserve for a second volume, this book provided new reflections on various topics. These included the subject of human knowledge, the place of fiction in American life, and the importance of mathematics, particularly for "the attainment of superior ability and skill, in the exercise of oratory." He also added an autobiographical narrative that traced his years as a teacher and his experiences as a public lecturer.[12]

Ogilvie wrote the book because, as he announced with breathtaking immodesty in its preface, he realized that all the celebrity he had achieved as an orator would be "worthless, or hopeless; without the acquisition of permanent and extended celebrity, as a philosophical writer." It was not a promising opening. And immodesty was not the book's only problem.[13]

Ogilvie's *Philosophical Essays* had the feel of a rambling, poorly conceived vanity project that the author published without benefit of editors or advice from friends with perspective. Considering that virtually no book editors existed in 1816 and that many books appeared because the author paid for publication, Ogilvie's book was certainly not the only poorly conceived self-published volume on the market. But it was the only one published by a national celebrity and public intellectual.[14]

His immodest presumptions began with the early advertising for the book. Before the book appeared from the press, wordy advertisements that stretched three-quarters of the way down the printed newspaper page suggested that the book might be deemed important enough to grant him a post at one of the nation's colleges. The ads reminded the public that Ogilvie had tested his ideas with his students at the South Carolina College and that readers of those ideas might now determine "how far he is qualified to discharge the duties of a philosophical lecturer" to "any faculty or board of trustees, however intelligent and respect-

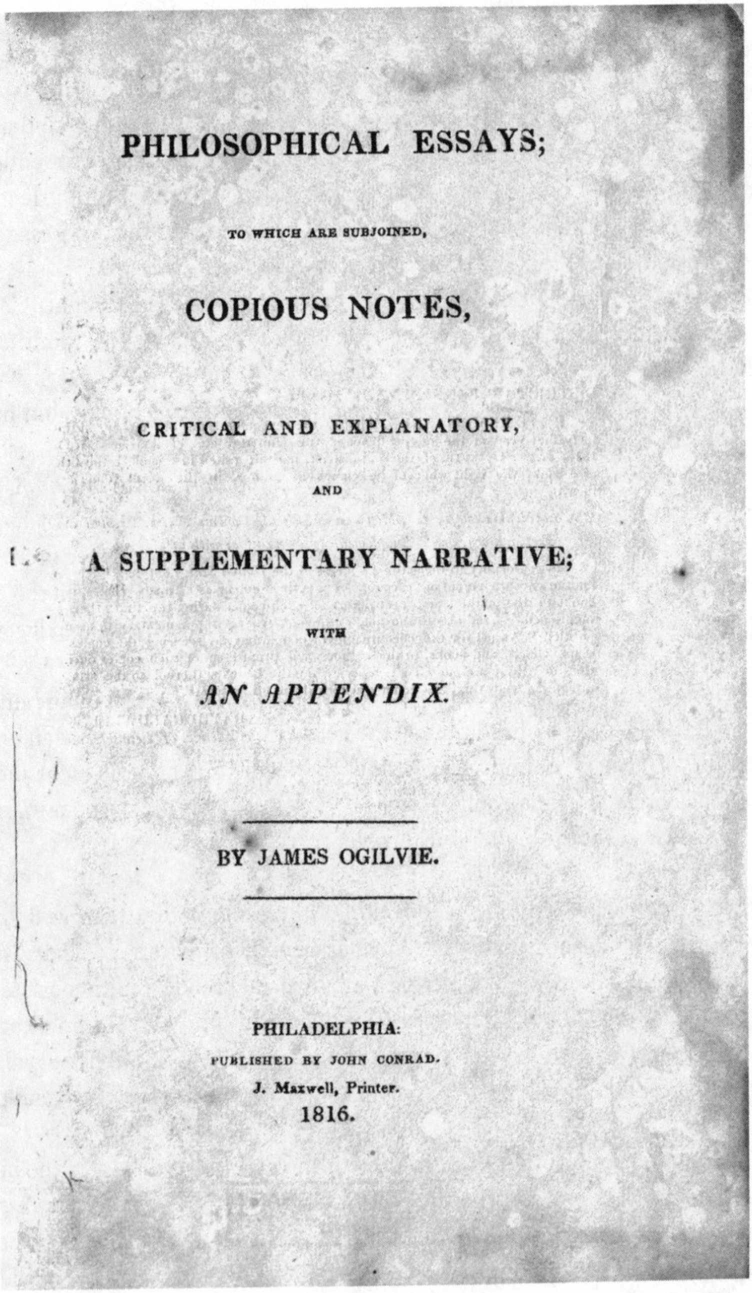

PHILOSOPHICAL ESSAYS;

TO WHICH ARE SUBJOINED,

COPIOUS NOTES,

CRITICAL AND EXPLANATORY,

AND

A SUPPLEMENTARY NARRATIVE;

WITH

AN APPENDIX.

BY JAMES OGILVIE.

PHILADELPHIA:
PUBLISHED BY JOHN CONRAD.
J. Maxwell, Printer.
1816.

Figure 44. Title page of James Ogilvie, Philosophical Essays . . . (Philadelphia, 1816).
The book's very title announced Ogilvie's outsized ambitions. In the preface, he explained
immodestly that with the book he sought to establish his "permanent and extended celebrity,
as a philosophical writer." Courtesy of the Library of Virginia, Richmond

able. It is the primary object of this volume to afford this direct and unequivocal evidence." Moreover, the ads explained, being able to read Ogilvie's ideas would show their intrinsic value without the added panache of his spoken eloquence and grace on stage. "No elegance of diction, no splendour of declamation, no artifice of rhetoric can, in an age like this, veil superficial thinking, or protect elementary error, from certain detection and ignominious exposure." With breathtaking hubris, he promised to make himself available to "any other American College" that invited him to reprise his success with the students in Columbia. And, because he concluded this advertisement by asking editors ("those more especially with whom Mr. Ogilvie has the pleasure of being personally acquainted throughout the United States") to reprint it, the same boastful text appeared in hundreds of papers, week after week, throughout the fall of 1816.[15]

Did he ever regret submitting such an ad for wide circulation? The resulting hubbub quickly overshadowed Ogilvie's recent schoolroom accomplishments with students and made the possibility of glamorous teaching engagements all the less likely.

Ogilvie's prose style compounded both the author's immodesty and the book's superficiality. He composed the essays in a baroque, belletristic style that might have sounded marvelous when spoken aloud but on the cold, hard page revealed the thinness of the underlying ideas covered over with the enthusiasm of rhetorical excess. His sentences stretched on for lines, sometimes more than a page at a time, with endless clauses and interjected thoughts. At times they read like the stream-of-consciousness essays written by students the night before a deadline, lacking order or logic. Two hundred years later it makes one cringe.[16]

Even the kindest readers of the book asked questions about Ogilvie's logical consistency. The book's three long essays drew heavily on other writing of the era, especially the work of David Hume, but mixed those ideas with contradictory ones from philosophers like John Locke and William Godwin. "He has suddenly dropped from the heights of idealism to the common level of realism," one critic wrote, noting other moments when he "abruptly" changed course or offered the odd "reversion of judgment." The book thus vacillated between passages that seemed derivative of other thinkers or contradictory, all bound up in verbose, sometimes repetitive language that exaggerated the divide between Ogilvie's vaulting ambitions and his chapters' more prosaic achievements.[17]

Worst of all was the strange, disorganized autobiography that concluded the volume. Written awkwardly in the third person (referring to himself as "the narrator") as if to affect modesty, this ninety-one-page narrative offered recollections of his years as a teacher and public speaker, describing memorable triumphs and poking uncomfortably at old embarrassments. His prose frequently

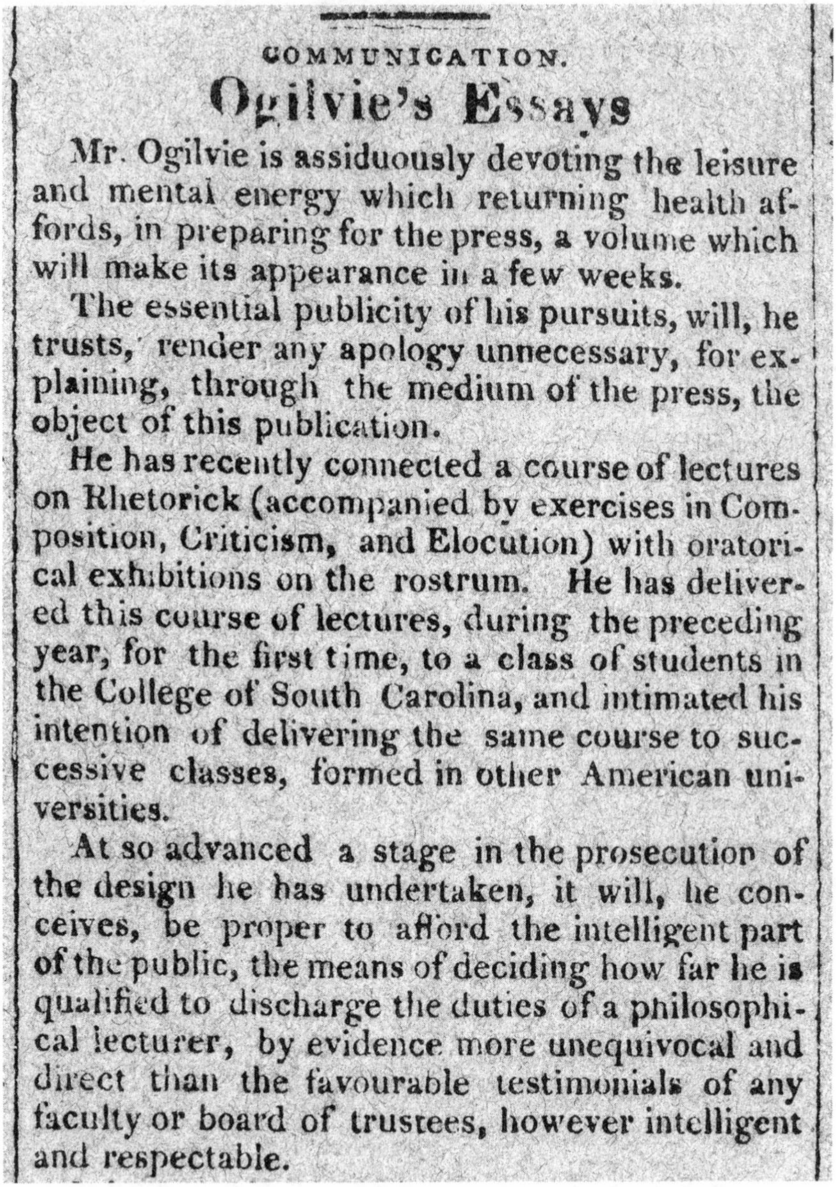

Ogilvie's Essays

Mr. Ogilvie is assiduously devoting the leisure and mental energy which returning health affords, in preparing for the press, a volume which will make its appearance in a few weeks.

The essential publicity of his pursuits, will, he trusts, render any apology unnecessary, for explaining, through the medium of the press, the object of this publication.

He has recently connected a course of lectures on Rhetorick (accompanied by exercises in Composition, Criticism, and Elocution) with oratorical exhibitions on the rostrum. He has delivered this course of lectures, during the preceding year, for the first time, to a class of students in the College of South Carolina, and intimated his intention of delivering the same course to successive classes, formed in other American universities.

At so advanced a stage in the prosecution of the design he has undertaken, it will, he conceives, be proper to afford the intelligent part of the public, the means of deciding how far he is qualified to discharge the duties of a philosophical lecturer, by evidence more unequivocal and direct than the favourable testimonials of any faculty or board of trustees, however intelligent and respectable.

Figure 45. "Ogilvie's Essays." From Poulson's American Daily Advertiser (Philadelphia), July 30, 1816, [3]. The first few paragraphs of the long advertisements that circulated throughout the country to announce Ogilvie's forthcoming book. The ads, like the book itself, would prove to suffer from a combination of false modesty and breathtaking hubris. Courtesy of the American Antiquarian Society, Worcester, Mass.

indulged in a combination of egotism and false modesty, as in this comparatively brief paragraph:

> He is quite aware, that he is expressing himself in language that will be distinctly understood only by one reader in a hundred, and expressing sensations which will awaken a vivid sympathy in the hearts of one only in a hundred readers, to whom this language will be clearly intelligible: yet this language is the idiosyncratic idiom, the spontaneous emanation of his feelings, and for the sake of the delicious sympathy of the few existing, and the many unborn minds to which this language will be delicious, he cheerfully subjects himself to the scorn, and, (if it so pleases them,) to the neglect, or even to the curse, of the mob of readers.

Confusing the narrative further, Ogilvie inserted long digressions into the footnotes that dot nearly every page. Two of these footnote detours stretched on for more than sixteen pages each. An eccentric autobiographical text like this may be a gold mine for a historian, offering a remarkable picture of his long school days, his struggles in the earliest months of his lecturing career, his use of opium. But his contemporaries dwelled on its lapses in judgment, often beginning their reviews with extended quotations from the autobiography, italicizing the most embarrassing lines lest their readers miss their sheer awfulness, and thus hoisting Ogilvie with his own petard.[18]

Philosophical Essays evoked howls immediately. Reviewers demolished the book. Nearly every one quoted the book's opening line about his seeking "permanent and extended celebrity, as a philosophical writer" with varying degrees of disgust or bemusement, turning those words against him. "The volume before us furnishes sufficient evidence that he has no pretensions whatsoever to the character of a philosophical writer," wrote a harsh reviewer for the magazine *Port Folio.* "Its numerous blemishes have nothing to redeem them; no strength of reasoning, no profound investigation, no enlarged or original knowledge, no splendid paradox, no specious or agreeable novelty, no captivating eloquence, none of that ethereal electricity which animates and embellishes every subject." The reviewer for the *Analectic Magazine*—rumored to be Ogilvie's friend, Washington Irving—was more generous, but still damned the book in a fifty-two-page review, so lengthy an account that the magazine divided it over the course of two issues. "Mr. Ogilvie forgets rather too often that he is not on the rostrum," this review complained, a lapse that led the book to ramble on in a manner "not at all calculated for the temperate and chaste disquisition of philosophical subjects." In addition, Ogilvie's professed desire for fame as a philosopher "is altogether incompatible with loose and negligent habits of writing." This review wasn't as mean as the one in the Port Folio but still concluded in its last lines that, "if we understand his characteristic temperament, we should advise him to abstain from composition whenever he has been taking opium, or reading Paradise Lost."[19]

When these reviews appeared in December 1816, Ogilvie lashed out in a Boston newspaper. He particularly attacked the Port Folio, and did so with the same vitriol as he believed he had received. "John E. Hall, the present editor of the Port Folio, has been so unusually and assiduously successful, in making public his incapacity to excel or even to obtain a moderate share of success in any liberal profession, or in the humblest walks of literary drudgery, that his incorrigible dullness and ignorance are [a] matter of general notoriety. He is unquestionably the most noted dunce in the United States." He held forth with such venom about Hall, often repeating his full name as if to mock his pretensions, that one suspects Ogilvie saw this as an affair of honor—even worthy of resorting to personal violence. "Mr. Ogilvie has threatened to gibbet the malignant dunce," he continued. More broadly, he accused magazine critics of being "a race of reptile-scribblers, ephemeral in their existence and odious in their instincts" who "prey only on carrion and putrescence." Even the Boston paper that published these words expressed embarrassment. It admitted he had been "treated with unmerited severity" but confessed, "We sincerely wish Mr. O. had not permitted his feelings so entirely to guide his pen."[20]

One can say many things about Ogilvie's angry rant, but it must be acknowledged that his writing improves remarkably when motivated by rage.

In dishing out this abuse, Ogilvie might have sought to channel the sharp pen of Lord Byron, who several years earlier had responded to critics by condemning them in poetry, which proved to be some of the best of his career at that point. In English Bards, and Scotch Reviewers (1809), Byron borrowed the satirical style of Alexander Pope's Dunciad—the very poem that had energized The Ogilviad back on the college grounds in Aberdeen in Ogilvie's youth—to skewer his Scottish critics in such a lively manner that it had won over many members of the public (and critics) to Byron's side. But, even if he'd been inspired by Byron's mockery of his naysayers, Ogilvie's tirade lacked Byron's good humor and larger vision "to make others write better." Rather than win over readers, he isolated himself further.[21]

Looking back at previous challenges to his honor—as a college student with The Ogilviad, the spat over politics and religion that lost him his teaching job in Fredericksburg, and his anger about John Rodman's satirical Fragments of a Journal of a Sentimental Philosopher—we can see a pattern. He read criticism as personal attack and responded with the same. He insisted on his book's significance, noting that he had "aspired to write a book, which when corrected and enlarged in a second edition, would be worthy of attentive perusal by every young person of either sex, who has been liberally educated; and become a philosophical manual in every college, established in either hemisphere" where English was spoken. He also claimed to want honest criticism. "Mr. O. has repeatedly declared, that he will be thankful to the sternest and severest critic, who with the spirit of a patriot, in the style of a philosopher and a scholar, and with the urbanity of a gentleman, will animadvert on the nature and objects of the enterprise which he has undertaken," he explained between barbs at Hall. Yet such a statement appeared disingenuous in the midst of an attack like this. Hall, meanwhile, corresponded with other editors to gauge their responses to the melee. "How does his book succeed with you?" he wrote to a Boston editor. "Here, it will soon be ranked among those quae legunt cacantes—his sheets will serve like those which honest Burton describes as used 'to put under pies, to lap spice in, and keep roast-meat from burning.'" (Hall was being coy when he translated the Latin as papers "to put under pies"; more accurately it reads, "things that people read while shitting.")[22]

Some members of the print media enjoyed the battle wholeheartedly. "The publick must certainly be very much indebted to Mr. Ogilvie and the 'Young Bostonian,' for the amusement they have furnished in these dull times," one editor wrote. Another opened his editorial saying that "we do not intend to review this work; because, in truth, we have not read the half of it, and, probably, never shall read the rest. . . . We suspect that those essays will do no harm; and it is probable that they can do no good." Some sought to defend the book, insisting on its instructive value and offering a defense of Ogilvie. But the majority preferred to join in the chorus of mocking his pretensions to permanent celebrity.[23]

The most damaging outcome was an emerging tendency by commentators to question not just Ogilvie's ideas and his talent as a writer but even his lectures and reputation as the nation's foremost orator. "It is absurd to call that eloquence which is only a mixture of mist and moonshine," one wrote. The reviewer for the Port Folio delivered the most damning appraisal. "Mr. Ogilvie seems to have aimed at what appeared to his distorted imagination, a glorious acquisition, but which, in soberness, is no more than the eclat that is due to a schoolboy who has spoken well. He acted the reciter, until he obtained the plaudits of the multitude." This writer suggested that the failures of Philosophical Essays were so profound that Ogilvie ought to cease delivering his own compositions during his performances. "If, however, he will still continue to deliver his own discourses from the rostrum, we think instead of demanding 'the erection of spacious and magnificent halls, in the principal cities of the American republic' . . . for his exercitations, he may be satisfied with those which have been usually allotted to him," suggesting that his campaign for the construction of such buildings had been entirely self-serving.[24]

Even his friends turned on him. Although Ogilvie had long carried on a warm correspondence with his former student Francis Walker Gilmer, by 1817 Gilmer had nothing good to say. In one letter written about a year after the publication of Gilmer's *Sketches of American Orators*, he referred to his former teacher as "that unhappy madman Ogilvie" who "never did, nor ever can read or understand Cicero, or any part of his works. He is utterly incapable of connecting in a natural order any two ideas, and is in every department of knowledge more perfectly a madman and a fool *secundum artem* [according to the accepted practice of a profession] than any one who ever enjoyed his reputation. I had some idea of putting an extinguisher on the smoke and dim flame of his stinking candle, but perhaps it is better to let him go out in his own feculence." The anger in Gilmer's letter was striking, as if he felt personally implicated by Ogilvie's dramatic public unmasking.[25]

The shift in opinion was profound. As one commentator recalled a few years later, "Unqualified praise was converted into unqualified condemnation; and those who looked upon every thing he said in the height of their extravagance as almost divine, now felt ashamed and wished to deny that they ever had admired his intellectual endowments." Some now behaved as if they had always known his shortcomings and had never been so naive as to admire his eloquence or his rhetorical prowess. Once, Ogilvie's cosmopolitanism and formidable reputation held up a mirror to his audiences, making them aware of their own provinciality and enhancing the sense of marvel at his performances. Now the denunciations of Ogilvie showed them a different image: they were not just provincial but also easily hoodwinked by a charlatan. The press filled with declarations professing never to have been convinced of his strange genius for oratory. It was as if the public had suddenly aged out of an embarrassing adolescent fixation and sought to put it behind them as quickly as possible.[26]

Abrupt public disenchantment with celebrities is a pattern we have come to know well. Celebrities whose lives seem to fall apart, whose racism or sexual abusiveness or addictions horrify us—all can lead to forms of shaming or banishment from the public eye. By the twenty-first century, Americans would have grown accustomed to a whipsaw pattern of celebrating and forgetting, adoring and then rejecting celebrities who no longer fit our ideas of whom we ought to admire and who we are now.[27]

That the early nineteenth-century United States lacked a celebrity culture such that Ogilvie had few peers means that we cannot neatly apply our familiarity with such disenchantments to his situation. His status had long been premised on two fundamental dynamics: an appreciation for his almost mystical oratorical talents that manifested in pure magic onstage, and Americans' sense of themselves as provincials. When they had opportunities to witness Ogilvie perform, the experience seemed to take them out of that relative regional isolation for the first time to appreciate true eloquence. If anyone doubted his talents and cosmopolitanism, they had only to scan local newspapers for stories of his triumphs, both locally and nationally, to find seemingly universal appreciation.

But faced with the spreading critical condemnation of his book, the public now had to reconsider. Whereas his appearances had once created anxious thoughts of "are we good enough? Are we respectable enough?" reports now asked, "Is *he* good enough?" For some critics, the answer was no. They now mocked his pretensions, his writing, his insufferable vanity. Print media had once confirmed his celebrity; now some of those writers transformed him into a fool. Some went so far as to proclaim that they had always doubted his talents. Others simply expressed an overwhelming desire to forget their prior naïveté. We have such a hard time forgiving those who expose our foolishness.[28]

If we step back from the awful progress of Ogilvie's fall from grace, we can see another side of this story: a disjunction between print and oratory as two primary forms of communication in this era. There are many reasons he had succeeded as an orator for so long, but one of these might have been that this medium had so few real experts, and correspondingly few expert critics. He gained power onstage not only because he had an unusual power to move his audiences but also because they had almost no one with whom to compare him. Without any real facility for criticizing oratory like Ogilvie's, newspaper editors were all the more inclined to join what seemed to be a chorus celebrating his talents. One Charleston critic had suggested as much. "It became extremely fashionable to admire Mr. Ogilvie, because a few persons in Charleston, imagining themselves qualified to dictate on all subjects of taste, had pronounced him excellent," this notice read. Meanwhile, the rest of the public "fall in with the prevailing taste or fashion, whatever they may be, and are impelled along with the general current, to admire, or condemn, without taste or discrimanation." In other words, few had any inclination or ability to gauge Ogilvie's skills because he had mastered an unusual mode of public speaking that did not resemble the styles of speech more familiar at the time, such as legal argument, political debate, religious exhortation, or even the famous oratory of the ancient world—and even if they had, they would have had to face the tide of opinion running in the opposite direction.[29]

But when Ogilvie decided to publish a book, he entered an arena filled with comparable texts and able critics. American commentators might have had little experience critiquing oratory, but they certainly knew how to read books—and many of them, particularly the young, hungry critics, had begun to build their reputations as ruthlessly uncompromising, witty and biting. Of course Ogilvie's book received a different level of criticism than his lectures. To have expected otherwise appears spectacularly egotistical or, at the very least, naive.[30]

One critic of *Philosophical Essays* put his finger on this gap between the practices of print and oratory. A lawyer and magazine editor (and brother of prominent minister William Ellery Channing), Edward Channing chastised Ogilvie for writing a book in a declamatory style that sober readers would instantly see through. "It should not be forgotten, that men are readers now," Channing wrote. "A habit of intelligent watchfulness is thus formed in the people, and the orator feels it. He aims less at forcing publick sentiment and drowning judgment in declamation. . . . We look about then for men in whom we can confide, not for the orator who glitters upon feast-days, who toils for effect." As an orator, Ogilvie was successful, but as a writer, incompetent—and the divide between the two forms of communication allowed Channing to tip the scales in terms of writing's preeminence. Oratory permitted a talented speaker to cloud the public's judgment with enthusiasm, eloquence, and personality. "We are ready to allow him all the license of poetry. We give ourselves up to illusions, and are not offended with inflated emptiness, if it only pour itself out in fine tones." The writer, in contrast, "must work through the judgment to the heart, and when he has reached and moved it, he will leave there a deep and inextinguishable energy."[31]

Unlike the *Port Folio*'s anonymous critic, Channing didn't indulge in grandstanding and sarcasm, and as a result he delivered a more serious blow. With measured, sober argument, he explained that Ogilvie's many failures in the book revealed the inferiority of one medium to the other. Within two years, Channing would assume the prominent Boylston Professorship of Rhetorick and Oratory at Harvard College—the very kind of job for which Ogilvie had advocated so strongly to enhance the role of oratory in American culture.

Even as *Philosophical Essays* met with a wall of criticism in the press, Ogilvie continued to deliver his usual lectures in New England and the mid-Atlantic states, receiving the usual rave reviews along the way. He spoke before six hundred auditors in New York and assisted a large number of ambitious young men there in making their debating society, the Forum, so prominent that notices of their meetings appeared in newspapers as far away as Kentucky. After performing at Harvard, the students presented him with a beautifully bound, twelve-volume set of classical Greek orations. On an invitation from a schoolteacher, he visited the Boston Latin School to witness the boys declaim. One of those boys, a thirteen-year-old Ralph Waldo Emerson, wrote to his brother enthusiastically about the day. "After the boys had spoken, Mr Ogilvie said a little *de oratore*—he told us, that it was as easy to teach youth dancing by diagrams as Eloquence by lecture; but that it was to be learnt by constant practice." (Emerson would go on, of course, to become one of the nation's most popular public speakers and would write extensively about eloquence as well as transcendentalist philosophy.) But Ogilvie also began to cancel lectures here and there, claiming "fatigue." "We are concerned to learn that the debility occasioned by extreme exertion has induced this worthy gentleman to suspend his rhetorical exhibitions for a short time," a New York paper noted, gracefully not mentioning Philosophical Essays at all.[32]

Ogilvie was hardly the first important personage to fall from grace in American culture. We can think of Benedict Arnold's defection to the British side during the American Revolution, Alexander Hamilton's public confession to having an affair with Maria Reynolds, or Aaron Burr's trial for treason. Yet those men had built their careers by amassing political clout going back years to their military service in the Revolution. Ogilvie, in contrast, now saw the very thing that had granted him celebrity—his eloquence—called into question, even if he continued to sell tickets to his performances.[33]

Ironically, the turn against Ogilvie provided one more step toward building a celebrity culture that would eventually emerge in the United States. If once his celebrity had provided a reason for a divided public to share interest in a single famous person, now the rising tide of antipathy against him gave Americans something new to share: the pleasure in collective condemnation and, perhaps, the possibility of moving collectively away from their previous preoccupation.

Ogilvie had had his fill of insults from American writers; it was time to leave. In March 1817, he boarded the ship Erin sailing to England. He had been in the United States for twenty-three years, his entire adult life. On the eve of departure, he sent a letter to a Virginia friend that made its way into the Richmond Enquirer and thence rapidly circulated through newspapers around the country. In it, he intimated a hope for "success in Great Britain as an Orator or as an Author" and dropped one line that received much attention. "I carry with me little money, but I carry proud and precious recollections, and no inconsiderable stock of practical experience," he wrote. Some editors who merely paraphrased the letter decided to embellish that point. "Though he might have amassed a fortune in America, he sailed for England with little more than sufficed to pay his passage, procure books and defray some necessary travelling expenses on his arrival," one commented, relishing the schadenfreude. As delicious as it might have been at the time to imagine him as practically broke, such accounts were certainly deceived by Ogilvie's overly modest assessment of his finances. Just a single night's ticket sales from his six-hundred-person New York event would have grossed a breathtaking six hundred dollars. No matter how imprudent he had been with his funds, he certainly had a healthy pocketbook by the time he left.[34]

It's more tempting to speculate on his expectations about continuing his speaking career in England, Scotland, and Ireland than to ponder the size of his wallet. Perhaps he hoped that his American celebrity would precede him. Alternately, he might have feared that the malicious accounts of Philosophical Essays would have crossed the Atlantic and prejudiced critics there. Whatever direction his thoughts took him, one thing is certain: somewhere along the way, between his days in Kentucky to his departure from New York, he had resumed taking opium.[35]

His friends had high hopes for him — and not just for his speaking career. He had conversed so frequently about his family's connections to the earldom of Findlater that his closest confidants believed he would find a fortune upon his arrival. "Ogilvie I hear is now Earl of Findlater," a friend wrote to Thomas Jefferson in 1814. In response, Jefferson expressed no doubts as to his becoming the new earl. "Mr. Ogilvie left us four days ago, on a tour of health," he replied, "which is to terminate at N. York from whence he will take his passage to Britain to recieve livery and seisin [an ancient ceremony to convey property] of his new dignities and fortunes."[36]

"New dignities and fortunes" — what better description of a man's high hopes for his future, what more glittering promise? Imagine Ogilvie's delight upon making his way to London, the largest city in the Western world, ten times the size of the United States' largest city, and the capital of Anglophone literature and culture — and reading a notice about himself in London's *Morning Post* that described him as having "for many years enjoyed a high reputation throughout the United States of America, for public recitations." Maybe things were looking up.[37]

CHAPTER 12

"A Very Extraordinary Orator" in Britain,

1817–1820

"We understand that a very extraordinary orator, by the name of OGILVIE, has recently arrived in England from America, where he has for some years past attracted great attention, by the power and peculiarity of his eloquence," London's *Morning Post* announced in June 1817, anticipating his first performance in the city. "This Gentleman is a native of Scotland," the writer continued, who "has only made use of the United States as a probationary school of practice." Americans might have agreed that London was the superior stage even as they would have bristled at the notion that James Ogilvie's long American career had merely been a trial run. In fact, he had tried to give the opposite impression on the eve of his departure from New York, when he had sent a letter to a friend, intending it for circulation in American papers. No matter how successful he might become in Great Britain, he wrote, "I cannot imagine, that any prospect of distinction or usefulness can present itself there, so attractive and delightful, as that of returning to the U. States a few years hence, and making a steady and systematic effort to promote the cultivation of Oratory."[1]

The forty-four-year-old Ogilvie did his best to characterize himself as "very extraordinary" for London readers, advertising how prominent he had become in the United States. He told London's *Morning Chronicle* that his American audiences had "repeatedly exceeded 900, and rarely, even in the smallest towns, fallen short of 200 respectable persons of both sexes, and of all denominations." A few months later when he spoke in Cheltenham, west of London, he told the local paper that "he has repeatedly addressed one thousand persons, often six hundred, and seldom fewer than three or four hundred." Both claims embroidered the facts. Glimpsing the gap between them (was it nine hundred or a thousand? "seldom fewer than" two hundred or three hundred?) captures Ogilvie's struggles to attract audiences of the same size across the Atlantic.[2]

He did not become a celebrity in Britain, which increasingly ate away at him despite the fact that his performances almost always succeeded during his three and a half years in England and Scotland. A different person might well have seen this ability to sell tickets and nearly always garner praise as success. But perhaps because of the savaging of his *Philosophical Essays* in the months before his departure from the United States, Ogilvie found it discouraging that he could not blaze through the British cultural scene as a shining star. Tracing his British successes and asking why they never brought him celebrity illuminates a great deal about the varied workings of celebrity on the two sides of the ocean during the 1810s. It also reveals unexpected differences between the two nations, especially their distinct media climates—elements that made it even harder for Ogilvie.[3]

Many of the particular pressures experienced by celebrities have become familiar in the twenty-first century, most of all the toxic combination of a growing narcissistic reliance on public adoration and the difficulty of maintaining one's reputation in the public eye. Likewise, we're familiar with the side effects: the drug busts, the breakdowns, the attempts to rebrand and reboot stalling careers. Ogilvie lived during an era that lacked those boom-and-bust whirligigs of later forms of celebrity culture. He had built his career without the aid of agents and handlers. Now, when he found himself earning less attention, he likewise had to manage those pressures on his own.[4]

He won praise in Britain. Praise, however, did not diminish his growing sense of dismay. As the months passed, James Ogilvie grew increasingly despairing in his quest for British celebrity.

Compared with those who helped with his American career, Ogilvie's British friends and patrons looked different. He had built his early American fame by using social networks of elites, starting in Virginia and spreading throughout the cities, towns, and communities of the new United States. He had used those networks to advance his career—their parlor gatherings, dinner parties, gossip and letter-writing networks, and, above all, their eagerness to assist a humble and talented man. Finding comparable patrons in Britain would have benefited his career in similar ways. He did not find them.[5]

The friends he did make in Britain, however, offered an intellectual intensity that offered its own pleasures. Almost immediately upon his arrival he arranged to meet his longtime hero, the political philosopher William Godwin, who helped to introduce Ogilvie to a dynamic circle of writers and critics. Ogilvie had been riveted by Godwin's *Political Justice* as a young man—an attraction to political radicalism and avowed atheism that had led to his losing his first teaching job in Fredericksburg two decades earlier. Now, with Godwin's help, he became acquainted with like-minded literary figures who gathered at the Godwin house. Indeed, at first, Ogilvie visited the house almost daily. Godwin's daughter Mary, who was deep into the writing of *Frankenstein*, shared her father's house with her husband, the poet Percy Bysshe Shelley. In turn, Ogilvie introduced Godwin to his American friends, including Washington Irving.[6]

A welcoming host, Godwin believed in the redemptive value of conversation. Discussion "is the road to truth; and the custom of speaking in public gradually imparts a facility of expressing sentiments impromptu. And the perception is shaped by dispute," another young man recalled Godwin telling him during such meetings. This guest found these conversations especially valuable because Godwin's aim seemed to be the pursuit of truth rather than "to shine as a talker." "He cared not to be lionized, or to lecture for the passing entertainment of people assembled in a drawing room to amuse themselves. . . . He never sharpened himself for display, nor did he seek to wrap himself up in the pomposity of the 'great man.'" For Ogilvie, those conversations took a different path than the ones he had engaged in for nearly a decade of courting patrons and supporters. Over the course of his first four months in London, he appears in Godwin's meticulous daily diary forty-nine times, making him one of Godwin's most frequent companions.[7]

Cultivating friendships with Godwin and his circle differed sharply from Ogilvie's courting of influential elites in the United States because, however notable as intellectuals, these figures had comparatively little social influence. Godwin's own social power had reached a notably low point. In fact, several years earlier, he had become so inconsequential in public life that Percy Shelley assumed he must be dead. Broke and barely able to hang onto his rented house in what one scholar generously termed a "not very salubrious" neighborhood near the Old Bailey prison where public executions took place, Godwin was simply in no position to help an aspiring performer find wealthy patrons in London. Ogilvie gained a great deal in the course of these many conversations with men he admired, but these contacts did not provide him with the social cachet that would raise his profile with influential elites.[8]

Some of his American patrons happened to be in London, but they too had little effect. Eight years earlier in Boston, John Quincy Adams had welcomed him into his home and introduced him to powerful elites, and he was now in London serving as the U.S. minister to Great Britain after the War of 1812. But when Ogilvie called on him, Adams was too busy to help him navigate the London social scene. Even if he had been available, however, as an outsider himself, Adams's own influence paled in comparison to what it had been in Boston. Likewise, Washington Irving offered companionship and commiseration but was busy seeking his own patronage and support. As a result, Ogilvie found himself working harder than he had in years to court elites, and English society proved much more difficult to crack. Back in the United States, one of the first to write letters of introduction for him had been the nation's president. But in Britain he found no equivalent to Thomas Jefferson; the social hierarchy appeared more intricate, attentive to divisions by class, and rife with subtle social codes unfamiliar to him.[9]

Well-connected friends might have warned him, for example, against initiating his lecture career during the dog days of summer in London, when so much of the ticket-buying public abandoned the city for cooler locales. He performed anyway every Saturday night in Freemason's Tavern through July and August 1817. At first his audiences were small, but his lectures gradually became more popular, and the early praise seemed promising. One newspaper announced that "we have never witnessed on any similar occasion, a more earnest and unbroken attention" given to a performer, and noted that his talk "drew forth loud and uncommon plaudits." Another explained: "At a season rendered peculiarly unpropitious, by the absence of that class of persons whose patronage and countenance are most essential to the success of every public exhibition, he had the satisfaction to address audiences, encreasing in number, and composed of respectable persons of both sexes, and of all denominations." Irving likewise reported to a mutual friend: "His lectures had been very well attended considering the season; his audiences applauded and the papers speak well of him." Ogilvie, according to Irving, "seems to be very well satisfied."[10]

He enjoyed his greatest success when he returned home to Aberdeen, Scotland, during late 1817 and the early weeks of 1818. Since he had left that city nearly twenty-five years earlier, he hadn't seen his family. His parents had died years earlier. Of his ten siblings, eight of whom survived to adulthood, none had married, none of the boys had followed their father and grandfathers into the ministry, and three had died while abroad (two in the West Indies and another in India). Now his three sisters lived together in an Aberdeen house, assisted financially by their youngest brother Simson, who lived nearby and had a successful career as an advocate (lawyer). Not long after his return to the city, the five remaining Ogilvie siblings developed a plan: he would perform just a single time in Aberdeen, giving his popular lecture on beneficence, after which he would donate all the proceeds to one of his sisters' many charities, the Society for Providing Clothes for the Destitute Poor. He would charge five shillings per ticket, comparable to the one dollar he had been charging in the United States. Despite his long-standing family ties to the city and the region, his advertisements insisted on calling him "Mr. Ogilvie, from America," perhaps because that designation gave his performance an extra sense of novelty.[11]

The lecture could not have gone better. Local papers rhapsodized about his talents and insisted that auditors would find themselves highly satisfied. "It rarely happens that public expectation is raised so high, and seldomer still that it is gratified so amply," the *Aberdeen Journal* wrote. The *Aberdeen Chronicle* professed that "it has never been our fortune to attend an entertainment more purely intellectual, or more highly subservient to the promotion of refined Taste and enlightened Benevolence, than was afforded the Inhabitants of this City by Mr. OGILVIE." These reviewers insisted that their appreciation was not easily won, particularly because of their distrust of American taste. "From whatever we had learned of American Society and Literature, we dreaded that a more highly sea-soned repast would be requisite for their palate, than the more chastened taste of British auditors could relish," the *Chronicle* continued. "It affords us great sat-isfaction to perceive, that our Trans-Atlantic Brethren have made such progress in one of the noblest of the arts, as to have justly appreciated his extraordinary attainments." The acclaim resulting from this lecture proved so overwhelming that he scheduled several more benefit lectures, including one for the Aberdeen Society for the Education of the Deaf and Dumb, which promptly voted to make him an honorary member.[12]

Success like this was a far cry from his impoverished college days as a scholar-ship student, when his singular intellectual achievement had been trying to one-up a rival with poetry in *The Ogilviad*. To win such applause must have been ex-hilarating—as if he had come full circle. His brother Simson was particularly impressed and resolved to set aside his law practice to join Ogilvie on his tour and help manage his career. According to a friend who clearly disapproved of the decision, Simson believed he might help his brother "secure the golden har-vest which his genius must necessarily produce, but which his philosophic in-difference to self would doubtless neglect." (This friend added sardonically that Ogilvie's "indifference" to money was a sham. "None could talk with greater con-tempt of money, but none knew the value of a shilling better.")[13]

He and Simson set off in mid-January 1818 for Edinburgh, where Ogilvie scheduled three evening performances at the Assembly Rooms, a grand venue on George Street in the city's fashionable New Town. Ogilvie had cultivated enough support from literary friends that he felt confident he would find "exactly such an audience as a man of talent could have desired" there. Surely, he believed, be-tween the ecstatic Aberdonian newspaper reviews and his friends' support, he might begin in earnest to build his fame.[14]

Edinburgh, a longtime literary and cultural capital in Great Britain (and home to the critics whom Lord Byron savaged in his satirical *English Bards, and Scotch Re-viewers*), had built the Assembly Rooms by public subscription several decades earlier as a site for dances, political meetings, social gatherings for drinking tea and playing cards, and musical performances. The building had been made even more elegant with the recent addition of crystal chandeliers, plaster ceiling roses, and mirrors. A renovation proposed in 1816 promised to create a dome with a magnificent lantern light at the center and other alterations designed to enhance the acoustics and the flow between rooms. One traveler described the interior of the main ballroom as "characterized by simplicity, lightness, and ele-gance, rather than by richness" and distinguished by "handsome fluted pilasters, of the Corinthian order, resting on the floor and supporting the cornice of the room; . . . The elegance of the whole is summed up in the rich cut crystal lustres suspended from the ceiling." The sheer size of the main ballroom, at 92 by 42 feet (3,864 square feet) with 40-foot ceilings, gave it an intimidating grandeur that announced Edinburgh's reputation for science and letters.[15]

Ogilvie did not succeed in Edinburgh, although the surviving records are so thin and contradictory that it's difficult to ascertain what went wrong. On the one hand, a friend reported that Ogilvie had returned to London afterward "full of health and spirits from his success in Scotland," an experience so stimulating that he had successfully "overcome his formidable enemy laudanum, and looks like another being" after kicking the opium habit. On the other hand, in a letter written several years later, another friend characterized Ogilvie's talks as a "catastrophe." Since neither man attended the lectures, a better measure might be reports in the local newspapers—except almost none exist. The *Caledonian Mercury* gave him a positive review following his first lecture, although it noted that Ogilvie's audience was "rather select than numerous." The bulk of the review enumerated the lecture's main contentions, largely without editorial comment, concluding that "he has a full and commanding voice, well adapted for recitation, and his general manner is extremely pleasing." The author noted that Ogilvie had been "repeatedly applauded by the audience." Such an account certainly paled in comparison to the enthusiastic reviews he had received after his Aberdeen performances—and it would be the last review to appear. Edinburgh newspapers and magazines simply ignored his final two performances, and Simson returned to his legal practice in Aberdeen.[16]

As tempting as it is to speculate about whether or how he had failed onstage—did he forget passages? did his opium habit inhibit his performance?—the more apt conclusion to draw from the contradictory reports is that, without the fulsome support of a crowd of elites who might soften the response to a poor performance, and without a terrific success in a cultural center like Edinburgh or London, he struggled to build his reputation on his own.

We can also see that for Ogilvie, receiving negative reviews would have better than nothing at all. Even vicious accounts would have created a sense of controversy: they might have prompted attendees to come witness what they anticipated to be a disaster, thus allowing Ogilvie to adjust after a bad night. Bad reviews might also have prompted his supporters to defend him in the papers. No matter how discouraging or enraging, poor reviews would have signaled that people nevertheless wanted to talk about him. No reviews at all amounted to the worst possible situation: it conveyed the message that he was best ignored.[17]

The silence of Edinburgh's newspapers was a glaring exception during Ogilvie's British tour. Following his other appearances, newspaper critics offered a consistent stream of reviews flattering and uncontroversial enough to herald a night's talk as a success, yet unexceptional enough to crush Ogilvie's dreams of rising to celebrity. In the United States, papers had compared him to Cicero and had marveled at his magical ability to transfix a room. English critics nearly always found his presentations original, commended his plan for the expansion of oratory, and admired his ideas and performances, but did so without hyperbole. An 1818 report in a London paper explained that "he was listened to throughout with the most profound attention, and received repeated testimonies of decided approbation from a numerous audience." The following year, the *Bath Chronicle* insisted that "it is scarcely possible, that any candidate for literary or oratorical distinction could have invited public attention in a manner more dignified, manly, and respectable; or have experienced a more flattering reception: nor will we impeach or disparage the liberality of Bath, by harbouring or expressing a doubt about this gentleman's success in this city." Ogilvie likely appreciated the kind words but would not have missed the hint in that last phrase that the author might indeed have a doubt about his lectures' success.[18]

He was anxious to spark more than polite compliments—in part because of shrinking audiences. By early 1820, his advertisements began to request that critics publish "whatever they may deem faulty, defective, or in any shape censurable in Mr. O's Lectures, Specimens of Oratory, Recitations, or Criticisms" and offered free admission to members of the press. Newspapers declined to offer that degree of criticism and instead lamented the public's inattention and offered even more praise to the orator. "Those who are capable of duly estimating the merits of this interesting branch of education," the *Bath & Cheltenham Gazette* explained, "cannot fail" to find his lectures "an exquisite source of mental enjoyment." Another local paper reported "with sentiments of mingled indignation and shame" that his audiences were so thin that he could not defray the expense of renting Bath's elegant Upper Assembly Rooms. As a result, Ogilvie dropped his ticket prices from five shillings to four, and then to three. The praise he received allowed his lectures to fade into the background, doomed to be neither adored nor hated.[19]

Without the help of patronage networks, ecstatic press, or a striking success in a major city, he fought an uphill battle. That kind of attention and support could have made up for a flaw in Ogilvie's plan: that oratory played a different role in Great Britain than it did in the United States.

The British certainly appreciated the spoken word. They published books on the subject, collected great speeches, organized debating societies, urged the spread of the elocutionary movement in schools, and attended lectures by learned speakers. If asked, most citizens would have attested that their nation's orators had achieved the greatest heights of eloquence since the ancient Romans. One of those who celebrated British oratory was Ogilvie's new acquaintance William Hazlitt, whose two-volume *Eloquence of the British Senate* had collected hundreds of parliamentary speeches to commemorate "the wisdom of the wise, and the strength of the strong, whose praises were inscribed on every window-shutter or brick-wall, or floated through the busy air, upborne by the shouts and huzzas of a giddy multitude." Their achievements in oratory served as one pillar of a British sense of superiority and national unity.[20]

Nevertheless, oratory played a different role in the United States not least because Americans had fewer illusions about their talents for public speech. For them, fostering eloquence was aspirational. To improve their national oratory appeared crucial for a republic that drew so much inspiration from the ancient republics. As Ogilvie began touring in 1808, his gifts for the spoken word appeared to answer inchoate American needs: desires for strong and eloquent leadership, spaces where women and men could gather and think together about matters of public importance, reasons to believe that oratory might become a hallmark of American national pride. No wonder his stated rationale for his lecture tour evolved over the course of those first few years. Whereas at first he simply displayed eloquence, he quickly came to suggest that his lectures constituted an argument for oratory itself in the American Republic; and by the 1810s he advocated for the construction of halls of oratory to better establish the medium of public speech as a part of urban American life. In other words, it was Americans' perceived shortcomings in oratory that made Ogilvie's performances so resonant, so symbolic, so influential. His performances had provided glimpses of how oratory might provide the cultural glue required to knit a vast, varied, and fractious nation together.[21]

Celebrity had also played a different role in the United States, where no true celebrity culture yet existed—those entrepreneurs, institutions, and media technologies that work together to heighten the public's fascination with women and men perceived to be talented and influential. Ogilvie's gifts for public speech and his celebrity grew up together in a comparatively primitive media climate, combining to provide new visions for how a dispersed United States might join together to discuss civic matters and, no matter how regionally disparate, admire together the talents of one of their own (naturalized) citizens. In contrast, Britain enjoyed a far more elaborate celebrity culture and a dense set of media networks. In London one could find any number of gossip rags detailing Lord Byron's sexual scandals, engravings that portrayed the actress Sarah Siddons in her most haunting roles, portraits of the most attractive members of the royal family, and information about the fashionable clothes worn by famous ladies and gentlemen.[22]

With the benefit of hindsight, we can see why he could have achieved success but not celebrity for his performances in Britain. We must remember, however, that Ogilvie lacked such perspective. His ambitions had only grown more acute over the years, and now he registered a deepening sense of failure.

There was one final way that he might have risen to stardom: if he had inherited the earldom of Findlater, about which he'd hinted to his American friends for years.[23]

To be sure, telling Americans that he was the heir to an earldom might have been the same kind of tall tale spun by other British ex-patriots to hoodwink or swindle gullible people. Ogilvie's motives might have been less underhanded; perhaps he had repeated the fib so many times during his fifteen years in the United States that he came to believe it was possible. Yet, again, Ogilvie's immediate family might have harbored fantasies of inheritance that led him to hold out hope. Rather than assume that he lied outright about his claim to the earldom, it's worth examining the widespread confusion about this title, and lines of descent more generally, that prevailed in Great Britain and its former colonies.[24]

Certainly the fate of the earldom of Findlater appeared uncertain. The previous earl, who also carried the title of earl of Seafield, had died childless and without male siblings in 1811, opening up the possibility that the title, the magnificent house in the north of Scotland, the lands, and all the associated wealth would pass to a different branch of the family. That wealth was significant. Newspapers estimated that the annual income from Findlater's estates alone amounted to some forty thousand pounds, which today would make him a millionaire many times over. In straightforward cases of descent, sons of deceased earls simply presented their family's diploma for the earldom, official coats of arms, and any other relevant documents to the Committee of Privileges within the House of Lords in London, the final arbiter of succession cases. But when no clear heir existed, determining which claimant should inherit was fraught with complications. In cases like the earldoms of Findlater and Seafield, with no children or younger brothers to assume the two titles, the case became opaque, resulting in a number of distant relatives submitting claims for each title. In this case, the Committee of Privileges granted the Findlater mansion, lands, and associated wealth to a second cousin who, because of the cousin's distinct line of descent, inherited only the title of the earl of Seafield. Although the committee passed the wealth associated with the earldom of Findlater to this cousin, it determined that the title of Findlater would become dormant, as no claimant had a clear line of succession.[25]

If Ogilvie had come back to Scotland with the intention of applying for the title, as he'd told his American friends, he left no evidence that he ultimately followed through with a claim. But if he had broached the topic with his lawyer brother Simson, he likely would have run up against the unspoken rules and procedures that shielded the British aristocracy, rules that he had ignored during his twenty-five years in the United States. These procedures were vague. Would a commoner like Ogilvie have been seriously considered for an earldom by the Committee of Privileges? In theory, yes, but probably not. By the eighteenth century one's ancestry ostensibly mattered most of all, yet virtually all successful titles passed to men who already possessed wealth, land, and high standing. In general, the committee usually held to the maxim that "one had to be able to hold up one's head." They ultimately granted all the Findlater wealth to the previous earl's cousin, a baronet's son, who had been declared "in the most hopeless case of mental derangement" more than a decade earlier. The new earl might be mad, but he came from the right class to inherit the title. Poorer distant relatives like Ogilvie rarely submitted claims for peerages, particularly as they would have had to bear the legal costs of advancing a well-documented genealogical case with slim hopes for triumphing in the end. To one who'd lived so long in the United States, which had no hereditary titles, such aristocratic gatekeeping must have felt exasperatingly archaic.[26]

Contemporary Britons found succession as confusing as it was compelling. Newspapers all over Great Britain breathlessly reported contradictory and usually false news about the fate of the earldom of Findlater during the 1810s. Several proclaimed that a clerk named Ogilvie in the War Office had been granted the title and lands. Others declared that a different Ogilvie from Inchmartine— or yet another Ogilvie from Boyne—had received the nod. Some papers reported that the two titles had been separated but provided inaccurate information about which family members would receive either one. Meanwhile, one member of the extended family sought to bribe officials to help him gain the earldom and wound up in Canongate Jail in Edinburgh instead. One member of this vast family simply pronounced himself the earl of Findlater and began racking up debts in that name, signing himself "Findlater" in grandiosely large, elegant lettering across the bottoms of his letters. Thus, even though the Committee of Privileges had rendered a decision in 1811, all this conflicting information permitted continued confusion in the public mind for years.[27]

Inheriting the earldom almost certainly would have boosted Ogilvie's career with a British public that followed such news. Indeed, Lord Byron's own celebrity status derived not only from his poetic talent but at least in part from the public's fascination with his exploits as a titled aristocrat. If Ogilvie had won a peerage, however improbably, it would have resolved certain problems: it would have guaranteed attendance by fashionable British social circles and far more enthusiastic interest from the print media, which had already shown such curiosity about the fate of the title of Findlater.[28]

Ogilvie never became the earl of Findlater, but he got lucky with an inheri-

tance after all. In a different story, this windfall might have been a deus ex ma-
china—one of those turns of events that suddenly and miraculously resolves all
of a protagonist's problems. This, however, is not that story.

As the family's oldest son, Ogilvie inherited half an estate called Dunnydeer,
about eighteen miles from Ogilvie's hometown in rural Aberdeenshire. In the
evocative, archaic legal boilerplate language of the sasine (a document that
Americans call a deed or conveyance), Ogilvie now shared possession with a
cousin of the estate "with all the Mill Lands, astrict Multures and Sequels of the
same, houses, bigging, Yards, orchyards, lofts, crofts, Mosses, Muirs, Marshes,
Fishings, Pasturages, with the pendicles thereof." Half of a small estate in Aberdeenshire might have been a far cry from the earldom of Findlater, but the money
was real, granting security. As Irving described it, the income from Dunnydeer
"is sufficient for all his moderate wants"—a kind of consolation prize that, by
1819, Ogilvie dearly needed. He would not have needed to live at Dunnydeer to
profit from the annual rents and other income from the estate. The notion that
he had inherited a Scottish estate might even have revived his credibility among
friends who'd long heard about Findlater. He was an heir, after all.[29]

But rather than turn events toward a happy ending, the inheritance played
only a small role in a life that was beginning to unravel.

First, he squandered his half of Dunnydeer by relinquishing it to his co-
inheritor cousin for a cash settlement of three thousand pounds, a considerable but not extravagant lump sum. He did so apparently without informing his
siblings, who doubtless would have disapproved because of the steady income
it could have provided. Of course, he had no experience as a landlord and landowner, nor an inclination to learn. The choice to settle for cash probably had
more to do with his eagerness to continue his lecture tour rather than help manage an estate or collect rents. It also gave him a financial cushion—but no bulwark against mounting frustrations.[30]

His friends agonized about how the decline in public attention would affect
his disposition. One former student visiting London explained: "I fear very much
that if he has not at least in part been successful that the disappointment will
prey upon his spirits. Should there however be one plank to lay hold of, his temper is so very sanguine as to induce him to persevere much longer than is usual."
In a similar fashion, Washington Irving wrote home to a friend in New York that
Ogilvie continued to deliver lectures even though he had "never had a fair chance
at the London folks. I think his success here very problematical, though vastly
his inferiors have succeeded; but there is a great caprice in public taste in London." Irving believed Ogilvie deserved better luck. "I see him frequently, and am
more convinced than ever of the pureness of his intentions, and goodness of his
heart. He is quite a visionary but a most interesting one."[31]

Ogilvie had undertaken a difficult task. He tried to move from the height of American celebrity to the British scene, a task fraught with difficulties. He arrived with expectations he simply did not have when he had begun the tour ten years earlier. In 1808, he had set off on his first journey to Staunton, Virginia, by modestly referring to it as a "romantic excursion"—and by "romantic" he conveyed unusual, fanciful, impractical—or, to use Irving's slightly more patronizing term, "visionary." No such modesty attended his trip to Britain. He appears to have placed faith in his own essential merit, believing that fame would eventually follow. Hence, when his inflated newspaper claims about his American audiences failed to pique British interest and fill his halls, the sense of slippage must have been humiliating. His friends increasingly distrusted his recollections of his American celebrity. One wrote bitterly that, although he believed Ogilvie had been successful across the Atlantic, it was "not nearly to the extent that his self-love had flatteringly told him."[32]

Irving's faith in his friend—filtered through the bemused characterization of Ogilvie as a visionary—was not shared by all. He had begun to alienate people as his moods changed with his vacillating success on the rostrum. William Godwin proved the most skeptical. He told a mutual friend angrily that Ogilvie had "failed totally in his exhibitions" and had "dropped his visits to me, I believe because I saw pretty clearly in what his endeavors would terminate." In contrast to the summer of 1817, when they had met forty-nine times in just four months, they saw each other only eight times during the first eight months of 1818, reflecting the chill between them. Ogilvie ultimately sought reconciliation. "I cannot close this letter," Ogilvie wrote to Godwin in early 1819, "without an expression of sincere regret, that the advantage and satisfaction of an occasional personal intercourse with you, have been so much interrupted by a tone of feeling and tone of conversation, which can produce only disadvantage and dissatisfaction," attempting to chalk up their disagreement to a combination of poor health and unfortunate circumstances. His apology worked enough for their friendly meetings to resume, and over the next twelve months Ogilvie appears seventy-six times in Godwin's diary, indicating that on average they met about every four or five days.[33]

Other friends found him growing narcissistic and prone to unrealistic expectations of success, a moodiness made worse by his return to heavy use of laudanum. One described him in shocking terms. Whereas once Ogilvie had appeared "a man of lively temper," he now seemed paranoid, "always jealous of not being respected as a luminary," and increasingly inclined to exaggerate his American successes. "He ever made the most favourable impression at first, [but] he was fickle and changeable in his friendships and acquaintances, while his temper was occasionally so fretful that it would have been impossible for any one to have been long intimate with him." This friend believed these changes in Ogilvie's personality resulted from his reliance on massive amounts of the opiate. "Before rising in the morning he generally took half a wine-glassful of laudanum, and, when he intermitted the practice he fell into a state of horror— 'loathing life and light of day.' Had you seen him thus!—It was not merely that a death like paleness overspread his features, and that his hollow eye was fixed and glazed, but that every sunk muscle had the apparent rigidity of a cor[p]se." Ogilvie had twice before succeeded in beating his need for opium—once in Kentucky during the late fall and winter of 1811, and again during the spring of 1818 after his successes in Aberdeen. This return to heavy use must have seemed an additional failure.[34]

For the first time, friends described Ogilvie as addicted to the drug. The term *addiction* was slowly coming into use in the late 1810s to describe compulsive use of substances like tobacco, alcohol, opium, and coffee, but it would take decades before the term brought together the combination of pity and disgust that it conveyed by the twentieth century. As a result, it's striking to see a friend describe Ogilvie in these terms. "You are aware of his having been adicted to the use of opium, but I apprehend that you never suspected the excess to which he carried this destructive species of debauchery, nor yet its dreadful effects," a mutual friend wrote to William Godwin. Users typically measured their laudanum consumption in drops, with medical reference works recommending between ten and fifty drops for various ailments; one of the most famous addicts of the day, Thomas De Quincey, confessed reaching a height of ten thousand drops per day at the same time that Ogilvie had apparently begun drinking it by the half-wineglassful. As De Quincey would explain in his *Confessions of an English Opium-Eater* in 1821, ingestion to this degree could not possibly grant the "spells of pleasure" and mental clarity it once did. Rather, users found they had to keep taking exorbitant amounts simply to avoid the "tortures" of withdrawal. De Quincey's descriptions of trying to withdraw paint horrific scenes. "Even when four months had passed" of gradually decreasing his daily ingestion of laudanum, he explained, he still spent his days "agitated, writhing, throbbing, palpitating, shattered," feeling like someone who'd been put to the rack. "I saw that I must die if I continued the opium," De Quincey confessed. "I determined, therefore, if that should be required, to die in throwing it off." Overly dramatic? Perhaps, but Ogilvie shared the propensity for drama. If *Confessions of an English Opium-Eater* became a touchstone narrative about succumbing to opium and slowly overcoming addiction, it also suggests how hard it would have been for Ogilvie to succeed in withdrawing one year only to slip back into habitual use the next.[35]

Gradually all of these concerns merged. Once a celebrated orator who sold hundreds of tickets to each performance, he now found himself drinking laudanum by the glassful, agonizing about his mixed success as a public figure, increasingly estranging himself from his friends and family, self-absorbed. In September 1820, he decided to return to Aberdeen, perhaps to revive some of his success on the rostrum and find comfort with his siblings. He stopped in Perth, a small city some forty miles north of Edinburgh on the way to Aberdeen, and rented a room. Perched on a bluff on the east side of the River Tay, the city was "elegant and well built" according to travelers' guidebooks, busy with linen- and cotton-weaving mills and import mercantile establishments. In all, it appeared a quintessential Scottish city: bustling, tidy, with a populace absorbed in business rather than culture.[36]

While he paused on his journey, he took the time to send a note to a friend explaining that the closer he got to Aberdeen, "the scene of his former triumph," the more he believed that "he must return with disgrace, [and] his heart died within him," as this friend explained afterward. He waited for his brother Simson to come from Aberdeen to meet him as he'd requested. They had fought over money, and Ogilvie might have wanted to resolve it. But when Simson ignored the letter, Ogilvie found himself waiting interminably, feeling "himself despised and neglected by all the world."[37]

On September 12, 1820, he walked out of his inn toward the river in what one friend later described as "a fit of despair." He crossed the dark granite bridge over the Tay, which rushed below, and headed toward Kinnoul Wood, which rose sharply over the city to provide grand views of river bend, the surrounding farmland, and distant hills. If you visit Perth and walk up to the Wood from downtown, you soon find yourself winded; it's easy to imagine how hard such a dramatic uphill hike would have been for the scrawny, laudanum-addicted, forty-seven-year-old Ogilvie. Nearly ten years earlier, while in self-imposed isolation in Kentucky, he had climbed a hill next to his cabin every day as part of his campaign to rid himself of the opium habit. Now, how many times did he stop to catch his breath? How did his physical weakness compound his fragile emotional state? Could he have made it all the way to the top?[38]

Once he got to the Wood, Ogilvie shot himself in the head.[39]

CHAPTER 13

The Meanings of Melancholy,

1780–1820

I was almost done with my research for this book when I stumbled across a letter that unsettled my views of James Ogilvie. Sitting in the Historical Society of Pennsylvania—a lovely, hushed, book-lined, high-ceilinged research library with a big arched window at one end—I opened up one more volume of letters, hoping to find information about one of Ogilvie's performances in Philadelphia. Instead, I found a letter that dated back to 1797, when Ogilvie was a twenty-three-year-old Virginia teacher. In it, he begged Benjamin Rush, the nation's most eminent physician, for medical help for his melancholy.[1]

Over the course of four closely written pages, Ogilvie described "a malady which has for some time past greatly alarmed and distressed me." He depicted going through periods of intense "elevated . . . spirits and intellect" during which he was "in sensible to fatigue and fearless of danger, happy in myself and anxious to promote the happiness of others." But these periods were "regularly followed by two and latterly by 3 or 4 months of deplorable melancholy and an almost total incapacity to write converse or even to think with vigour and satisfaction." "At times," he wrote, "my consciousness is absolutely suspended for any other purpose except presenting a dreary distresful and disconsolate sense of impotency; My nerves are extremely irritable and the very semblance of mental or bodily exertion painful." These periods of dark melancholy were so excruciating, he confessed, that he had contemplated suicide. Moreover, "for the last twelve-months this malady has increased very alarmingly and in spite of every effort I can make [it] continues to bow down my fortitude and mangle my happiness."[2]

After reading this, I sat back in my chair, stunned. For I recognized that, if Ogilvie had been alive today, he might be diagnosed with what we now call manic depression or bipolar disorder.[3]

Ogilvie had mentioned his melancholy in other letters, but I had disregarded it—because to me, as well as to his friends, the word failed to convey the seriousness of his agony. I had, in essence, viewed his condition through the eyes of his peers. One friend, a Scottish historian named George Brodie, wrote to William Godwin trying to reconsider what he knew about Ogilvie's melancholy in the light of his suicide. "When he told me that he was subject to low spirits, I naturally concluded that he merely complained of an evil to which most men are more or less exposed." Brodie explained that he was shocked to find that "the same language had conveyed a very different picture to each—that mine was a slight shade, his an appalling gloom." With only terms like *low spirits* or *melancholy* to encompass everything from mild sadness to deep depression, even a writer as hyperbolic as Ogilvie could not communicate the depths of his despair. He had delivered lectures on the topic of suicide since 1803, yet, despite telling his friends about his propensity for melancholy, no one realized that he struggled with suicidal ideation himself. Only by scrutinizing the nineteenth-century meanings of melancholy closely can we appreciate the role it played throughout his life. We need to take melancholy seriously.[4]

I wouldn't blame you for wondering why I held this information back, saving it for the end of the book. Perhaps this decision even makes it seem that I've pulled the rug out from under you. This chapter is intended to convince you otherwise. If you had known from the beginning of this book that Ogilvie suffered so, it would have been hard for you to avoid an armchair diagnosis, one that would delimit our understanding of an earlier era with such different ideas about health. You might have interpreted his entire life through the modern lens of a bipolar diagnosis, a term that did not exist for more than a century after his death. Perhaps you would have applied other terms: you would have thought of him as *mentally ill* or concluded that he lived with a *mental disorder* (or even that he was *crazy*), concepts that Ogilvie's contemporaries never applied to him.

Definitions of what we now call "mental health" are historically bound. In Ogilvie's day, no one used the terms *normal* and *abnormal*. These words, along with *crazy*, can belittle or pathologize people in the past in a way that they did not experience during their lifetimes. If you had known from the outset that he experienced such dramatic mood swings, you might have found it difficult to reconcile the fact that, far from hiding or feeling ashamed, Ogilvie revealed these swings to dozens of friends and even to his audiences. In other words, he experienced these highs and lows in an era that confounds us because we live in such a different time, conditioned by medical, pharmaceutical, psychiatric, and therapeutic ideas that did not exist in the early nineteenth century.

"I have been afflicted more or less ever since I can remember," Ogilvie explained in his 1797 letter to Rush, but recently his malady had "encreased in frequency, duration, and virulency." His crashes into "deplorable melancholy" had become so oppressive that "suicide too often obtrudes itself on my mind as my last refuge and my only remedy." Having already sought out at least one local doctor in Virginia, he still lacked solutions. His letter carefully laid out the details of his case to provide Rush with as much information as possible so he might provide help, as he had for others.

Ogilvie described himself as an ambitious, intellectual young man with an uncommonly active imagination, contrasting his melancholic episodes with periods of exceptional good health. "For a week and sometimes a fortnight I seem to possess an almost unlimited command over my facultys," he explained. "I can recal my ideas with great promptitude, combine them with facility and vivacity into any form that the subject requires, words flow at will." His physical health mirrored his excited thoughts and intellectual productivity. "I eat and drink little and with little appetite, my spirits are delightfully chearful and sleep to which I resign myself with reluctance is short, but very refreshing and accompany'd with gay and animating dreams." The value of such a state for an intellectual made his descents into melancholy all the more distressing. For as many as four months "my whole organization is deadened, it distresses me even to articulate and I am unable not only to promote or partake but even to attend to conversation." With these periods of melancholy increasing in duration, no wonder he admitted to Rush that, "if my present disorder proves incurable and much more if it proves progressive, I shall consider life in the light rather of a penalty than a privilege, rather to be endured than enjoy'd."

The letter revealed that he did not believe his periods of terrific energy, creativity, and purpose were part of the problem; these he portrayed as notable but still essential to his baseline intellectual temperament. "All my organs and members participate in the glow of ardour that flashes from my mind," he wrote. These periods were so exhilarating, such perfect experiences of lucidity and intellectual productivity, that they made the melancholic crashes ever more horrifying. The problem was the crippling melancholy.[5]

The very form of his letter was revealing. Written like the case studies that appeared in other medical writing of the day, it indicated that Ogilvie was unusually familiar with published work on the topic. He began the letter in an organized, methodical manner. "In order to convey as precise and compleat a notion of my disorder as I can I will state, first, the condition of mind and body that forerun its recurrences. I will next describe the disorder itself and lastly its principle concomitants which very probably make a part of it." The orderliness of this depiction suggested that he developed the letter over the course of several drafts to ensure that it would provide Rush with the information he might need. Such care might also convince Rush to take his case seriously: Ogilvie portrayed himself as both educated and familiar with medical diagnosis. He described in detail the quality of his digestion and his tendency toward costiveness (constipation), which many doctors linked to melancholy. Such detail suggests that Ogilvie had spent time seeking to understand and resolve his condition and that he placed his faith in science for answers.

By this point, anyone familiar with the broad outlines of what we now call bipolar disorder will have seen the ways that Ogilvie's condition lined up with a psychological diagnosis that only became more common late in the twentieth century. One might well wonder: Why not call it bipolar? What might we learn about Ogilvie by applying more recent psychology?

The terms manic depression and bipolar disorder were coined in the 1950s and 1960s, respectively, to establish a category for a specific range of mood disorders and temperaments that distinguish this condition from others, such as schizophrenia. As they are currently defined, the symptoms include unusual changes in mood, energy, and sleep, ranging between deep depression and unusually high energy or full mania. Depressive periods can lead to suicidal thoughts as well as attempts; they can also lead to abuse of alcohol and narcotics, especially opioids, likely as a means of self-medicating. In contrast, one's high energy periods can include intense creativity, rapid thought and speech, excited sleeplessness, a tendency toward grandiosity, and lack of impulse control, such as reckless spending or hypersexuality. This condition seems to have a strong genetic component, reappearing within families and across generations. Over time, researchers have come to refer to a bipolar spectrum or continuum to encompass the many manifestations of these conditions. Indeed, the several editions of the American Psychiatric Association's *Diagnostic and Statistical Manual of Mental Disorders* (DSM) has broken this diagnosis into four, then five, subgroupings to capture general differences, to acknowledge the capaciousness of this spectrum.[6]

Many individuals suffering from manic depression cycle through both excited highs and depressive lows as Ogilvie did, even as each person's experience might vary in degree of intensity. For some, those highs can range all the way up to a full mania so serious that it can demand hospitalization. The author and clinical psychologist Kay Redfield Jamison describes her own manic periods in conflicted terms, for they start with a wonderful period of euphoria and energy. "When you're high it's tremendous. The ideas and feelings are fast and frequent like shooting stars, and you follow them until you find better and brighter ones. Shyness goes, the right words and gestures are suddenly there, the power to captivate others a felt certainty." Her highs are attended by "feelings of ease, intensity, power, well-being, financial omnipotence, and euphoria." Who wouldn't want to feel like that? Psychologists currently call this hypomania; people in this elevated state can still function on their own and might not be distinguishable as being on the bipolar spectrum. But for Jamison and others, this period of hypomania is fleeting, as full mania commences. "Somewhere, this changes," she continues. "The fast ideas are far too fast, and there are far too many; overwhelming confusion replaces clarity. Memory goes. Humor and absorption on friends' faces are replaced by fear and concern." When people reach these manic states and demonstrate marked impairment in functioning, the DSM advises immediate treatment in the form of hospitalization or medication. A major depressive episode often follows. "Everything previously moving with the grain is now against—you are irritable, angry, frightened, uncontrollable, and enmeshed totally in the blackest caves of the mind," Jamison writes. In her case, her depressions are "awful beyond words or sounds or images." At other points along the spectrum, people encounter fewer highs, milder highs and lows, or suffer primarily deep, long-lasting periods of depression without the ecstatic periods of hypomania. Given this enormous range, one wouldn't be surprised to find future DSM revisions breaking the bipolar spectrum into a series of discrete diagnoses.[7]

These broad outlines of twenty-first-century understandings of the bipolar spectrum certainly capture a range of Ogilvie's self-described conditions: his dramatic highs and lows, his propensity for opium use, his suicidal thoughts. Viewing him as bipolar might shed some light on his experience because it leads us to speculate that these various aspects of his life were interconnected, all looking strikingly similar to a condition that, according to recent estimates, affects between 3 and 5 percent of the populations in the United States and Great Britain today.

Such speculations can be alluring. Some of the elements that we now associate with bipolar disorder raise questions about other parts of Ogilvie's life. When he racked up impossibly high debts during his marriage in 1804 and 1805, could any of that spending have resulted from the lack of impulse control that we find among people today who experience hypomania and mania? His minister-poet father published a popular poem, "Ode to Melancholy," and invoked the theme in dozens of other poems; could this indicate a hereditary thread in the Ogilvie family and perhaps give us hints about why he alone among his many siblings married? Was it a propensity for grandiosity that led him to make such immodest claims about the quality of his *Philosophical Essays*? For that matter, what might such a diagnosis suggest about his marriage, about which we know so little?[8]

The problem with speculations like these is that they tempt us to pick selective moments out of Ogilvie's biography, elements that might confirm this hypothesis, often without much firm evidence—and, in doing so, reduce his life to a psychological diagnosis. Did he run into deep debt during his wife's illness? Bipolar. Did his father write poetry about melancholy? Bipolar. As tempting as those associations are, they lead us to presume that the bundle of symptoms we now call *manic depression* was his "real" condition, and *melancholy* was merely a signpost illustrating his culture's regrettable ignorance. We're tempted to feel distress, wondering how he might have benefited if only people at the time had known this "truth."

The problem with such diagnoses is that they stop us from asking different questions.[9]

To drive this point home, consider one element of Ogilvie's experiences often tied to twenty-first-century presentations of bipolar disorder: narcotics addiction and addiction to opioids in particular. How might we understand his laudanum habit if we see it as linked to his manic depression? Research over the past fifty years has examined the close connection between substance abuse and people on the bipolar spectrum, who are currently believed to be among the most likely of all sufferers of psychiatric disorders to turn to alcohol and narcotics. Opiates are a common choice. Researchers speculate that such abuse likely results from an attempt to moderate the periods of depression and perhaps stop the acceleration from hypomania to full mania. They disagree about whether such self-medication works. Some find that narcotics make the mood shifts even more radical and increase the likelihood of hospitalization for both mania and depression. Other studies indicate that opiates might help alleviate some forms of depression, although funding to advance that research has proved difficult to obtain—not surprising, given concerns about addiction.[10]

Drawing overly tidy parallels between past and present obscures that the opiates used today and the opium- and wine-based laudanum of the nineteenth century differ radically. Laudanum produced highly specific chemical responses. For some ambitious and creative individuals, laudanum seemed to have brought about something like what we now call hypomania, which was how Ogilvie described his earliest use of it. Recall one doctor's description of it: "Its first and most common effect is to excite the intellect, stimulate the imagination, and exalt the feelings into a state of great activity and buoyancy, producing unusual vivacity and brilliancy in conversation." Ogilvie indicated that he took it (at least at first) to bring about that coveted energy and intellectual clarity rather than to moderate his depression or knock himself out at the end of the day. Whereas people today may take opiates to blunt the sharpest edges of their highs and lows, Ogilvie's laudanum habit might have resulted as much from the promise of having on demand an enthusiastic state of mental sharpness—a motivation apparently common among some laudanum users. Without evidence one way or the other (modern drug studies have no reason to study an archaic drug like laudanum), we simply can't know.[11]

Historians hate it when we put people in the past on the psychologist's couch for two main reasons. First, it encourages a false sense of superiority about the present—to lament that Ogilvie lived in an age lacking "real" mental illness diagnoses, or to believe that what we currently call *bipolar* is the "accurate" diagnosis. It's tempting to believe that if he had received a better explanation of and treatment for his condition, he might have survived the worst of his suffering, even though such an explanation did not appear for more than 130 years. He might have found along the way a community of others who likewise struggled with these radical vacillations of mood. But is the modern era so superior to the past? If he had lived in the 1950s or 1960s, he might have been subject to cures like crippling electroshock therapy or lobotomy. Even now it often takes months or years to find treatments that moderate the worst of the manic highs and depressive lows. Lithium, once hailed as a wonder drug, works for fewer than half of those who try it. Other mood stabilizers are likewise finicky and, like so many products on the pharmaceutical market, come with a battery of side effects.[12]

The second reason historians hate armchair diagnoses is that they discourage us from understanding a person's actual experience. Consider what else he might have received along with a term like *bipolar spectrum* in the twentieth century: stigma. "It is much harder telling people that I have bipolar disorder than it was telling them I had anxiety and depression," one representative recent account explains. "The stigma against speaking out about mental illness is causing me more harm than the mental illness itself is." Whereas anxiety and depression have become common enough ailments that they have ceased to seem unusual (even as they, too, vary in seriousness), many even in our allegedly more enlightened world continue to consider mental health conditions like manic depression and schizophrenia as potentially dangerous or violent—as abnormal, perhaps even psychotic. Say what you will about the misleading capaciousness of *melancholy* in the nineteenth century: no one felt stigmatized by it.[13]

Thinking of Ogilvie as bipolar ultimately clouds our understanding of his experience and the world he inhabited. We learn far more if we set aside our twenty-first-century ideas about mental health and take nineteenth-century melancholy seriously.

How could I have missed the seriousness of Ogilvie's melancholy? He wrote about it *all the time*. Everyone seems to have known. He referenced it in his letters; his students, friends, and patrons remarked on it to one another; newspapers made note of it in their columns. He even described his "very anomalous fluctuations of spirits and mental energy" in the long autobiography included in his 1816 *Philosophical Essays*, in which he bemoaned his low periods: "His frozen heart, benumbed faculties, palsied tongue, leaden eye, pallid cheek, Hippocratic face, flaccid arteries and feeble pulse, exhibit the appearance of something spectral and sepulchral, and are accompanied by an unassured consciousness, and a faintness of vital energy." Looking back, I realized that his very openness about his emotions led me to make assumptions that I now found inaccurate. Largest of all was the mistaken assumption that, if his melancholic episodes were truly as terrible as he often described, he would seek to hide them from others. In other words, I needed to come to grips with the fact that he appears to have felt no stigma. In fact, to consider yourself melancholic in the nineteenth century rather than bipolar in the twenty-first had real advantages.[14]

Perhaps one reason I failed to grasp the seriousness of his melancholy was that he so frequently used poetry to describe it. Over and over in his letters, Ogilvie called melancholy his "dim-eyed fiend," a quotation from a book-length eighteenth-century poem called *The Art of Preserving Health* that reads:

> There madness enters; and the dim-eyed fiend,
> Sour melancholy, night and day provokes
> Her own eternal wound. The sun grows pale;
> A mournful, visionary light o'erspreads
> The cheerful face of nature; earth becomes
> A dreary desert, and heaven frowns above.

Ogilvie described visitations by this "fiend" throughout his life. In 1810, he wrote to a friend that "by the most terrible visitation of morbid melancholy and [illegible] apathy I have ever suffered—Day after Day have I languished under the gripe of the 'dim-eyed Fiend' with a restless mind and palsied tongue." In the wake of the misery of those days, however, he had begun "to feel indications of convalescence and renovation and am permitted to anticipate a glorious burst of energy and animation." Again in 1813, he quoted the full "dim-eyed fiend" passage in a letter to a former student in which he described being "under the gripe of one of these overwhelming visitations of collapse and atomy [an emaciated, withered state] to which I am organically and irreversibly liable.—In the endless degrees and varieties of painful sensations, I cannot imagine any much more infernally adapted to test human fortitude, than these, which I now endure." Reconsidering passages like these, I can see why I discounted his descriptions of his condition: it appeared one more affectation of his flamboyant persona and his effusive quality as a letter writer—and many of us are not in the habit of viewing poetically depicted emotional states as deadly serious. Now I saw that his suffering and his propensity to perform his emotions melodramatically were twinned. Human beings enact and describe their emotional states in historically specific ways. To understand emotions in the past requires a thoroughgoing exploration of the historical contexts in which people lived.[15]

No matter how much he suffered during his dark melancholic periods, he did not view his condition as one that he ought to hide from the world. Ogilvie tended to be so open about his condition that even the newspapers commented on his health. A Rhode Island newspaper reported on "the delicate state of the Orator's health" during one performance, stating frankly that his gloom "seemed to hang like a dead weight on his exertions." Yet the writer insisted that

Ogilvie's talents for oratory were "still sufficient to arouse and awaken admiration and delight" from the audience. Shortly thereafter, the same paper described a subsequent performance by stating, "We rejoice to find that the Orator's health and spirits were so far confirmed, that he was capable of *appearing like himself*" and that as a result "the audience felt the magnetick versatility of the Orator's powers, which was capable of attracting smiles or tears at his command." In newspapers' frank dissemination of such personal information, we see glimpses of an early nineteenth-century world in which one might be unafraid to tell acquaintances—even listening audiences—about one's impaired "health and spirits" and to display one's melancholy hanging "like a dead weight" around one's neck.[16]

I'm glad I didn't find this letter until the very end of my research, for it allowed me to see Ogilvie as everyone else did at the time.

Seeing him through the lens of his own world also prevented me from pathologizing the other side of his fluctuating moods: what psychologists now assign the highly clinical term *hypomania*. In contrast, Ogilvie liked to refer to his "powers." In one letter bemoaning a recent bout of melancholy while in Baltimore, he described being "not in full possession of my powers" while on stage, but, "in spite of all these adverse circumstances, my success was incomparably more brilliant than at any former period in the progress of my excursion." Imagine how his performances might have sparkled when in full possession of those powers. He could become more exuberant, more charming, more compelling onstage. His propensity for word associations and alliteration increased, along with his already impressive capacity for quoting poetry; he likely demonstrated improvisational flexibility in his thinking as he made unusual, evocative, even gymnastic intellectual connections. His decreasing inhibitions would have granted terrific expansiveness to his gestures and movements, and his rich, resonant voice would have spanned its full register. To call such "powers" *hypomania*, and thereby to discount them as one aspect of what later generations categorized as a mental disorder, diminishes what Ogilvie and his auditors found magical about his talents.[17]

Recall how his friend Washington Irving captured those powers in a lightly fictionalized version of Ogilvie nearly two decades later. Irving described him as having a "meagre, pallid countenance" and behaving with "an awkward and embarrassed manner" in society. But, once inspired in conversation, he energetically warmed to the discussion of ideas, "facts, theories, and quotations." "These, in a moment of excitement, would be, as it were, melted down, and poured forth in the lava of a heated imagination," Irving continued. "At such moments, the change in the whole man was wonderful. His meagre form would acquire a dignity and grace; his long, pale visage would flash with a hectic glow;

his eyes would beam with intense speculation; and there would be pathetic tones and deep modulations in his voice, that delighted the ear, and spoke movingly to the heart." Even recognizing the distorting lens of Irving's fond memories, we might see how riveting such a transformation might be when transferred to a rostrum in a room lit by flickering candles.[18]

No one at the time would have seen Ogilvie's strange genius for performance as associated with a mental disorder, and when he committed suicide, no one chalked it up to his melancholy, even when they discussed it openly in their eulogies. A Boston paper downplayed his condition entirely. "The melancholy to which he was constitutionally liable, was untinged with any shade of misanthropy—for, in his periods of depression as of excitement, his heart, his voice, and his pecuniary aid, were ever at the service of humanity," the writer explained with approval. Another newspaper described him as "alternately the prey to hope or despondency[;] at one time he would be full of delusive chimeras, in which he saw nothing but Elysian joys; again, all the horror of despair would suddenly rush upon his mind and extinguish every glimmering of hope—he was in consequence a miserable man." Yet after providing such a description of Ogilvie's melancholy, this writer joined a chorus of eulogies that attributed Ogilvie's suicide to a "despondency" resulting from his failure on tour in Britain. Eulogies appearing in American newspapers, even those written by avowed friends, repeated time and again that his British lectures had "failed" and that those disappointments had crushed an ego that had grown dependent on praise from others. In other words, far from leading commentators to reconsider the severity of his melancholy, his suicide led them to explain it as a result of circumstances. Instead they invented a narrative of failure and crushed pride—a narrative that, as we have seen, did not wholly align with Ogilvie's experiences.[19]

Why didn't his friends and correspondents express concern when he discussed these miseries? We might expect to find among his educated and comparatively wealthy circles those individuals most knowledgeable about such vacillations of temperament and most able to determine the difference between melancholy as a burden and one so serious it required intervention. Yet none of this correspondence expressed alarm, even as those friends acknowledged their familiarity with Ogilvie's "so great an alternation of feeling" from high to low.[20]

Instead, they called him *eccentric*, but his eccentricities didn't inhibit people from coming to his performances or lead people to call him *mad*. His occasional weirdness appears in an exchange between a Philadelphia matron and her future son-in-law, Nicholas Biddle, who lived temporarily in Lancaster, the Pennsylvania state capital, as a young state legislator. While Ogilvie packed his bag to return to Philadelphia after several lectures, Biddle asked him to shepherd a letter to Mrs. Craig, as personal deliveries of letters could be faster and safer than the regular mail. But upon his arrival in the metropolis, the task slipped Ogilvie's mind for a few days, such that he wound up on the Craigs' doorstep, distraught about his mistake. "He left [it] at the door whilst we were at dinner, with a long and highly polished apology much improved as you may suppose by the graceful delivery and flowing diction" of the Craigs' French servant, Antoine, who tried to mimic the orator's performance later. That wasn't enough; Ogilvie returned later that evening. "I recd. a note from him much longer than the letter he brought which was a second apology for not having delivered the letter sooner," an apology that "was warmed up by a finished eulogium on you." She found the whole series of encounters both odd and improper according to social rules that prevented familiarities without formal introductions, especially between the sexes. None of this changed her mind about his upcoming performances, however. "My curiosity is so much excited to see and hear this accomplished prodigy that I must certainly go to his recitations on Thursday," she concluded. At another point, dressed to the nines while at a dinner party in New York, Ogilvie surprised the guests when he felt "his head a little too warm" and "without any ceremony pulled off his wig in the face of the company, and began to rub his half bald pate vociferously," as one guest reported. "I never in my life was much more astounded." As an eccentric, Ogilvie might lead his acquaintances to scratch their heads or smile at him behind his back on occasion without leading them to consider him manic or crazy, particularly in a culture that lacked a drive to diagnose permutations of character difference as medical problems.[21]

His friends also called him *philosophical* and *visionary*—meaning an enthusiast, one who indulges in impractical ideas or speculations. He had "a kind of philosophic chivalry, in imitation of the old peripatetic sages, and was continually dreaming of romantic enterprises in morals, and splendid systems for the improvement of society," Washington Irving wrote about him. At an earlier point in their friendship, Irving described Ogilvie as an "amusing, philosophical Quixote" prone to "harmless eccentricities and visionary speculations." This wasn't the first time Ogilvie had been likened to Quixote. Irving's London-based artist friends Charles Robert Leslie and Gilbert Stuart Newton, for whom Ogilvie had sat as a model, transformed his visage into versions of Quixote during the early 1820s, after his death. One might speculate that likening him to the man of La Mancha amounted to a kind of code for dismissing Ogilvie as crazy, deluded. But many early nineteenth-century readers romanticized Quixote as a noble, if misguided, opponent of the corruptions of modern society. Irving's and others' portrayals of Ogilvie thus walked a line between admiration and bemusement. To many, Quixote might have seen things that weren't there, but in tilting at windmills he sought to correct the wrongs of the world.[22]

Ogilvie's educated and wealthy friends might not have been able to discern

Figure 46. Don Quixote. By Charles Robert Leslie. Circa early 1820s. Leslie used Ogilvie as a model for the painting. Courtesy of the National Museums Northern Ireland, Ulster

the gravity of his suffering because they were the most likely to be caught up in the eighteenth-century culture of sensibility, a British and American movement that privileged a unique sensitivity or responsiveness to emotions, literature, and art. This movement held that such sensitivity marked one's greater capacity to perceive beauty, higher thought, and moral truth. Some could take such sensitivity to an extreme. Medical experts even fretted that the extreme poles of sensibility could harm one's health. Jane Austen gently mocked this culture in her novel *Sense and Sensibility* (1811) by portraying the younger sister Marianne as an embodiment of this culture of sensibility. She gave full range to her feelings—from her passion for Romantic poetry to her despair over a feckless suitor—to a degree that she ultimately suffered a breakdown. The novel traced her evolution

Figure 47. Don Quixote and Dorothea. By Charles Robert Leslie. Circa 1825, oil on panel.
Leslie used Ogilvie as a model for the painting. © Victoria and Albert Museum, London

as she gradually learned to rein in her passions and display as much sense as
sensibility, just as it shows that Marianne's more stoic sister Elinor might benefit from expressing her feelings more openly. Seen in the light of the culture of
sensibility among wealthy people and self-identified intellectuals, Ogilvie's propensity for radical "alternation of feeling" might have been viewed as emblem-
atic of his superior capacity for philosophical, moral, and poetical ideas. For
many, the radical extremes of sensibility from exaltation to melancholy would
actually have been seen as morally and aesthetically superior to a more moderate, limited range of emotion. They would not have seen Ogilvie's sensitivity as
a disorder at all.[23]

In fact, in some circles, melancholy became positively fashionable as an emotion, further muddying the distinction between depth of feeling and illness. The
Romantic literature and poetry that Ogilvie recited so frequently was preoccupied with melancholy as a theme and a quality of feeling that gave its sufferers a
heightened understanding that relentlessly cheerful types could not experience.
More than a hundred poems appeared during Ogilvie's lifetime with *melancholy*

Figure 48. John Philip Kemble in Character. A British engraving illustrating
the dramatic scene in Joseph Addison's play Cato in which the titular character kills
himself rather than succumb to tyranny in Rome. Courtesy of the Rare Book &
Manuscript Library, University of Illinois at Urbana-Champaign

in the title (*On Melancholy, Ode to Melancholy, The Pleasures of Melancholy*); thousands more invoked the word in their stanzas. No wonder his friends might have seen Ogilvie's "dim-eyed fiend" as something more complicated than a cry for help. His melancholy could be simultaneously a dire condition, a sign of temperamental superiority, a depth of feeling capable of producing the highest and most evocative of ideas, and a stylish sensitivity to emotions. A close reading of his own letters suggests that Ogilvie found melancholy to be simultaneously an affliction and a gift.[24]

That era's writers also had a propensity to romanticize and even popularize suicide. Suicides appeared frequently in Romantic literature, as well as in the lives of writers of that period. The most vivid of these was Goethe's wildly popular novel *The Sorrows of Young Werther* (1774), whose protagonist's sorrows and ultimate suicide were so expressive of fine sensibility that a "Werther-mania" led hundreds of young Europeans to kill themselves and dozens of novelists to bring their own protagonists to suicide. Writers could also frame suicide as a final act of nobility, human rights, and individual self-determination. The toga-wearing Cato in Joseph Addison's popular, classically themed play killed himself at the end because he despaired the departure of virtue in the Roman republic. William Godwin likewise weighed in on the topic in the midst of a widespread cultural and political debate on suicide. As a result of this deluge of writing justifying and sometimes romanticizing the act of killing oneself, the prevailing legal and religious prohibitions on suicide appeared as only one side of a much more complicated Anglo-American conversation. Indeed, it's impossible to think of Ogilvie committing suicide by shooting himself in the head without considering that the fictional Werther's death was identical.[25]

It might be tempting to call Ogilvie *bipolar*, to trace a direct line from his life to the present, and believe we can make sense of his life by giving our own name to it. Yet doing so clouds over the fact that concepts of health are always historically specific — situated in historical moments when people make sense of their health and spirits in ways that can seem foreign to us. *Bipolar* isn't the "right" way to categorize this set of symptoms. It's just our own word, reflective of our world with its own medical and psychological frameworks for understanding health. Setting that aside and using *melancholy* instead, and prying open the full range of meanings of melancholy unique to the early nineteenth century, illuminates why no one near him sounded the alarm about his temperament, why his melancholy might have appeared a lamentable but necessary aspect of the life of an intellectual, and why his contemporaries might even have idealized his vacillating moods as a fit quality for a man of fine feeling. Understanding people in the past on their own terms rather than by twenty-first-century measures illuminates the rich complexities of past cultures and helps us tease out how indi-

Figure 49. Don Quixote. 1823. The engraving drawn from Leslie's painting, using
Ogilvie as a model. Courtesy of the Maryland Historical Society, MS194

viduals made choices of their own even as the range of their choices was shaped by the cultures around them.

Finally, understanding prevailing medical theories of and therapies for melancholy of two hundred years ago grants us one last revelatory level of insight into Ogilvie's life and choices.

Theories about and treatments for melancholy demonstrate a prevailing truth about the era: there was no distinction between mental health and physical health. When American newspapers commented on Ogilvie's fluctuating "health and spirits," they saw those two things as intertwined. Melancholy wasn't seen merely as an ailment of the spirits; it was an illness of both body and spirits, an understanding shared by everyone from the most elite medical experts to Americans and Britons who never visited a doctor in their lives. This conception of health conjoining body and mind went back centuries. When Ogilvie sought advice for resolving his melancholy from doctors, they prescribed both medical and behavioral therapies that addressed what Benjamin Rush called "the reciprocal influence of the body and mind upon each other."[26]

Ogilvie's letters provided a glimpse into the solutions he found successful. In the middle of his Kentucky visit in 1813, when he successfully withdrew from heavy opium use by drinking spring water and climbing a hill every day, he wrote a letter to a former student that brimmed with enthusiasm and hopefulness. Over and over he used words depicting physical *activity*, *exertion*, and *energy*, all associated with a powerful sense of will and ambition. He believed that this activity might forestall melancholy. "Constituted as I am, to enjoy any degree of happiness, even to avert intolerable misery, I must be intensely active," he wrote. "This activity can only be exerted and kept alive by powerful motives, and these motives can be supplied only by a generous, persevering, heroic struggle with the sort of difficulties and dangers with which I am ready and armed to contend." He portrayed himself as a man of terrific willpower, driven by the carrot of ambition and the stick of needing to avoid "intolerable misery." With diligence and force of will, he could keep his melancholy at bay. The early nineteenth-century world that saw mind and body as an organic, unified system led sufferers like Ogilvie to believe they had significant ability to manage their own conditions.[27]

Starting in the early eighteenth century, medical experts had begun a serious reconsideration of older views of the root causes of melancholy. Whereas once they had attributed it to an imbalance of the humors—an excess of black bile that left the body overly cold and dry and the mind dejected—changing concepts of human biology offered new ways of understanding melancholy's cause. Instead of ascribing it to an overactive gall bladder, they now blamed sluggish blood flow or problems in the lymphatic and nervous systems. Others suggested that melancholy resulted from a decrease in the body's quantum of electrical excitement.[28]

But if new theories about its cause abounded, therapies to treat melancholy changed little from earlier centuries. Even if a doctor knew of cutting-edge explanations for the causes of the condition, their treatments remained the same. Some of these solutions were called heroic because they asked doctors to take aggressive measures to adjust bodily imbalances in their patients, such as bloodletting or blistering the skin to activate blood flow. They also prescribed ingesting large amounts of spring water or laxatives to cleanse the body, vomiting to resolve blocked digestion, and medicines like mercury to produce a large amount of saliva. In tandem with these medical solutions, doctors suggested behavioral therapies to invigorate the "health and spirits" and restore full health. These included recommendations to exercise, take baths, and divert the mind.[29]

One of the prevailing experts on melancholy, a Swiss doctor with the delicious name S. A. D. Tissot (also internationally famous for his warnings about the dangers of masturbation), helped to popularize the prevailing belief that melancholy and digestive problems were interwoven. Melancholy disproportionately affected learned and literary people, Tissot argued, in part because they did not exercise enough. In his *Essay on Diseases Incident to Literary and Sedentary Persons*, he proposed that "the perpetual labours of the mind" together with "the constant inaction of the body" could result in severe, if not fatal, debility for both stomach and emotions. Intense study "begins by impairing the stomach; and that if the complaint is not relieved, it may degenerate into melancholy." Tissot acknowledged that "melancholy may be useful to learning, because melancholy persons, being fixed to one idea, are able to consider the same object in all its views, and without having their attention diverted." The problem, he suggested, was both the intellectual's sedentary lifestyle and the fixity of his thoughts, which produced the terrible combination of physical ailments and depression. To drive the point home, Tissot recounted an arresting case of a history professor "who suffered for a long time, and was not cured till he had voided a mass of the form and colour of the intestines. It was a kind of gluish viscous substance, formed by his sedentary life, which had gradually filled up the intestinal tube; and becoming putrid, had disordered the whole animal œconomy." Turning such people away from their preoccupations and providing regular exercise resolved the inextricable, conjoined problems of poor digestion and melancholy.[30]

S. A. D. Tissot's recommendations, alongside those of a wide range of other writers whose suggestions appeared in everything from cheap almanacks to home medical guidebooks to cutting-edge medical treatises, advised melancholic people to engage in diverting and energetic activities. Spend more time with others rather than in solitude. Go outside more often. Get a change of scenery. "Melancholia is characterized by inactivity of body and mind," one wrote in a representative passage.[31]

These prescriptions could be contradictory and, frankly, amusing, and reveal how often they were directed at wealthy elites prone to a class-specific kind of low spirits. One doctor might recommend drinking wine, another abstaining from all drink. One gave a patient opium to help her sleep, while another refused. Some suggested engaging in light conversation, others to spend time with people more depressed than you are. Some recommended cold baths, others hot ones— but keep in mind that, in an era when almost no one had running water, the recommendation of frequent baths was labor-intensive to the point of being nearly impossible. (Even quite comfortable Americans sponged themselves with water, perhaps from a basin, and usually without soap, which was reserved for washing clothes. When bathtubs became slightly more common in the 1830s, people generally bathed in cold water.) One doctor recommended that his patients brush themselves with a "flesh-brush" over the "legs, arms, trunk of the body, and abdomen," for such friction "is a kind of exercise that strengthens, [and] promotes circulation." The very notion that one might add exercise or horse riding to one's day, purchase a flesh-brush, or engage in "light conversation" must have seemed a slap in the face to nonelite women and men whose days revolved around the physical labor of washing, farming, managing homes full of children, chopping wood, and working with farm animals.[32]

James Ogilvie wrote to Benjamin Rush in 1797 because, as the nation's most preeminent doctor, Rush had vast experience with treating the ailments of the body and mind. Rush's advice for those who wrote him about melancholy largely followed that of his contemporaries: avoid "solitude, and vacancy of employment. If all fail, a long Journey, or a salivation" by taking mercury, alongside more familiar recommendations involving diet, exercise, and baths.[33]

Two therapies stood out for Ogilvie's case. Over and over, medical experts advised people prone to melancholy to travel and to engage in public speaking. Travel and oratory as treatments for melancholy: let that sit with you for a moment.

Travel and public speech were, of course, the two activities Ogilvie had practiced constantly for the last thirteen years of his life. Reading and speaking aloud, said another writer, "has an excellent effect . . . [for it] not only exercises the lungs, but almost the whole body. Hence studious people are greatly benefited by delivering discourses in public." "Nothing has done more service than agreeable company, daily exercise, especially travelling, and a variety of amusements," another medical book suggested. Rush reported that some of his patients revealed "talents for eloquence": "A gentleman whom I attended in our hospital in the year 1810 often delighted, as well as astonished, the patients and officers of our hospital, by his displays of oratory, in preaching from a table in the hospital yard every Sunday." Such displays might help people suffering from melancholy in the same way traveling did: oratory exercised the body, diverted the mind, and forced one to engage dynamically with others.[34]

After discovering Ogilvie's 1797 letter and studying melancholy in the nineteenth century, I found this association of travel and public speaking as frequently touted solutions for melancholy a revelation. I went back to his earliest advertisements, published in newspapers in 1808 just as he began making his way northward out of Virginia for the first time. And there it is: he described himself as "travelling for the restoration of that health which has been impaired by laborious study and persevering application." When Thomas Jefferson wrote letters of introduction on his behalf, he explained that Ogilvie had set out on his journey as a result of "considerations of health" and discussed Ogilvie's "tour of health" with mutual friends in more casual correspondence. We have to consider the possibility that Ogilvie's entire career as a traveling lecturer began as both an avenue by which an ambitious man might make his name in the world and, quite simply, a survival strategy.[35]

Sometimes when we look backward to previous eras, we're tempted to offer patronizing pronouncements, such as "he suffered from what we would call manic depression"—as if that diagnosis is the correct one, and as if such a pronouncement gets at the truth of the experience of someone in the past. Certainly, Ogilvie's symptoms seemed to line up with a diagnosis we now find familiar, an insight that grants new seriousness to his many discussions of the depths of his depressive periods and invites evocative speculations about his performances, his sensitivity to words and sounds and images, his family and marriage, his use of opium. But seeing his condition instead on his terms, as melancholy, reveals much more.

In the early nineteenth century, melancholy was both a medical condition and a fashionable capacity for deep emotional resonance, both an affliction and a sign of superior fine feeling. That "dim-eyed fiend" could produce agonies and generate reams of Romantic poetry. Its very fashionable and productive elements meant that no one felt the need to hide their torments from the world. Just the opposite: they developed an elaborate poetic lexicon for discussing melancholy—so elaborate that it would lead later generations unfamiliar with that language to discount the suffering that inspired it. We shouldn't judge their views of and treatments for melancholy as better or worse than our own culture's understanding of manic depression. Instead, we should explore those nineteenth-century meanings of melancholy as illuminating lost worlds of medical and emotional understanding, for they grant us keen historical perspective.

Ogilvie and his contemporaries saw melancholy, not as a mental illness, but as a disorder of both body and mind that he might be able to adjust—a mind / body connection that, ironically, has come back in the field of twenty-first-century neurobiology as some researchers have begun to displace older psychological paradigms. But to a degree that we rarely see today, nineteenth-century physicians gave melancholics hope that they might take control of their own "health and spirits" and that by purposeful action rather than fatalism they might limit the unbearable extremes of their spectrum of vacillating temperaments. In setting himself a grueling schedule of public performances intermixed with miserably long days of travel, Ogilvie took the reins of his own treatment. "To avert intolerable misery, I must be intensely active," he wrote during the War of 1812, with the enthusiasm of one who believed he had discovered the secret.[36]

James Ogilvie never escaped his melancholy; perhaps it ultimately caused his suicide. But the same culture that termed his condition *melancholy* gave him therapies that took him out into the world, told him that with willpower and energy he might recover his own health. Knowing that he might suffer all his life from melancholy did not lead him to conceal his condition or believe it amounted to a death sentence. It liberated him from the stultifying life of a schoolteacher and helped him realize a long career that even allowed him to deliver passionate orations on his darkest demon, suicide.

{ EPILOGUE }
Celebrating and Forgetting

Not a single British paper reported James Ogilvie's death or offered a eulogy, perhaps because suicide remained both illegal in civil law and immoral in Christian thought. In fact, it took seven months before the news reached the United States via gossip networks. The earliest American notices of his death brought together verifiable information alongside wild speculation and confirmed the rumors that he had killed himself. They offered varying explanations. Some attributed his suicide to the opium habit; others to his purported failure onstage in Britain or to his continued embarrassment over his *Philosophical Essays*. To add poignancy to his death, American eulogies also claimed—generously, fantastically, falsely—that Ogilvie had received the title of earl of Findlater. One announced that he had committed suicide on his new estate.[1]

For several years after Ogilvie's death, reminders of his career appeared with some regularity in the press. His imitators especially invoked his name, making their debts to him explicit—perhaps to increase attendance. When the orator Mr. Hazelton announced his forthcoming performances in Saratoga, New York, the paper explained that "it is believed that his efforts in the eloquence of the Rostrum would not be unworthy of OGILVIE, his distinguished model." Hazelton and his fellow imitators delivered orations on Ogilvie's own subjects (dueling, gambling) and recited the same poetry afterward. One imitator's advertisements noted that he would declaim the passage on the battle of Flodden Field from Sir Walter Scott's poem *Marmion* "after the manner of his friend, the late JAMES OGILVIE"; Hazelton announced he would wear a Roman toga and recite Thomas Campbell's poetic account of the Battle of Culloden "in imitation of the late James Ogilvie." Was it nostalgia for the late Ogilvie that brought audiences to these performances, or was it their ongoing appreciation of this form of the spoken word? One commentator felt it must be the former. "We have known a hundred attempts at Lectures made here," a writer for the *National Intelligencer* explained skeptically, "none of which were ever crowned with the success necessary to compensate the Lecturer, except perhaps Mr. Ogilvie's. There was a novelty and freshness about his undertaking, which drew large audiences around him."[2]

But those reminders of Ogilvie's celebrity faded quickly. Most simply found other orators to admire. By the time the promoters of the new lyceum movement began touting entertaining lectures designed to give American society "an intellectual, moral, and of course an elevated character" during the mid-1820s, none chose to remember that Ogilvie had been the first to recommend such lectures, nor that his supporters a decade earlier had recommended the creation of "*Schools* of improvement" they called lyceums. These local institutions that sponsored weekly lectures on entertaining and educational topics like science, philosophy, and travel mushroomed in popularity. By 1831, perhaps as many as a thousand town lyceums had been established, most of which assembled in the same buildings where Ogilvie had spoken: schoolrooms, assembly rooms, taverns, and churches. The movement's founder, Josiah Holbrook, began recommending the construction of purpose-built lyceum halls in 1832 in nearly every issue of his new magazine, the *Family Lyceum*. "A place of general intellectual and social resort," he wrote, would be "a bulwark to our nation's liberties and a monument to our nation's glory," perhaps an unconscious nod to Ogilvie's arguments during the 1810s. By 1839, Americans had established some five thousand local lyceums and built dozens of lyceum halls, and the movement had begun to cultivate star lecturers whose eloquence and celebrity allowed them to command top earnings. By the 1850s, the lyceum had become so widespread that 5 percent of the white adult population in the Northeast and Midwest attended lectures every week.[3]

Among the most successful of the stars of lyceum lecturing was Ralph Waldo Emerson, who earned his fame in part by delivering orations on the topic of eloquence itself. Eloquence, he stated, had the capacity to change the hearts and minds of listeners, to illustrate new ways of contemplating problems, and to model the noble conviction to address those problems. "If the speaker utter a noble sentiment, the attention deepens, a new and highest audience now listens, and the audiences of the fun and of facts and of the understanding are all silenced and awed," Emerson intoned. That dynamic between speaker and audience ultimately rose to something magical, he believed. "An audience is not a simple addition of the individuals that compose it." Rather, that combination of people together in a room energized them and the orator just as "a battery is charged" with electricity. "No one can survey the face of an excited assembly, without being apprised of new opportunity for painting in fire human thought, and being agitated to agitate." With passages like that, Emerson held up the importance of eloquence in bringing people together in a room, generating ideas and imaginations together in rituals of civic enchantment. If those ideas sound familiar, perhaps it was because Emerson heard them expressed in an Ogilvie lecture back in 1817. Or, more likely, they had become such common knowledge that the ideas only required Emerson's finesse as a writer and speaker to invest them with fresh life.[4]

Emerson was preaching to the choir. By the 1840s, when he delivered "Eloquence" from the lyceum stage, the spoken word had grown in significance.

Grand speechmaking had become so crucial in national politics that American newspapers had begun to hire stenographers who sat in the halls of Congress taking shorthand to record the pronouncements of great orators like Daniel Webster and Henry Clay or the debates between Abraham Lincoln and Stephen Douglas. Political figures competed with one another to get their speeches picked up by newspapers and reprinted throughout the country. Success enabled them to dominate the conversation about the political subjects at hand and burnish their reputations as exceptionally gifted speakers in a crowded field. To underline the public significance of such figures, artists continued to portray Henry Clay and others in togas, and American schoolbooks reprinted those speeches for memorization and recitation by generations of children.[5]

Social reformers and evangelicals also relied on public speech to dramatize the urgency of their movements. Many innovated new rhetorical styles of argument and self-presentation. Eager to display the hopelessness of a gradualist approach to ending slavery, for example, abolitionists demonized the colonization movement as evil—equal even to the evil of slavery itself. They demanded that their listeners "hear" the misery of slavery so invoked in their speeches the clanking sound of chains, the crack of the whip, the cries of the enslaved calling for freedom, the abiding misery of the songs they sang in the fields. In doing so, abolitionists portrayed themselves as unstinting in their righteousness, fearless in their opposition to a shadowy, moneyed, and elite "slave power" as well as the apathy of a majority of the public. That self-presentation proved infectious and, to some, insufferable; abolitionists encountered riots, violence, the burning of the halls where they tried to speak, the destruction of their businesses. Their confrontational and obnoxious style succeeded nevertheless in bringing the subject of emancipation to the forefront of public discussions, and offered some women and men new modes of identifying and living as moral Christians. Abolitionism would also generate new questions and social movements, including the drive for women's rights.[6]

Orators galvanized other movements as well at all points on the political and social spectrum. The Tennessee frontiersman David Crockett became a political phenomenon because of his colorful and alternately funny, racist, and vindictive campaigning from the stump. His self-presentation proved so compelling that mythologizers would embroider even more color onto a fictionalized Davy Crockett for use in tall tales published in cheap almanacs, a Davy who claimed to be "half horse, half alligator, [and a] little touched with the snapping turtle— can wade the Mississippi, leap the Ohio, ride upon a streak of lightning, and slip without a scratch down a honey locust." Meanwhile, members of the Know-Nothing political movement, which agitated against immigration, Catholics, and the abolition of slavery, likewise used speechmaking as a means of energiz-

Figure 50. A Song for the Man: A Henry Clay Ballad. 1844. A piece of sheet music that portrays Clay in the quintessentially American (that is, convoluted) mix of modern dress and what contemporaries thought of as a toga. Courtesy of the Susan H. Douglas Political Americana Collection, #2214, Division of Rare and Manuscript Collections, Cornell University Library, Ithaca, N.Y.

ing its adherents and articulating a vision of the United States that contrasted sharply with that of the abolitionists and women's rights advocates.[7]

The growing importance of public speech after Ogilvie's death reveals the long afterlife of his ideas about the importance of eloquence "at this time, and in this country." He had promoted eloquence to Americans as a spur to youthful ambition and as a source of cultural pride in a new republic anxious to distinguish itself among nations. In his most optimistic moods he had imagined oratory serving as a social glue for a fractious, disparate United States—an optimism echoed in Emerson's "Eloquence"—even though Ogilvie's own experience weathering scandal (and Emerson's perspective on the intense political divisions of the 1840s) revealed a less utopian reality. Oratory had not magically erased the many points of national discord; indeed, it had served as one of the media that amplified that discord. But it had nevertheless fulfilled one of Ogilvie's dreams by offering occasions for community discussions, sites for thinking together if not arriving at consensus.[8]

The performance of the spoken word also created new oratorical celebrities, whose fame grew in part with the behind-the-scenes efforts of new agents, publishers, and technologies. Traveling lyceum star lecturers like Emerson, Susan B. Anthony, and Anna Dickinson commanded lucrative lecturing fees and saw their travel and advertising arranged by lyceum booking agents. Entrepreneurial photographers and printmakers published thousands of copies of the portraits of Frederick Douglass, Sojourner Truth, Daniel Webster, and other distinguished orators, which allowed anyone with discretionary income to feel a greater intimacy with those figures and to study the nobility of their faces and the forthrightness of their gazes. Gossip columns increasingly appeared in periodicals, eager to expose the private lives of the famous or to reveal in excruciating detail scandals, as when Henry Ward Beecher, the nation's most famous minister and lyceum star, was accused of adultery with the wife of a friend. Some cultivated reputations for possessing what they began to call *personal magnetism* (and eventually *charisma*) that drew followers in ways that provoked both imitation and new concerns about Americans' unsettling propensity to be wooed by powerful speakers.[9]

Flocking to see a powerful performer can still prompt some of the same emotions, identifications, and tensions. We still believe that a person's celebrity continues to reflect on us—about our collective capacity to judge excellence, our ability to see through trickery, our power to grant authority to the right people. We still experience thrills when we submit to the charms of a dynamic speaker, at least until we come to doubt that person's worth or honesty. The ebbs and flows of oral performance still create a sense of shared identity within the audience—and, sometimes, generate animosity against other audiences. When our tastes change, or when we recognize the flaws that make a performer no longer worthy of our adoration, we continue to pursue the acts of rejection, forgetting, and finding new idols. How do these performances still evoke a sense of a shared past, call forth a vision of a bright future, demand action in the present? Ultimately, we continue to believe that the drama of celebrity tells us something important about us, good, bad, or indifferent.

If noticing these continuities casts light on our own culture, this story about a long-forgotten celebrity also points to a very different lesson: the value of understanding the peoples and cultures of the past on their own terms.

Ogilvie's career was shaped by forces unique to his time and place, and only by appreciating those differences can we truly understand this forgotten man and his world. The poetic duel he fought in the pages of *The Ogilviad*, the Roman toga he donned, the hatred of Indians that spurred his entering the militia during the War of 1812, the melancholy that both motivated and tormented him— all illuminate profound gaps between his world and ours. Even his infatuation with laudanum, which helped to fuel his ambitions but later demanded painful withdrawals, defies easy analogies to present-day concerns about opiate addiction. Noticing these differences helps recapture a United States in the midst of invention.

When Americans forgot James Ogilvie, they also chose to forget the slow process of invention. They gradually settled on new narratives about the early Republic—narratives that overlooked those awkward years. Instead, they spun new narratives, fantasies that emphasized national unity, internal improvements, progress.

Fond memories of Ogilvie were replaced with derisive ones. In 1832, Benjamin Rush's son James, who had begun to organize his father's letters and manuscripts with the goal of guaranteeing his historical legacy, came across the letter that Ogilvie had written nearly two generations earlier, begging Rush's father for help with his melancholy. Despite James Rush's own medical training (and a formidable reputation of his own), he felt compelled to trivialize Ogilvie's life in an annotation on the back of the letter. "Mr. Ogilvie was an unfortunate genius of the erratic kind—who loved *idleness* not the usefulness of contemplation," Rush wrote. "He used to take opium immoderately [and] he died I don't know where."[10]

Case dismissed.

Reopening that case need not lead to pat conclusions about Ogilvie or bemusement at the many women and men who admired and supported him, Benjamin Rush among them. Simply because so many chose later to forget him should not blind us to how much his career reveals about the early Republic. Just as Ogilvie's melancholy allowed him to believe he had a strange genius for erudition and performance, so his audiences' faith in eloquence allowed them to see in him a kind of national destiny. We should take seriously that early nineteenth-century world not merely for its limitations but also for the possibilities it opened.

{ ACKNOWLEDGMENTS }

When James Ogilvie finished writing *Philosophical Essays* in 1816, he told his readers how hard it was to write a book. He explained that he "has found the anxious, monotonous, life-consuming, soul-chilling drudgery of transcribing and revising for the press, and of correcting proof-sheets, injurious to his health and spirits," noting that he had "suspended social intercourse and bodily exercise" to do it. "It has been the destiny of the Author of this volume to traverse a pathless, and often dreary wilderness, without a guide to conduct, or a compass to direct him" (xciv, xcvi).

My experience was different than his. In fact, I'm not sure I will ever enjoy writing a book as much as I did this one. It has been my good fortune to have paths, compasses, and guides.

Exceptional teachers and mentors have helped to shape my curiosity and my writing (and my tennis game) throughout my life. I don't know how to thank them for all they did except to acknowledge them here, in the order I encountered them: Elizabeth Eitzen Barsoom, Chris Cook, Gail Hutchinson, Herbert Shinn, Bonnie Folkers Huebert, John Dizikes, Donald Wilcox, Jonathan Beecher, Toby Ditz, Amy Greenberg, and Jan Ellen Lewis.

When Paula McDowell invited me to New York University to give a talk almost a decade ago, I took the opportunity to pull together some early ideas on Ogilvie, thinking I might write an article. As I began to think of it as a book, I've benefited from presentations at Northwestern University, the College of Charleston, the Zuckerman Salon at the McNeil Center for Early American Studies, and the Triangle Early American History Seminar; conferences sponsored by the Society for Historians of the Early American Republic, the European Early American Studies Association, the American Studies Association, and the Society for the History of Authorship, Reading, and Publishing; and the conferences "The Cosmopolitan Lyceum" (sponsored by the American Antiquarian Society, 2011) and "Celebrity Encounters: Transatlantic Fame in Nineteenth-Century Britain and America" (sponsored by the University of Portsmouth, 2014). In the wake of the latter, Páraic Finnerty and Rod Rosenquist edited my article "The Transatlantic Celebrity of Mr. O: Oratory and the Networks of Reputation in Early Nineteenth-Century Britain and America" for a special issue of *Comparative American Studies* (XIV [2016], 7–20), threads of which appear throughout this book.

I developed a serious interest in Ogilvie's story at about the time I moved to Richmond—a lucky break. For not only is this city full of libraries and archives that helped me understand his years as a teacher in Virginia, it also features a wealth of early Americanists and early modernists who read early drafts and alternately cheered and fought with me along the way. For their help I thank Claire Bourne, Leigh Ann Craig, Michael Dickinson, Eric Garberson, Richard Godbeer, Terri Halperin, Catherine Ingrassia, Kate Nash, Marion Nelson, Brooke Newman, Andrew O'Shaughnessy, Kate Roach, Samantha Seeley,

Ryan Smith, Greg Smithers, Peter Stone, Brent Tarter, and the other members of regional seminars (Virginia Commonwealth University's Premodern History and Culture Reading Group, the Fall Line Early Americanists, and the colloquia of the Omohundro Institute of Early American History and Culture). Farther afield, Susan Boettcher, Jeremy Dibbell, Cassie Good, Charlene Boyer Lewis, Meredith Neuman, and Angela Ray answered my calls to talk me through conceptual snags, and Karen Rader offered good cheer and advice at all turns.

For help with archives, I particularly thank Richard Candee and Ronan Donohoe at the Portsmouth Athenaeum; Michelle Gait at the University of Aberdeen's Special Collections Centre; James Green, Connie King, Sarah Weatherwax, and Linda August at the Library Company of Philadelphia; Martha King at the Papers of Thomas Jefferson; Alison Lindsay at the National Records of Scotland; and Brian Cuthrell at the South Caroliniana Library. Bill MacLehose and Affy Athanasiou, Sarah Pearsall, Rebecca Whitley and Hugh Small, Michelle and Roderick McDonald, Emma Hart, and Mara Keire and Chris McKenna provided help with housing and good company while conducting research. My Richmond friends—Natalie Draper and Peter Stone, Mary Cosby and Rob Williams, Meredith Katz and Antonio Espinoza, Brooke Newman and Greg Smithers, and Diana Westbrook— offered reasons to stop working at the end of the day.

Virginia Humanities and Virginia Commonwealth University's Humanities Research Center and College of Humanities and Sciences's scholarly leave program each provided release from teaching to develop the manuscript. Grants and fellowships from the American Philosophical Society, the International Center for Jefferson Studies at Monticello, the Library Company of Philadelphia, VCU's Department of History (including its Schilling Fund), VCU's Humanities Research Center, and VCU-Globe's program at Harris Manchester College, Oxford, provided funding for research trips throughout the United States and Great Britain. Special thanks to John Kneebone and John Powers who, as chairs of the Department of History, steered a little of its tiny budget toward helping me attend conferences and co-sponsor a manuscript workshop. Lacey Guest and Anne McCrery offered brilliant, careful research at an early stage.

So much of my work stands on the shoulders of giants, starting with the writings of Richard Beale Davis. Davis believed Ogilvie to be a fool, but his terrific research got me started. Jennifer Eastman provided nuanced Latin translations and classical expertise, and she talked me through my very earliest ideas about what to make of Ogilvie's melancholy; Kelly Gray and Jonathan Jones allowed me to read their unpublished work about opium; Catherine Jones gave painstaking readings to the book's first two chapters; Alex Maxwell Findlater advised me on the Scottish law of succession; and Jonathan Sadowsky offered eleventh-hour thoughts on my chapter on melancholy. During our weekly boot camp phone calls, Antonia Lant and Scott Desposato asked all the right questions and formed a cheering section when I needed it. When I was about halfway along with this manuscript, Jolie Olcott, Kathleen DuVal, and I formed a writing group—which meant that they read about half the chapters in first draft, entirely out of order, even when we were all pulling out our hair during busy semesters. What a difference it made. I still see passages here that work only because of their advice.

Jill Kneerim and especially Lucy Cleland of Kneerim & Williams read my material so effectively that they made it possible to sign with the Omohundro Institute, for which I'll always be grateful. This book matured because I worked with people who really know how to make that happen. Cathy Kelly and Brandon Proia took the lead in shepherding a manuscript that looked a little bit different than the OI's usual list, and they were backed up by Virginia Chew, Catherine Preus, Emily Suth, and the OI's famously thorough source checkers.

And speaking of Cathy Kelly: Where do I begin? She offered advice on the flow of chapters, pushed back on sections that needed more elaboration, offered felicitous word changes, and took my calls when I got stuck. You have no idea what it means to have an editor with this kind of prowess in your corner. Thank you.

The hardest part about writing a book is figuring out what the story is, what kind of narrative arc you're developing, and whether it works—and there's nothing like having colleagues with that big-picture vision who can offer feedback. I owe a deep debt to those who read the entire manuscript at crucial stages: Ann Fabian, François Furstenberg, Mary Kelley, Cathy Kelly, James E. Lewis, Jr., Brandon Proia, Katy Shively, Alan Taylor, and Nadine Zimmerli. It feels so wrong that Rebecca Plant, Frances Clarke, and Tom Foster, whose friendships and writing advice now stretch back nearly a quarter century (!), don't live within three blocks of me anymore, but their combined talent for reading manuscripts continues to shape how and why I write.

When I was little, my father used to tell us that all we had to do was write a page a day, and by the end of the year we'd have a book. He was thus rightly baffled when this one took a while. Jeannie and Roger Eastman and Jennifer Eastman and Michael Clark asked a lot of questions about when this book would get done, for which they are forgiven. I have written this book for them.

Kevin Shupe is averse to public displays of affection (even as he has a confounding weakness for romantic comedies), so this book is simply dedicated to him, because it's ours together. Allons-y.

{ NOTES }

INTRODUCTION

1. Ogilvie visited Portsmouth three times during the summer and early fall of 1809. For examples of events taking place at the Assembly House, see "Mr. Turner . . . ," *Portsmouth Oracle*, June 14, 1806, [3]; "Readings and Recitations . . . ," *New-Hampshire Gazette* (Portsmouth), Dec. 16, 1806, [3]; "G. Dame's Academy for Dancing . . . ," *Portsmouth Oracle*, Apr. 23, 1808, [3]; and "Exhibition . . . Theatrical Performance, and Ventriloquism," ibid., May 20, 1809, [3]. In 1810, Portsmouth was the twentieth-largest city in the United States, with a population of about seven thousand. See U.S. census tables listing urban places by decade, accessed Apr. 22, 2016, www.census.gov/population/www/documentation /twps0027/tab04.txt. Washington diary and information about the Assembly Room is from James Leo Garvin, "Academic Architecture and the Building Trades in the Piscataqua Region of New Hampshire and Maine, 1715–1815" (Ph.D. diss., Boston University, 1983), 257–259. Garvin's discussion of the room's decor relies in part on the memories of Sarah Parker Rice Goodwin that appeared in *The Portsmouth Book* (Boston, 1898). For a description of that year's Fourth of July celebration, see "4th July, 1809. The 33d Anniversary," *Portsmouth Oracle*, July 8, 1809, [3].

2. Quotes from the oration come from [Ogilvie], "On Suicide as Justifiable," MS oration, n.d., Jonathan Clark Letters, MSS A/C 593d 6, folder 4, Filson Historical Society, Louisville, Ky. These passages rest on numerous accounts of Ogilvie's performances discussed throughout this book and use some of their language describing him (awkward, sepulchral, electric, soft blue eyes, his powers, his penchant for alliteration) and audience response (goosebumps, drunken attendees, tears, mouths open).

3. Ibid. ("man is but a shadow").

4. Historians, too, have largely forgotten Ogilvie. By the twentieth century, he appeared a foolish figure to scholars and his success an indictment of a period when Americans were so naive as to find him compelling. He found his way into a few histories nevertheless, often cast as a bit character or the comic relief: the overly dramatic, oratory-spouting, deluded man who, like the fictional character of Don Quixote, sought to tilt at windmills. Scholars expressed bemusement when they discussed him, spurred by the mid-twentieth-century writings of Richard Beale Davis, the only scholar to discuss Ogilvie in detail. Davis was a meticulous researcher, yet he still portrayed Ogilvie as "eccentric and egocentric to the verge of ridiculous." "Perhaps no better comment may be made upon the 'literary' taste of the American republic at the time than the fact that Ogilvie's proposals were taken most seriously." See Richard Beale Davis, "James Ogilvie, an Early American Teacher of Rhetoric," *Quarterly Journal of Speech*, XXVIII (1942), 289 ("egocentric"); Davis, *Francis Walker Gilmer: Life and Learning in Jefferson's Virginia* (Richmond, Va., 1939), 23 ("most seriously"). See also his "James Ogilvie and Washington Irving," *Ameri-*

cana Illustrated, XXXV (1941), 435–458; and *Intellectual Life in Jefferson's Virginia, 1790–1830* (Chapel Hill, N.C., 1964). Subsequent scholars who wrote about Ogilvie have displayed some of the same bemusement. These include Andrew Burstein, *The Original Knickerbocker: The Life of Washington Irving* (New York, 2007), 90–91, 135, 150; Patrick Scott, "From Rhetoric to English: Nineteenth Century English Teaching at South Carolina College," *South Carolina Historical Magazine,* LXXXV (1984), 233–243; and Alan Taylor, *Thomas Jefferson's Education* (New York, 2019), 175–180.

5. H., "For the Times: Mr. Ogilvie," *Times* (Charleston), Mar. 6, 1811, [3] ("Mr. Ogilvie's genius"); "Communication," *Enquirer* (Richmond), June 25, 1811, [2]; An Admirer, "Mr. Ogilvie," *Poulson's American Daily Advertiser* (Philadelphia), Nov. 15, 1813, [3] ("Standing forth"); "Mr. Ogilvie," *Salem Gazette,* Oct. 16, 1809, [3] ("His style"); "Mr. Ogilvie," *Repertory* (Boston), Dec. 5, 1809, [2]; "The Rostrum," *Daily National Intelligencer* (Washington, D.C.), Mar. 15, 1814, [3] ("peculiar powers"); "James Ogilvie," *Georgia Journal* (Milledgeville), June 5, 1821, [1] ("the force").

6. For maps showing roads, see Simeon De Witt, *Map of the State of New York* ([Albany?], 1804), Library of Congress; and Henry Charles Carey, *The State Map of New York,* in *Carey's General Atlas . . .* (Philadelphia, 1814), digital.library.pitt.edu/islandora/object/pitt%3A31735060440892/viewer#page/2/mode/2up. See also Allan S. Everest, "Early Roads and Taverns of the Champlain Valley," *Vermont History,* XXXVII (1969), 247–255. A steamboat arrived at Lake Champlain in 1809, but it, too, moved at five or six miles per hour.

7. My emphasis in these passages on self-representation and self-fashioning reflects my dedication to scholarship that focuses less on trying to uncover a "true" self than on exploring how people in the past performed themselves and how that representation of self is always conditioned by the wider culture, even when one is an *eccentric* who rejects conventional mores. That Ogilvie spent half his adult life on a literal stage and seeking auditors for his performances demanded that he represent himself in appealing ways. For more on these influential historical, theoretical, and especially feminist approaches to subjectivity, see Marilyn Booth and Antoinette Burton, "Critical Feminist Biography," *Journal of Women's History,* XXI, no. 3 (Fall 2009), 7–12; Judith Butler, *Gender Trouble: Feminism and the Subversion of Identity* (New York, 1990); Natalie Zemon Davis, *The Return of Martin Guerre* (Cambridge, Mass., 1983); Stephen Greenblatt, *Renaissance Self-Fashioning: From More to Shakespeare* (Chicago, 1980); Kali Israel, *Names and Stories: Emilia Dilke and Victorian Culture* (New York, 2002), esp. 13–17; Israel, "Style, Strategy, and Self-Creation in the Life of Emilia Dilke," in George Levine, ed., *Constructions of the Self* (New Brunswick, N.J., 1992), 213–245; Jo Burr Margadant, ed., *The New Biography: Performing Femininity in Nineteenth-Century France* (Berkeley, Calif., 2000), esp. editor's introduction and essays by Margadant and Mary Louise Roberts; Joan W. Scott, "The Evidence of Experience," *Critical Inquiry,* XVII (1991), 773–797; Carolyn Steedman, *Landscape for a Good Woman: A Story of Two Lives* (London, 1986); and Scott, "La Théorie qui n'en est pas une; or, Why Clio Doesn't Care," in Ann-Louise Shapiro, ed., *Feminists Revision History* (New Brunswick, N.J., 1994), 73–94.

8. On Washington as a symbol, icon, or celebrity, see Patricia A. Anderson, *Promoted*

to Glory: The Apotheosis of George Washington (Northampton, Mass., 1980); Marcus Cunliffe, *George Washington: Man and Monument* (New York, 1958); Catherine E. Kelly, *Republic of Taste: Art, Politics, and Everyday Life in Early America* (Philadelphia, 2016), chap. 6; Paul K. Longmore, *The Invention of George Washington* (Berkeley, Calif., 1988); Trevor Parry-Giles, "Fame, Celebrity, and the Legacy of John Adams," *Western Journal of Communication*, LXXII (2008), 83–101; Barry Schwartz, *George Washington: The Making of an American Symbol* (New York, 1987); Wendy C. Wick, *George Washington, an American Icon: The Eighteenth-Century Graphic Portraits* (Washington, D.C., 1982). No one helped construct that image more than Mason Locke Weems, whose affordable biography invented the story of the cherry tree (*Life of Washington* [1809; rpt. Cambridge, Mass., 1962]). On that subject, see François Furstenberg, *In the Name of the Father: Washington's Legacy, Slavery, and the Making of a Nation* (New York, 2006), 123–138; and John J. Garcia, "The 'Curiousaffaire' of Mason Locke Weems: Nationalism, the Book Trade, and Printed Lives in the Early United States," *Papers of the Bibliographical Society of America*, CVIII (2014), 453–475.

On other political celebrities of that generation, see Jon Kukla, *Patrick Henry: Champion of Liberty* (New York, 2017); Stanley J. Idzerda, Anne C. Loveland, and Marc H. Miller, *Lafayette, Hero of Two Worlds: The Art and Pageantry of His Farewell Tour of America, 1824–1825* (Flushing, N.Y., 1989); Jan Lewis and Peter S. Onuf, "Review Essay: American Synecdoche: Thomas Jefferson as Image, Icon, Character, and Self," *American Historical Review*, CIII (1998), 125–136; Merrill D. Peterson, *The Jefferson Image in the American Mind* (New York, 1960); and Lin-Manuel Miranda and Jeremy McCarter, eds., *Hamilton: The Revolution: Being the Complete Libretto of the Broadway Musical . . .* (New York, 2016). On Whitefield, see Robert E. Cray, Jr., "Memorialization and Enshrinement: George Whitefield and Popular Religious Culture, 1770–1850," *Journal of the Early Republic*, X (1990), 339–361; Thomas S. Kidd, *George Whitefield: America's Spiritual Founding Father* (New Haven, Conn., 2014); Jessica M. Parr, *Inventing George Whitefield: Race, Revivalism, and the Making of a Religious Icon* (Jackson, Miss., 2015); Nancy Ruttenburg, "George Whitefield, Spectacular Conversion, and the Rise of Democratic Personality," *American Literary History*, V (1993), 429–458; Harry S. Stout, *The Divine Dramatist: George Whitefield and the Rise of Modern Evangelicalism* (Grand Rapids, Mich., 1991); and Stout, "Religion, Communications, and the Ideological Origins of the American Revolution," *William and Mary Quarterly*, 3d Ser., XXXIV (1977), 519–541. On Dow and his contemporaries, see Nathan O. Hatch, *The Democratization of American Christianity* (New Haven, Conn., 1989); Marianne Perciaccante, *Calling Down Fire: Charles Grandison Finney and Revivalism in Jefferson County, New York, 1800–1840* (Albany, N.Y., 2003); and Leigh Eric Schmidt, *Hearing Things: Religion, Illusion, and the American Enlightenment* (Cambridge, Mass., 2000). And for information on Franklin, Wheatley, Rush, and their contemporaries, see Stephen Fried, *Rush: Revolution, Madness, and the Visionary Doctor Who Became a Founding Father* (New York, 2018); Charlene M. Boyer Lewis, *Elizabeth Patterson Bonaparte: An American Aristocrat in the Early Republic* (Philadelphia, 2012); Etta Madden, "'To Make a Figure': Benjamin Rush's Rhetorical Self-Construction and Scientific Authorship," *Early American Literature*, XLI (2006), 241–272; Nian-Sheng Huang and Carla Mulford, "Benjamin Franklin and the

American Dream," in Mulford, ed., *The Cambridge Companion to Benjamin Franklin* (New York, 2008), 145–158; Mulford, "Figuring Benjamin Franklin in American Cultural Memory," *New England Quarterly*, LXXII (1999), 415–443; Andrew M. Schocket, "Benjamin Franklin in Memory and Popular Culture," in David Waldstreicher, ed., *A Companion to Benjamin Franklin* (New York, 2011), 479–498; and Gordon S. Wood, *The Americanization of Benjamin Franklin* (New York, 2004).

9. Ogilvie to Benjamin Rush, Feb. 21, 1797, Rush Family Papers, 1748–1876, XXV, LCP. in.HSP.134, Historical Society of Pennsylvania, Philadelphia ("instrumental"). On Revolutionary era figures' seeking simultaneously to offer public service and receive public accolades, see Brandon Brame Fortune, "Portraits of Virtue and Genius: Pantheons of Worthies and Public Portraiture in the Early American Republic, 1780–1820" (Ph.D. diss., University of North Carolina at Chapel Hill, 1986), 2–3, 34–38, 90–92, 112; Kelly, *Republic of Taste*, 168–177; and Leo Braudy, *The Frenzy of Renown: Fame and Its History* (New York, 1986), 315–380. Charles L. Ponce de Leon, *Self-Exposure: Human-Interest Journalism and the Emergence of Celebrity in America, 1890–1940* (Chapel Hill, N.C., 2002), is particularly adept with the topic of public ambivalence toward celebrities later in the nineteenth and twentieth centuries. On transitions from early forms of fame or renown into more modern incarnations of celebrity, Richard Schickel once declared that the phenomenon of celebrity could not exist before the twentieth century, with the arrival of dense, overlapping media cultures like radio, film, fan magazines, photography, and gossip columns. See Schickel, *Intimate Strangers: The Culture of Celebrity* (1985; rpt. Garden City, N.Y., 2000), 23. Subsequent scholars have challenged that view, finding similarly dense celebrity cultures in places like eighteenth-century London and Paris, where a combination of print, images, and venues for performance propelled some figures to levels of public attention theretofore unseen. See Laura Engel, *Fashioning Celebrity: Eighteenth-Century British Actresses and Strategies for Image Making* (Columbus, Ohio, 2011); Antoine Lilti, *Figures publiques: L'invention de la célébrité, 1750–1850* (Paris, 2014); Tom Mole, ed., *Romanticism and Celebrity Culture, 1750–1850* (Cambridge, 2009); and Elizabeth Barry, ed., "Celebrity, Cultural Production and Public Life," special issue of *International Journal of Cultural Studies*, XI (2008), 251–376.

10. On the possibility of celebrity being fragile, see Lilti, *Figures publiques*, introduction and chap. 5; and Sharon Marcus, *The Drama of Celebrity* (Princeton, N.J., 2019), 3–8, and chap. 7. Here, I draw a finer distinction between Washington's and Ogilvie's celebrity than Lilti does. See also Ari Adut, *On Scandal: Moral Disturbances in Society, Politics, and Art* (New York, 2008); Páraic Finnerty and Rod Rosenquist, eds., "Transatlantic Celebrity: European Fame in Nineteenth-Century America," special issue of *Comparative American Studies*, XIV (2016), 1–89; Sara Lampert, *Starring Women: Celebrity, Patriarchy, and American Theater, 1790–1850* (Urbana, Ill., forthcoming); Tom Mole, *Byron's Romantic Celebrity: Industrial Culture and the Hermeneutic of Intimacy* (New York, 2007); Mole, ed., *Romanticism and Celebrity Culture, 1750–1850* (Cambridge, 2009); and Stella Tillyard, "Celebrity in Eighteenth-Century London," *History Today*, LV, no. 6 (June 2005), 20–27.

11. Edward G. Parker, *The Golden Age of American Oratory* (Boston, 1857). On the subject

of public speech in early America, see Thomas Augst, "Temperance, Mass Culture, and the Romance of Experience," *American Literary History*, XIX (2007), 297–323; Gregory Clark and S. Michael Halloran, eds., *Oratorical Culture in Nineteenth-Century America: Transformations in the Theory and Practice of Rhetoric* (Carbondale, Ill., 1993); Kenneth Cmiel, *Democratic Eloquence: The Fight over Popular Speech in Nineteenth-Century America* (1990; rpt. Berkeley, Calif., 1991); Carolyn Eastman, *A Nation of Speechifiers: Making an American Public after the Revolution* (Chicago, 2009); Eastman, "Oratory and Platform Culture in Eighteenth- and Nineteenth-Century America and Britain," in Colin Burrow, ed., *Oxford Handbooks Online* (July 2016), www.oxfordhandbooksonline.com; Eastman, "Reading Aloud: Editorial Societies and Orality in Magazines of the Early American Republic," *Early American Literature*, LIV (2019), 163–188; Jay Fliegelman, *Declaring Independence: Jefferson, Natural Language, and the Culture of Performance* (Stanford, Calif., 1993); Sandra M. Gustafson, *Eloquence Is Power: Oratory and Performance in Early America* (Williamsburg, Va., and Chapel Hill, N.C., 2000); Gustafson, *Imagining Deliberative Democracy in the Early American Republic* (Chicago, 2011); Jane Kamensky, *Governing the Tongue: The Politics of Speech in Early New England* (New York, 1997); Angela G. Ray, *The Lyceum and Public Culture in the Nineteenth-Century United States* (East Lansing, Mich., 2005); Ray and Paul Stob, eds., *Thinking Together: Cultures of Lecturing, Learning, and Difference in the Long Nineteenth Century* (State College, Pa., 2019); Joseph R. Roach, *The Player's Passion: Studies in the Science of Acting* (Ann Arbor, Mich., 1993); Schmidt, *Hearing Things*; James Perrin Warren, *Culture of Eloquence: Oratory and Reform in Antebellum America* (State College, Pa., 1999); Tom F. Wright, *Lecturing the Atlantic: Speech, Print, and an Anglo-American Commons, 1830–1870* (New York, 2017); and Wright, ed., *The Cosmopolitan Lyceum: Lecture Culture and the Globe in Nineteenth-Century America* (Amherst, Mass., 2013).

12. On the phenomenon of how the media both unified the early United States and yet raised awareness of provinciality, see William J. Gilmore, *Reading Becomes a Necessity of Life: Material and Cultural Life in Rural New England, 1780–1835* (Knoxville, Tenn., 1989); and, albeit for the twentieth-century context, Pierre Bourdieu, *Distinction: A Social Critique of the Judgement of Taste*, trans. Richard Nice (Cambridge, Mass., 1984). See also Richard L. Bushman, *The Refinement of America: Persons, Houses, Cities* (New York, 1992); and Eran Zelnik, "Yankees, Doodles, Fops, and Cuckolds: Compromised Manhood and Provincialism in the Revolutionary Period, 1740–1781," *Early American Studies*, XVI (2018), 514–544. Scholarship that analyzes the culture of oratory a few decades later also points to the unifying tendency of lyceum lecturers. See, especially, Mary Kupiec Cayton, "The Making of an American Prophet: Emerson, His Audiences, and the Rise of the Culture Industry in Nineteenth-Century America," *AHR*, XCII (1987), 597–620; Ray, *Lyceum and Public Culture*; and Donald M. Scott, "The Popular Lecture and the Creation of a Public in Mid-Nineteenth-Century America," *Journal of American History*, LXVI (1980), 791–809. Although this use of the word *fan* appeared as early as the seventeenth century, the *Oxford English Dictionary Online* shows it came into popular usage in the late nineteenth century. I should also note that the word *charismatic* was unknown in the early American Republic. See Jeremy C. Young, *The Age of Charisma: Leaders, Followers, and Emotions in American Society, 1870–1940* (Cam-

bridge, 2017); see also Tom F. Wright, "The Birth of Charisma: Languages of Mass Persuasion, 1820–1910" (unpublished manuscript).

13. In framing this as a drama, I rely on Marcus, *Drama of Celebrity.*

14. Whether those records might have been preserved by successive generations or archival institutions compounds the problem. In addition, many archival documents burned during the Civil War battles that took place in Virginia and other points in the South.

15. E., "Communication," *Poulson's American Daily Advertiser,* Oct. 20, 1808, [3]. Painting the newspaper into the portrait permitted Peale to make some clever choices, for this version of the newspaper is a creative composite of real and invented advertisements. He solved the problem of where to place his own signature by inventing an ad for himself, dated Oct. 20, 1808 (in reality, he never advertised in *Poulson's*). I'm grateful to James Green and Wendy Woloson of the Library Company of Philadelphia for sharing these images as well as their thoughts and research on the portrait (email correspondence with the author, Nov. 9, 2011).

16. Hew Scott, *Fasti Ecclesiae Scoticanae: The Succession of Ministers in the Parish Churches of Scotland from the Reformation, A.D. 1560, to the Present Time* (Edinburgh, 1871), III, part 2, 538; Scott, *Fasti Ecclesiae Scoticanae . . .* , new ed. (Edinburgh, 1926), VI, 108 (biography of Rev. Ogilvie); [Grigor Grant and James Ogilvie], *The Ogilviad, an Heroic Poem, with Its Answers: Being a Dispute between Two Gentlemen at King's College* (Aberdeen, U.K., 1789). The only known copy survives at Special Collections, Sir Duncan Rice Library, University of Aberdeen, U.K. William Walker, *The Bards of Bon-Accord, 1375–1860* (Aberdeen, U.K., 1887), 262–265, offers an appreciation of several passages.

CHAPTER ONE

1. Jonathan C. Cooper, "The Scarlet Gown: History and Development of Scottish Undergraduate Dress," *Transactions of the Burgon Society,* X (2010), 14. The quote is from the 1695 Covenanting Commission that sought to reform the Scottish universities. For college rules, see Colin A. McLaren, *Aberdeen Students, 1600–1860* (Aberdeen, U.K., 2005), 79–82, 169–170. The riot took place in 1781.

2. Grigor Grant, quoted in [Grant and James Ogilvie], *The Ogilviad, an Heroic Poem, with Its Answers: Being a Dispute between Two Gentlemen at King's College* (Aberdeen, U.K., 1789), [7] ("*great Ogilvie*"). Throughout this book, I attribute authorship of the lines alternately to Grant and Ogilvie, abbreviating them hereafter as GG and JO. One of the print shop's compositors misspelled Ogilvie's name as Ogilvy on the even-numbered pages; I have corrected those spellings. On Pope et al., see Richmond P. Bond, "-iad: A Progeny of the *Dunciad,*" *Publications of the Modern Language Association,* XLIV (1929), 1099–1105; Ritchie Robertson, *Mock-Epic Poetry from Pope to Heine* (Oxford, 2009), 99–101.

3. Laura J. Rosenthal, "'Trials of Manhood': Cibber, *The Dunciad,* and the Masculine Self," in Catherine Ingrassia and Claudia N. Thomas, eds., *"More Solid Learning": New Perspectives on Alexander Pope's "Dunciad"* (Lewisburg, Pa., 2000), 81–105. Grant and Ogilvie fol-

lowed Pope's example in using paired, rhyming couplets, often called heroic couplets because they could easily stand alone, facilitating memorization. See, for example, William Bowman Piper, *The Heroic Couplet* (Cleveland, Ohio, 1969).

4. GG, 8 ("battle fell"), JO, 8 ("unequal"), GG, 10 ("pseudo-poet"), in [Grant and Ogilvie], *Ogilviad.*

5. "David Gelston's Account of an Interview between Alexander Hamilton and James Monroe," July 11, 1797, in Harold C. Syrett et al., eds., *The Papers of Alexander Hamilton*, XXI (New York, 1974), 159–161 (quotations on 161); Joanne B. Freeman, *Affairs of Honor: National Politics in the New Republic* (New Haven, Conn., 2001), 174–178; Paul A. Gilje, *To Swear Like a Sailor: Maritime Culture in America, 1750–1850* (New York, 2016), 19–22.

6. JO, 8, in [Grant and Ogilvie], *Ogilviad.* Ogilvie borrowed the phrase "jingling verse" from Virgil. See *The Georgicks of Virgil*, trans. J. M. King (London, 1843), 58.

7. On public speech in early modern Britain, see Adam Fox, *Oral and Literate Culture in England, 1500–1700* (Oxford, 2000); Martin Hewitt, "Aspects of Platform Culture in Nineteenth-Century Britain," *Nineteenth-Century Prose*, XXIX, no. 1 (Spring 2002), 1–32; Josephine Hoegaerts, "Speaking Like Intelligent Men: Vocal Articulations of Authority and Identity in the House of Commons in the Nineteenth Century," *Radical History Review*, no. 121 (January 2015), 123–144; Paula McDowell, *The Invention of the Oral: Print Commerce and Fugitive Voices in Eighteenth-Century Britain* (Chicago, 2017); Joseph S. Meisel, *Public Speech and the Culture of Public Life in the Age of Gladstone* (New York, 2001); Judith Pascoe, *The Sarah Siddons Audio Files: Romanticism and the Lost Voice* (Ann Arbor, Mich., 2011); and Mary Thale, "The Case of the British Inquisition: Money and Women in Mid-Eighteenth-Century London Debating Societies," *Albion*, XXXI (1999), 31–48. On British education more generally, see Charles Bradford Bow, "The Science of Applied Ethics at Edinburgh University: Dugald Stewart on Moral Education and the Auxiliary Principles of the Moral Faculty," *Intellectual History Review*, XXIII (2013), 207–224; Jan Golinski, *Science as Public Culture: Chemistry and Enlightenment in Britain, 1760–1820* (Cambridge, 1992); Alan Richardson, *Literature, Education, and Romanticism: Reading as Social Practice, 1780–1832* (New York, 1994); W. B. Stephens, *Education in Britain, 1750–1914* (New York, 1998); and H. Lewis Ulman, ed., *The Minutes of the Aberdeen Philosophical Society, 1758–1773* (Aberdeen, U.K., 1990), 22.

8. James Beattie to Mrs. Montagu, Apr. 3, 1777, MS 30/1/121–130, Special Collections, Sir Duncan Rice Library, University of Aberdeen, U.K. (hereafter cited as UA) ("learned to fence"); Dictates [class notes] from James Beattie's class on moral philosophy, Marischal College, late eighteenth century, MS 30/49a, 223 ("barbarous"), 224 ("provincial accent"), 225 ("better than himself"), UA. In his letter to Montagu, Beattie gratefully acknowledges her compliment that he "write[s] English as well as an Englishman" but seems unwilling to believe it. As Paul B. Wood notes, Beattie (who taught at Aberdeen's Marischal College) and other Scottish college professors thus demonstrated their loyalty to the British crown through their spoken language, and therefore their opposition to any remaining Scots who opposed British rule or maintained sympathy for the Jacobite movement. See Wood, *The Aberdeen Enlightenment: The Arts Curriculum in the Eighteenth Century* (Aberdeen, U.K., 1993),

128–129. See also Roger L. Emerson, *Professors, Patronage, and Politics: The Aberdeen Universities in the Eighteenth Century* (Aberdeen, U.K., 1992), chap. 5; Donald J. Withrington, "What Was Distinctive about the Scottish Enlightenment?" 9–19, David Hewitt, "James Beattie and the Languages of Scotland," 251–260, and Joan H. Pittock, "Rhetoric and *Belles Lettres* in the North East," 276–281, all in Jennifer J. Carter and Pittock, eds., *Aberdeen and the Enlightenment: Proceedings of a Conference Held at the University of Aberdeen* (Aberdeen, U.K., 1987); and R. Bruce Taylor, "Student Days in Glasgow University, 1887–1891," *Journal of the Presbyterian Historical Society*, XXXVII (1959), 193–207. Although a tiny number of sources professed finding Ogilvie's accent difficult, the vast majority never mentioned it. Nor should this surprise us. During a period in which the United States had a large number of Scottish immigrants, it's likely his accent was familiar to people in many parts of the country.

9. Hewitt, "James Beattie," in Carter and Pittock, eds., *Aberdeen and the Enlightenment*, 255.

10. Wood, *Aberdeen Enlightenment*, 119, 161–162; Philip Hicks, *Neoclassical History and English Culture: From Clarendon to Hume* (New York, 1996), chap. 7.

11. Pryse Lockhart Gordon, *Personal Memoirs; or, Reminiscences of Men and Manners at Home and Abroad . . .*, 2 vols. (London, 1830), I, 30 ("sonorous voice"). On language and elocution, see Hans Aarsleff, *The Study of Language in England, 1780–1860* (Princeton, N.J., 1967); Carolyn Eastman, *A Nation of Speechifiers: Making an American Public after the Revolution* (Chicago, 2009); Jay Fliegelman, *Declaring Independence: Jefferson, Natural Language, and the Culture of Performance* (Stanford, Calif., 1993); Wilbur Samuel Howell, *Eighteenth-Century British Logic and Rhetoric* (Princeton, N.J., 1971); and Catherine Packham, "Cicero's Ears, or Eloquence in the Age of Politeness: Oratory, Moderation, and the Sublime in Enlightenment Scotland," *Eighteenth-Century Studies*, XLVI (2013), 499–512.

12. GG, 14, in [Grant and Ogilvie], *Ogilviad*.

13. Thomas Pennant, *A Tour in Scotland*, 4th ed. (London, 1775), I, 173, quoted in Henry Grey Graham, *The Social Life of Scotland in the Eighteenth Century*, 2d ed. (London, 1901), 361–362 ("narrow"). See comparably low rates for English clergy: Francis Godwin James, "Clerical Incomes in Eighteenth Century England," *Historical Magazine of the Protestant Episcopal Church*, XVIII (1949), 311–325. Estimating the value of this income in today's money is notoriously difficult; for contrast, in 1810 the minimum salary for a minister in Scotland was raised to £150. James states drily that "the economic position of the lesser clergy was not enviable" (311). See also Robert T. D. Glaister, "A Comparative Study of Estates of Ministers and Schoolmasters in Roxburghshire in the Nineteenth Century," *Scottish Historical Review*, LXII (1983), 150–152. See also Valerie Morgan, "Agricultural Wage Rates in Late Eighteenth Century Scotland," *Economic History Review*, XXIV (1971), 181–201. Male laborers made about eight to ten pounds per year; female laborers, about three to four pounds.

14. Wallace Jackson, "Introduction," in John Ogilvie, *An Essay on the Lyric Poetry of the Ancients* (1762), ed. Jackson (Los Angeles, 1970); Douglas L. Patey, "Ogilvie, John (1733–1813)," in A. C. Grayling, Naomi Goulder, and Andrew Pyle, eds., *The Continuum Encyclopedia of British Philosophy*, 4 vols. (Bristol, U.K., 2006), III, 2370–2371; Douglas Lane Patey, *Proba-*

bility and Literary Form: Philosophic Theory and Literary Practice in the Augustan Age (Cambridge, 1984), chap. 8.

15. Robert Chambers, ed., A Biographical Dictionary of Eminent Scotsmen, rev. and cont. Thomas Thomson (London, 1875), half-vol. V, 222 ("incident"); John Bulloch, "Historic Scenes in Aberdeenshire," Dundee Courier & Argus and Northern Warder, Dec. 28, 1883, [7] ("voluminous"); M. C. T., "John Ogilvie," Aberdeen Journal, Apr. 5, 1909, [3] ("noble wild prospects").

16. Adam Fox, Oral and Literate Culture in England, 1500–1700 (Oxford, 2000); Paula McDowell, The Invention of the Oral: Print Commerce and Fugitive Voices in Eighteenth-Century Britain (Chicago, 2017); and Adam Fox and Daniel Woolf, eds., The Spoken Word: Oral Culture in Britain, 1500–1850 (Manchester, U.K., 2002).

17. Marischal College Records, MS M 366, n.p. ("PESSIMUM"), UA; John Ogilvie, The Fane of the Druids: A Poem (London, 1787). I'm grateful to Rev. Elspeth McKay, the current minister for Midmar and Echt, for providing information about the region's history, the standing stones, and Ogilvie's church.

18. Francis Douglas, A General Description of the East Coast of Scotland, from Edinburgh to Cullen ... (Paisley, U.K., 1782), 118–119. See also R. A. Houston, Scottish Literacy and the Scottish Identity: Illiteracy and Society in Scotland and Northern England, 1600–1800 (Cambridge, 1985); and W. B. Stephens, "Literacy in England, Scotland, and Wales, 1500–1900," History of Education Quarterly, XXX (1990), 545–571.

19. Gordon, Personal Memoirs, I, 21 ("good teacher"); "Inventory of the Writes of Redhyths Mortification," Seafield Papers, GD 248/680/7, National Records of Scotland (NRS), Edinburgh ("poor and such"). On the details of the bursary, see Evidence, Oral and Documentary, Taken and Received by the Commissioners Appointed by His Majesty George IV., July 23d, 1826 ... for Visiting the Universities of Scotland (London, 1837), IV, 202–204. Initially, the Redhyth Bursary had also been designated for children of the servants and tenants at Redhyth, as well as boys with the surname Sharp. See Evidence, Oral and Documentary, 203; King's College Bursars Books, 1753–1822, MS K 28, 128, UA. On Scottish education, see Donald J. Withrington, "Education and Society in the Eighteenth Century," in N. T. Phillipson and Rosalind Mitchison, eds., Scotland in the Age of Improvement: Essays in Scottish History in the Eighteenth Century (Edinburgh, 1996), 169–199; and Houston, Scottish Literacy.

20. McLaren, Aberdeen Students, 81–82 ("Diligence"), 96 ("mark of inferiority"); Gordon, Personal Memoirs, I, 14 ("many colours" and "aristocrats").

21. Petition of John Ogilvie, Seafield Papers, GD 248/680/7, NRS ("tollerable"); Petition of Sir John Grant, ibid; sample presentation to a bursar at the School of Fordyce, ibid ("having undoubted right").

22. Gordon, Personal Memoirs, I, 16; McLaren, Aberdeen Students, 74, 84.

23. In 1786, James Ogilvie was one of four students who received £1 11s. 6d. for his bursary, whereas the remaining twelve bursars only got £1 2s. 2d. See King's College Bursars Book, 1753–1822, MS K 28, 128, UA. Pryse Lockhart Gordon, who attended about ten years earlier than Ogilvie, offers an enumerated account of his first year's expenses at

King's College, which added up to £17 4s. 3d. (*Personal Memoirs*, I, 15–16). For details on the city of Aberdeen, see "Introduction," in Ulman, ed., *Minutes of the Aberdeen Philosophical Society, 1758–1773* (Aberdeen, U.K., 1990), 14–17.

24. Hew Scott, *Fasti Ecclesiae Scoticanae: The Succession of Ministers in the Church of Scotland from the Reformation*, new ed. (Edinburgh, 1926), VI, 358.

25. James Boswell, quoted in Ian Charles Cargill Graham, *Colonists from Scotland: Emigration to North America, 1707–1783* (Ithaca, N.Y., 1956), 21. Not all moved to America; some went to Germany, Ulster in Northern Ireland, Australia, and the Scottish Lowlands, among other locales. For published treatises on the out-migration of Scots, see Alexander Irvine, *An Inquiry into the Causes and Effects of Emigration from the Highlands and Western Islands of Scotland* . . . (Edinburgh, 1802); Robert Brown, *Strictures and Remarks on the Earl of Selkirk's Observations on the Present State of the Highlands of Scotland, with a View of the Causes and Probable Consequences of Emigration* (Edinburgh, 1806); and [Edward Satchwell Fraser?], "On Emigration from the Scottish Highlands and Isles," circa 1803, MS 9646, National Library of Scotland, Edinburgh.

26. "The Public are hereby informed . . . ," *Virginia Herald, and Fredericksburg Advertiser*, Dec. 19, 1793, [4].

27. Graham, *Colonists from Scotland*, 23–25; G. MacLaren Brydon, "Letter of the Rev. James Ogilvie to Colonel John Walker of Belvoir, Virginia, April 26, 1771," *Historical Magazine of the Protestant Episcopal Church*, I (1932), 32–36; James Ogilvie to Thomas Jefferson, Mar. 28, 1770, Jefferson to Peyton Randolph, July 23, 1770, Jefferson to James Ogilvie, Feb. 20, 1771, James Ogilvie to Jefferson, Apr. 26, 1771, John Ogilvie to Jefferson, July 19, 1771, all in James P. McClure and J. Jefferson Looney, eds., *The Papers of Thomas Jefferson Digital Edition*, Main Series (Charlottesville, Va., 2008–2020), I, 38–40, 49–51, 62–64, 67–68, 75–76, https://rotunda.upress.virginia.edu/founders.

28. James Ogilvie, "The Preface," *Sermons on Various Subjects* (London, 1786), [ii]. Rev. Ogilvie subsequently served as a chaplain for the man-of-war *Vigilant* and thereafter as the curate at Egham. See also Ogilvie's eulogy in *Monthly Magazine* (London), XXVI, no. 179 (January 1809), 607–608. In his claim to the Loyalist Claims Commissioners, Ogilvie professed to have earned £240 per year as the rector of Westover Parish. A letter in the same file from Jonathan Boucher attested, "I know of no American Property so ascertainable, and so easily desirable, as the Value of a Virginia Living." See Rev. James Ogilvie, Memorial to the Loyalist Claims Commissioners, 1784, Auditor's Office 13/134, Public Record Office, London, Virginia Colonial Records Project, reel 262, Library of Virginia.

29. Seth Cotlar, *Tom Paine's America: The Rise and Fall of Transatlantic Radicalism in the Early Republic* (Charlottesville, Va., 2011). For Ogilvie's views on the United States, see James Ogilvie, *Cursory Reflexions on Government, Philosophy, and Education* (Alexandria, Va., 1802), 39–40; "J. Ogilvie's Oration," *Richmond Examiner*, July 9, 1803, [2]; James Ogilvie, *Philosophical Essays* . . . (Philadelphia, 1816), ii For other Scots inspired by the radical promise of the new United States, see Gail Bederman, "Revisiting Nashoba: Slavery, Utopia, and Frances Wright in America, 1818–1826," *American Literary History*, XVII (2005), 438–459.

30. Philip Vickers Fithian, *Journal and Letters of Philip Vickers Fithian, 1773–1774: A Plantation Tutor of the Old Dominion*, ed. Hunter Dickinson Farish (Williamsburg, Va., 1943), 39. See also Franklin E. Court, *The Scottish Connection: The Rise of English Literary Study in Early America* (Syracuse, N.Y., 2001).

31. J. M. Bumsted, "The Scottish Diaspora: Emigration to British North America, 1763–1815," in Ned C. Landsman, ed., *Nation and Province in the First British Empire: Scotland and the Americas, 1600–1800* (Lewisburg, Pa., 2001), 143–144, 146.

32. Jedidiah Morse, *The American Universal Geography* . . . , 3d ed. (Boston, 1796), I, 620.

33. Franklin [pseud.], "The present moment is a crisis," *Republican Citizen*, Mar. 1, 1797, [4].

34. Ogilvie to Benjamin Rush, Feb. 21, 1797, Rush Family Papers, 1748–1876, LCP. in.HSP.134, XXV, Historical Society of Pennsylvania, Philadelphia.

CHAPTER TWO

1. James Ogilvie, "To the Inhabitants of Richmond and Its Vicinity," *Examiner* (Richmond), Mar. 9, 1803, [3].

2. Nancy Beadie, *Education and the Creation of Capital in the Early American Republic* (New York, 2010); Lawrence A. Cremin, *American Education: The National Experience, 1783–1876* (New York, 1980); and Rita Koganzon, "'Producing a Reconciliation of Disinterestedness and Commerce': The Political Rhetoric of Education in the Early Republic," *History of Education Quarterly*, LII (2012), 403–429. See also Johann N. Neem, *Democracy's Schools: The Rise of Public Education in America* (Baltimore, 2017).

3. James Ogilvie, "Supplementary Narrative," in Ogilvie, *Philosophical Essays* . . . (Philadelphia, 1816), vii–viii (quotations on viii) (hereafter cited as PE). In Ogilvie, "The public are respectfully informed . . . ," *Virginia Herald, and Fredericksburg Advertiser* (Fredericksburg), Sept. 25, 1795, [1], he explains his preference for ages eight through fourteen but promises that "youth will find ample and profitable employment in this seminary till twenty or twenty-one years of age." For notices about Ogilvie's schools, including details on the subjects he taught, see "On Monday the 15th instant," *Virginia Herald, and Fredericksburg Advertiser*, Dec. 25, 1794, [3]; "To the Public," *Aurora General Advertiser* (Philadelphia), Dec. 24, 1799, [4] ("the principles"); and "For the National Intelligencer," *National Intelligencer, and Washington Advertiser* (Washington, D.C.), Mar. 8, 1802, [3].

4. "Course of Juvenile Education," *Enquirer* (Richmond), Apr. 9, 1805, [3]. In Tappahannock in 1799, he started a school with former star pupil Thomas Ritchie, who went on to found the Richmond *Enquirer* in 1804. See Bert Marsh Mutersbaugh, "Jeffersonian Journalist: Thomas Ritchie and the Richmond *Enquirer*, 1804–1820" (Ph.D. diss., University of Missouri, 1973), 16–21.

5. "On Monday the 15th instant," *Virginia Herald, and Fredericksburg Advertiser*, Dec. 25, 1794, [3] ("extraordinary progress"). See similar praise after he left Stevensburg Academy in "Letter to J. Ogilvie," *Virginia Gazette & General Advertiser* (Richmond), Jan. 22, 1803, [3]; [Thomas Ritchie?], "Mr. Ogilvie," *Enquirer*, May 1, 1821, [3] ("unparalleled"); H. of Rich-

mond [James Heath?], "Recollections of James Ogilvie, Earl of Findlater . . . ," *Southern Literary Messenger*, XIV (1848), 534–535 ("consummate skill"). Some of Ogilvie's most famous students include Sen. William S. Archer; Rep. John S. Barbour; Brig. Gen. George Mercer Brooke; William Pope Duval, governor of Florida; Gen. Roger Jones; Commander Thomas ap Catesby Jones; Sen. Benjamin Watkins Leigh; Sen. William Cabell Rives; Commander Winfield Scott; and William W. Seaton, editor of the *National Intelligencer, and Washington Advertiser* (Washington, D.C.). On his students, see Allen C. Clark, "Colonel William Winston Seaton and His Mayoralty," *Records of the Columbia Historical Society, Washington, D.C.*, XXIX–XXX (1928), 3; Jay B. Hubbell, "William Wirt and the Familiar Essay in Virginia," *William and Mary Quarterly*, 2d Ser., XXIII (1943), 140; and Winfield Scott, *Memoirs of Lieut.-General Scott, LL.D* (New York, 1864), 8–9.

6. Eran Shalev, *Rome Reborn on Western Shores: Historical Imagination and the Creation of the American Republic* (Charlottesville, Va., 2009), 2 ("of, through, and with"), and chap. 5; Caroline Winterer, *The Culture of Classicism: Ancient Greece and Rome in American Intellectual Life, 1780–1910* (Baltimore, 2002). See also Cremin, *American Education*; and Robert Middlekauff, *Ancients and Axioms: Secondary Education in Eighteenth-Century New England* (New Haven, Conn., 1963).

7. Ogilvie, "Fellow-Citizens," *Virginia Herald, and Fredericksburg Advertiser*, July 3, 1795, [2]. Some of Ogilvie's improvements were inspired by innovations taking place in Scottish higher education, as Franklin E. Court shows about the rising importance of English in *The Scottish Connection: The Rise of English Literary Study in Early America* (Syracuse, N.Y., 2001).

8. Ogilvie, "Course of Juvenile Education," *Enquirer*, Apr. 9, 1805, [3]; Cremin, *American Education*, 117–181.

9. For information on the Young Ladies' Academy, dame schools, and the Cherokee school, see Carolyn Eastman, *A Nation of Speechifiers: Making an American Public after the Revolution* (Chicago, 2009), 66–67, 89. On the African Free School, see Anna Mae Duane, "'Like a Motherless Child': Racial Education at the New York African Free School and in *My Bondage and My Freedom*," *American Literature*, LXXXII (2010), 461–488; and "New-York, Nov. 16," *Virginia Herald and Fredericksburg & Falmouth Advertiser* (Fredericksburg), Nov. 25, 1796, [2], which describes the New York African Free School's impressive "dialogues, speeches, and other select pieces, pronounced by some of the scholars" with such skill that "the most prejudiced advocate of African slavery, if present, could have felt his favourite argument weakened." On school exhibitions, see Eastman, *A Nation of Speechifiers*, 22–27; Jay Fliegelman, *Declaring Independence: Jefferson, Natural Language, and the Culture of Performance* (Stanford, Calif., 1993), 28–35; Sandra M. Gustafson, *Eloquence Is Power: Oratory and Performance in Early America* (Williamsburg, Va., and Chapel Hill, N.C., 2000), chap. 4; Mary Kelley, *Learning to Stand and Speak: Women, Education, and Public Life in America's Republic* (Williamsburg, Va., and Chapel Hill, N.C., 2006), 92–102; Catherine E. Kelly, *Republic of Taste: Art, Politics, and Everyday Life in Early America* (Philadelphia, 2016), 50–53; and J. M. Opal, *Beyond the Farm: National Ambitions in Rural New England* (Philadelphia, 2008), 100–103.

10. Ogilvie, "To the Public," *Virginia Herald, and Fredericksburg Advertiser*, Aug. 7, 1795, [3]

("necessary"); Ogilvie, "To the Public," *Aurora General Advertiser* (Philadelphia), Dec. 24, 1799, [4] ("habits of clear"). On the importance of oratory in Virginia during the early Republic, see Richard Beale Davis, *Intellectual Life in Jefferson's Virginia, 1790–1830* (Chapel Hill, N.C., 1964), 363–386.

11. Ogilvie to Jefferson, [before July 3, 1795], Jefferson to Mann Page, Aug. 30, 1795, both in James P. McClure and J. Jefferson Looney, eds., *The Papers of Thomas Jefferson Digital Edition*, Main Series (Charlottesville, Va., 2008–2020), XXVIII, 401–404 ("the right road," 403), 434–435 (declines to attend), https://rotunda.upress.virginia.edu/founders (hereafter cited as *PTJ*, Main); Martha Walker Divers to Mary (House) Gilmer, June 18, 1807, Peachy Ridgway Gilmer Papers, 1790–1889, Mss1 G4216 a, Virginia Museum of History and Culture (VMHC), Richmond ("conspicuous figure"); Gene A. Smith, *Thomas ap Catesby Jones: Commodore of Manifest Destiny* (Annapolis, Md., 2000), 7 (leaving William and Mary). For Ogilvie's learned pamphlet, see Ogilvie, *Cursory Reflexions on Government, Philosophy, and Education* (Alexandria, Va., 1802). On educational innovation, see Alan Taylor, *Thomas Jefferson's Education* (New York, 2019). I'm grateful to Taylor for sharing an early version of his material on Ogilvie.

12. Joseph M. Cabell to William H. Cabell, Mar. 14, 1807, MS 2C11147a, VMHC ("has now elapsed"); Samuel J. Cabell, Jr., to Joseph C. Cabell, Oct. 15, 1806, Joseph Carrington Cabell Papers, 1790–1890, Acc. no. 38–111c, Albert and Shirley Small Special Collections Library, University of Virginia, Charlottesville (hereafter cited as UVA) ("self command").

13. Benjamin Rush, "Of the Mode of Education Proper in a Republic," in *Essays, Literary, Moral and Philosophical* (Philadelphia, 1798), 7 ("adapt our modes"). See also Benjamin Henry Latrobe, "Thoughts on National System of Education" [a letter to Ferdinand Fairfax, 1798], in J. H. B. Latrobe, ed., *Journal of Latrobe* (New York, 1905), 65–82; Cremin, *American Education*; Eastman, *Nation of Speechifiers*, chap. 1; and Taylor, *Thomas Jefferson's Education*, chap. 6.

14. "Mr. Ogilvie," *Enquirer*, May 1, 1821, [3] ("light and liberty"); Ogilvie to Jefferson, [before July 3, 1795], *PTJ*, Main, XXVIII, 401–404 ("felicity of mankind," 401). On republican radicalism, see Seth Cotlar, *Tom Paine's America: The Rise and Fall of Transatlantic Radicalism in the Early Republic* (Charlottesville, Va., 2011), 5, chap. 2; Cotlar, "Languages of Democracy in America from the Revolution to the Election of 1800," in Joanna Innes and Mark Philp, eds., *Re-imagining Democracy in the Age of Revolutions: America, France, Britain, Ireland, 1750–1850* (Oxford, 2013), 13–27; Matthew Rainbow Hale, "Regenerating the World: The French Revolution, Civic Festivals, and the Forging of Modern American Democracy, 1793–1795," *Journal of American History*, CIII (2017), 891–920; Armin Mattes, *Citizens of a Common Intellectual Homeland: The Transatlantic Origins of American Democracy and Nationhood* (Charlottesville, Va., 2015); Andrew Shankman, *Crucible of American Democracy: The Struggle to Fuse Egalitarianism and Capitalism in Jeffersonian Pennsylvania* (Lawrence, Kans., 2004); and Sean Wilentz, *The Rise of American Democracy: Jefferson to Lincoln* (New York, 2005).

15. "Perdition Seize That Democratic Society," *General Advertiser* (Philadelphia), May 16, 1794, [3] ("Citizen implies"); Ogilvie, "Fellow-Citizens," *Virginia Herald, and Fredericksburg Ad-*

vertiser, July 3, 1795, [1]; Ogilvie to Jefferson, Oct. 29, 1802, PTJ, Main, XXXVIII, 597–598 ("fellow Citizen," 598); Ogilvie to Francis Walker Gilmer, Feb. 1, 1813, in Richard Beale Davis, *Francis Walker Gilmer: Life and Learning in Jefferson's Virginia* (Richmond, Va., 1939), 375 ("citizen"). For Virginia's naturalization law, see "An Act Declaring Who Shall Be Deemed Citizens," Dec. 23, 1792, *The Statutes at Large of Virginia* . . . , I (Richmond, Va., 1835–1836), 148. On republican newspapers, see Jeffrey L. Pasley, *The Tyranny of Printers: Newspaper Politics in the Early American Republic* (Charlottesville, Va., 2001), chap. 1.

16. William Wirt to Dabney Carr, May 14, 1821, in John P. Kennedy, *Memoirs of the Life of William Wirt, Attorney-General of the United States*, new and rev. ed. (New York, 1872), II, 108 ("blood runs cold"). On celebrating the French Revolution, see Simon P. Newman, *Parades and the Politics of the Street: Festive Culture in the Early American Republic* (Philadelphia, 1997), chap. 4; Terry Bouton, *Taming Democracy: "The People," the Founders, and the Troubled Ending of the American Revolution* (New York, 2007); Susan Branson, *These Fiery Frenchified Dames: Women and Political Culture in Early National Philadelphia* (Philadelphia, 2001); François Furstenberg, *When the United States Spoke French: Five Refugees who Shaped a Nation* (New York, 2014); Hale, "Regenerating the World," *JAH*, CIII (2017), 891–920; Mattes, *Citizens of a Common Intellectual Homeland*; Simon Schama, *Citizens: A Chronicle of the French Revolution* (New York, 1989); and Adam I. P. Smith, "The 'Fortunate Banner': Languages of Democracy in the United States, c. 1848," in Innes and Philp, eds., *Re-Imagining Democracy in the Age of Revolutions*, 28–39.

17. Hale, "Regenerating the World," *JAH*, CIII (2017); Annie Jourdan, "Les discours de la terreur à l'époque révolutionnaire (1776–1798): Etude comparative sur une notion ambiguë," *French Historical Studies*, XXXVI (2013), 52–81.

18. Ogilvie, "Fredericksburg Academy," *Virginia Herald, and Fredericksburg Advertiser*, July 10, 1795, [3] ("duties of a freeman"); Ogilvie, *A Speech Delivered in Essex County in Support of a Memorial, Presented to the Citizens of that County and Now Laid before the Assembly, on the Subject of the Alien and Sedition Acts* (Richmond, Va., 1798), 5 ("rights of a freeman"); William Godwin, *An Enquiry concerning Political Justice*, ed. Mark Philip (1793; rpt. Oxford, 2013), 317 ("gradually prepared"). For data on enslaved people, see Ira Berlin, *Slaves without Masters: The Free Negro in the American South* (1974; rpt. New York, 1992), 46–47. The percentage of black men and women who were enslaved dropped slightly between 1790 and 1800, from 96 percent to 95 percent, thanks to a state law that made it easier to free enslaved people. Half the enslaved people in the United States lived in Virginia in 1790. See Alan Taylor, *The Internal Enemy: Slavery and War in Virginia, 1772–1832* (New York, 2014), 7–9.

19. Godwin, *Political Justice*, 16 ("progressive improvement"); "Extract of a Letter from W. Godwin to James Ogilvie," *National Intelligencer, and Washington Advertiser*, Apr. 16, 1802, [3], reprinted in the *Democratic Republican; or, Anti-Aristocrat* (Baltimore), May 8, 1802, [1–2]. See also Burton R. Pollin, "Godwin's Letter to Ogilvie, Friend of Jefferson, and the Federalist Propaganda," *Journal of the History of Ideas*, XXVIII (1967), 432–444; and "We are promised . . . ," *Alexandria Expositor, and the Columbian Advertiser*, May 9, 1803, [2]. Ogilvie was hardly alone in appreciating *Political Justice*. Many young men were inspired by the book, and it

gained particular traction on college campuses. About the Virginia-born John James Marshall, Jr. (the son of John Marshall, the chief justice of the U.S. Supreme Court), one friend recalled: "He was the most intrepid infidel in College and avowed his creed on all occasions. Godwin's *Political Justice* was his Bible." See Steven J. Novak, *The Rights of Youth: American Colleges and Student Revolt, 1798–1815* (Cambridge, Mass., 1977), 91 (quotation), and chap. 5; and Taylor, *Thomas Jefferson's Education*, 86, 88.

20. Thomas Paine, *The Age of Reason, Being an Investigation of True and Fabulous Theology* (New York, 1898), 175 ("thing called Christianity"). For reaction to Ogilvie's use of Godwin, see Crito, "To the Editor," *Gazette of the United States, & Daily Advertiser* (Philadelphia), Sept. 24, 1801, [2]. On Ogilvie's skepticism, see Ogilvie to Walter Jones, Jan. 19, 1798 [1799], Gallatin Papers, New-York Historical Society Library (NYHS); [John Rodman], *Fragment of a Journal of a Sentimental Philosopher* ... (New York, 1809), 14; Ogilvie to Francis Walker Gilmer, Feb. 1, 1813, in Davis, *Francis Walker Gilmer*, 374; and H. of Richmond [James Heath?], "Recollections of James Ogilvie," *Southern Literary Messenger*, XIV (1848), 536. On Paine's earlier popularity, see Trish Loughran, "Disseminating *Common Sense*: Thomas Paine and the Problem of the Early National Bestseller," *American Literature*, LXXVIII (2006), 1–28. On religious changes, see Jon Butler, *Awash in a Sea of Faith: Christianizing the American People* (Cambridge, Mass., 1990); Christopher Grasso, *Skepticism and American Faith: From the Revolution to the Civil War* (New York, 2018); Edward G. Gray, *Tom Paine's Iron Bridge: Building a United States* (New York, 2016), chaps. 10–12; Herbert M. Morais, *Deism in Eighteenth-Century America* (1934; rpt. New York, 1960); Eric R. Schlereth, *An Age of Infidels: The Politics of Religious Controversy in the Early United States* (Philadelphia, 2013); Leigh Eric Schmidt, *Hearing Things: Religion, Illusion, and the American Enlightenment* (Cambridge, Mass., 2000); and James Turner, *Without God, without Creed: The Origins of Unbelief in America* (Baltimore, 1985). Thomas Jefferson's daughter, Martha Jefferson Randolph, found deism appealing enough that she determined not to have her sons baptized during this era (although she did arrange for her daughters' baptisms). She later professed to regret that decision. See Martha Jefferson Randolph to Benjamin F. Randolph, Jan. 27, 1836, Family Letters, University of Virginia, Charlottesville, http://tjrs.monticello.org/letter/2334.

21. Thomas Jefferson's Bible, Smithsonian Institution, http://americanhistory.si.edu /JeffersonBible. Jefferson also deleted extraneous words and corrected the grammar. See also Grasso, *Skepticism and American Faith*; David L. Holmes, *The Faiths of the Founding Fathers* (New York, 2006), chap. 8; and Constance B. Schulz, "'Of Bigotry in Politics and Religion': Jefferson's Religion, the Federalist Press, and the Syllabus," *Virginia Magazine of History and Biography*, XCI (1983), 73–91. Most of Jefferson's contemporary founders weren't deists but followed a more conventional Christianity. See also Mark David Hall, "Were Any of the Founders Deists?" in Barbara A. McGraw, ed., *The Wiley Blackwell Companion to Religion and Politics in the U.S.* (Chichester, U.K., 2016), 51–63; and Daniel L. Dreisbach and Mark David Hall, eds., *Faith and the Founders of the American Republic* (New York, 2014). Jefferson's deism was so notorious that it became important during the presidential election of 1800, when some called him an "infidel enemy of Christ" and believed his candidacy amounted to a

referendum on Christianity. Many Americans believed his election would unleash a vast rejection of Christianity and would lead to the burning of Bibles. See Grasso, *Skepticism and American Faith*, 14, 138, 155.

22. Monitor, "Mr. Green, on a perusal of your paper . . . ," *Virginia Herald, and Fredericksburg Advertiser*, July 14, 1795, [3] ("pedantic puffings"); Ogilvie, "Mr. Green," *Virginia Herald, and Fredericksburg Advertiser*, July 17, 1795, [3] ("abortive malignity"); Ogilvie, "Mr. Green," from a supplement to the *Virginia Herald, and Fredericksburg Advertiser*, July 31, 1795, [2] ("mental imbecility"); "Monitor and Mr. Ogilvie," *Virginia Herald, and Fredericksburg Advertiser*, Sept. 1, 1795, [3].

23. Ogilvie to Walter Jones, Jan. 19, 1798 [1799], Gallatin Papers, NYHS.

24. Senex, "To the Editor of the Virginia Gazette," *Virginia Gazette* (Richmond), Oct. 1, 1803, [2] ("gross and open"); Ogilvie, "Mr. Davis," *Virginia Gazette*, Oct. 5, 1803, [3] ("cheerfully alter"); "On no occasion . . . ," *Examiner*, Oct. 5, 1803, [2] ("species of infidelity"). The immoderate style and word choices appear to be distinctively Ogilvie's, and the editor, Meriweather Jones, was one of his friends.

25. Thomas Cooper to Jefferson, Mar. 20, 1814, PTJ, Retirement Series, VII, 257–259.

26. Ogilvie was not the only man during the early Republic to encounter controversy or even failure only to rebound and find subsequent success. See Edward J. Balleisen, *Navigating Failure: Bankruptcy and Commercial Society in Antebellum America* (Chapel Hill, N.C., 2001); Jane Kamensky, *The Exchange Artist: A Tale of High-Flying Speculation and America's First Banking Collapse* (New York, 2008); Scott A. Sandage, *Born Losers: A History of Failure in America* (Cambridge, Mass., 2005); and Ryan K. Smith, *Robert Morris's Folly: The Architectural and Financial Failures of an American Founder* (New Haven, Conn., 2014).

27. Of course, Richmond had ultimately suffered attack, too. See Harry M. Ward and Harold E. Greer, Jr., *Richmond during the Revolution, 1775–1783* (Charlottesville, Va., 1977), 8, 77–78; Marie Tyler-McGraw, *At the Falls: Richmond, Virginia, and Its People* (Chapel Hill, N.C., 1994), 60.

28. William Loughton Smith, "Journal of William Loughton Smith, 1790–1791," Massachusetts Historical Society, *Proceedings*, 3d. Ser., LI (1917–1918), 65; Hilary Louise Coulson, "The Penitentiary at Richmond: Slavery, State Building, and Labor in the South's First State Prison" (Ph.D. diss., University of California, San Diego, 2016).

29. [Samuel Mordecai], *Richmond in By-Gone Days: Being Reminiscences of an Old Citizen* (Richmond, Va., 1856), 45, 129, 205–206 ("Tooth-Drawer" and local color); Johann David Schoepf, quoted in Ward and Greer, *Richmond during the Revolution*, 50 ("talking ribaldry"). Details about Richmond found in Richmond Common Council, cited in Marianne Patricia Buroff Sheldon, "Richmond, Virginia: The Town and Henrico County to 1820" (Ph.D. diss., University of Michigan, 1975), 253, 411; *Richmond Directory, Register and Almanac* (Richmond, Va., 1819), [3]; *Catalogue of Books Belonging to the Richmond Library* (Richmond, Va., 1801); and Coulson, "The Penitentiary at Richmond."

30. "J. Ogilvie's Oration," *Examiner*, July 9, 1803, [2]. The speech is printed over the course of the next several issues: July 13, 16, and 20 ("reign of error"), and I'm grateful

to Anne McCrery for transcribing it. See also Isaac A. Coles to Joseph C. Cabell, Nov. 1, 1804, Joseph Carrington Cabell Papers, 1790–1890, Acc. no. 38–111c, box 3, folder 12, UVA ("whole mass of talents"). Thomas Ritchie and William Brockenbrough were five years younger than Ogilvie; John Brockenbrough was the same age. Ritchie was the Brockenbrough brothers' cousin. Ogilvie ultimately published three essays for *The Rainbow*. Coles calls Ritchie's *Enquirer* "perhaps the best news paper in America or even in the world." Jay B. Hubbell found an unpublished memorandum of George Tucker's that names Ogilvie as the originator of the Rainbow Association (Hubbel, "William Wirt and the Familiar Essay," *WMQ*, 2d Ser., XXIII [1943], 140). This group included William Wirt, George Tucker, Peyton Randolph, Meriwether and Skelton Jones, the Brockenbrough brothers, and Ritchie; they published essays weekly throughout 1804 and 1805 (*The Rainbow; First Series* . . . [Richmond, Va., 1804]). See Davis, *Intellectual Life in Jefferson's Virginia*, 281–284.

31. James Ogilvie, "To the Friends of Literary and Moral Improvement," *Virginia Gazette*, Mar. 12, 1803, [3] ("ability and eloquence"). It's difficult to gauge the relative value of the cost of Ogilvie's tickets because a Virginia guinea was worth far less than a British guinea. My best guess is that in today's money the subscription would cost about forty or fifty dollars, and individual lectures about five to seven dollars.

32. "Richmond has long been in want . . . ," *Examiner*, Apr. 30, 1803, [3] ("popular governments"), reprinted in the *Virginia Argus* on the same date; "Richmond, (Virginia)," *National Intelligencer, and Washington Advertiser* (Washington, D.C.), Mar. 28, 1804, [2] ("nervous"). Calling a speech "nervous" was a common way to compliment a speaker's dynamic presentation. On Ogilvie's application to the South Carolina College, see Ogilvie to James Madison, Mar. 9, 1804, in J. C. A. Stagg, ed., *Papers of James Madison Digital Edition*, Secretary of State Series (Charlottesville, Va., 2010), VI, 575, https://rotunda.upress.virginia.edu /founders; Ogilvie to Jefferson, Mar. 11, 1804, and Jefferson to Ogilvie, Mar. 17, 1804, PTJ, Main, XLIII, 4, 42.

33. Ogilvie, "Supplementary Narrative," PE, viii ("'think for himself'"); Ogilvie to Benjamin Rush, Feb. 21, 1797, Rush Family Papers, 1748–1876, LCPinHSP.134, XXV, Historical Society of Pennsylvania, Philadelphia ("restless and ardent"). To complicate his schedule even further, he took on private pupils, which helped to enhance his income. At one point in 1795 he promised to visit those students at their homes "four times a week, from seven till nine at night." See Ogilvie, "The public are respectfully informed . . . ," *Virginia Herald, and Fredericksburg Advertiser*, Sept. 25, 1795, [1].

CHAPTER THREE

1. James Ogilvie, "Supplementary Narrative," in Ogilvie, *Philosophical Essays* . . . (Philadelphia, 1816), vii, ix (hereafter cited as PE).

2. "Collectanea," *Wilmingtonian, and Delaware Advertiser* (Wilmington), Feb. 2, 1826, [1] ("infatuation"); Benjamin Rush to Bushrod Washington, May 2, 1812, Bushrod Washington Papers, Fred W. Smith National Library for the Study of George Washington, http:// catalog.mountvernon.org/digital/collection/p16829coll22/id/168 (emphasis mine), ("At-

tachment"). David T. Courtwright's *Forces of Habit: Drugs and the Making of the Modern World* (Cambridge, Mass., 2001); Richard Davenport-Hines's *Pursuit of Oblivion: A Global History of Narcotics* (London, 2001); Thomas Dormandy's *Opium: Reality's Dark Dream* (New Haven, Conn., 2012); and Lucy Inglis's *Milk of Paradise: A History of Opium* (New York, 2019) provide the historical view of opium over the centuries, offering some of the relatively rare, if brief, analyses of opium use in the long eighteenth century. In general, historians have been primarily concerned with uncovering the origins of the idea of addiction and opium as a public health problem, beginning these studies in the 1820s at the earliest following the publication of Thomas De Quincey's addiction memoir, *Confessions of an English Opium-Eater* (1821). See, for example, Marcus Aurin, "Chasing the Dragon: The Cultural Metamorphosis of Opium in the United States, 1825–1935," *Medical Anthropology Quarterly*, XIV, no. 3 (September 2000), 414–441; Courtwright, *Dark Paradise: A History of Opiate Addiction in America*, rev. ed. (Cambridge, Mass., 2001); and Joseph L. Zentner, "Opiate Use in America during the Eighteenth and Nineteenth Centuries: The Origins of a Modern Scourge," *Studies in History and Society*, V, no. 2 (Spring 1974), 40–54. I'm grateful to Elizabeth Kelly Gray for sharing *Habit Forming: Drug Addiction in America, 1776–1914* (New York, forthcoming); and to Jonathan S. Jones for sharing parts of "A Mind Prostrate: Opiate Addiction in the Civil War's Aftermath" (Ph.D. diss., Binghamton University, forthcoming), as well as his "The 'Worst Species of Inebriety': Opiate Addiction in Antebellum NYC," *Gotham: A Blog for Scholars of NYC History* (Mar. 12, 2019), www.gothamcenter.org/blog. The *Oxford English Dictionary* now finds several uses of *addiction* in the eighteenth century linked to the concept of compulsive use of substances ("addiction to the bottle" or to tobacco), but these are rare. Historians lack an adequate history of changing word usage about addiction during this era. William L. White's "The Lessons of Language: Historical Perspectives on the Rhetoric of Addiction," in Sarah W. Tracy and Caroline Jean Acker, eds., *Altering American Consciousness: The History of Alcohol and Drug Use in the United States, 1800–2000* (Amherst, Mass., 2004), 33–60, is vague on chronological shifts, focusing primarily on terms that appeared after 1819. On "had fallen in love," no data on opium use exists before 1842. Courtright suggests that commenters increasingly refer to the problem of habitual use starting around 1830 (*Forces of Habit*, 95). Anglo-American writers occasionally likened love to a drug, and more specifically to opium, during this era as well. See, for example, Rowland Rugeley, *Miscellaneous Poems and Translations from La Fontaine and Others* (Cambridge, 1763), 219: "To these you need not add above / Two, or three grains at most, of Love, / (A drug we seldom now prescribe) / With which Assurance mix *ad lib*."

3. Oliver Wendell Holmes, "Currents and Counter-Currents in Medical Science," in Holmes, *Medical Essays, 1842–1882* (Boston, 1891), 202.

4. Next to laudanum, concocted with wine, paregoric was probably the second most popular opiate tincture used by doctors and druggists. Paregoric had many of the same curative qualities as laudanum but was prepared with honey and camphor and was believed to particularly help asthma sufferers.

5. John Awsiter, *An Essay on the Effects of Opium: Considered as a Poison . . .*, 2d ed. (London,

1767), 6 (laudable). On the import of smoking opium, see John R. Haddad, *America's First Adventure in China: Trade, Treaties, Opium, and Salvation* (Philadelphia, 2013), chap. 5.

6. *The Medical Vade Mecum: Containing Approved Directions for the Use* . . . (Charleston, S.C., 1800), 7 ("wonderful and divine"); Elizabeth Kelly Gray, paper for the roundtable "Drugs, Alcohol, and Gendered and Racial Experiences of Addiction" (presented at the annual meeting of the Society for Historians of the Early American Republic, Philadelphia, July 18, 2014) ("most widely used drug"). Americans used alcohol and tobacco in larger quantities but did not view those substances as drugs. See also Zentner, "Opiate Use in America," *Studies in History and Society*, V, no. 2 (Spring 1974), 40–54. On histories of pain, see Rob Boddice, ed., *Pain and Emotion in Modern History* (Houndmills, U.K., 2014); Joanna Bourke, *The Story of Pain: From Prayer to Painkillers* (Oxford, 2014); Elaine Forman Crane, "'I Have Suffer'd Much Today': The Defining Force of Pain in Early America," in Ronald Hoffman, Mechal Sobel, and Fredrika J. Teute, eds., *Through a Glass Darkly: Reflections on Personal Identity in Early America* (Williamsburg, Va., and Chapel Hill, N.C., 1997); Mark Johnson, *The Body in the Mind: The Bodily Basis of Meaning, Imagination, and Reason* (Chicago, 1987); Kathleen Kennedy, "On Writing the History of the Body in Pain," *Cultural History*, IV (2015), 87–106; and Roselyne Rey, *The History of Pain*, trans. Louise Elliott Wallace, J. A. Cadden, and S. W. Cadden (Cambridge, Mass., 1995). Undiagnosed and untreated rheumatic fever remains life-threatening today in some countries with political and economic barriers to effective health care. It was later renamed strep throat for the group A streptococcus bacteria. See Laurel Thatcher Ulrich, *A Midwife's Tale: The Life of Martha Ballard, Based on Her Diary, 1785–1812* (New York, 1990), 44–45. Household medical guides regularly recommended laudanum for rheumatism. See, for example, Samuel Hemenway, *Medicine Chests, with Particular Directions* (Salem, Mass., 1800), [2].

7. Laudanum as cure-all: "Cure for the Tooth-Ache," *Washingtonian* (Leesburg, Va.), July 24, 1810, [2]; "A Cure for Sore Eyes," *Alexandria Herald* (Va.), June 3, 1811, [4]; Hugh Smith, *The Female Monitor Consisting of a Series of Letters to Married Women on Nursing and the Management of Children* . . . (Wilmington, N.C., 1801), 258; see also Dormandy, *Opium*, 10, 32, 34, 99. On laudanum for animals, see "Extract from the English Sporting Magazine for June 1810," *Alexandria Daily Gazette* (Va.), Mar. 20, 1811, [3]; and "From the London Papers," *Enquirer* (Richmond), July 12, 1805, [4]. On medicine chests, see Hemenway, *Medicine Chests*, [2]. John Harrison, a Philadelphia druggist, recorded selling opium specifically for his customers' family medicine chests. See Harrison daybooks, 1800–1804, Amb. 4258, Historical Society of Pennsylvania (HSP), Philadelphia.

8. John DuVal records, Mutual Assurance Society of Virginia General Business Records, 1795–1965, Acc. no. 28135, Library of Virginia, Richmond. Many merchants and doctors also sold raw opium. Recipes for making one's own laudanum proliferated in home health guidebooks; some users might have skipped this stage entirely and ingested it directly or dissolved it in wine, despite its bitter taste.

9. Dormandy, *Opium*, 70. For a detailed account of the growth and harvesting of the sap of white poppy plants, see ibid., 12–16. Barbara Hodgson estimates that the morphine

content of raw opium could vary from 3 to 17 percent. See Hodgson, *In the Arms of Morpheus: The Tragic History of Laudanum, Morphine, and Patent Medicines* (Buffalo, N.Y., 2001), 2. On its cost, see De Quincey, *Confessions*, 41–42. Kendal's Black Drop, a laudanum brand marketed in England, was notoriously more potent than its competitors, so much so that writers like Lord Byron referred to it in their poetry. See, for example, Byron's *Don Juan* (1823). Coleridge also used Kendal's Black Drop (Dormandy, *Opium*, 88–89).

10. *Medical Vade Mecum*, 7–8.

11. Franklin Scott, *Experiments and Observations on the Means of Counteracting the Deleterious Effects of Opium* ... (Philadelphia, 1803), 7–22 (quotation on 7).

12. "Last evening's paper ... ," *Newburyport Herald, and Country Gazette* (Mass.), Sept. 18, 1801, [3] ("guilty conscience"); "Poisonous Drugs," *Alexandria Herald*, Sept. 3, 1819, [2] (British bill).

13. Nathan Allen, *An Essay on the Opium Trade* ... (Boston, 1850), 23 ("brilliancy"); Hast Handy, *An Inaugural Dissertation on Opium* ... (Philadelphia, 1791), 11 ("So does opium"); Robert Carter, *An Inaugural Essay, Being a Comparative Inquiry into the Properties and Uses of Opium* (Philadelphia, 1803), 18 (studying late at night); Ogilvie, "Supplementary Narrative," PE, viii ("most important subjects"). These passages use the terms *stimulant* and *sedative*, which appear in medical and popular writing about laudanum at the time, with the assumption that contemporaries experienced the drug through the lens of the culture around them. Gray displays a more skeptical view in *Habit Forming*, holding that laudanum was not a stimulant even though people at the time thought it was (email correspondence with the author, May 15, 2019).

14. De Quincey, *Confessions*, 42 ("exquisite order"); J. H. to Benjamin Rush, fall 1795, quoted in Gray, *Habit Forming*, chap. 1 ("intellects were more brilliant").

15. Mike Jay, *Emperors of Dreams: Drugs in the Nineteenth Century*, rev. ed. (Cambridgeshire, U.K., 2011), 47–50; Dormandy, *Opium*, 86–91 (opium dreams); De Quincey, *Confessions*, 7 ("talk of oxen").

16. Ogilvie, "Supplementary Narrative," PE, ix.

17. De Quincey, *Confessions*, 42–47 (study drug). Women who became "infatuated" with opium also often appear to have developed their habit after using the drug for medical reasons, although evidence for their use is even more scanty than for men. See Jonathan S. Jones, " 'So Dreadful an Evil': Elite Women and Opiate Misuse in Antebellum American Medical Discourse" (unpublished paper circulated to the Upstate Early American History Workshop, Dec. 2, 2016), used with permission from the author. On self-made men in the nineteenth century, see John G. Cawelti, *Apostles of the Self-Made Man* (Chicago, 1965); Louis P. Masur, ed., *The Autobiography of Benjamin Franklin* (Boston, 1993), 1–18; Irvin G. Wyllie, *The Self-Made Man in America: The Myth of Rags to Riches* (1954; rpt. New York, 1966).

18. Ogilvie, "Supplementary Narrative," PE, vii, ix.

19. Elbridge Boyden, *Reminiscences of Elbridge Boyden, Architect* (Worcester, Mass., 1890), 3. He recalls his youth in the 1810s and 1820s. Lucy Inglis also draws a comparison to alcohol in *Milk of Paradise*, 135–142.

20. Sarah Hand Meacham, *Every Home a Distillery: Alcohol, Gender, and Technology in the Colonial Chesapeake* (Baltimore, 2009), chap. 1; W. J. Rorabaugh, *The Alcoholic Republic: An American Tradition* (New York, 1979).

21. When the fledgling United States government created a brand-new tax on domestically produced whiskey in the early 1790s—a tax intended to pay off Revolutionary War debts—farmers in the trans-Appalachian west staged tax protests that came to be called the Whiskey Rebellion. See Terry Bouton, *Taming Democracy: "The People," the Founders, and the Troubled Ending of the American Revolution* (New York, 2007). See also John J. McCusker, "The Rum Trade and the Balance of Payments of the Thirteen Continental Colonies, 1650–1775," *Journal of Economic History*, XXX (1970), 24–27; and Frederik H. Smith, *Caribbean Rum: A Social and Economic History* (Gainesville, Fla., 2005). On high consumption rates, see Matthew Warner Osborn, *Rum Maniacs: Alcoholic Insanity in the Early American Republic* (Chicago, 2014), 14–17; Rorabaugh, *Alcoholic Republic*, ix.

22. Masur, ed., *Autobiography of Benjamin Franklin*, 61–62 ("detestable"). Individuals in New York in 1808 and Boston in 1813 launched fledgling efforts to encourage moderation in drinking by establishing temperance societies, a movement that would pick up speed in 1826 with a national society dedicated to the cause. See Rorabaugh, *Alcoholic Republic*, 191–193; see also *A Report of a Committee of the Humane Society Appointed to Inquire into the Number of Tavern Licenses . . .* (New York, 1810). More than any other writer, the preeminent Philadelphia physician Benjamin Rush began advocating for temperance as early as the 1780s after witnessing the social and health effects of heavy drinking in his patients as well as one of his sons. Over the course of several decades, he developed the view that habitual drinking amounted to a "disease of the will." Very few of his contemporaries joined in to point medical thinking toward the concept of addiction. See Osborn, *Rum Maniacs*, 15–22; James Green, "Popular Medicine," *The Annual Report of the Library Company of Philadelphia for the Year 2013* (Philadelphia, 2014), 29–38. On Franklin's use of opium, see Gray, *Habit Forming*, chap. 1; and Jones, "A Mind Prostrate," chap. 1. Parts of Franklin's narrative were published starting in 1791 and have a bizarre publication history; many of the early English-language versions printed in the United States were actually re-translations of a French edition. A complete version of the book did not appear until 1828. See Christopher Hunter, "From Print to Print: The First Complete Edition of Benjamin Franklin's 'Autobiography,'" *The Papers of the Bibliographical Society of America*, CI (2007), 481–505.

23. Osborn, *Rum Maniacs*, chap. 2. In 1816, a story that circulated through some American newspapers entitled "Abuse of Laudanum" lamented its overuse by doctors and lay people, explaining that it was "an invaluable medicine in the hands of a discreet physician, but worse than the plague of Egypt in the hands of quacks, ignorant pretenders, and foolish nurses," but it did not make mention of chronic or habitual use as one of the drug's problems. See Ratio, "Abuse of Laudanum," *Columbian* (New York), July 17, 1816, [2]; reprinted in *Poulson's American Daily Advertiser* (Philadelphia), July 30, 1816, [3], among others.

24. Scott, *Experiments* (Philadelphia, 1803), 45–46 (anecdote about Turks). These sources sometimes explained that the Turks believed opium granted courage upon

marching into battle. See Samuel Crumpe, *An Inquiry into the Nature and Properties of Opium* ... (London, 1793), 48–50. One sign of the way opium seemed to be regarded as a negligible product rests in the fact that American traders initially showed no eagerness to muscle in on British control of the Turkish and Indian opium trades. If they had anticipated good profits, they might have jumped at the chance, especially to get access to opium via Chinese merchants, who managed the export of Indian opium. Despite having engaged in an active trade with China for a generation, bringing back tea, porcelain, silk, furniture, and other goods, American ships only began importing opium from China in about 1806. Until that point, Americans purchased opium exclusively from British traders, who sold them about a quarter of the opium they imported from Turkey, perhaps, in part, because that opium tended to be more effective than the Indian product. See Eric Jay Dolin, *When America First Met China: An Exotic History of Tea, Drugs, and Money in the Age of Sail* (New York, 2012), 118–123; Charles Clarkson Stelle, *Americans and the China Opium Trade in the Nineteenth Century* (New York, 1981).

25. Rush to Bushrod Washington, May 2, 1812, Bushrod Washington Papers ("lessen the dose"); De Quincey, *Confessions*, 4–5 ("fascinating enthrallment"), 64 ("intense perspirations"), 79 ("tortures").

26. "Married," *Enquirer*, Dec. 28, 1803, [3]. The archivists at the Library of Virginia have even created a document explaining the loss of documents: www.lva.virginia.gov/public /guides/rn30_lostrecords.pdf. More Civil War battles took place in Virginia than in any other state; even census records for the region were destroyed. Those losses help explain why even finding genealogical data and tax records on the Wilkinson family has proved so difficult. Nevertheless, I'm grateful to the genealogists of the New Kent County Genealogical Project for their assistance. New Kent lies roughly halfway between Richmond and Williamsburg.

27. "To be Rented," *Enquirer*, Apr. 16, 1805, [3] ("large and commodious"); Ogilvie, "To the Public," *Virginia Gazette, and General Advertiser*, Jan. 7, 1804, [3] ("pretenders and pedants"); Ogilvie, "For the Virginia Gazette," *Virginia Gazette, and General Advertiser*, Mar. 21, 1804, [3] (defense of increased fees).

28. The literature on marriage's significance to manhood is vast. See, for example, Thomas A. Foster, *Sex and the Eighteenth-Century Man: Massachusetts and the History of Sexuality in America* (Boston, 2006), chap. 1; Dana D. Nelson, *National Manhood: Capitalist Citizenship and the Imagined Fraternity of White Men* (Durham, N.C., 1998), chap. 1; J. M. Opal, *Beyond the Farm: National Ambitions in Rural New England* (Philadelphia, 2008), 30–35; and Lisa Wilson, *Ye Heart of a Man: The Domestic Life of Men in Colonial New England* (New Haven, Conn., 1999), chaps. 2–3.

29. "Observations subjoined . . . ," *Enquirer*, Mar. 15, 1805, [3] (brief trip); "Died," *Enquirer*, Mar. 12, 1805, [3] (eulogy).

30. John Taylor to Peter Carr, Sept. 18, 1806, Mss2 P1424 b 29, Virginia Museum of History and Culture (VMHC). This was not the only debt that went unpaid. In Milton in 1807, he purchased materials for his school amounting to £28 4s, a bill that he didn't

pay until 1815. See Thomas Wells v. James Ogilvie (1815), Albemarle County Chancery Records, index no. 1815-004, case no. 583 29, Library of Virginia, Richmond. See also Samuel Pleasants, Jr., to James Ogilvie, Dec. 22, 1808, Lea and Febiger Records, Coll. 0227B, box 64, folder 3, HSP. It is notoriously difficult to compare monetary values from the early Republic to the modern United States, as the value of wages and the costs of rents and goods varied so much from the cost of living today. Nevertheless, twelve hundred dollars is a staggering debt for a schoolteacher to have amassed in an era when laborers earned roughly a dollar per day.

31. John Harrison daybooks, 1800–1804, Amb. 4258, HSP.

32. Taylor to Carr, Sept. 18, 1806, Mss2 P1424 b 29, VMHC ("catastrophe of his sufferings"); Thomas Jefferson to James Ogilvie, June 23, 1806, (Randolph affair), Jefferson to Ogilvie, Jan. 31, 1806 (borrowing books), both in *Founders Online*, National Archives, https://founders.archives.gov; Isaac A. Coles to Joseph C. Cabell, June 10, 1808, Joseph Carrington Cabell Papers, 1790–1890, Acc. no. 38–111c, box 5, folder 37, Small Special Collections Library, University of Virginia, Charlottesville ("equally free in lending"). Jefferson might have recognized that Ogilvie and Randolph shared highly emotional personalities and quick tempers, making Ogilvie an unusual but effective adviser in this case. See Cynthia A. Kierner, *Martha Jefferson Randolph, Daughter of Monticello: Her Life and Times* (Chapel Hill, N.C., 2012), 132–135.

33. Ogilvie, "Supplementary Narrative," PE, v–vi ("most respectable citizens"), vii ("works of Cicero"); Francis Walker Gilmer to Peachy Gilmer, Nov. 3, 1807, Peachy Ridgway Gilmer Papers, 1790–1889, Mss1 G4216 a (Sundays for deists), Dr. Charles Everette letter fragment to Peachy Gilmer, n.d., Mss1 G4216 a 9 ("delights beyond measure"), VMHC. I'm grateful to Alan Taylor for pointing me to the Everette letter.

34. Ogilvie, "Supplementary Narrative," PE, v ("affectionate admonition"), ix ("exhibition of oratory").

35. Ogilvie, "Supplementary Narrative," PE, x ("deranged"). On Eliza Harriot O'Connor, an educational lecturer in the 1780s, see Granville Ganter, "Women's Entrepreneurial Lecturing in the Early National Period," in Angela G. Ray and Paul Stob, eds., *Thinking Together: Lecturing, Learning, and Difference in the Long Nineteenth Century* (University Park, Pa., 2018), chap. 2. On the "Walking Stewart," aka John Stewart, the Traveller, see Kirsten Fischer, "Cosmic Kinship: John Stewart's 'Sensate Matter' in the Early Republic," *Commonplace: The Journal of Early American Life*, http://commonplace.online/article/cosmic-kinship.

CHAPTER FOUR

1. James Ogilvie, "Supplementary Narrative," in Ogilvie, *Philosophical Essays . . .* (Philadelphia, 1816), ix ("prophetic glance"), x ("from the moment"), xi (hereafter cited as PE).

2. Anne Cary Randolph to Thomas Jefferson, Mar. 4, 1808 ("Mr. Ogilvie"), and Ellen Wayles Randolph to Jefferson, Mar. 18, 1808 ("much ashamed"), both in *Founders Online*, National Archives, https://founders.archives.gov.

3. Ogilvie to Jefferson, [June 20, 1808], *Founders Online*.

4. Ogilvie to Francis Walker Gilmer, Feb. 4, 1814, in Richard Beale Davis, *Francis Walker Gilmer: Life and Learning in Jefferson's Virginia* (Richmond, Va., 1939), 381. On the lyceum and booking agencies, see Angela G. Ray, *The Lyceum and Public Culture in the Nineteenth Century* (East Lansing, Mich., 2005), 39–40; Carl Bode, *The American Lyceum: Town Meeting of the Mind* (New York, 1956), 248–249; and Sara Lampert, *Starring Women: Celebrity, Patriarchy, and American Theater, 1790–1850* (Urbana, Ill., forthcoming), chap. 6. The Northwestern Lecture Association (renamed the Associated Western Literary Societies) was formed in 1864 and was followed by the American Literary Bureau and James Redpath's Boston Lyceum Bureau.

5. John Edwards Caldwell, *A Tour through Part of Virginia, in the Summer of 1808; in a Series of Letters . . .* (New York, 1809), 14.

6. Alexander Anderson diary, Sept. 9, 1797, MS 1861, Rare Book and Manuscript Library, Butler Library, Columbia University, New York ("feats with cards"); Peter Benes, *For a Short Time Only: Itinerants and the Resurgence of Popular Culture in Early America* (Amherst, Mass., 2016), 345 (he finds at least 179 penmanship teachers between about 1790 and 1826); Richardson Wright, *Hawkers and Walkers in Early America: Strolling Peddlers, Preachers, Lawyers, Doctors, Players, and Others, from the Beginning to the Civil War* (Philadelphia, 1927). See also Valentijn Byvanck, "Public Portraits and Portrait Publics," *Explorations in Early American Culture*, special issue of *Pennsylvania History: A Journal of Mid-Atlantic Studies*, LXV (1998), 199–242; James Delbourgo, *A Most Amazing Scene of Wonders: Electricity and Enlightenment in Early America* (Cambridge, Mass., 2006), chap. 7; Granville Ganter, "Before the Lyceum: Entrepreneurial Lecturing in the Early National Period, 1784–1826" (unpublished manuscript, cited courtesy of the author); Ganter, "Women's Entrepreneurial Lecturing in the Early National Period," in Angela G. Ray and Paul Stob, eds., *Thinking Together: Lecturing, Learning, and Difference in the Long Nineteenth Century* (University Park, Pa., 2018); Ian Inkster, "The Public Lecture as an Instrument of Science Education for Adults—The Case of Great Britain, c. 1750–1850," *Paedagogica Historica*, XX (1980), 80–107; David Jaffee, *A New Nation of Goods: The Material Culture of Early America* (Philadelphia, 2010), chaps. 1, 4, 6; Jaffee, "Peddlers of Progress and the Transformation of the Rural North, 1760–1860," *Journal of American History*, LXXVIII (1991), 511–535; Jack Larkin, *The Reshaping of Everyday Life, 1790–1840* (New York, 1988), 208–211; Brett Mizelle, "'I Have Brought My Pig to a Fine Market': Animals, Their Exhibitors, and Market Culture in the Early Republic," in Scott C. Martin, ed., *Cultural Change and the Market Revolution in America, 1789–1860* (New York, 2005), 181–216; Yvette R. Piggush, "Modernity, Gender, and the Panorama in Early Republican Literature," *Early American Literature*, XLVIII (2013), 425–456; Tamara Plakins Thornton, *Handwriting in America: A Cultural History* (New Haven, Conn., 1996).

7. "Literary Amusements," *Aurora General Advertiser* (Philadelphia), Sept. 29, 1808, [1]; "Ogilvie's Orations," *Political and Commercial Register* (Philadelphia), Oct. 21, 1808, [3] ("progress and prospects").

8. These categories never fully satisfied everyone, and it was difficult to draw neat lines

among them, yet they remained in popular use throughout the eighteenth and nineteenth centuries. Indeed, as early as the first century CE, Quintilian reported widespread debate on this system, yet it remained in place. See Carolyn Eastman, "Oratory and Platform Culture in Britain and North America, 1740–1900," in Colin Burrow, ed., *Oxford Handbooks Online* (July 2016), www.oxfordhandbooksonline.com; Adam Fox, *Oral and Literate Culture in England, 1500–1700* (Oxford, 2000), 117, 127; Alan G. Gross and Arthur E. Walzer, *Rereading Aristotle's Rhetoric* (Carbondale, Ill., 2000), introduction; Joseph R. Roach, *The Player's Passion: Studies in the Science of Acting* (Newark, Del., 1985), 23–27.

9. Pictor [Charles Brockden Brown], "For the American Daily Advertiser," *Poulson's American Daily Advertiser* (Philadelphia), Oct. 22, 1808, [2] ("reasoning"). For the identification of the author, see Elijah Brown, Sr., Commonplace book, 1808–1809, [iii], Brown Family Papers, coll. 84, XI, Historical Society of Pennsylvania (HSP), Philadelphia; Alice G. Waters et al., eds., *The Diary of William Bentley, D. D.*, 4 vols. (Salem, Mass., 1905–1914), Dec. 1, 1809, III, 482 ("more in favour") (hereafter cited as DWB).

10. "Dear Parents and Relatives," *New-Hampshire Sentinel* (Keene), June 1, 1805, [3] ("self-murder" and laudanum). See also Richard Bell, *We Shall Be No More: Suicide and Self-Government in the Newly United States* (Cambridge, Mass., 2012), 36–42; Bell, "The Moral Thermometer: Rush, Republicanism, and Suicide," *Early American Studies*, XV (2017), 308–331; R. A. Houston, *Punishing the Dead? Suicide, Lordship, and Community in Britain, 1500–1830* (Oxford, 2010); Eric Vallee, "'A Fatal Sympathy': Suicide and the Republic of Abjection in the Writings of Benjamin Rush and Charles Brockden Brown," *EAS*, XV (2017), 332–351.

11. [Ogilvie], "On Suicide as Justifiable," and "On Suicide as Not Justifiable," MS orations, n.d., Jonathan Clark Letters, MSS A/C 593d 6, folders 4 and 6, Filson Historical Society, Louisville, Ky. See also orations "On Sincerity," "On Love," and, ironically, "On the Practicality of Reforming Vicious Habits and the Most Effectual Means of Reformation."

12. "Slave Trade," *Poulson's American Daily Advertiser*, Jan. 1, 1808, [3] ("*human flesh*"), quoted in Randy J. Sparks, "Blind Justice: The United States's Failure to Curb the Illegal Slave Trade," *Law and History Review*, XXXV (2017), 53. David N. Gellman, *Emancipating New York: The Politics of Slavery and Freedom, 1777–1827* (Baton Rouge, La., 2006); Manisha Sinha, *The Slave's Cause: A History of Abolition* (New Haven, Conn., 2016), chapters 4–5; Paul J. Polgar, *Standard-Bearers of Equality: America's First Abolition Movement* (Williamsburg, Va., and Chapel Hill, N.C., 2019), chap. 2. Congress did little to combat a number of American merchants who flouted the 1808 law by continuing for decades to smuggle enslaved people from Africa and the Caribbean. See Kenneth Morgan, "Proscription by Degrees: The Ending of the African Slave Trade to the United States," in David T. Gleeson and Simon Lewis, eds., *Ambiguous Anniversary: The Bicentennial of the International Slave Trade Bans* (Columbia, S.C., 2012), 1–10. Because the law constricted the market in human beings, it raised the relative value of the people they owned, particularly as new markets for enslaved people opened up in Kentucky and Tennessee and in the new Mississippi and Louisiana Territories. There planters would develop a vast new industry in cotton. See Edward E. Baptist, *The Half Has*

Never Been Told: Slavery and the Making of American Capitalism (New York, 2014); Daina Ramey Berry, *The Price for Their Pound of Flesh: The Value of the Enslaved, from Womb to Grave, in the Building of a Nation* (Boston, 2017).

13. "Mr. Ogilvie's Orations," *Baltimore Patriot & Evening Advertiser*, Feb. 23, 1814, [2] ("matter or manner"); "Mr. Ogilvie," *Poulson's American Daily Advertiser*, Nov. 18, 1808, [3] ("strength of argument"); "The Rostrum," *Daily National Intelligencer* (Washington, D.C.), Mar. 15, 1814, [3] ("peculiar powers").

14. "James Ogilvie," *Star* (Raleigh, N.C.), June 28, 1811, 102 ("captive"); Washington Irving, "Mountjoy: Or Some Passages out of the Life of a Castle-Builder," *Knickerbocker, or New-York Monthly Magazine*, XIV (1839), 404–405 ("pathetic tones"). The character of Glencoe was based on Ogilvie. See Richard Beale Davis, "James Ogilvie and Washington Irving," *Americana Illustrated*, XXXV (1941), 435–458.

15. Daniel Adams, *The Understanding Reader; or, Knowledge Before Oratory*, 3d ed. (Leominster, Mass., 1805), iii ("modulations of the voice"); Gilbert Austin, *Chironomia; or, A Treatise on Rhetorical Delivery . . .* (London, 1806), 488 ("horror"), 497 ("understanding"); Carolyn Eastman, *A Nation of Speechifiers: Making an American Public after the Revolution* (Chicago, 2009); Jay Fliegelman, *Declaring Independence: Jefferson, Natural Language, and the Culture of Performance* (Stanford, Calif., 1993), 65–72, 189–195.

16. E., "Communication," *Poulson's American Daily Advertiser*, Oct. 20, 1808, [3] ("partial illumination"). On Indian eloquence, see Sandra M. Gustafson, *Eloquence Is Power: Oratory and Performance in Early America* (Williamsburg, Va., and Chapel Hill, N.C., 2000); Eastman, *Nation of Speechifiers*, chap. 3; Edward G. Gray, *New World Babel: Languages and Nations in Early America* (Princeton, N.J., 1999).

17. "Discourse on Luxury and Domestic Manufactures," *Federal Republican* (Baltimore), Sept. 9, 1808, [3] ("pathetick effusions"); "Ogilvie's Orations," *Political and Commercial Register* (Philadelphia), Oct. 21, 1808, 3 ("humorous effusion"). On recitation and memorization, see Catherine Robson, *Heart Beats: Everyday Life and the Memorized Poem* (New York, 2012), 42–57; Carolyn Eastman, "Reading Aloud: Editorial Societies and Orality in Magazines of the Early American Republic," *Early American Literature*, LIV (2019), 163–188; Ronald J. Zboray and Mary Saracino Zboray, *Everyday Ideas: Socioliterary Experience among Antebellum New Englanders* (Knoxville, Tenn., 2006), 127–130.

18. "Explanations," *New York Evening Post*, May 8, 1810, [2] ("this country"); Ogilvie, "Preface," v ("dignity, grandeur"), "Supplementary Narrative," xxii ("partially"), both in *PE*.

19. "Mr. Ogilvie," *National Advocate* (New York), Nov. 25, 1813, [3] ("ancient rostrum"); "Extracts from the Columbia paper . . . ," *Star*, Aug. 16, 1811, 132 ("drops his sceptre").

20. Increase Cooke, *The American Orator; or, Elegant Extracts in Prose and Poetry; Comprehending a Diversity of Oratorical Specimens . . . Principally Intended for the Use of Schools and Academies* (New Haven, Conn., 1811), 85; Peter Gibian, "Walt Whitman, Edward Everett, and the Culture of Oratory," *Intellectual History Newsletter*, XVI (1994), 20; Michelle Sizemore, *American Enchantment: Rituals of the People in the Post-Revolutionary World* (New York, 2018), 81–82.

21. An Admirer of Eloquence, "Mr. Editor," *Aurora General Advertiser*, Jan. 19, 1811, [3]

("pathos and energy"); "Public Halls," *Southern Patriot* (Charleston), Dec. 6, 1815, [2] ("RE-PUBLICAN AMERICA"). On the magic of public assembly, see Sizemore, *American Enchantment*, 8–12.

22. Emerson, quoted in James Perrin Warren, *Culture of Eloquence: Oratory and Reform in Antebellum America* (University Park, Pa., 1999), 24 ("common soul"); see also Mary Kupiec Cayton, "The Making of an American Prophet: Emerson, His Audiences, and the Rise of the Culture Industry in Nineteenth-Century America," *American Historical Review*, XCII (1987), 597–620. On public assembly, see Judith Butler, *Notes toward a Performative Theory of Assembly* (Cambridge, Mass., 2015), chap. 5; Ray, *The Lyceum and Public Culture*; Donald M. Scott, "The Popular Lecture and the Creation of a Public in Mid-Nineteenth-Century America," *JAH*, LXVI (1980), 791–809.

23. Sandra Frink, "'Strangers are Flocking Here': Identity and Anonymity in New Orleans, 1810–1860," *American Nineteenth Century History*, XI (2010), 155–181. Two of the most famous of these autobiographies are Stephen Burroughs, *Memoirs of Stephen Burroughs* (Hanover, N.H., 1798), which appeared in many reprintings through 1820; and Henry Tufts, *A Narrative of the Life, Adventures, Travels, and Sufferings of Henry Tufts* (Dover, N.H., 1807). See also Karen Halttunen, *Confidence Men and Painted Women: A Study of Middle-Class Culture in America, 1830–1870* (New Haven, Conn., 1982); Peter Jaros, "Personating Stephen Burroughs: The Apparitions of a Public Specter," *EAL*, XLIV (2009), 569–603; and Larzer Ziff, *Writing in the New Nation: Prose, Print, and Politics in the Early United States* (New Haven, Conn., 1991), chap. 4.

24. Ogilvie, "Supplementary Narrative," PE, xiii ("twenty or thirty"); Jefferson to Martha Jefferson Randolph, June 21, 1808, ("very unequal"), *Founders Online*.

25. Ogilvie, "Supplementary Narrative," PE, xiv–xvi.

26. Ogilvie to Jefferson, [June 20, 1808], ("romantic excursion"), Jefferson to John Glendy, June 21, 1808, ("friendly attachment"), *Founders Online*; Alexander Graydon, *Memoirs of a Life, Chiefly Passed in Pennsylvania* (Harrisburg, Pa., 1811), quoted in François Furstenberg, *When the United States Spoke French: Five Refugees who Shaped a Nation* (New York, 2014), 144 ("my respect"). These passages rest on important scholarship on letter writing, including Eve Tavor Bannet, *Empire of Letters: Letter Manuals and Transatlantic Correspondence, 1688–1820* (Cambridge, 2005); Konstantin Dierks, *In My Power: Letter Writing and Communications in Early America* (Philadelphia, 2009); Toby L. Ditz, "Shipwrecked; or, Masculinity Imperiled: Mercantile Representations of Failure and the Gendered Self in Eighteenth-Century Philadelphia," *JAH*, LXXXI (1994), 51–80; Ditz, "Secret Selves, Credible Personas: The Problematics of Trust and Public Display in the Writing of Eighteenth-Century Philadelphia Merchants," in Robert Blair St. George, ed., *Possible Pasts: Becoming Colonial in Early America* (Ithaca, N.Y., 2000), 219–242; and Furstenberg, *When the United States Spoke French*, 137–152.

27. Alexander J. Dallas to Nicholas Biddle, Jan. 5, 1811, Biddle Family Papers, Coll. 2146, box 7, folder 6, HSP ("fullest audience"); on Lancaster, see U.S. census tables listing urban places by decade, accessed Apr. 22, 2016, www.census.gov/population/www/documen

tation/twps0027/tab04.txt (hereafter cited as USC-1810). This size made Lancaster the twenty-seventh-largest city in the nation, larger than Savannah and only slightly smaller than New Haven and Schenectady. For information about networks, see Joseph M. Adelman, *Revolutionary Networks: The Business and Politics of Printing the News, 1763–1789* (Baltimore, 2019); Ryan Cordell, "Reprinting, Circulation, and the Network Author in Antebellum Newspapers," *American Literary History*, XXVII (2015), 417–445; Furstenberg, *When the United States Spoke French*, chap. 3; John J. Garcia, "Networks," *EAS*, XVI (2018), 721–727; Caroline Levine, *Forms: Whole, Rhythm, Hierarchy, Network* (Princeton, N.J., 2015); and Lindsay O'Neill, *The Opened Letter: Networking in the Early Modern British World* (Philadelphia, 2015).

28. DWB, Oct. 13, 1809, Oct. 21, 1809, III, 468 (mention of father), 469 ("much entertainment"); see also Oct. 14, 1809, III, 468. Ogilvie writes "I courted no one" in his letter to Francis Walker Gilmer, Feb. 4, 1814, in Davis, *Francis Walker Gilmer*, 381.

29. *The Diaries of John Quincy Adams: A Digital Collection*, www.masshist.org/jqadiaries /php, XXVII, Jan. 1, 1803–Aug. 4, 1809, entries for Apr. 28 (Adams lecture), May 1 ("small party"), May 2 ("get a place"), and May 15, 1809 (dinner with Ogilvie).

30. Letter transcribed in David Ramsay, *Memoirs of the Life of Martha Laurens Ramsay*, 2d ed. (Charleston, S.C., 1812), 269 ("in *propria persona*"); Margaret Bayard Smith to Jane Bayard Kirkpatrick, Mar. 13, 1814, in Gaillard Hunt, ed., *The First Forty Years of Washington Society Portrayed by the Family Letters of Mrs. Samuel Harrison Smith (Margaret Bayard) from the Collection of Her Grandson* (New York, 1906), 97–98 ("cultivated taste"); Judith S. Graham et al, eds., *Diary and Autobiographical Writings of Louisa Catherine Adams*, I (Cambridge, Mass., 2013), May 1809, 281–282. See also Catherine Allgor, *Parlor Politics: In Which the Ladies of Washington Help Build a City and a Government* (Charlottesville, Va., 2000).

31. Ogilvie, "Supplementary Narrative," PE, xviii–xix (quotations on xviii). The quote is from Alexander Pope and was a favorite of Ogilvie's.

32. George Ticknor, *Life, Letters, and Journals of George Ticknor* (Boston, 1876), 8–9 ("effective recitations"); Hunt, ed., *First Forty Years*, 98 (declines to recite).

33. "Mr. Ogilvie," *North American, and Mercantile Daily Advertiser* (Baltimore), Aug. 27, 1808, [3] ("rich embellishments"); "We were pleased to find . . . ," ibid., Aug. 30, 1808, [2] ("universal satisfaction"); Philopatris, "From the Box," *Montréal Gazette*, Oct. 29, 1810, [2] ("new aera"). Colonial theater companies sometimes used similar strategies to build their own audiences. See Odai Johnson, *Absence and Memory in Colonial American Theatre: Fiorelli's Plaster* (New York, 2006), chap. 4.

34. On this subject, see David S. Shields, *Civil Tongues and Polite Letters in British America* (Williamsburg, Va., and Chapel Hill, N.C., 1997), 262–266.

35. USC-1810; Susan Branson, *These Fiery Frenchified Dames: Women and Political Culture in Early National Philadelphia* (Philadelphia, 2001); Nina Reid-Maroney, *Philadelphia's Enlightenment, 1740–1800: Kingdom of Christ, Empire of Reason* (Westport, Conn., 2001).

36. Ogilvie to Jefferson, Nov. 5, 1808 ("extensive apparatus"), *Founders Online*; Esther Cox to Mary Chesnut, Nov. 10, 1808, Papers of the Cox and Chesnut Families, 1792–1858, MSS Plb. 5–FWS–9–2, folder 24, South Caroliniana Library, University of South Caro-

lina, Columbia ("Theatre is open"); Charles Durang, "History of the Philadelphia Stage," a scrapbook of Durang's collected newspaper essays published in the *Philadelphia Sunday Dispatch* between 1854 and 1863, Library Company of Philadelphia (Antipodean Whirligig). On other scientific and educational lecturers, see Delbourgo, *Most Amazing Scene*; and Ganter, "Before the Lyceum."

37. A. B. [Charles Brockden Brown], "Communication," *Relf's Philadelphia Gazette & Daily Advertiser*, Oct. 15, 1808, [3]. This letter also appeared in the *Aurora General Advertiser*, Oct. 18, 1808, [2], and *Poulson's American Daily Advertiser*, Oct. 17, 1808, [3].

CHAPTER FIVE

1. "Literary Amusements," *Aurora General Advertiser* (Philadelphia), Sept. 29, 1808, [1] ("approbation"); Philologus, "Communication," *United States' Gazette* (Philadelphia), Oct. 22, 1808, [3] ("accomplished scholar"); A. B. [Charles Brockden Brown], "Communication," *Relf's Philadelphia Gazette & Daily Advertiser*, Oct. 15, 1808, [3] ("reputation and influence"), reprinted in *Poulson's American Daily Advertiser* (Philadelphia), Oct. 17, 1808, [3], and *Aurora General Advertiser*, Oct. 18, 1808, [2].

2. Philologus, "Communication," *United States' Gazette*, Oct. 22, 1808, [3] ("modest and unassuming") (this letter appeared simultaneously in the *Political and Commercial Register* [Philadelphia], Oct. 22, 1808, [3]; and *Poulson's American Daily Advertiser*, Oct. 22, 1808, [3]); A. B. [Charles Brockden Brown], "Communication" ("side of morality"), and Maskell M. Carll, "Reading and Recitation" ("useful accomplishment"), both in *Poulson's American Daily Advertiser*, Oct. 18, 1808, [4].

3. James Ogilvie, "Supplementary Narrative," in Ogilvie, *Philosophical Essays . . .* (Philadelphia, 1816), xxiii, xxv (hereafter cited as PE). Ogilvie's reference to "stony eyes" comes from the Edmund Spenser poem *The Faerie Queene* (1590).

4. Jon Butler, *Awash in a Sea of Faith: Christianizing the American People* (Cambridge, Mass., 1990); Christopher Grasso, *Skepticism and American Faith: From the Revolution to the Civil War* (New York, 2018); Nathan O. Hatch, *The Democratization of American Christianity* (New Haven, Conn., 1989); Herbert Morais, *Deism in Eighteenth-Century America* (1934; rpt. New York, 1960); Eric R. Schlereth, *An Age of Infidels: The Politics of Religious Controversy in the Early United States* (Philadelphia, 2013); Leigh Eric Schmidt, *Hearing Things: Religion, Illusion, and the American Enlightenment* (Cambridge, Mass., 2000); Jonathan Sheehan, "Enlightenment, Religion, and the Enigma of Secularization: A Review Essay," *American Historical Review*, CVIII (2003), 1061–1080; James Turner, *Without God, Without Creed: The Origins of Unbelief in America* (Baltimore, 1985).

5. "Literary Amusements," *Aurora General Advertiser*, Sept. 29, 1808, [1] ("carefully avoided"); Ogilvie to Thomas Jefferson, [June 20, 1808] ("abstain scrupulously"), *Founders Online*, National Archives, https://founders.archives.gov; Ogilvie, "Supplementary Narrative," PE, xviii ("classes and denominations").

6. Crito, "To the Editor of the Gazette . . . ," *Gazette of the United States, & Daily Advertiser* (Philadelphia), Sept. 24 ,1801, [2]. That this information circulated as far away as Philadel-

phia is less surprising when we recall that Ogilvie had regularly submitted notices about the high quality of his schools to newspapers in Washington, D.C., and Philadelphia as he sought students.

7. "Mr. Ogilvie's Discourses," *Washington Federalist* (Georgetown), June 16, 1808, [2] ("we acknowledge"); Ogilvie, "Supplementary Narrative," PE, xxvii ("religious persuasion").

8. Philologus, "Communication," *United States' Gazette*, Oct. 22, 1808, [3].

9. John F. Berens, *Providence and Patriotism in Early America, 1640–1815* (Charlottesville, Va., 1978); Timothy Roberts and Lindsay DiCuirci, gen. eds., *American Exceptionalism*, III, *Millennial Aspirations and Providentialism*, ed. DiCuirci (London, 2014); Carolyn Eastman, *A Nation of Speechifiers: Making an American Public after the Revolution* (Chicago, 2009), chap. 5; Nicholas Guyatt, *Providence and the Invention of the United States, 1607–1876* (Cambridge, 2007), 150–169.

10. A. B. [Charles Brockden Brown], "For the Aurora," Oct. 22, 1808, *Aurora General Advertiser*, [2] ("potent interference"); Denver Brunsman, *The Evil Necessity: British Naval Impressment in the Eighteenth-Century Atlantic World* (Charlottesville, Va., 2013); Robert E. Cray, Jr., "Remembering the U.S.S. Chesapeake: The Politics of Maritime Death and Impressment," *Journal of the Early Republic*, XXV (2005), 445–474; Paul A. Gilje, *Free Trade and Sailors' Rights in the War of 1812* (New York, 2013); Donald R. Hickey, *The War of 1812: A Forgotten Conflict*, bicentennial ed. (Urbana, Ill., 2012), 18–21; and Burton Spivak, *Jefferson's English Crisis: Commerce, Embargo, and the Republication Revolution* (Charlottesville, Va., 1979). On Philadelphia's docks, see Priscilla Ferguson Clement, *Welfare and the Poor in the Nineteenth-Century City: Philadelphia, 1800–1854* (Rutherford, N.J., 1985), 26–27.

11. James Hay Beattie, "The Hermit," *The Minstrel: In Two Books; with Some Other Poems* . . . (Philadelphia, 1809), 97–99; Ogilvie, "Supplementary Narrative," PE, xxiii ("not flying away").

12. Ogilvie, "Supplementary Narrative," PE, xxiv.

13. Ibid., xxiii–xxiv.

14. Ogilvie, "Supplementary Narrative," PE, xxiii ("forbear"). Ogilvie's own text for the "Progress and Prospects" lecture has not survived; I have reconstructed the flow of the argument from numerous descriptions of it, including PE; "Mr. Ogilvie," *Mercantile Advertiser* (New York), June 2, 1810, [2]; and "Communication," *Augusta Chronicle*, June 14, 1811, [3].

15. Ogilvie, "Supplementary Narrative," PE, xxv ("abrupt cessation"). On these debates, see Frederick C. Beiser, *The Fate of Reason: German Philosophy from Kant to Fichte* (Cambridge, Mass., 1987); Nathalie Caron and Naomi Wolf, "American Enlightenments: Continuity and Renewal," *Journal of American History*, XCIX (2013), 1072–1091; Jonathan I. Israel, *Radical Enlightenment: Philosophy and the Making of Modernity, 1650–1750* (Oxford, 2001); Margaret C. Jacob, *The Radical Enlightenment: Pantheists, Freemasons, and Republicans* (London, 1981); Nina Reid-Maroney, *Philadelphia's Enlightenment, 1740–1800: Kingdom of Christ, Empire of Reason* (Westport, Conn., 2001); Schlereth, *Age of Infidels*; Sheehan, "Enlightenment, Religion, and the Enigma of Secularization," AHR, CVIII (2003).

16. Plan of Estate in Fourth Street, circa 1806, Archives General Pre-1820 Collection, Box 2023, University Archives and Records Center, University of Pennsylvania, http://hdl.library.upenn.edu/1017/d/archives/20140904002; John C. Evans, Insurance Survey of the Old College, Jan. 2, 1818, Philadelphia Contributionship Digital Archives, www.philadelphiabuildings.org/contributionship/ho_display.cfm?RecordId=CONTRIB-US00367&CFID=32247454&CFTOKEN=9f93a7afbb10d0e6-1A4EF46F-155D-0A04-06D2AD96A6954C2D. See also William L. Turner, "The College, Academy, and Charitable School of Philadelphia: The Development of a Colonial Institution of Learning, 1740–1779" (Ph.D. diss., University of Pennsylvania, 1952), 169–174. I'm grateful to John Pollack and Jim Duffin for helping me find these materials.

17. Ogilvie, "Supplementary Narrative," PE, xxii, xxv ("in a place").

18. Ibid., xxvi (quotations), xxvii.

19. "Mr. Ogilvie," *Poulson's American Daily Advertiser*, Nov. 18, 1808, [3] ("omitting"); [Ogilvie], "Mr. Poulson," ibid., Nov. 19, 1808, [3] (Ogilvie's decline). The practice of holding occasional benefit performances was common in American theater, but actors used benefits to raise funds for a specific performer rather than for a local charity. See Sara Lampert, *Starring Women: Celebrity, Patriarchy, and American Theater, 1790–1850* (Urbana, Ill., forthcoming), chap. 1. See also Odai Johnson, *Absence and Memory in Colonial American Theatre: Fiorelli's Plaster* (London, 2006).

20. Ogilvie, "Supplementary Narrative," PE, xxvi.

21. *Temple of Reason* (Philadelphia), Jan. 1, 1803, [1] (quote on masthead); Schlereth, *Age of Infidels*, chap. 2; Christopher Grasso, "Deist Monster: On Religious Common Sense in the Wake of the American Revolution," *JAH*, XCV (2008), 43–68; Grasso, *Skepticism and American Faith*; and Kerry S. Walters, ed., *The American Deists: Voices of Reason and Dissent in the Early Republic* (Lawrence, Kans., 1992).

22. *Temple of Reason*, June 3, 1801, [1] quoted in Schlereth, *Age of Infidels*, 73 ("good of mankind"); Seth Cotlar, *Tom Paine's America: The Rise and Fall of Transatlantic Radicalism in the Early Republic* (Charlottesville, Va., 2011); Christopher Grasso, "The Religious and the Secular in the Early American Republic," *JER*, XXXVI (2016), 359–388; Henry F. May, *The Enlightenment in America* (New York, 1976); Amanda Porterfield, *Conceived in Doubt: Religion and Politics in the New American Nation* (Chicago, 2012); Schlereth, *Age of Infidels*; and Schmidt, *Hearing Things*.

23. *Temple of Reason*, Dec. 13, 1800, cited in Schlereth, *Age of Infidels*, 70 ("standard of Reason"); Elizabeth Sandwith Drinker, *The Diary of Elizabeth Drinker: The Life Cycle of an Eighteenth-Century Woman*, ed. Elaine Forman Crane, II (Boston, 1991), Dec. 3, 1802, 1596 ("Poor Philadelphia"). Drinker, a Quaker, is now best known for her exceptionally detailed diary of Philadelphia life during the Revolutionary era and the early Republic. See Richard Godbeer, *World of Trouble: A Philadelphia Quaker Family's Journey through the American Revolution* (New Haven, Conn., 2019).

24. Schlereth, *Age of Infidels*, 6–7.

25. "Address: From the Committee of the Friends of the Constitution," *Poulson's American Daily Advertiser*, Sept. 29, 1808, [2] ("live by Scandal"). On the Ross scandal, see Schlereth, *Age of Infidels*, 1, 127.

26. John B. Boles, *The Great Revival: Beginnings of the Bible Belt* (1972; rpt. Lexington, Ky., 1996); Paul K. Conkin, *Cane Ridge: America's Pentecost* (Madison, Wis., 1990); Sylvia R. Frey and Betty Wood, *Come Shouting to Zion: African American Protestantism in the American South and British Caribbean to 1830* (Chapel Hill, N.C., 1998); Hatch, *Democratization of American Christianity*; Thomas S. Kidd, *The Great Awakening: The Roots of Evangelical Christianity in Colonial America* (New Haven, Conn., 2007); Mark A. Noll, *America's God: From Jonathan Edwards to Abraham Lincoln* (Oxford, 2002); Michael J. McClymond, "Issues and Explanations in the Study of North American Revivalism," in McClymond, ed., *Embodying the Spirit: New Perspectives on North American Revivalism* (Baltimore, 2004), 1–46; and John H. Wigger, *Taking Heaven by Storm: Methodism and the Rise of Popular Christianity in America* (Urbana, Ill., 1998).

27. "Camp-Meeting," *Kline's Carlisle Weekly Gazette* (Pa.), Aug. 5, 1808, [3] ("sober judgment"). On camp meetings, see Leigh Eric Schmidt, *Holy Fairs: Scotland and the Making of American Revivalism*, 2d ed. (Grand Rapids, Mich., 2001); Ann Taves, *Fits, Trances, and Visions: Experiencing Religion and Explaining Experience from Wesley to James* (Princeton, N.J., 1999); Douglas L. Winiarski, "Seized by the Jerks: Shakers, Spirit Possession, and the Great Revival," *William and Mary Quarterly*, 3d Ser., LXXVI (2019), 111–150; Winiarski, "Shakers and Jerkers: Letters from the 'Long Walk,' 1805, Part I," *Journal of East Tennessee History*, LXXXIX (2017), 90–110.

28. "Review," *Literary Miscellany, Including Dissertations and Essays* . . . II, no. 1 (December 1806), 391 ("fanaticism"); "From the Salem Register," *Pennsylvania Correspondent, and Farmer's Advertiser* (Doylestown), July 30, 1805, [2] ("wrath and malice"). For accounts of camp meetings, see "Baltimore, Sept. 16," *Kline's Carlisle Weekly Gazette*, Oct. 5, 1804, [3]; "A Camp Meeting," ibid., July 31, 1807, [3].

29. Susan Juster, "Demagogues or Mystagogues? Gender and the Language of Prophecy in the Age of Democratic Revolutions," AHR, CIV (1999), 1575. See also Juster, *Doomsayers: Anglo-American Prophecy in the Age of Revolution* (Philadelphia, 2006).

30. On this subject, see Sandra M. Gustafson, *Eloquence Is Power: Oratory and Performance in Early America* (Williamsburg, Va., and Chapel Hill, N.C., 2000), xv–xix.

31. Schmidt, *Holy Fairs*, chaps. 1–2.

32. Ogilvie to Joseph Cabell, Nov. 17, 1808, Rare Books and Manuscripts, Boston Public Library.

CHAPTER SIX

1. [John Rodman], *Fragment of a Journal of a Sentimental Philosopher* . . . (New York, 1809), 3, 7–8, 11 (hereafter cited as FOAJ).

2. Noel Ignatiev, *How the Irish Became White* (New York, 1995); Peter Way, *Common Labour: Workers and the Digging of America's Canals, 1780–1860* (Cambridge, 1993), 63. Scots at American colleges included President John Witherspoon of the College of New Jersey (now

Princeton University) and Provosts William Smith and John McDowell of the University of Pennsylvania. Many others served as professors. Scots made up a little more than 10 percent of Virginia's population and about 7 to 8 percent of New York's. See Celeste Ray, "Scottish Immigration and Ethnic Organization in the United States," in Celeste Ray, ed., *Transatlantic Scots* (Tuscaloosa, Ala., 2005), 50–51; James C. Docherty, *Scottish Migration since 1750: Reasons and Results* (Lanham, Md., 2016), chap. 3; and, for a slightly later era, Juliana F. Gilheany, "Subjects of History: English, Scottish, and Welsh Immigrants in New York City, 1820–1860" (Ph.D. diss., New York University, 1989), chap. 5.

3. "Mr. Ogilvie's Orations," *Public Advertiser* (New York), Jan. 5, 1809, [2] ("awful gratitude"); "Ogilvie's Orations," *Evening Post* (New York), Jan. 4, 1809, [2] ("in compliance"); Humanitas, "Communication," *American Citizen* (New York), Jan. 19, 1809, [2] ("Ogilvie's celebrity"). See also Richard Beale Davis, "James Ogilvie and Washington Irving," *Americana Illustrated*, XXXV (1941), 439–440; FOAJ, 11–12.

4. FOAJ, 3. On the pamphlet, see Andrew Burstein, *The Original Knickerbocker: The Life of Washington Irving* (New York, 2007), 90–91; and Richard Beale Davis, "James Ogilvie, an Early American Teacher of Rhetoric," *Quarterly Journal of Speech*, XXVIII (1942), 289–297.

5. FOAJ, 8.

6. Ibid., 18 ("German tale"), 32 ("sublimest flights"), 37 ("art of oratory").

7. Ibid., 11 ("Godwinian school"), 12 ("marks"), 19 ("the game," "not fashionable").

8. Ibid., 8 ("languish"), 12 ("wash my hands"), 14 ("*soft blue eyes*"); Grigor Grant, quoted in [Grant and James Ogilvie], *The Ogilviad, an Heroic Poem, with Its Answers: Being a Dispute between Two Gentlemen at King's College* (Aberdeen, U.K., 1789), 11 ("dirty den").

9. FOAJ, 3–4.

10. FOAJ, 13 ("proceed with caution"), 14 ("*divine origin*"), 15–16 ("conduct of women"), 30 ("disciples"). These passages are indebted to Ari Adut, *On Scandal: Moral Disturbances in Society, Politics, and Art* (Cambridge, 2008), 24–27, 77–82.

11. FOAJ, 11, 12 ("has genius"); Burstein, *Original Knickerbocker*, 90. See also James E. Lewis, Jr., *The Burr Conspiracy: Uncovering the Story of an Early American Crisis* (Princeton, N.J., 2017), 291–338; R. Kent Newmyer, *The Treason Trial of Aaron Burr: Law, Politics, and the Character Wars of the New Nation* (Cambridge, 2012), 66–73, 81–86; and Stanley T. Williams, *The Life of Washington Irving*, 2 vols. (1935; rpt. New York, 1971), I, 125. Thanks to Sean Casey of the Boston Public Library's Rare Books and Manuscripts for hunting down this copy of the pamphlet, which had been misplaced. Other figures targeted in the pamphlet included Irving confidante Anthony Bleecker, lawyer Cadwallader D. Colden, and Dr. Edward Miller, a physician with a hand in magazine editing and publishing.

12. Irving's friends included Josiah O. Hoffman, John Ward Fenno, and Gulian Verplanck, the latter two of whom are mocked in the Journal. See Davis, "James Ogilvie and Washington Irving," *Americana Illustrated*, XXXV (1941), 439–440.

13. It's also worth noting that Ezra Sargeant, in whose bookstore Irving met, was the publisher of Rodman's pamphlet. In addition, Burstein notes that it is difficult to characterize Irving's own politics without understanding the ways that the political parties dif-

fered by state and by city and the way Irving might embrace a uniquely New York variety of Republicanism that maintained some ties to the Federalists. See Burstein, *Original Knickerbocker,* 19–20. Several years after he published *FOAJ,* Rodman delivered a Fourth of July address before an associated group of Republican and workingmen's organizations: *An Oration Delivered before the Tammany Society, or Columbian Order, Tailor's, Hibernian Provident, Columbian, Cordwainers, and George Clinton Societies, in the City of New-York, on the Fifth Day of July, 1813* (New York, 1813).

14. This account appears in a letter from John Howard Payne to Thomas Ritchie, Dec. 13, 1810, discussed in Williams, *Life of Washington Irving,* I, 125 ("injudiciously"); Mores, "For the Commercial Advertiser," *Commercial Advertiser* (New York), Mar. 25, 1809, [2] ("lynx-eyed"); "For the Commercial Advertiser," ibid., Mar. 28, 1809, [2] ("neat things"). At the time that Williams wrote *Life,* the Payne letter was in the private collection of T. F. Madigan of New York. See also Wayne R. Kime, "Introduction," *Complete Works of Washington Irving: Miscellaneous Writings, 1803–1859* (Boston, 1981), xxv. On the politics of published insults between men, see Joanne B. Freeman, *Affairs of Honor: National Politics in the New Republic* (New Haven, Conn., 2001), chaps. 2–3. "Satiric thong" is drawn from the William Cowper poem *The Task.*

15. Liberalitas, "For the Evening Post," *Evening Post,* Mar. 27, 1809, [3].

16. *New-York Review; or Critical Journal* (New York, 1809), 103 ("painful duties"), 105 ("Ironmonger"), 108 ("full yelp"), 116 ("religious zeal").

17. *New-York Review,* 117 ("censorious"), 117–118 ("multitudes"), 119 ("interlopers"). Jennifer Kristene Sherer points out that Irving used Rodman's central conceit—the idea of finding a fragment of a document—in his *History of New York* that he published later in 1809. See Sherer's "Mining America: Antiquarian Authorship and U.S. Empire, 1800–1850" (Ph.D. diss., University of Iowa, 2008), 49. On riding the rail, see Benjamin H. Irvin, "Tar, Feathers, and the Enemies of American Liberties, 1768–1776," *New England Quarterly,* LXXVI (2003), 197–238; and Maya Jasanoff, *Liberty's Exiles: American Loyalists in the Revolutionary World* (New York, 2011).

18. In the intervening years, Rodman became a lawyer and ultimately served as a district attorney in Manhattan.

19. [James Ogilvie], *Explanations Relative to the Nature and Objects of the Pursuit in Which Mr. Ogilvie Is Now Engaged* (New York, 1810), broadside, SY 1810, no. 44, New-York Historical Society.

20. Irving to John Howard Payne, Nov. 2, 1809, in Williams, *Life of Washington Irving,* I, 84–85.

21. Ibid.; Joseph W. Donohue, Jr., ed., *The Theatrical Manager in England and America: Player of a Perilous Game* (Princeton, N.J., 1971); and Odai Johnson, *Absence and Memory in Colonial American Theatre: Fiorelli's Plaster* (New York, 2006). See also Richard Butsch, *The Making of American Audiences: From Stage to Television, 1750–1990* (New York, 2000); Andrew Davis, *America's Longest Run: A History of the Walnut Street Theater* (University Park, Pa., 2010); Weldon B. Durham, ed., *American Theatre Companies, 1749–1887* (Westport, Conn., 1986);

David Grimsted, *Melodrama Unveiled: American Theater and Culture, 1800–1850* (Chicago, Ill., 1968); Odai Johnson and William J. Burling, *The Colonial American Stage, 1665–1774: A Documentary Calendar* (Madison, Wis., 2001), 21–70; Sara Lampert, *Starring Women: Celebrity, Patriarchy, and American Theater, 1790–1850* (Urbana, Ill., forthcoming), chap. 1; Lawrence W. Levine, *Highbrow / Lowbrow: The Emergence of Cultural Hierarchy in America* (Cambridge, Mass., 1988); and Heather S. Nathans, *Early American Theatre from the Revolution to Thomas Jefferson: Into the Hands of the People* (Cambridge, 2003).

22. James Ogilvie to Henry Wheaton, [March or April 1809], Henry Wheaton Letters and Papers, Pierpont Morgan Library, New York ("even delightful"); Robert Means, Jr., to Charles Stewart Daveis, Aug. 14, 1809, S0840, Manuscript Collections, Portsmouth Athenaeum, N.H. (Exeter performance). On hotels, see Jane Kamensky, *The Exchange Artist: A Tale of High-Flying Speculation and America's First Banking Collapse* (New York, 2008), 71–114; A. K. Sandoval-Strausz, *Hotel: An American History* (New Haven, Conn., 2007), 11–44. On New England's urban places, see U.S. census tables listing urban places by decade for 1810, accessed Apr. 22, 2016, www.census.gov/population/www/documentation/twps0027/tw ps0027.html (hereafter cited as USC-1810). Twelve urban places were in Massachusetts; New Hampshire and the District of Maine had one each.

23. On the gradual development of criticism and the professionalization of criticism, see Adam Gordon, *Prophets, Publicists, and Parasites: Antebellum Print Culture and the Rise of the Critic* (Amherst, Mass., 2020), chap. 1; Gerald Graff, *Professing Literature: An Institutional History* (Chicago, Ill., 1987); Catherine O'Donnell Kaplan, *Men of Letters in the Early Republic: Cultivating Forums of Citizenship* (Williamsburg, Va., and Chapel Hill, N.C., 2008); Tim Lanzendörfer, *The Professionalization of the American Magazine: Periodicals, Biography, and Nationalism in the Early Republic* (Paderborn, Ger., 2013); Bryan Waterman, *Republic of Intellect: The Friendly Club of New York City and the Making of American Literature* (Baltimore, 2007).

24. Alice G. Waters et al., eds., *The Diary of William Bentley, D. D.*, 4 vols. (Salem, Mass., 1905–1914), Oct. 13, Oct. 21, Nov. 8, Nov. 18, Dec. 10, 1809, III, 468–484 (hereafter cited as DWB). See also USC-1810 for information about Salem's size relative to other U.S. cities. On female asylums and other female-run charitable organizations, see Anne M. Boylan, *The Origins of Women's Activism: New York and Boston, 1797–1840* (Chapel Hill, N.C., 2002); Faye Dudden, *Serving Women: Household Service in Nineteenth-Century America* (Middletown, Conn., 1983); Carole S. Lasser, "The Domestic Balance of Power: Relations between Mistress and Maid in Nineteenth-Century New England," *Labor History*, XXVIII (1987), 5–22; Lasser, "A 'Pleasingly Oppressive' Burden: The Transformation of Domestic Service and Female Charity in Salem, 1800–1840," *Essex Institute Historical Collections*, CXVI (1980), 156–175; Susan Lynne Porter, "The Benevolent Asylum—Image and Reality: The Care and Training of Female Orphans in Boston, 1800–1840" (Ph.D. diss., Boston University, 1984); and Porter, "Gendered Expectations: Orphans and Apprenticeship in Antebellum New England," in Peter Benes, ed., *The Worlds of Children, 1620–1920*, Dublin Seminar for New England Folklife, Annual Proceedings 2002 (Boston, 2004), 112–129.

25. "Mr. Ogilvie," *Portsmouth Oracle*, Oct. 14, 1809, [3] ("chastened and corrected"); "Mr.

Ogilvie," *Newburyport Herald*, Sept. 26, 1809, [3], reprinted from the *Portsmouth Oracle* ("all smoke"); Amelia E. Russell, diary (1814–1815), box 5, folder 2, Jonathan Russell Papers, Manuscript Collections, Massachusetts Historical Society (MHS) ("whip sillybub"); *DWB*, Nov. 18, 1809, III, 478 ("sophimore").

26. John Gallison, Diary B (1808–1810), Nov. 1, 1809, MHS ("He directed"); [John Gallison], "For the Salem Gazette," *Salem Gazette*, Nov. 3, 1809, [3] ("praise her advocate").

27. "Mr. Ogilvie," *Newburyport Herald*, Sept. 29, 1809, [2] ("unbiassed opinions"); "Mr. Ogilvie," *Salem Gazette*, Oct. 16, 1809, [3] ("manly, dignified"); [Gallison], "For the Salem Gazette," Nov. 3, 1809, [3] ("philosophic truth").

28. One of the most active critics published in the Charleston, South Carolina, *Southern Patriot* in 1815 under the pseudonym of "Veritas," writing a series of lecture-by-lecture critiques. Like Gallison and the others in the northern New England papers described here, Veritas took a somber tone and sought to display a finer critical sense of what amounted to oratorical excellence than what he saw performed on Ogilvie's stage. See, for example, Veritas, "Mr. Ogilvie's Second Oration on Oratory," *Southern Patriot, and Commercial Advertiser*, Nov. 23, 1815, [2].

29. Ogilvie to Francis Walker Gilmer, Feb. 4, [1814] ("abject coward"), in Richard Beale Davis, *Francis Walker Gilmer: Life and Learning in Jefferson's Virginia* (Richmond, Va., 1939), 382; Freeman, *Affairs of Honor*, chap. 4.

30. David Waldstreicher, *In the Midst of Perpetual Fetes: The Making of American Nationalism* (Williamsburg, Va., and Chapel Hill, N.C., 1997).

CHAPTER SEVEN

1. Edwin J. Scott, *Random Recollections of a Long Life, 1806 to 1876* (Columbia, S.C., 1884), 33 ("split spoons"). Estimates on traveling are notoriously difficult to ascertain, but considering that about 80 percent of American families engaged in farming, few had opportunities to travel far from home. See Donald H. Parkerson, "How Mobile Were Nineteenth-Century Americans?" *Historical Methods*, XV (1982), 99–109; Jack Larkin, *The Reshaping of Everyday Life, 1790–1840* (New York, 1988), 15–16. A poll by Ipsos in 2016 found recent data, www.ipsos.com/en-us/average-american-has-visited-just-12-states.

2. "Oration on Duelling," *Ordeal; a Critical Journal of Politicks and Literature* (Boston), I, no. 16 (Apr. 22, 1809), 256 ("eminently distinguished"); "Mr. Ogilvie's Orations," *Times* (Charleston, S.C.), Feb. 27, 1811, [3] ("respectable audiences").

3. On Americans' provincialism, see John Clive and Bernard Bailyn, "England's Cultural Provinces: Scotland and America," *William and Mary Quarterly*, 3d Ser., XI (1954), 200–213; David Jaffe, "The Village Enlightenment in New England, 1760–1820," ibid., XLVII (1990), 327–346; David B. Knight, "Identity and Territory: Geographical Perspectives on Nationalism and Regionalism," *Annals of the Association of American Geographers*, LXXII (1982), 514–531; Ned C. Landsman, *From Colonials to Provincials: American Thought and Culture, 1680–1760* (New York, 1997); Landsman, ed., *Nation and Province in the First British Empire: Scotland*

and the Americas, 1600–1800 (Lewisburg, Pa., 2001); Landsman, "AHR Forum: Nation, Migration, and the Province in the First British Empire: Scotland and the Americas, 1600–1800," *American Historical Review*, CIV (1999), 463–475; John M. Murrin, "A Roof without Walls: The Dilemma of American National Identity," in Richard Beeman, Stephen Botein, and Edward C. Carter II, eds., *Beyond Confederation: Origins of the Constitution and American National Identity* (Williamsburg, Va., and Chapel Hill, N.C., 1987), 333–348; J. M. Opal, *Beyond the Farm: National Ambitions in Rural New England* (Philadelphia, 2008); Joseph Rezek, "Cooper and Scott in the Anglophone Literary Field: *The Pioneers, The Heart of Mid-Lothian*, and the Effects of Provinciality," *ELH: English Literary History*, LXXVIII (2011), 891–916; and David Waldstreicher, *In the Midst of Perpetual Fetes: The Making of American Nationalism, 1776–1820* (Williamsburg, Va., and Chapel Hill, N.C., 1997).

4. "Western Railway," *American Traveller* (Boston), Nov. 25, 1828, [1] ("there is more travelling"); Albert Gallatin, *Report of the Secretary of the Treasury, on the Subject of Public Roads and Canals . . .* (Washington, D.C., 1808), 55 ("artificial roads"). See also John Lauritz Larson, *Internal Improvement: National Public Works and the Promise of Popular Government in the Early United States* (Chapel Hill, N.C., 2001).

5. [Stephen Ravenel?], travel diary, 1803, Ravenel Family Papers, SCHS 1027.00, 12/342/2, South Carolina Historical Society Manuscripts, Special Collections, College of Charleston Library, S.C. ("of the roads"); Bradford Perkins, ed., *Youthful America: Selections from Henry Unwin Addington's Residence in the United States of America, 1822, 23, 24, 25* (Berkeley, Calif., 1960), 75 ("the wreck"). For a similar account of broken coaches, see Francis Hall, *Travels in Canada, and the United States, in 1816 and 1817* (Boston, 1818), 240, among other primary sources; Donald B. Klein and John Majewski, "Economy, Community, and Law: The Turnpike Movement in New York, 1797–1845," *Law and Society Review*, XXVI (1992), 469–512; John Lauritz Larson, "A Bridge, a Dam, a River: Liberty and Innovation in the Early Republic," *Journal of the Early Republic*, VII (1987), 351–375; Larson, *Internal Improvement*; and Greg Laugero, "Infrastructures of Enlightenment: Road-Making, the Public Sphere, and the Emergence of Literature," special issue of *Eighteenth-Century Studies*, XXIX (1995), 45–67.

6. John Melish, *Travels in the United States of America, in the Years 1806 and 1807, and 1809, 1810, and 1811 . . .* , 2 vols. (Philadelphia, 1812), I, 82 ("turnpike to Providence"); William Brisbane, "Account of My Travels through the United States of America and in Great Britain and Other Parts of Europe," 1801–1807, MS 16, 13, Manuscript Collections, Charleston Library Society, S.C. ("insulting travellers"). On the differences between traveling in urban and rural areas, see Jason M. Opal, "Enterprise and Emulation: The Moral Economy of Turnpikes in Early National New England," special issue of *Early American Studies*, VIII (2010), 627.

7. Ogilvie to Henry Wheaton [March or April 1809], Henry Wheaton Letters and Papers, Pierpont Morgan Library, New York; Melish, *Travels in the United States*, II, 52 (Pittsburgh expenses), II, 17 ("great dispatch"). Melish reported that the cost of the stage to Pittsburgh was twenty dollars, plus about seven dollars for all the other charges along the

way (tavern rooms and meals); the cost of traveling by wagon was about five dollars, plus twelve dollars in other charges.

8. Wayland Fuller Dunaway, *History of the James River and Kanawha Company* (New York, 1922), 28; Gallatin, *Report*, 55. On Gallatin and the National Road, see Larson, *Internal Improvement*, chap. 2. On local opposition to tolls, see Opal, "Enterprise and Emulation," *EAS*, VIII (2010), 633–636. On steamboats, see Ross Thomson, *Structures of Change in the Mechanical Age: Technological Innovation in the United States, 1790–1865* (Baltimore, 2009). Historians sometimes refer to a "transportation revolution" that "swept across" the nation during these decades of the early Republic. But we should not assume that their use of the term *revolution* implies "radical changes in the speed, scale and experience of traveling." See Carol Sheriff, *The Artificial River: The Erie Canal and the Paradox of Progress, 1817–1862* (New York, 1996), 4; Larkin, *Reshaping of Everyday Life*, 204; Larson, *Internal Improvement*, introduction.

9. *An Act to Establish the Post-Office and Post-Roads, within the United States* ([Philadelphia], 1792), [6]; Richard R. John, *Spreading the News: The American Postal System from Franklin to Morse* (Cambridge, Mass., 1995). See also Joseph M. Adelman, *Revolutionary Networks: The Business and Politics of Printing the News, 1763–1789* (Baltimore, 2019); David M. Henkin, *The Postal Age: The Emergence of Modern Communications in Nineteenth-Century America* (Chicago, 2006); Richard R. John, "American Historians and the Concept of the Communications Revolution," in Lisa Bud-Frierman, ed., *Information Acumen: The Understanding and Use of Knowledge in Modern Business* (London, 1994), 98–110; and John, "Expanding the Realm of Communications," in Robert A. Gross and Mary Kelley, eds., *A History of the Book in America*, II, *An Extensive Republic: Print, Culture, and Society in the New Nation, 1790–1840* (Chapel Hill, N.C., 2010), 211–220.

10. "As was mentioned in a late Repertory . . . ," *Portland Gazette, and Maine Advertizer*, June 19, 1809, [3] ("difficult to speak"); "It is with much pleasure we announce . . . ," *Salem Gazette* (Mass.), Sept. 19, 1809, [3] ("must be heard"); H., "For the Times: Mr. Ogilvie," *Times*, Mar. 6, 1811, [3] ("ineffable state," "magic"). For examples of "genius," see "Mr. Ogilvie," *Eastern Argus* (Portland, Maine), June 22, 1809, [3]; "Mr. Ogilvie," *Baltimore Patriot & Evening Advertiser*, Sept. 28, 1813, [3]; and "The Rostrum," *Daily National Intelligencer* (Washington, D.C.), Mar. 15, 1814, [3]. It's also worth noting that the feint of "must be heard to be conceived" was also used to describe subsequent effective speakers, as Thomas Augst reveals in his "Temperance, Mass Culture, and the Romance of Experience," *American Literary History*, XIX (2007), 297–323, esp. 311.

11. Ben Paul Lafferty, "Joseph Dennie and *The Farmer's Weekly Museum*: Readership and Pseudonymous Celebrity in Early National Journalism," *American Nineteenth Century History*, XV (2014), 67–87; David S. Shields, *Civil Tongues and Polite Letters in British America* (Williamsburg, Va., and Chapel Hill, N.C., 1997), 262–266; Victoria Smith Ekstrand and Cassandra Imfeld Jeyaram, "Our Founding Anonymity: Anonymous Speech during the Constitutional Debate," *American Journalism*, XXVIII, no. 3 (Summer 2011), 35–60; Myron F. Wehtje, "Controversy over the Legal Profession in Post-Revolutionary Boston," *Historical Journal of Massachusetts*, XX (1992), 133–142.

12. "Ogilvie," *Middlesex Gazette* (Middletown, Conn.), July 26, 1810, [3] ("depth of his knowledge"); "Communication: The Rostrum," *Poulson's American Daily Advertiser* (Philadelphia), Jan. 29, 1814, [3] ("graceful action"). See also Carolyn Eastman, *A Nation of Speechifiers: Making an American Public after the Revolution* (Chicago, 2009), 8–9, chap. 1 (hereafter cited as NOS). William J. Gilmore argues that readers did not necessarily see the profusion of new printed materials as signs of inevitable progress. See Gilmore, *Reading Becomes a Necessity of Life: Material and Cultural Life in Rural New England, 1780–1835* (Knoxville, Tenn., 1989), chaps. 5 and 6.

13. "Mr. Ogilvie," *Portland Gazette, and Maine Advertizer*, June 19, 1809, [3] ("dissolve the charm"); Nicholas Biddle to A. J. Dallas (copy), Jan. 12, 1811, Biddle Family Papers, coll. 2139, box 7, folder 6, Historical Society of Pennsylvania, Philadelphia ("up to their eyes"). This letter was subsequently excerpted and published in *Poulson's American Daily Advertiser*, Jan. 17, 1811, [3]. These passages are indebted to practices of reading for readers and their responses to literature, and most of all to Cathy N. Davidson's *Revolution and the Word: The Rise of the Novel in America* (New York, 1986), part II. Other influential sources include Robert A. Gross, "Reading for an Extensive Republic," in Gross and Kelley, eds., *History of the Book in America*, II, 516–544; and James L. Machor, "Fiction and Informed Reading in Early Nineteenth-Century America," *Nineteenth-Century Literature*, XLVII (1992), 320–348.

14. Samuel Emerson to George Barrell Emerson, July 1, 1820, George Barrell Emerson Papers, MS N-188, box 11, volume I, Massachusetts Historical Society ("small man"); Joseph R. Anthony, *Life in New Bedford a Hundred Years Ago: A Chronicle of the Social, Religious, and Commercial History of the Period as Recorded in a Diary Kept by Joseph R. Anthony*, ed. Zephaniah W. Pease (New Bedford, Mass., 1922), Jan. 22, 1823, 14 ("please my taste"); Sarah Noyes to Holbrook Curtis, Apr. 11, 1814, in Elizabeth Curtis, ed., *Letters and Journals* (New York, 1926), 61 ("much dignity"). See also NOS, chap. 1; and Meredith Marie Neuman, *Jeremiah's Scribes: Creating Sermon Literature in Puritan New England* (Philadelphia, 2013), chap. 1. Some American newspapers also recorded information about the content and structure of weekly sermons.

15. James Perrin Warren, *Culture of Eloquence: Oratory and Reform in Antebellum America* (University Park, Pa., 1999), introduction; NOS, chap. 1. In 1790, the U.S. census designated 94.9 percent of Americans as living in rural areas, a number that dropped slightly in successive decades to 93.9 percent in 1800 to 92.7 percent in 1810. It ticked up slightly in 1820 to 92.8 percent. See U.S. census tables listing urban places by decade for 1810 and 1820, accessed Apr. 22, 2016, www.census.gov/population/www/documentation/twps0027/tw ps0027.html (hereafter cited as USC-1810).

16. Gerald F. Moran and Maris A. Vinovskis, "Schools," in Gross and Kelley, eds., *History of the Book in America*, II, 286–303; and J. M. Opal, "Exciting Emulation: Academies and the Transformation of the Rural North, 1780s–1820s," *Journal of American History*, XCI (2004), 445–470.

17. "We observe with pleasure . . . ," *Rhode-Island American, and General Advertiser* (Providence), May 22, 1810, [3], quoting from the *Democratic Press* ("taste and intelligence");

"Mr. Ogilvie," *Enquirer* (Richmond, Va.) Sept. 28, 1813, [3], quoting from Baltimore papers ("instructed and delighted"); "Mr. Ogilvie's Orations," *Kentucky Gazette* (Lexington), July 9, 1811, [3] ("degree of delicacy"); "Mr. Ogilvie, last evening," *Columbian* (New York), Dec. 3, 1813, [3] ("highly respectable"). For Lexington's population, see USC-1810.

18. "Mr. Ogilvie's Oration on Public Libraries," *Mercantile Advertiser* (New York), Apr. 10, 1810, [2] ("unquestionable partiality"). Ogilvie discusses raising his fees in James Ogilvie to Francis W. Gilmer, Feb. 4, 1814, in Richard Beale Davis, *Francis Walker Gilmer: Life and Learning in Jefferson's Virginia* (Richmond, Va., 1939), 380.

19. "For the Times: Mr. Ogilvie," *Times*, Mar. 6, 1811, [3]; Clive and Bailyn, "England's Cultural Provinces," *WMQ*, 3d Ser., XI (1954); Knight, "Identity and Territory," *Annals of the Association of American Geographers*, LXXII (1982); and Murrin, "A Roof without Walls," in *Beyond Confederation*, 333–348.

20. "Mr. Ogilvie," *Eastern Argus*, June 22, 1809, [3] ("quota"); "We observe with pleasure . . . ," *Rhode-Island American*, May 22, 1810, [3] ("taste and intelligence"); "It is with the greatest pleasure . . . ," *Columbian*, June 12, 1811, [2], reprinted from "a Savannah paper," ("in proportion"), my emphasis. On Portland's size, see USC-1810.

21. "Communication: The Rostrum," *Poulson's American Daily Advertiser*, Jan. 29, 1814, [3] ("uncommonly"); "Mr. Ogilvie," *Newport Mercury*, Mar. 10, 1810, [3] ("fully attended").

22. "For the Times. Mr. Ogilvie," *Times*, Mar. 6, 1811, [3]. See also Veritas, "Mr. Ogilvie," *Southern Patriot* (Charleston), Mar. 18, 1815, [2]; and Veritas, "Mr. Ogilvie's Oration on Oratory," ibid., Nov. 10, 1815, [2].

23. "Extracts from the Columbia paper. Mr. Ogilvie," *Star* (Raleigh, N.C.), Aug. 16, 1811, 132 ("light of genius"). On remediation, see Thomas Augst, "The Temperance Lecture, Between Speech and Print" (paper delivered at the annual meeting of the Society for the History of Authorship, Reading, and Publishing, Washington, D.C., July 2011); Jay David Bolter and Richard Grusin, *Remediation: Understanding New Media* (Cambridge, Mass., 1999); Lisa Gitelman, *Always Already New: Media, History, and the Data of Culture* (Cambridge, Mass., 2006); Kate Lacey, *Listening Publics: The Politics and Experience of Listening in the Media Age* (Cambridge, 2013).

24. "This Day Published," *Massachusetts Spy, or Worcester Gazette*, Feb. 10, 1808, [4] ("learned and evangelical"); "Antisthenes," *Litchfield Gazette* (Conn.), July 13, 1808, [4] ("Athenian philosopher"); "For the Monitor," *Monitor* (Washington, D.C.), July 21, 1808, [1] ("consequential celebrity"); "The Exhibition of Wax-Figures," *Spirit of the Press* (Philadelphia), June 1, 1808, [3] ("figures"); Dinah Maria Mulock Craik, *The Ogilvies: A Novel* (London, 1849), I, 45, quoted in Tom Mole, "Introduction," *Romanticism and Celebrity Culture, 1750–1850* (Cambridge, 2009), 2 ("as you call"). Newspaper advertisements also used the terms *celebrity* and *celebrated* to refer to patent medicines. "The above Medicines with many others of equal celebrity have been received, and are now offered for sale," one New York druggist announced of such medicines as Harvey's Grand Restorative Balsam, Infallible Ague and Fever Pills, and Velnoe's Genuine Bilious Pills. See "Disorders Cured," *Daily Advertiser* (New York), Jan. 4, 1809, [4]. See also Kenneth Cohen, "Tracking the Language

of Celebrity in the Early Republic" (paper presented at the annual meeting of the Society for Historians of the Early American Republic, Cleveland, July 2018). When a Baltimore beauty named Elizabeth Patterson married the youngest brother of Napoleon Bonaparte in 1803, she earned international celebrity as a result, particularly after Bonaparte himself sought to have the marriage annulled and his brother remarried to European royalty. See Charlene M. Boyer Lewis, *Elizabeth Patterson Bonaparte: An American Aristocrat in the Early Republic* (Philadelphia, 2012).

25. Humanitas, "Communication," *American Citizen* (New York), Jan. 19, 1809, [2] ("the great body"); "The Orator—Ogilvie," *Albany Register*, Dec. 25, 1810, [2] ("so high a degree"); H., "For the Times. Mr. Ogilvie," *Times*, Mar. 6, 1811, [3] ("well merited"); James Ogilvie, "Preface," in Ogilvie, *Philosophical Essays . . .* (Philadelphia, 1816), [iii], ("permanent and extended") (hereafter cited as PE); Ogilvie to Mr. Tart, Apr. 23 (catalogued as 1813, but should read 1811), Letters regarding Charles Brockden Brown, MSS 6349-b, Small Special Collections Library, University of Virginia, Charlottesville ("Johnson[']s claims"); Samuel Johnson, "The Impotence of Wealth: The Visit of Serotinus to the Place of His Nativity," Oct. 15, 1751, in Johnson, *The Rambler, a Periodical Paper, Published in 1750, 1751, 1752* (London, 1825), 284 ("enriched in proportion"). On Johnson, see Kurt Heinzelman, "Lord Byron and the Invention of Celebrity," *Southwest Review*, XCIII (2008), 489. On other applications of *celebrity* to Ogilvie, see, for example, "Mr. Ogilvie," *Enquirer*, May 25, 1814, [3], a story reprinted in the *Daily National Intelligencer* and the *Rhode-Island American* in subsequent weeks.

26. Whether to use the term *celebrity* for early historical contexts like the eighteenth and early nineteenth centuries (and even earlier) used to be controversial among scholars. On the early modern phenomenon, see Elizabeth Barry, ed., "Celebrity, Cultural Production, and Public Life," special issue of *International Journal of Cultural Studies*, XI (2008), 251–376, esp. essays by Barry, Uta Kornmeier, and Tom Mole; Edward Berenson and Eva Giloi, eds., *Constructing Charisma: Celebrity, Fame, and Power in Nineteenth-Century Europe* (New York, 2010), esp. essays by Dana Gooley, Martin Kohlrausch, and Stephen Minta; Brian Cowan, "Histories of Celebrity in Post-Revolutionary England," *Historical Social Research / Historische Sozialforschung*, no. 32, Supplement, *Celebrity's Histories: Case Studies and Critical Perspectives* (2019), 83–98; Eric Eisner, *Nineteenth-Century Poetry and Literary Celebrity* (Houndmills, U.K., 2009); Laura Engel, *Fashioning Celebrity: Eighteenth-Century British Actresses and Strategies for Image Making* (Columbus, Ohio, 2011); Páraic Finnerty and Rod Rosenquist, eds., "Transatlantic Celebrity: European Fame in Nineteenth-Century America," special issue of *Comparative American Studies*, XIV (2016), 1–89, esp. essays by Finnerty and Holly Gale Millette; Fred Inglis, *A Short History of Celebrity* (Princeton, N.J., 2010); Antoine Lilti, *Figures publiques: L'invention de la célébrité, 1750–1850* (Paris, 2014); Sharon Marcus, *The Drama of Celebrity* (Princeton, N.J., 2019); P. David Marshall, ed., *The Celebrity Culture Reader* (New York, 2006); Tom Mole, *Byron's Romantic Celebrity: Industrial Culture and the Hermeneutic of Intimacy* (New York, 2007); Mole, ed., *Romanticism and Celebrity Culture*; Pramod K. Nayar, *Seeing Stars: Spectacle, Society, and Celebrity Culture* (New Delhi, 2009); Joseph Roach, "Celebrity Erotics: Pepys, Performance, and Painted Ladies," *Yale Journal of Criticism*, XVI (2003), 211–230; and Stella

Tillyard, "Celebrity in 18th-Century London," *History Today*, LV, no. 6 (June 2005), 20–27. For a survey, see Leo Braudy, *The Frenzy of Renown: Fame and Its History* (New York, 1986).

27. "Mr. Ogilvie, we understand . . . ," *Mercantile Advertiser* (New York), June 2, 1810, [2] ("throng of fashion"); "Mr. Ogilvie," *Repertory* (Boston), May 16, 1809, [2] ("private circles").

28. James Spear Loring, *The Hundred Boston Orators Appointed by the Municipal Authorities . . . ,* 4th ed. (Boston, 1855), 559 (gerrymander); "The ode on . . . ," *Columbian*, Feb. 4, 1812, [3] (Tippecanoe). Both claims are likely false, considering that both *gerrymander* and the song appeared while Ogilvie was far away in Kentucky. Even more than they used the term *celebrity*, writers for newspapers referred to Ogilvie's *genius*. "Standing forth in all the proud originality of his genius, he claimed the privilege of criticism and boldly asserted her rights," explained one representative account. See "Mr. Ogilvie," *Poulson's American Daily Advertiser*, Nov. 15, 1813, [3].

29. "From the Utica Patriot," *Balance, & New-York State Journal* (Albany), Oct. 5, 1810, [3] ("SHAKESPEARE"); "Mr. Ogilvie," *Newburyport Herald* (Mass.), Sept. 8, 1809, [2] ("*forget all time*"). For additional examples, see "It is with much pleasure . . . ," *Salem Gazette*, Sept. 19, 1809, [3]; "For the Times: Mr. Ogilvie," *Times*, Mar. 6, 1811, [3]; and "Mr. Ogilvie," *Baltimore Patriot*, Sept. 28, 1813, [3]. See also Michelle Sizemore, *American Enchantment: Rituals of the People in the Post-Revolutionary World* (New York, 2018).

30. Irving to William Van Ness, June 24, 1809, Thomas F. Madigan Collection, MSS Col 1831, box 1, folder 17, Manuscripts and Archives Division, New York Public Library ("Ogilvian oration"); "As I passed by the house of a friend . . . ," *Cynick* (Boston) I, no. 9 (Nov. 23, 1811), 151 ("force of rhetorick"); "Readings and Recitations," *Balance, & New-York State Journal*, Mar. 19, 1811, 90 ("every body crazy"); "On Wednesday Evening," *Public Advertiser* (New York), June 20, 1812, [2] ("young Mr. Ogilvie").

31. Engel, *Fashioning Celebrity*, chap. 1; Lilti, *Figures publiques*, chap. 2; and Mole, *Byron's Romantic Celebrity*, chap. 1.

32. James Ogilvie, "Supplementary Narrative," PE, xiii ("mortifying interruption"), xxxi ("Kentucky"), xxxii ("declamation"). On heckling, see Faye E. Dudden, *Women in the American Theatre: Actresses and Audiences, 1790–1870* (New Haven, Conn., 1994); Sara E. Lampert, *Starring Women: Celebrity, Patriarchy, and American Theater, 1790–1850* (Champaign, Ill., forthcoming); Lawrence W. Levine, *Highbrow / Lowbrow: The Emergence of Cultural Hierarchy in America* (Cambridge, Mass., 1988), chap. 1; and Joseph Roach, "Performance; or, Answering a Call from the Nineteenth Century," *J19: The Journal of Nineteenth-Century Americanists*, VI (2018), 418–426. For different eras, see Eileen Curley, "Mutual Profiteering: Sensational Journalism, Society Columns, and Mrs James Brown Potter's Theatrical Debuts," *Nineteenth Century Theatre and Film*, XLVI (2019), 73–98; Richard deCordova, *Picture Personalities: The Emergence of the Star System in America* (Urbana, Ill., 1990); Caroline Heim, *Audience as Performer: The Changing Role of Theatre Audiences in the Twenty-First Century* (London, 2016); and Charles L. Ponce de Leon, *Self-Exposure: Human-Interest Journalism and the Emergence of Celebrity in America, 1890–1940* (Chapel Hill, N.C., 2002).

33. "We understand . . . ," *New-York Evening Post*, Dec. 21, 1808, [3] ("impudence"); "One Hundred Dollars Reward," *Reporter* (Washington, Pa.), Aug. 23, 1813, [3] ("respectable audience").

34. "Mr. Ogilvie," *Something; Edited by Nemo Nobody, Esquire*, Jan. 6, 1810, 117–118.

35. "On Friday evening last," *Rhode-Island American*, Feb. 27, 1810, [3] ("pleasures"); "On Tuesday evening last . . . ," *Rhode-Island American*, Mar. 23, 1810, [3] ("*appearing like himself*").

36. Ogilvie to Charles Stewart Daveis, March 1810, Special MS Collection Daveis, Rare Book and Manuscript Library, Butler Library, Columbia University, N.Y.

37. Others, too, found it possible to suffer seemingly devastating setbacks only to find new opportunities during the early Republic. See, for example, Edward J. Balleisen, *Navigating Failure: Bankruptcy and Commercial Society in Antebellum America* (Chapel Hill, N.C., 2001); Jane Kamensky, *The Exchange Artist: A Tale of High-Flying Speculation and America's First Banking Collapse* (New York, 2008); and Scott A. Sandage, *Born Losers: A History of Failure in America* (Cambridge, Mass., 2005).

38. John, "Expanding the Realm of Communications," in Gross and Kelley, eds., *History of the Book*, II, 211–220; see also George N. Gordon, *The Communications Revolution: A History of Mass Media in the United States* (New York, 1977), 25–36; and John, *Spreading the News*. My view of the situation is more in keeping with that described by Trish Loughran, who insists that we should continue to view the circulation of print as remaining overwhelmingly localized and sporadic until at least the 1830s. See Loughran, *The Republic in Print: Print Culture in the Age of U.S. Nation Building, 1770–1870* (New York, 2007).

CHAPTER EIGHT

1. "The Rostrum," *Morning Post* (London), Aug. 5, 1817, [3] ("appropriate costume"); "The Rostrum," *Providence Patriot* (R.I.), Oct. 25, 1823, [3] ("Roman Toga"). One scholar would later find the idea of "the toga in which he wrapped himself to orate" so ridiculous that he characterized it as one of the most obvious reasons why Ogilvie's performances "show the worst side of the elocutionary movement": a comical delusion of oratorical grandeur. That perspective might reflect twentieth-century views but utterly misses an understanding of the early nineteenth-century context. See Patrick Scott, "From Rhetoric to English: Nineteenth-Century English Teaching at South Carolina College," *South Carolina Historical Magazine*, LXXXV (1984), 236.

2. Carl J. Richard, *The Founders and the Classics: Greece, Rome, and the American Enlightenment* (Cambridge, Mass., 1994), 39, 43–47, 57–66. This chapter also draws on Viccy Coltman, *Fabricating the Antique: Neoclassicism in Britain, 1760–1800* (Chicago, 2006); Chloe Chard, "Effeminacy, Pleasure, and the Classical Body," in Gill Perry and Michael Rossington, eds., *Femininity and Masculinity in Eighteenth-Century Art and Culture* (Manchester, U.K., 1994), 142–161; John W. Eadie, ed., *Classical Traditions in Early America* (Ann Arbor, Mich., 1976); Paul A. Rahe, "Cicero and the Classical Republican Legacy in America," in Peter S. Onuf and Nicholas P. Cole, eds., *Thomas Jefferson, the Classical World, and Early America* (Charlottesville, Va., 2011), 248–264; Rahe, *Republics Ancient and Modern: Classical Republicanism and the Ameri-*

can Revolution (Chapel Hill, N.C., 1992); Eran Shalev, Rome Reborn on Western Shores: Historical Imagination and the Creation of the American Republic (Charlottesville, Va., 2009); Caroline Vout, "The Myth of the Toga: Understanding the History of Roman Dress," Greece and Rome, XLIII (1996), 205–215; Caroline Winterer, The Culture of Classicism: Ancient Greece and Rome in American Intellectual Life, 1780–1910 (Baltimore, 2002); and Winterer, "From Royal to Republican: The Classical Image in Early America," Journal of American History, XCI (2005), 1264–1290.

3. William C. Allen, "Senators Poindexter, Davis, and Stennis: Three Mississippians in the History of the United States Capitol," Journal of Mississippi History, LXV (2003), 193–196. In fact, Greenough's statue was based on the statue of Zeus at Olympia, known principally via a description by Pausanius, a second-century travel writer. Pausanius refers to the robe worn by the statue as a himation, the Greek predecessor of the toga, which revealed more of the man's upper body and, with different folds, could also be worn by women. I'm grateful to Peter Stone for clarifying these details.

4. Quintilian, Institutio Oratoria, 11.6.137, in Harold Edgeworth Butler, ed., Quintilian, with an English Translation (Cambridge, Mass., and London, 1922), Perseus Digital Library, ed. Gregory R. Crane, www.perseus.tufts.edu. This confirms Paul Rahe's point that the founding generation was prone to choose selectively from classical models. See Rahe, Republics Ancient and Modern, 191.

5. One of the rare exceptions, Basil Kennett's Romae Antiquae Noticia; or, The Antiquities of Rome (London, 1696), a less expensive pocket-sized book, was reprinted in dozens of editions and included a brief chapter on Roman clothing as well as a foldout panel of idealized figures in togas. According to Caroline Winterer, Kennett's book appeared in colonial American libraries and remained in use into the nineteenth century. See Winterer, "From Royal to Republican," JAH, XCI (2005), 1279. Robert von Spalart's expensive, illustrated, multi-volume work on historical costume, Versuch über das Kostum der vorzüglichsten Völker des Alterthums . . . , appeared in its original German in 1796 and was translated into French in 1804. This work does not appear in known catalogues of American libraries or in bookstores' newspaper advertisements. Another expensive two-volume set with lavish illustrations, Thomas Hope's Costume of the Ancients, appeared from a London publisher in 1809 and found its way into newspaper advertisements in the United States. Many thanks to Jeremy Dibbell of the Libraries of Early America project (www.librarything.com/groups /PLEA) for his assistance in searching for these materials.

6. Studying under Benjamin West gave Peale access to West's library of illustrated volumes as well as his collection of Old Masters, a valuable resource of images in an era when publicly accessible art was rare. See Giles Waterford, ed., Palaces of Art: Art Galleries in Britain, 1790–1990 (London, 1991), 17–18.

7. "Statue of Washington," Repertory (Boston), June 3, 1821, [1]; this story was reprinted in numerous papers throughout the country. See also Margaret French Cresson, "First in Toga, First in Sandals," American Heritage, VIII, no. 2 (February 1957), www.american heritage.com/first-toga-first-sandals. Jefferson had not always advised sculptors to place American leaders in classical dress. In 1787, he approved of the decision by the sculptor

Jean-Antoine Houdon to create a sculpture of Washington in contemporary dress for the Virginia Capitol building. See John S. Hallam, "Houdon's Washington in Richmond: Some New Observations," *American Art Journal*, X (1978), 76; Maurie D. McInnis, "George Washington: Cincinnatus or Marcus Aurelius?" in Onuf and Cole, eds., *Thomas Jefferson*, 128–168.

8. Shalev, *Rome Reborn on Western Shores*, 2 ("of, through, and with"). See also Winterer, *Culture of Classicism*; Robert Middlekauff, *Ancients and Axioms: Secondary Education in Eighteenth-Century New England* (New Haven, Conn., 1963); and Carolyn Eastman, *A Nation of Speechifiers: Making an American Public after the Revolution* (Chicago, 2009), 8–9, 19–29 (hereafter cited as NOS). Estate inventories demonstrate that even some of the poorest families in the rural Northeast owned these anthologies. See William J. Gilmore, *Reading Becomes a Necessity of Life: Material and Cultural Life in Rural New England* (Knoxville, Tenn., 1989), 146, 152, 172, 198–199, 201.

9. Criticus, "Ogilvie," *Middlesex Gazette* (Middletown, Conn.), July 26, 1810, [3] ("genius of Tully" [Tully was another name for Marcus Tullius Cicero]); "Outline of Ogilvie," *Federal Republican & Commercial Gazette* (Baltimore), Aug. 21 1810, [2] ("animated zeal"; this article refers to Plutarch's description of Caius); Philopatris, "From the Box," *Montréal Gazette*, Oct. 29, 1810, [2] ("inimitable eloquence"; this letter appeared simultaneously in the *Québec Mercury*, Oct. 29, 1810, [3]); "Outline of Ogilvie," *Federal Republican & Commercial Gazette*, Aug. 21, 1810, [2] ("*ille regit*"; thanks to Jennifer Eastman for the graceful translation). Few notices described Ogilvie's toga, but one letter describes the suit he wore to a party in New York in 1809: "black velvet edged with red, and a cloak of the same lined with Scarlet velvet." James Kirke Paulding sardonically called it "the dress of Oratory." Clearly, Ogilvie had come far since his college days, when he wore hand-me-down clothes. See Paulding to Peter Kemble, Jr., Jan. 8, 1809, in Washington Irving, *Letters*, I, *1802–1823*, ed. Ralph M. Aderman, Herbert L. Kleinfield, and Jenifer S. Banks (Boston, 1978), 271 n. 9.

10. "The Orator—Ogilvie," *Albany Register*, Dec. 25, 1810, [2] ("modern Cicero"); "Mr. Ogilvie," *Maryland Gazette* (Annapolis), Apr. 21, 1814, [3] ("his whole attention"). In his work on Lord Byron, Tom Mole refers to this phenomenon of tying an aspect of a figure's visual appearance to their celebrity as an early form of branded identity. See Mole, *Byron's Romantic Celebrity: Industrial Culture and the Hermeneutic of Intimacy* (Houndmills, U.K., 2007), 16–22.

11. Quintilian, *Institutio Oratoria*, 12.1.1 ("good man"). For examples of the frequent reproduction of this line, see Caleb Bingham, *The Columbian Orator: Containing a Variety of Original and Selected Pieces . . .* (1797), 6th Troy ed. (Troy, N.Y., 1815), 10; for a paraphrase, see *The American Orator: Containing Rules and Directions . . .* (Lexington, Ky., 1807), 50. See also Richard, *Founders and the Classics*, chap. 3. George Washington, a famously reluctant orator, gave the text of his address directly to a Philadelphia newspaper in 1796. Thereafter, schoolbooks reprinted it so often that it became a familiar text for children's memorization and recitation. Those books didn't mention that it had never been delivered orally and in fact implied that it had by flanking the address with descriptions of Washington as an orator. See NOS, 51. The togate portrait of Samuel Myers contrasted with his experiences

as a young adult. As Alan Taylor recounts, as a college student Myers struggled to avoid "dissipated company," nearly dueled with his roommate, and after graduating shot and killed another rival. See Taylor, *Thomas Jefferson's Education* (New York, 2019), 91–92.

12. On the Warren speech, see Sandra M. Gustafson, *Eloquence Is Power: Oratory and Performance in Early America* (Williamsburg, Va., and Chapel Hill, N.C., 2000), 195–199; Shalev, *Rome Reborn*, 119–128; and Shalev, "Dr. Warren's Ciceronian Toga," *Commonplace: The Journal of Early American Life*, http://commonplace.online/article/dr-warrens-ciceronian-toga. On Kemble, see Shearer West, *The Image of the Actor: Verbal and Visual Representation in the Age of Garrick and Kemble* (New York, 1991), 68–89. See also Philippa M. Spoel, "The Science of Bodily Rhetoric in Gilbert Austin's *Chironomia*," *Rhetoric Society Quarterly*, XXVIII (1998), 5–27.

13. Quintilian, *Institutio Oratoria*, 11.6.13. Glenys Davies, "What Made the Roman Toga Virilis?" in Liza Cleland, Mary Harlow, and Lloyd Llewellyn-Jones, eds., *The Clothed Body in the Ancient World* (Oxford, 2005), 121–130, refers to the toga as "the ultimate in power-dressing" (127). See also Alice T. Christ, "The Masculine Ideal of 'the race that Wears the Toga,'" *Art Journal*, LVI (1997), 24–30.

14. Quintilian, *Institutio Oratoria*, 11.6.141 ("breadth at the chest"), 144 ("throw back the toga"), 146 ("air of vigour"); "Outline of Ogilvie," *Federal Republican & Commercial Gazette*, Aug. 21, 1810, [2] ("smites himself"). On Kemble, see Shearer West, "Thomas Lawrence's 'Half-History' Portraits and the Politics of Theater," *Art History*, XIV (1991), 235. See also Michael Squire, *The Art of the Body: Antiquity and Its Legacy* (New York, 2011), 56–65.

15. For examples of "manly eloquence," see "Saturday's Intelligencer," *Alexandria Daily Gazette, Commercial & Political*, Apr. 16, 1811, [3]; "Mr. Cheves' Speech," *Connecticut Herald* (New Haven), Dec. 29, 1812, [2]; and "Able Review," *Boston Gazette*, Apr. 4, 1814, [1]. For quotation, see "Mr. Ogilvie," *National Advocate* (New York), Nov. 25, 1813, [3]. See also "Extracts from the Columbia Paper, Mr. Ogilvie," *Star* (Raleigh, N.C.), Aug. 16, 1811, 132; and [Francis Walker Gilmer], *Sketches of American Orators . . .* (Baltimore, 1816), 36.

16. That association between women and unreason has persisted, as Susan J. Douglas demonstrates about the screaming, crying, and fainting female fans of Elvis Presley and the Beatles. See Douglas, *Where the Girls Are: Growing Up Female with the Mass Media* (New York, 1994), 113–116.

17. John Kingston, *The Reader's Cabinet: Consisting of More than a Hundred Papers, Original and Extract* (Baltimore, 1809), 131. On the subject of Scottish Enlightenment effects on female education, see Sarah Knott and Barbara Taylor, eds., *Women, Gender, and Enlightenment* (Houndmills, U.K., 2005), esp. essays by Silvia Sebastiani, Sylvana Tomaselli, and Jane Rendall; Carroll Smith-Rosenberg, "The Republican Gentleman: The Race to Rhetorical Stability in the New United States," in Stefan Dudink, Karen Hagemann, and John Tosh, eds., *Masculinities in Politics and War: Gendering Modern History* (Manchester, U.K., 2004), 64; and Rosemarie Zagarri, "The Rights of Man and Woman in Post-Revolutionary America," *William and Mary Quarterly*, 3d Ser., LV (1998), 203–230. Indeed, many manners guidebooks advised young men to learn the art of conversation and the expression of true feeling from

the brilliant women in their midst. Books like these even proposed that George Washington had learned his talents for engaging in society from matrons in his circles. Manners guidebooks often drew on Lord Chesterfield's *Letters to His Son* (1774) in heralding the value of intelligent women's beneficial influence on men (see *Lord Chesterfield's Maxims; or, A New Plan of Education, on the Principles of Virtue and Politeness ... Being the Substance of the Earl of Chesterfield's Letters, to His Son, Philip Stanhope, esq.* [London, 1774]). See, for example, Carolyn Eastman, "The Female Cicero: Young Women's Oratory and Gendered Public Participation in the Early American Republic," *Gender and History*, XIX (2007), 260–283.

18. James Ogilvie, "Supplementary Narrative," in Ogilvie, *Philosophical Essays ...* (Philadelphia, 1816), xviii–xix (hereafter cited as PE). Since the premature death of his wife in 1805, not a murmur had emerged connecting him to women, nor about his relationships with men, although some correspondents pointed to his propensity for close friendships with younger men. "Ogilvie is particular in his enquiries after you," Robert Means, Jr., wrote to a man fifteen years Ogilvie's junior. "I think he feels a stronger attachment for you than any other young man in New England." See Robert Means, Jr., to Charles Stewart Daveis, Aug. 14, 1809 (S0840), Manuscript Collections, Portsmouth Athenaeum, N.H.

19. Means to Daveis, Aug. 14, 1809. In an early Republic so redolent with classicism, it's no surprise to find daughters with classical names like Lucretia and Dolly (Dorothea).

20. Cassandra A. Good, *Founding Friendships: Friendships between Men and Women in the Early American Republic* (New York, 2015), chap. 4.

21. Ogilvie, "Supplementary Narrative," PE, v ("modern Cornelia"); Mary E. Fenno to Gulian Verplanck, Jan. 16, [likely 1811], Gulian Crommelin Verplanck Papers, box 4, folder 2, New-York Historical Society (Mrs. Hopkinson); Charles Brockden Brown to Mary Brown, summer 1809, in William Dunlap, *The Life of Charles Brockden Brown ...*, 2 vols. (Philadelphia, 1815), II, 87 (Mrs. Ellis); James Ogilvie to Henry Wheaton, March or April 1809, Henry Wheaton Letters and Papers, MS 995, Literary and Historical Manuscripts Collection, Pierpont Morgan Library (Mrs. Humphreys); Victoria Myers, David O'Shaughnessy, and Mark Philp, eds., *The Diary of William Godwin*, Jan. 2, 1819 (Mrs. Dixon), Apr. 4, 1819 (Mrs. Hamilton), http://godwindiary.bodleian.ox.ac.uk/index2.html. Ogilvie's cultivation of female attendees stretched back to his teaching days in Virginia; see Martha Walker Divers to Mary (House) Gilmer, June 18, 1807, Peachy Ridgway Gilmer Papers, Mss1 G4216 a, Virginia Museum of History and Culture, Richmond. I'm grateful to Cassie Good for helping parse the dynamics of these friendships.

22. "The Rostrum," *Aurora General Advertiser* (Philadelphia), Nov. 18, 1813, [3] ("radical importance"); "For the Times," *Times* (Charleston, S.C.), Mar. 6, 1811, [2] ("sentimental associate"). See also the extended discussion of Ogilvie's lecture on female education in "For the Times: Mr. Ogilvie," *Times*, Mar. 6, 1811, [3]; and, more broadly, Zagarri, "Rights of Man and Woman," *WMQ*, 3d Ser., LV (1998), 203–230.

23. "For the Times: Female Character," *Times*, Mar. 9, 1811, [2] ("no small degree"); subsequent parts appeared Mar. 16, 23, 30, 1811, all on [2]. Girls could not attend college

until Oberlin College opened its doors to women in 1833, but expensive academy educations for girls sometimes differed little from that for boys of the same rank. On this subject, see Nancy F. Cott, *The Bonds of Womanhood: "Woman's Sphere" in New England, 1780–1835* (New Haven, Conn., 1977), 101–125; NOS, chap. 2; Mary Kelley, *Learning to Stand and Speak: Women, Education, and Public Life in America's Republic* (Williamsburg, Va., and Chapel Hill, N.C., 2006), chaps. 2–3; Kelley, "Vindicating the Equality of Female Intellect: Women and Authority in the Early Republic," *Prospects*, XVII (1992), 1–27; Catherine E. Kelly, *Republic of Taste: Art, Politics, and Everyday Life in Early America* (Philadelphia, 2016); Linda K. Kerber, *Women of the Republic: Intellect and Ideology in Revolutionary America* (Williamsburg, Va., and Chapel Hill, N.C., 1980), chap. 7; Jan Lewis, "The Republican Wife: Virtue and Seduction in the Early Republic," *WMQ*, 3d Ser., XLIV (1987), 689–721; Margaret A. Nash, "The Historiography of Education for Girls and Women in the United States," in William J. Reese and John L. Rury, eds., *Rethinking the History of American Education* (New York, 2008), 143–160; Nash, "Rethinking Republican Motherhood: Benjamin Rush and the Young Ladies' Academy of Philadelphia," *Journal of the Early Republic*, XVII (1997), 171–191; and Nash, *Women's Education in the United States, 1780–1840* (New York, 2005), chaps. 2–4.

24. Ogilvie to the Commissioners of the Orphan House, Apr. 14, 1811, Commissioners Correspondence, box 58 ("unalloy'd pleasures"); and Minute Book of the Commissioners of the Charleston Orphan House (1810–1814), Apr. 25, 1811, Microfilm COH 1, both housed in the Records of the Commissioners of the Charleston Orphan House, City of Charleston Records, Charleston County Public Library, S.C. By 1816, his twenty-six benefit evenings had allowed him to donate an estimated $3,935 (equivalent to approximately $72,500 today). Each event raised between $50 and $500. This estimate is based on Ogilvie, "Supplementary Narrative," PE, xxxiv–xxxv, plus additional information from newspaper reports of his donations. Ogilvie had not originated the idea of benefit evenings, though his charitable giving was new. These were common practices among troupes of actors, although those benefits were usually held for individual members of the troupe to provide for them during the theater's summer hiatus. On theater benefits, see Andrew Davis, *America's Longest Run: A History of the Walnut Street Theatre* (University Park, Pa., 2010), 29; Sara Lampert, *Starring Women: Celebrity, Patriarchy, and American Theater, 1790–1850* (Urbana, Ill., forthcoming 2020), chap. 1. On female-run charities, see Carole Lasser, "A 'Pleasingly Oppressive' Burden: The Transformation of Domestic Service and Female Charity in Salem, 1800–1840," *Essex Institute Historical Collections*, CXVI (1980), 156–175; Susan Lynne Porter, "The Benevolent Asylum—Image and Reality: The Care and Training of Female Orphans in Boston, 1800–1840" (Ph.D. diss., Boston University, 1984); and Porter, "Gendered Expectations: Orphans and Apprenticeship in Antebellum New England," in Peter Benes, ed., *The Worlds of Children, 1620–1920*, Dublin Seminar for New England Folklife Annual Proceedings 2002 (Boston, 2004), 112–129.

25. "Oration on Beneficence," *Republican* (Savannah, Ga.), May 4, 1811, [3] ("550 dollars"); "It is with the greatest pleasure ...," *Columbian* (New York), June 12, 1811, [2] (Savannah benefit). Savannah had 5,215 residents, according to the 1810 census; Charleston had

nearly 25,000. See U.S. census tables listing urban places by decade, accessed Apr. 22, 2016, www.census.gov/population/www/documentation/twps0027/tab04.txt.

26. "From the Columbia S. C. State Gazette," *Enquirer* (Richmond, Va.), June 25, 1811, [2].

27. Ogilvie to Charles Stewart Daveis, May 6, [1811], Special MS Collection Daveis, Rare Book and Manuscript Library, Butler Library, Columbia University, New York ("in a few weeks"); Ogilvie to James Madison, May 18, 1810, James Madison Papers, microfilm reel 12, Library of Congress ("love of gold").

CHAPTER NINE

1. [Freeman Hunt], "Mr. Ogilvie," *American Anecdotes: Original and Select, by an American*, 2 vols. (Boston, 1830), I, 151–153.

2. Samuel R. Brown, *The Western Gazetteer; or Emigrant's Directory* . . . (Auburn, N.Y., 1817), 91 ("bespeaking the taste"); George Washington Rancke, *Lexington Kentucky: Its Early Annals and Recent Progress* . . . (Cincinnati, Ohio, 1872), 128 ("garden spot"); Thomas Ashe, *Travels in America, Performed in the Year 1806* . . . (London, 1809), II, 149–150 ("the canaille"); John Jordan, Jr., to Thomas Jefferson, Sept. 1, 1811, in James P. McClure and J. Jefferson Looney, eds., *The Papers of Thomas Jefferson*, Retirement Series (Charlottesville, Va., 2008–2020), IV, 113–114 ("No State," 113), https://rotunda.upress.virginia.edu/founders (hereafter cited as *PTJ, RS*). F. Cuming, *Sketches of a Tour to the Western Country* . . . (Pittsburgh, 1810), 184–188, describes the city's achievements and institutions. For the relative size and growth of these cities, see U.S. census tables listing urban places by decade for 1810 and 1820, accessed Apr. 22, 2016, www.census.gov/population/www/documentation/twps0027/tab04.txt and www.census.gov/population/www/documentation/twps0027/tab05.txt. See also Stephen Aron, *How the West Was Lost: The Transformation of Kentucky from Daniel Boone to Henry Clay* (Baltimore, 1996); James C. Klotters and Craig Thompson Friend, *A New History of Kentucky* (Lexington, Ky., 2018); Friend, *Along the Maysville Road: The Early American Republic in the Trans-Appalachian West* (Knoxville, Tenn., 2005); Arthur K. Moore, *The Frontier Mind: A Cultural Analysis of the Kentucky Frontiersman* (Lexington, Ky., 1957), 11–24; and Honor Sachs, *Home Rule: Households, Manhood, and National Expansion on the Eighteenth-Century Kentucky Frontier* (New Haven, Conn., 2015).

3. James Ogilvie to Charles Stewart Daveis, May 6, [1811], Special MS Collection Daveis, Rare Book and Manuscript Library, Butler Library, Columbia University, N.Y. ("painful and protracted"); "Extracts," *Kentucky Gazette* (Lexington), July 16, 1811, [2] ("celebrated Orator"); Henry Clay to Ogilvie, July 9, 1811, in James F. Hopkins and Mary W. M. Hargreaves, eds., *The Papers of Henry Clay: The Rising Statesman* (Lexington, Ky., 1959), I, 563–565 ("eminently displayed"); Anthony Butler to Andrew Jackson, Sept. 28, Oct. 12, 1811, in Daniel Feller, ed., *The Papers of Andrew Jackson Digital Edition* (Charlottesville, Va., 2015–2020), II, 265–266 ("to a stranger," 265), 267–268. For papers that reprinted flattering accounts from elsewhere, see "Elocution," *Palladium* (Frankfort, Ky.), July 13, 1811, [2], which quotes at length from a much-reprinted story that originated in the *South-Carolina State Gazette*,

and *Columbian Advertiser.* See, for example, "From the Columbia S.C. State Gazette," *Enquirer* (Richmond, Va.), June 25, 1811, [2]; "James Ogilvie," *Kentucky Gazette,* July 16, 1811, [1], which quotes from the *Enquirer.*

4. "Maccoun, Tilford, & Co. have just received . . . ," *Kentucky Gazette,* Aug. 6, 1811, [4] ("an introduction"); "The Quotist," *Palladium,* Apr. 22, 1812, [2–3] ("Essay"). "There never was a time in American history when flamboyant oratory had a greater effect upon public opinion in the West than in the first two decades of the nineteenth century"; see Thomas D. Clark, *Frontier America: The Story of the Westward Movement,* 2d ed. (New York, 1969), 263. For debating societies, etc., see Alfred Tischendorf and E. Taylor Parks, eds., *The Diary and Journal of Richard Clough Anderson, Jr., 1814–1826* (Durham, N.C., 1964), 7–9; Robert Pettus Hay, "A Jubilee for Freemen: The Fourth of July in Frontier Kentucky, 1788–1816," *Register of the Kentucky Historical Society,* LXIV, no. 3 (July 1966), 169–195. Clay had already served briefly as an interim replacement in the U.S. Senate in 1806.

5. William Little Brown diary (1805–1814), II, November 1810 ("unnatural and unmanly"), Apr. 9, 1812 ("Study law"), June 11, 1812 ("poetic images"), MSS Col. 417, Manuscripts and Archives Division, New York Public Library. Brown went on to have a long career as a lawyer, judge, and legislator in Tennessee. See Albert V. Goodpasture, "William Little Brown," *American Historical Magazine and Tennessee Historical Society Quarterly,* VII (1902), 97–111.

6. "Mr. Ogilvie's Orations," *Kentucky Gazette,* July 9, 1811, [3] ("peculiarly gratifying"); James Ogilvie, "Supplementary Narrative," in Ogilvie, *Philosophical Essays . . .* (Philadelphia, 1816), xxiii ("deep and dead") (hereafter cited as PE).

7. Ogilvie to Jefferson, Nov. 24, [1811], PTJ, RS, IV, 276–277 ("temporary seclusion," 276); "A Letter from 'Seer Rolf,'" *Park City Daily News* (Bowling Green, Ky.), Aug. 12, 1885 ("cold spring water"). See transcription from the Kentucky Historical Society (KHS), research files for the state historical marker erected near Chameleon Springs and Chalybeate Springs, 2016. Ogilvie rented the cabin from Benjamin Temple, a Virginia transplant who had purchased two hundred acres of land in 1807 (Ogilvie, "Supplementary Narrative," PE, xlix–li).

8. Joseph F. Kett, *The Formation of the American Medical Profession: The Role of Institutions, 1780–1860* (New Haven, Conn., 1968); Kathryn Shively Meier, *Nature's Civil War: Common Soldiers and the Environment in 1862 Virginia* (Chapel Hill, N.C., 2013); Charles E. Rosenberg, "The Therapeutic Revolution: Medicine, Meaning, and Social Change in Nineteenth-Century America," in Rosenberg and Morris J. Vogel, eds., *The Therapeutic Revolution: Essays in the Social History of American Medicine* (Philadelphia, 1979), 3–26; and John Harley Warner, *The Therapeutic Perspective: Medical Practice, Knowledge, and Identity in America, 1820–1885* (Cambridge, Mass., 1986), 85–86.

9. Dr. Charles Everette to Wilson C. Nicholas, Aug. 25, 1808, Edgehill-Randolph / Wilson Cary Nicholas Papers, #5533, Albert and Shirley Small Special Collections Library, University of Virginia Library, Charlottesville (hereafter cited as UVA), quoted in

Charlene M. Boyer Lewis, *Ladies and Gentlemen on Display: Planter Society at the Virginia Springs, 1790–1860* (Charlottesville, Va., 2001), 70.

10. Letter from Dr. J. M. Briggs, June 21, 1844, transcription in KHS research files for the state historical marker erected near Chameleon Springs and Chalybeate Springs, 2016. Chalybeate springs are natural mineral springs that contain iron salts. Not until the 1890s would an entrepreneur build a summer resort hotel at Chameleon Springs promising "Healthfulness Unsurpassed—Scenery Unequaled" and offering "Music and amusements first class." See "Delightful Summer Resort," *Park City Daily News*, Aug. 2, 1897, transcription ibid.

11. Ogilvie letter transcribed in "Collectanea," *Wilmingtonian, and Delaware Advertiser* (Wilmington), Feb. 2, 1826, [1].

12. For accounts of people seeking to wean themselves off laudanum, see Benjamin Rush to Bushrod Washington, May 2, 1812, Bushrod Washington Papers, Fred W. Smith National Library for the Study of George Washington, http://catalog.mountvernon.org /digital/collection/p16829coll22/id/168; Thomas De Quincey, *Confessions of an English Opium-Eater* (1821; rpt. University Park, Pa., 2004), 94–95. On the cost of laudanum during the embargo, see [John Rodman], *Fragment of a Journal of a Sentimental Philosopher* ... (New York, 1809), 12; "Robert Harris, Jr., Druggist," *Kentucky Gazette*, Feb. 2, 1813, [1].

13. "A Card," *Palladium*, May 27, 1812, [3].

14. Justice, "Mr. Ogilvie," *Reporter* (Lexington, Ky.), June 27, 1812, [3] ("genuine eloquence"); Ogilvie to Francis Walker Gilmer, June 20, [1813], Correspondence of Francis Walker Gilmer, MSS 38–588, box 1, folder 34, UVA (lost wallet).

15. "At a meeting ... ," *Kentucky Gazette*, Aug. 13, 1811, [2] ("British scheme"). Kentuckians' Indian-hating stretched back decades. See Aron, *How the West Was Lost*; and Sachs, *Home Rule*, 101–104.

16. On similar anti-Indian narratives, see Jill Lepore, *The Name of War: King Philip's War and the Origins of American Identity* (New York, 1998); Peter Silver, *Our Savage Neighbors: How Indian War Transformed Early America* (New York, 2008); and Richard Slotkin, *Regeneration through Violence: The Mythology of the American Frontier, 1600–1860* (Middletown, Conn., 1973).

17. Donald R. Hickey, *The War of 1812: A Forgotten Conflict*, bicentennial ed. (Urbana, Ill., 2012), chap. 3 (Baltimore riots); Alan Taylor, *The Civil War of 1812: American Citizens, British Subjects, Irish Rebels, and Indian Allies* (New York, 2010), (conspiracy theories). See also Paul A. Gilje, *Free Trade and Sailor's Rights in the War of 1812* (New York, 2013); Nicole Eustace, *1812: War and the Passions of Patriotism* (Philadelphia, 2012); Matthew Rainbow Hale, "For the Love of Glory: Napoleonic Imperatives in the Early American Republic," in Nicole Eustace and Fredrika J. Teute, eds., *Warring for America: Cultural Contests in the Era of 1812* (Williamsburg, Va., and Chapel Hill, N.C., 2017), 205–249; John Grenier, *The First Way of War: American War Making on the Frontier, 1607–1814* (Cambridge, 2005); David Waldstreicher, *In the Midst of Perpetual Fetes: The Making of American Nationalism, 1776–1820* (Williamsburg, Va., and Chapel Hill, N.C., 1997); and other essays in *Warring for America*, including those by James M.

Greene, Jonathan Todd Hancock, Tim Lanzendörfer, and Nathaniel Millett. Fearmongering about Native Americans had also been a common theme in some regions during the American Revolution, when shared hatred of Indians and African Americans had cultivated a common cause. See Robert G. Parkinson, *The Common Cause: Creating Race and Nation in the American Revolution* (Williamsburg, Va., and Chapel Hill, N.C., 2016).

18. "At a meeting . . . ," *Kentucky Gazette*, Aug. 13, 1811, [2] ("British scheme"). See Gregory Evans Dowd, *A Spirited Resistance: The North American Indian Struggle for Unity, 1745–1815* (Baltimore, 1992); Dowd, "Thinking and Believing: Nativism and Unity in the Ages of Pontiac and Tecumseh," *American Indian Quarterly*, XVI (1992), 309–335; Gilje, *Free Trade*, chap. 11; Jonathan Todd Hancock, "Widening the Scope on the Indians' Old Northwest," in Eustace and Teute, eds., *Warring for America*, 359–385; Hickey, *War of 1812*, 22–25; Adam Jortner, *The Gods of Prophetstown: The Battle of Tippecanoe and the Holy War for the American Frontier* (Oxford, 2012); Taylor, *Civil War of 1812*; Karim M. Tiro, "The View from Piqua Agency: The War of 1812, the White River Delawares, and the Origins of Indian Removal," *Journal of the Early Republic*, XXXV (2015), 25–54; and Richard White, *The Middle Ground: Indians, Empires, and Republics in the Great Lakes Region, 1650–1815* (Cambridge, 1991), 495–517.

19. *Reporter*, Mar. 14, 1812, quoted in Hickey, *War of 1812*, 25 ("KNIFE and TOMA-HAWK"); Charles Scott, *Reporter*, Dec. 7, 1811, quoted in James Wallace Hammack, Jr., "Kentucky and Anglo-American Relations, 1803–1815" (Ph.D. diss., University of Kentucky, Lexington, 1974), 201–202 ("British intrigue"). See also Grenier, *First Way of War*, 10–12, 204–220; and Parkinson, *Common Cause*.

20. "News of the Declaration of War," *Kentucky Gazette*, June 30, 1812, [3] (firing cannons); Hay, "A Jubilee for Freemen," *Register of the Kentucky Historical Society*, LXIV, no. 3 (July 1966), 190–191 (toasts); Clay to [James Monroe], July 29, 1812, in Hopkins and Hargreaves, eds., *Papers of Henry Clay*, I, 697 ("sensibility"). According to the *Gazette* article cited here, the people of Winchester, Richmond, and Nicholasville also spent the night firing off their guns. For another report of "a second decree of Independence," see M. D. Hardin to Isaac Shelby, June 26, 1812, Shelby Family Papers, Library of Congress, cited in Hammack, "Kentucky and Anglo-American Relations," 5–6. Nicole Eustace argues that these hyperbolic accounts performed "a kind of emotional alchemy" when they "recast suffering as elevation and calamity as mental enlargement." It was via such emotional appeals that many in the United States "came to view the war as a positive good" (Eustace, *1812*, xiii [quotations], 29–31).

21. "Toasts, &c.," *Kentucky Gazette* Aug. 4, 1812, [3] (Ogilvie toast); *Reporter*, July 1, 1812, [2] (Declaration), July 18, 1812, [2] (lives of Revolutionary leaders). Godwin's original language, from Book IV, Chapter 1 ("Of Resistance"), was slightly different: "ripe for its reception, and competent to its assertion." See William Godwin, *Enquiry concerning Political Justice, and Its Influence on Morals and Happiness*, 3d ed., corr., 2 vols. (London, 1798), I, 256.

22. Ogilvie to Francis Walker Gilmer, Feb. 1, 1813, in Richard Beale Davis, *Francis Walker Gilmer: Life and Learning in Jefferson's Virginia* (Richmond, Va., 1939), 374–375 ("roused by feelings"), 375 ("marching in arms"), 376 ("vicinity of Danville") (hereafter cited as FWG);

Ogilvie, "Supplementary Narrative," PE, xlii ("howling wilderness"). For his unit, see Minnie S. Wilder, comp., *Kentucky Soldiers of the War of 1812*, introduction by G. Glenn Clift (Baltimore, 1969), 243. Ogilvie reported that he ultimately served for three months. See also Parkinson, *Common Cause*; Ed Gilbert, *Frontier Militiaman in the War of 1812: Southwestern Frontier* (Oxford, 2008).

23. Jonathan Ball Nichols to William S. Nichols, Oct. 27, 1812, Jonathan Ball Nichols Papers, M-577, Special Collections, University of Kentucky (UKY) ("Linsey Coats"); *Boston Patriot*, reprinted in the *Reporter*, Dec. 4, 1813, cited in Hammack, "Kentucky and Anglo-American Relations," 247–248 ("considered glorious"); Thomas Smith, "To my Friends and Patrons," *Kentucky Gazette*, Aug. 18, 1812, [3] ("all my companions"). See a similar report of "men of all ages fathers and Sons step'd into the ranks together" in Nichols to Nichols, Oct. 27, 1812, Ball Nichols Papers. See also Hammack, *Kentucky and the Second American Revolution: The War of 1812* (Lexington, Ky., 1976), 19–20.

24. Major William Trigg to Robert Alexander, Oct. 4, 1812, Alexander Family Papers, MSS 93, box 5, folder 5, KHS (hereafter cited as AFP) ("employed in Organizing"); Hammack, "Kentucky and Anglo-American Relations," 254, 247.

25. James Winchester logbook, Aug. 28, 1812, 87m14, UKY ("Court Martial"); G. Glenn Clift, ed., "War of 1812 Diary of William B. Northcutt," *Register of the Kentucky Historical Society*, LVI, no. 2 (April 1958), 167 ("Soldier's life").

26. Trigg to Alexander, Sept. 28, 1812, AFP ("oritori[c]al robe"); Ogilvie to Gilmer, Feb. 1, 1813, FWG, 376 ("profoundly conscious"). General Hopkins would soon after call him "the famous Ogilvie." See Samuel Hopkins to the Secretary of State [James Monroe], Aug. 27, 1815, in Clarence Edwin Carter, comp. and ed., *The Territorial Papers of the United States*, XVII, *The Territory of Illinois, 1814–1818, Continued* (Washington, D.C., 1950), 209. See also A. C. Quisenberry, "Kentucky Troops in the War of 1812," *Register of the Kentucky State Historical Society*, X, no. 30 (September 1912), 49–66.

27. Ogilvie to Gilmer, Feb. 1, 1813, FWG, 377; William Shakespeare, *Henry V*, 4.3.56–58.

28. Isaac Shelby to William Henry Harrison, Sept. 26, 1812, Letter Book "A" of the official correspondence of Governor Shelby, transcript of the original, Isaac Shelby Papers, 1765–1826, M-590, UKY.

29. Shelby to Harrison, Nov. 1, 1812, Letter Book "A," Isaac Shelby Papers, 1765–1826, M-590, UKY ("bad news"); Ogilvie to Gilmer, Feb. 1, 1813, FWG, 376 ("disappointed"); Hammack, "Kentucky and Anglo-American Relations," 282. Hammack estimates that, although Kentuckians represented only 4.6 percent of the troops who served in the War of 1812, they represented 64 percent of all Americans killed during the conflict (Hammack, *Kentucky and the Second American Revolution*, 112).

30. Taylor, *Civil War of 1812*, 6–10; Hammack, *Kentucky and the Second American Revolution*, 23–24; Hickey, *War of 1812*; and Waldstreicher, *In the Midst of Perpetual Fetes*.

31. Ogilvie to Gilmer, Feb. 1, 1813, FWG, 376.

32. Ogilvie to Gilmer, July 12, 1813, FWG, 379–380 ("Constituted as I am"); Trigg to Alexander, Sept. 28, 1812, AFP ("kill an Indian").

33. Ogilvie to Gilmer, Feb. 4, 1814, FWG, 382.

34. Ogilvie to Gilmer, July 12, 1813, FWG, 379 ("magnitude of the design"); [James Ogilvie], "Eloctuion [sic]: Instruction in Rhetoric, Philosophical Criticism, and Elocution," Port Folio, 3d Ser., II, no. 3 (September 1813), 288. He was not the only writer in the nineteenth century to quote the line "a log house beyond the mountains," which came from Fisher Ames's 1796 speech in Congress opposing the Jay Treaty. See Works of Fisher Ames; Compiled by a Number of His Friends ... (Boston, 1809), 86.

CHAPTER TEN

1. "Mr. Huntington," Alexandria Gazette (Va.), June 30, 1814, [3], reprinted from Charleston's City Gazette ("Moral Lectures"); "A Mr. Flagg ...," New-England Palladium (Boston), Jan. 24, 1815, [2] ("Ogilvie school"); "Mr. Walter," Alexandria Herald, Jan. 10, 1823, [3], and "The Rostrum," Providence Patriot (R.I.), Oct. 25, 1823, [3] ("after the manner"); "Mr. Huntingdon [sic]," Palladium (Frankfort, Ky.), June 3, 1812, [3] (cost of ticket). These men charged fifty cents, while Ogilvie's tickets cost a dollar. See also "Mr. Hazelton," Saratoga Sentinel (Saratoga Springs, N.Y.), July 25, 1821, [3].

2. Edward G. Parker, The Golden Age of American Oratory (Boston, 1857).

3. Thomas Jefferson to Martha Jefferson Randolph, June 21, 1808, Founders Online, National Archives, https://founders.archives.gov.

4. Catherine Mitchill to [Margaret Miller], Apr. 3, 1806, Dec. 19, 1808, quoted in Jan Lewis, "Politics and the Ambivalence of the Private Sphere: Women in Early Washington, D.C.," in Donald R. Kennon, ed., A Republic for the Ages: The United States Capitol and the Political Culture of the Early Republic (Charlottesville, Va., 1999), 134–135. See also Catherine Allgor, Parlor Politics: In Which the Ladies of Washington Help to Build a City and a Government (Charlottesville, Va., 2000), chap. 2.

5. James Sterling Young, The Washington Community, 1800–1828 (New York, 1966), 24, 44, 74–75. I have also drawn from James M. Banner, Jr., "The Capital and the State: Washington, D.C., and the Nature of American Government," in Kennon, ed., Republic for the Ages, 64–86; Kenneth R. Bowling, Creating the Federal City, 1774–1800: Potomac Fever (Washington, D.C., 1988); Adam Costanzo, George Washington's Washington: Visions for the National Capitol in the Early American Republic (Athens, Ga., 2018); Constance McLaughlin Green, Washington, I, Village and Capital, 1800–1878 (Princeton, N.J., 1962); Howard Gillette, Jr., ed., Southern City, National Ambition: The Growth of Early Washington, D.C., 1800–1860 (Washington, D.C., 1995); and Frank Freidel and William Pencak, eds., The White House: The First Two Hundred Years (Boston, 1994).

6. [Charles Jared Ingersoll], Inchiquin, the Jesuit's Letters, during a Late Residence in the United States of America ... (New York, 1810), 31–32 ("scattered hamlets"); Henry Adams, The Education of Henry Adams, ed. Ernest Samuels (1918; rpt. Boston, 1974), 44 ("deserted Syrian city"); Charles William Janson, The Stranger in America: Containing Observations Made During a Long Residence in That Country ... (London, 1807), 202 ("grotesque"). Ingersoll, a Philadelphian, wrote his book in the persona of an Irish Jesuit.

7. Margaret Bayard Smith to [Jane Bayard] Kirkpatrick, Mar. 13, 1814, in Gaillard Hunt, ed., *The First Forty Years of Washington Society: Portrayed in the Family Letters of Mrs. Samuel Harrison Smith (Margaret Bayard)* (New York, 1906), 96 (hereafter cited as MBS), quoted in Lewis, "Politics and the Ambivalence of the Private Sphere," in Kennon, ed., *Republic for the Ages*, 141.

8. Margaret Bayard Smith, *A Winter in Washington; or, Memoirs of the Seymour Family* (New York, 1824) I, 147–148 ("He rose"); Smith to Kirkpatrick, Jan. 26, 1830, MBS, 310 ("present arena").

9. "Mr. Ogilvie," *National Advocate* (New York), Nov. 25, 1813, [3].

10. "We should do injustice to Mr. Ogilvie . . . ," *United States' Gazette* (Philadelphia), Jan. 28, 1814, [3] ("unbreathing attention"); Crito, "Mr. Ogilvie's Orations," *Baltimore Patriot*, Feb. 23, 1814, [2] ("riveted"); "A Card," *Daily National Intelligencer* (Washington, D.C.), Mar. 9, 1814, [3] ("gentlemen of the Bar").

11. Jefferson to Benjamin Henry Latrobe, Sept. 8, 1805, *Founders Online* ("handsomest room"); Janson, *Stranger in America*, 204 ("truly elegant"). See also C. M. Harris, "Jefferson, the Concept of the Modern Capitol, and Republican Nation-Building," in Kenneth R. Bowling and Donald R. Kennon, eds., *Establishing Congress: The Removal to Washington, D.C., and the Election of 1800* (Athens, Ohio, 2005), 72–101; and Mark R. Wenger, "Thomas Jefferson and the Virginia State Capitol," *Virginia Magazine of History and Biography*, CI (1993), 77–102. It might have been a beautiful room, but the glass skylights leaked badly on rainy days and the hot-air furnaces installed underneath the room overheated it to a noxious degree in the winter (Young, *Washington Community*, 45). See also Peter S. Onuf, "Ancients, Moderns, and the Progress of Mankind: Thomas Jefferson's Classical World," in Onuf and Nicholas Cole, eds., *Thomas Jefferson, the Classical World, and Early America* (Charlottesville, Va., 2011), 35–55.

12. "The Rostrum," *Daily National Intelligencer*, Mar. 15, 1814, [3].

13. Ibid. ("free people"); "Mr. Ogi[l]vie," *Maryland Gazette* (Annapolis), Apr. 21, 1814, [3] ("public utility").

14. Smith to Kirkpatrick, Mar. 13, 1814, MBS, 95–98. See also Allgor, *Parlor Politics*, chap. 3; and Lewis, "Politics and the Ambivalence of the Private Sphere," in Kennon, ed., *Republic for the Ages*, 122–151. On the wider phenomenon of a celebrity career crowning, see Joseph Roach, *It* (Ann Arbor, Mich., 2007); and Sharon Marcus, *The Drama of Celebrity* (Princeton, N.J., 2019).

15. Smith to Kirkpatrick, Mar. 13, 1814, MBS, 98 ("more rational"); "Mr. Ogilvie," *Charleston Courier*, Feb. 24, 1815, 1 ("new era"); "Mr. Huntington," *Alexandria Gazette*, June 30, 1814, [3] ("eloquent Ogilvie").

16. Paul A. Rahe, "Cicero and the Classical Republican Legacy in America," in Onuf and Cole, eds., *Thomas Jefferson*, 248–264; Eran Shalev, *Rome Reborn on Western Shores: Historical Imagination and the Creation of the American Republic* (Charlottesville, Va., 2009); Caroline Winterer, *The Culture of Classicism: Ancient Greece and Rome in American Intellectual Life, 1780–1910* (Baltimore, 2002).

17. "Elocution," *Poulson's American Daily Advertiser* (Philadelphia), Sept. 24, 1813, [1] (Abercrombie); "Mr. Dennison's," ibid., Nov. 1, 1813, [3] ("elegant Reading"); "Recitation," *Aurora General Advertiser* (Philadelphia), Dec. 31, 1813, [3] (Dennison's recitations); Constitution and By-Laws of the Philadelphia Literary Association, Am. 3117, 1813, Historical Society of Pennsylvania (HSP), Philadelphia; Henry Troth diary, 40, Mar. 30, Am. 172, 1814, HSP ("useful knowledge"); "At a meeting of the Members of the New York Forum . . . ," *New-York Evening Post*, Nov. 21, 1816, [3] ("free discussion"); "The Forum," *Daily National Intelligencer*, Nov. 27, 1816, [3] ("ancient Forum"). After this group managed to persuade Ogilvie himself to attend their first debate and deliver an oration, reports of the high quality of their meetings circulated as far away as Kentucky. Meanwhile, Ogilvie's lectures on the importance of creating Halls of Eloquence prompted an active discussion in Charleston, where one newspaper commentator marveled at what such a hall might allow. "It should be a sphere for the exhibition of every species of talents — for the Poet, the Painter, the Orator, the Moralist," this writer suggested. "Our native city will set the example of honourable ambition," he concluded. See "Public Halls," *Southern Patriot, and Commercial Advertiser* (Charleston), Dec. 6, 1815, [2]. In *A Nation of Speechifiers: Making an American Public after the Revolution* (Chicago, 2009), 40–41 (hereafter cited as NOS), I make a related point: that, during the 1810s, American schoolbooks began to include significant numbers of speeches by Americans alongside the previously overwhelming offerings of classical and British oratory. See also the 1814 correspondence of Henry Wheaton, Henry Wheaton Letters and Papers, MA 995, at the Pierpont Morgan Library, New York, which discusses his attempts at public speaking. More broadly, this phenomenon is discussed in Gregory Clark and S. Michael Halloran, eds., *Oratorical Culture in Nineteenth-Century America: Transformations in the Theory and Practice of Rhetoric* (Carbondale, Ill., 1993), esp. essays by Gregory Clark, Nan Johnson, and Ronald E. Reid; and James Perrin Warren, *Culture of Eloquence: Oratory and Reform in Antebellum America* (University Park, Pa., 1999), chap. 1.

18. NOS, chap. 1; Jay Fliegelman, *Declaring Independence: Jefferson, Natural Language, and the Culture of Performance* (Stanford, Calif., 1993); Frederick W. Haberman, "English Sources of American Elocution," in Karl R. Wallace, ed., *History of Speech Education in America: Background Studies* (New York, 1954), 105–126; Winifred Bryan Homer and Kerri Morris Barton, "The Eighteenth Century," in Homer, ed., *The Present State of Scholarship in Historical and Contemporary Rhetoric* (Columbia, Mo., 1990), 126; and Wilbur Samuel Howell, *Eighteenth-Century British Logic and Rhetoric* (Princeton, N.J., 1971).

19. [William Wirt], *The Letters of the British Spy*, 4th ed. (Baltimore, 1811), 45 ("scarcity"), 50 ("Timotheus"), 52 ("seventh heaven"); Marie Tyler-McGraw, *At the Falls: Richmond, Virginia, and Its People* (Chapel Hill, N.C., 1994), 81 ("whip syllabub"). Wirt's newspaper essays were first collected in a volume in Richmond in 1803 and subsequently appeared in at least fifteen more printings throughout the United States and London by 1812. On "The Rainbow," see Isaac A. Coles to Joseph C. Cabell, Nov. 1, 1804, Joseph Carrington Cabell Papers, 1790–1890, Acc. No. 38-111c, box 3, folder 12, Albert and Shirley Small Special Collections Library, University of Virginia, Charlottesville (hereafter cited as UVA); Jay B.

Hubbell, "William Wirt and the Familiar Essay in Virginia," *William and Mary Quarterly*, 2d Ser., XXIII (1943), 136–152; and Richard Beale Davis, *Intellectual Life in Jefferson's Virginia, 1790–1830* (Chapel Hill, N.C., 1964), 370–386. On Wirt and the Burr trial, see James E. Lewis, Jr., *The Burr Conspiracy: Uncovering the Story of an Early American Crisis* (Princeton, N.J., 2017), chap. 4. For more on Wirt, see Andrew Burstein, "The Political Character of Sympathy," *Journal of the Early Republic*, XXI (2001), 601–632; Judy Jones Hample, "William Wirt: A Study of Rhetorical Stance" (Ph.D. diss., Ohio State University, 1974); Hample, "William Wirt's Familiar Essays: Criticism of Virginian Oratory," *Southern Speech Communication Journal*, XLIV (1978), 25–41; Jon Kukla, "Reflections: Orator of Nature: William Wirt's *Sketches of the Life and Character of Patrick Henry*," *Reviews in American History*, XLIV (2016), 517–523; and Kukla, *Patrick Henry: Champion of Liberty* (New York, 2017).

20. [Wirt], *The Letters of the British Spy*, 60 ("powerful engine"); William Wirt to Jefferson, Jan. 18, 1810, in James P. McClure and J. Jefferson Looney, eds., *The Papers of Thomas Jefferson Digital Edition*, Retirement Series (Charlottesville, Va., 2008–2020), II, 155–156 ("republic must soon devolve," 156), https://rotunda.upress.virginia.edu/founders (hereafter cited as PTJ, RS). Because the Henry speech is a reconstruction, scholars tend to attribute the text to Wirt and St. George Tucker, an eyewitness to the speech who sent Wirt extensive recollections in approximately 1805, a document that has not survived. See Judy Hample, "The Textual and Cultural Authenticity of Patrick Henry's 'Liberty or Death' Speech," *Quarterly Journal of Speech*, LXIII (1977), 298–310; Kukla, *Patrick Henry*, chap. 14; David A. McCants, "The Authenticity of William Wirt's Version of Patrick Henry's 'Liberty or Death' Speech," *VMHB*, LXXXVII (1979), 395; Stephen Taylor Olsen, "A Study in Disputed Authorship: The 'Liberty or Death' Speech" (Ph.D. diss., Penn State University, 1976).

21. Wirt to Francis Walker Gilmer, Oct. 9, 1806, Correspondence of Francis Walker Gilmer, MSS 38–588, box 1, folder 4, UVA ("admiring crowd"). Gilmer would later recycle some of this advice for his younger brothers George and Thomas Walker Gilmer. See letters dated May 4, 1816, and Mar. 24, 1821, in Francis Walker Gilmer Letters, Acc. No. 18783, Library of Virginia, Richmond. See also Richard Beale Davis, *Francis Walker Gilmer: Life and Learning in Jefferson's Virginia* (Richmond, Va., 1939) (hereafter cited as FWG). Gilmer was the younger brother of Wirt's first wife, Mildred Gilmer, who died in 1799.

22. [Francis Walker Gilmer], *Sketches of American Orators* (Baltimore, 1816), 13–14. Gilmer apparently intended this to be the first of a series of sketches. After his premature death in 1826 at the age of thirty-five, his friends published a revised and expanded edition. The 1816 edition includes sketches of a mix of Federalists and Republicans, but with a heavy emphasis on Virginia orators: four of the six sketches focus on Virginians. In writing it, Gilmer borrowed from several contemporary British anthologies that celebrated British eloquence, including Thomas Browne, *The British Cicero* . . . (London, 1808); and William Hazlitt, *The Eloquence of the British Senate* . . . (London, 1810), both of which codified Britain's claims to historic oratorical excellence. One American publication had sought to imitate this model: S.C. Carpenter's *Select American Speeches, Forensic and Parliamentary* (Philadelphia, 1815). But, whereas those authors were able to compile the texts of full speeches, Gilmer

did not have such documents. See also Davis, *Intellectual Life in Jefferson's Virginia*, 371–374; and *NOS*, 43–48.

23. Gilmer, *Sketches*, 7–8, 36. See also *FWG*, 289–307.

24. Gilmer, *Sketches*, 5 ("any one who can"); Hugh Legaré to Gilmer, Oct. 10, 1816, MSS 38–588, box 2, folder 5, UVA ("anonymous"). Gilmer's authorship became an open secret when he sent complimentary copies to the men he described in the book. See, for example, John Randolph of Roanoke to Gilmer, Mar. 15, 1817, Acc. No. 3553-b, UVA.

25. Ogilvie to Gilmer, June 20, [1812], MSS 38–588, box 1, folder 34 ("intellectual accomplishments"), Ogilvie to Gilmer, May 23, [1811], MSS 38–588, box 1, folder 33 ("betrayed"), Ogilvie to Gilmer, Feb. 4, [1814], MSS 38–588, box 1, folder 45 (number of attendees, "affectionate friend"), all in Correspondence of Francis Walker Gilmer, UVA. Ogilvie was not the only contemporary who felt so strongly about Gilmer's intellectual gifts. See John Gilmer Speed, *The Gilmers in America* (New York, 1897), 52–71, for transcriptions of similar compliments from Thomas Jefferson and others; *FWG*, 255–264.

26. Parker, *Golden Age of American Oratory*, 2. These passages draw on *NOS*, 39–52.

27. Latrobe to Jefferson, July 12, 1815, *PTJ*, RS, VIII, 591–596 ("so intense," 594); Janson, *Stranger in America*, 202–204 ("elegant" and "grotesque"). On the burning of the city and its slow rebuilding, see Donald R. Hickey, *The War of 1812: A Forgotten Conflict*, bicentennial ed. (Urbana, Ill., 2012), 205–210.

28. "The Peace," *Daily National Intelligencer*, Feb. 16, 1815, [2] ("powerful nations"); James Madison, "The following most interesting Message . . . ," ibid., Feb. 21, 1815, [2] ("most brilliant"). On American boosterism, see Hickey, *War of 1812*; Alan Taylor, *The Civil War of 1812: American Citizens, British Subjects, Irish Rebels, and Indian Allies* (New York, 2010).

CHAPTER ELEVEN

1. James Ogilvie, "Supplementary Narrative," in Ogilvie, *Philosophical Essays . . .* (Philadelphia, 1816), lv (hereafter cited as PE).

2. [James Ogilvie], "Eloctuion [*sic*]: Instruction in Rhetoric, Philosophical Criticism, and Elocution," *Port Folio*, 3d Ser., II, no. 3 (September 1813), 285–290.

3. Ogilvie, "Supplementary Narrative," PE, lvii ("melancholy"), lxii ("improvement"), "Appendix," civ ("exercises in elocution"), cix ("public mind"), cx (classes growing in size), cxi ("crouded and brilliant"). Jonathan Maxcy's public letter of July 11, 1815, together with supporting accounts from the rest of the faculty, appeared in dozens of newspapers and magazines throughout the United States, including *American Beacon & Commercial Diary* (Norfolk, Va.), Aug. 11, 1815; *Repertory* (Boston), Aug. 15, 1815; and *Analectic Magazine*, VI (September 1815), 261–262. Maxcy had previously served as president and professor of belles lettres of Rhode Island College (later renamed Brown University) and Union College in Schenectady, N.Y. See Wayne K. Durrill, "The Power of Ancient Words: Classical Teaching and Social Change at South Carolina College, 1804–1860," *Journal of Southern History*, LXV (1999), 469–498; Romeo Elton, ed., *The Literary Remains of the Rev. Jonathan Maxcy . . .* (New York, 1844); Patrick Scott, "From Rhetoric to English: Nineteenth-Century

English Teaching at South Carolina College," *South Carolina Historical Magazine*, LXXXV (1984), 234–236; and Scott, "Jonathan Maxcy and the Aims of Early Nineteenth-Century Rhetorical Teaching," *College English*, XLV (1983), 21–30; Ogilvie, "Supplementary Narrative," PE, lv. For a detailed account of Ogilvie's career at the College of South Carolina, see Richard Beale Davis, "James Ogilvie, an Early American Teacher of Rhetoric," *Quarterly Journal of Speech*, XXVIII (1942), 289–297.

The college's debating societies were important to college life. The Philomathic Society was the first to be established on campus, but it soon afterward split into the Clariosophic and Euphradian Societies, which competed with one another. For more on college debating societies, see J. Jefferson Looney, "Useful without Attracting Attention: The Cliosophic and American Whig Societies of the College of New Jersey, 1765–1896," *Princeton University Library Chronicle*, LXIV (2003), 389–423; James McLachlan, "The Choice of Hercules: American Student Societies in the Early Nineteenth Century," in Lawrence Stone, ed., *The University in Society*, II, *Europe, Scotland, and the United States from the Sixteenth to the Twentieth Century* (Princeton, N.J., 1974), 472; and Carolyn Eastman, "'The Powers of Debate Should Be Sedulously Cultivated': The Importance of Eloquence in Early American Education and the University of Virginia," in John A. Ragosta, Peter S. Onuf, and Andrew J. O'Shaughnessy, eds., *The Founding of Thomas Jefferson's University* (Charlottesville, Va., 2019), 287–305. Ogilvie arrived in Columbia shortly after student riots had created havoc at the college. On a single night in February 1814, students had stoned the windows of two professors' homes and burned a third professor in effigy. (The college had a total of four professors at the time; the only one not attacked was President Maxcy.) In the end, it required the Columbia town militia to quell the student unrest that night, and successive student "disorders" continued for the rest of the year. See Edwin L. Green, *A History of the University of South Carolina* (Columbia, S.C., 1916), 28. In this regard, students at the college resembled those at universities throughout the United States. See Howard Miller, *The Revolutionary College: American Presbyterian Higher Education, 1707–1837* (New York, 1976), 259–280; Mark A. Noll, "The Response of Elias Boudinot to the Student Revolt of 1807: Visions of Honor, Order, and Morality," *Princeton University Library Chronicle*, XLIII (1981), 1–22; and Steven J. Novak, *The Rights of Youth: American Colleges and Student Revolt, 1798–1815* (Cambridge, Mass., 1977), chap. 6.

4. Ogilvie, "Supplementary Narrative," PE, lxii ("magnificent halls"), lxvi ("'into thin air'"). See also House Journal (Nov. 27–Dec. 8, 1815), Dec. 8, 1815, Ser. S165085, South Carolina House of Representatives, South Carolina Department of Archives and History, Columbia. The Bartlet Professorship of Pulpit Eloquence was created in 1809 at the Andover Theological Seminary. See Edward D. Griffin, *An Oration Delivered June 21, 1809, on the Day of the Author's Induction into the Office of Bartlet Professor of Pulpit Eloquence* ... (Boston, 1810); see also "Pulpit Eloquence," *Comet* (Boston), Dec. 14, 1811, 97–99; and "Pulpit Eloquence," *Universalist Magazine*, I (1819), 20. Little scholarly work has examined this push for the teaching of pulpit eloquence in the early nineteenth-century United States. See Alan Brinton, "Hugh Blair and the True Eloquence," *Rhetoric Society Quarterly*, XXII (1992), 30–42.

5. Ogilvie, "Supplementary Narrative," PE, lxvi–lxxi ("republican government" on lxxi); "Mr. Ogilvie," *Poulson's American Daily Advertiser* (Philadelphia), Apr. 1, 1815, [3] (*"Ladies' feet"*); "For the Courier," *Charleston Courier*, Nov. 14, 1815, [2] (respectable audience).

6. "Public Halls," *Southern Patriot* (Charleston), Dec. 6, 1815, [2] ("REPUBLICAN AMERICA"). See also "Mr. Ogilvie," *Charleston Courier*, Nov. 25, 1815, [2]; and "Public Halls," *Southern Patriot*, Mar. 27, 1816, [2]. On elite support, see Ogilvie, "Supplementary Narrative," PE, lxxxviii. These supporters included Gen. Wade Hampton, a veteran of both the Revolution and the War of 1812 and a two-term member of the U.S. House of Representatives.

7. Ogilvie, "Supplementary Narrative," PE, lxxvi–lxxxi.

8. J. Hamilton Moore, *The Young Gentleman and Lady's Monitor, and English Teacher's Assistant; Being a Collection of Select Pieces from Our Best Modern Writers . . .*, 5th ed. (New York, 1787), 129 ("same method"). Moore's book, originally published in London in 1780, was reprinted dozens of times in the United States over four decades. The scholarly literature on female education is vast. See Lynne Templeton Brickley, "Sarah Pierce's Litchfield Female Academy, 1792–1833" (Ed.D. diss., Harvard Graduate School of Education, 1985); Carolyn Eastman, *A Nation of Speechifiers: Making an American Public after the Revolution* (Chicago, 2009), chap. 2 (hereafter cited as NOS); Mary Kelley, *Learning to Stand and Speak: Women, Education, and Public Life in America's Republic* (Williamsburg, Va., and Chapel Hill, N.C., 2006), chaps. 1, 2; Kelley, "'Vindicating the Equality of Female Intellect': Women and Authority in the Early Republic," *Prospects*, XVII (1992), 1–27; Catherine E. Kelly, *Republic of Taste: Art, Politics, and Everyday Life in Early America* (Philadelphia, 2016), chap. 1; Linda K. Kerber, *Women of the Republic: Intellect and Ideology in Revolutionary America* (Williamsburg, Va., and Chapel Hill, N.C., 1980), chap. 7; Margaret A. Nash, "'Cultivating the Powers of Human Beings': Gendered Perspectives on Curricula and Pedagogy in Academies of the New Republic," *History of Education Quarterly*, XLI (2001), 239–250; Nash, *Women's Education in the United States, 1780–1840* (New York, 2005), chap. 2; Glenda Riley, "Origins of the Argument for Improved Female Education," *History of Education Quarterly*, IX (1969), 455–470; Kathryn Kish Sklar, "The Schooling of Girls and Changing Community Values in Massachusetts Towns, 1750–1820," ibid., XXXIII (1993), 511–542; Kim Tolley, "Science for Ladies, Classics for Gentlemen: A Comparative Analysis of Scientific Subjects in the Curricula of Boys' and Girls' Secondary Schools in the United States, 1794–1850," ibid., XXXVI (1996), 129–153; and Rosemarie Zagarri, "The Rights of Man and Woman in Post-Revolutionary America," *William and Mary Quarterly*, 3d Ser., LV (1998), 203–230. On female education's ties to Wollstonecraft, see Chandos Michael Brown, "Mary Wollstonecraft, or, The Female Illuminati: The Campaign Against Women and 'Modern Philosophy' in the Early Republic," *Journal of the Early Republic*, XV (1995), 389–424; Michèle Cohen, "Gender and the Private / Public Debate on Education in the Long Eighteenth Century," in Richard Aldrich, ed., *Public or Private Education? Lessons from History* (London, 2004), 15–24; NOS, chap. 2; R. M. Janes, "On the Reception of Mary Wollstonecraft's *A Vindication of the Rights of Woman*," *Journal of the History of Ideas*, XXXIX (1978), 293–302; Kelley, *Learning to Stand and Speak*, 47–51; David Lundberg

and Henry F. May, "The Enlightened Reader in America," *American Quarterly*, XXVIII (1976), 262–93; Marcelle Thiébaux, "Mary Wollstonecraft in Federalist America, 1791–1802," in Donald H. Reiman, Michael C. Jaye, and Betty T. Bennett, eds., *The Evidence of the Imagination: Studies of Interactions between Life and Art in English Romantic Literature* (New York, 1978), 195–235; and Zagarri, "Rights of Man and Woman," *WMQ*, 3d Ser., LV (1998), 205–211.

9. "Amusing: Woman; an Apologue," *Boston Weekly Magazine*, II, no. 22 (Mar. 24, 1804), 86 ("learned women"). On women becoming ill from too much study, see Margaret Duncan Greene, "The Growth of Physical Education for Women in the United States in the Early Nineteenth Century" (Ed.D. diss., UCLA, 1950), 13–22; and Rebecca Noel, "'No Wonder They Are Sick, and Die of Study': European Fears for the Scholarly Body and Health in New England Schools before Horace Mann," *Paedagogica Historica*, LIV (2018), 134–153. In "'A Vapour Which Appears but for a Moment': Elocution for Girls during the Early American Republic," in David Gold and Catherine Hobbs, eds., *Rhetoric, History, and Women's Oratorical Education: American Women Learn to Speak* (New York, 2013), 38–59, I trace some of the ways in which female oratorical education explicitly delimited the potential role of women in American culture. On Americans' response to the Wollstonecraft biography, see Andrew Cayton, *Love in the Time of Revolution: Transatlantic Literary Radicalism and Historical Change, 1793–1818* (Williamsburg, Va., and Chapel Hill, N.C., 2013), chaps. 5–6; Seth Cotlar, *Tom Paine's America: The Rise and Fall of Transatlantic Radicalism in the Early Republic* (Charlottesville, Va., 2011), 204–205; Rosemarie Zagarri, *Revolutionary Backlash: Women and Politics in the Early American Republic* (Philadelphia, 2007), chap. 1.

10. "A Card," *Southern Patriot*, Mar. 16, 1816, [2]. On other forms of educational reform, see Martin Brückner, *The Geographic Revolution in Early America: Maps, Literacy, and National Identity* (Williamsburg, Va., and Chapel Hill, N.C., 2006); Lawrence A. Cremin, *American Education: The National Experience, 1783–1876* (New York, 1980), part 4; NOS, chap. 1; Carl F. Kaestle, *Pillars of the Republic: Common Schools and American Society, 1780–1860* (New York, 1983), chaps. 2–3; and Elaine Weber Pascu, "From the Philanthropic Tradition to the Common School Ideal: Schooling in New York City, 1815–1832" (Ph.D. diss., Northern Illinois University, 1980).

11. A Friend of Youth, "Mr. Ogilvie's Plan of Education," *Southern Patriot*, Apr. 30, 1816, [2].

12. Ogilvie, "On the Cardinal Importance of the Study of Mathematical Science, as a Branch of Liberal Education, and as Connected with the Attainment of Superior Ability and Skill, in the Exercise of Oratory," PE, 9.

13. Ogilvie, "Preface," PE, [iii]. He actually repeats this line almost verbatim in the book's final pages—and adds emphasis ("To the Candid Reader," xcv).

14. Lara Langer Cohen, *The Fabrication of American Literature: Fraudulence and Antebellum Print Culture* (Philadelphia, 2012), chap. 1; Ann Fabian, *The Unvarnished Truth: Personal Narratives in Nineteenth-Century America* (Berkeley, Calif., 2000); Stephen Mihm, *A Nation of Counterfeiters: Capitalists, Con Men, and the Making of the United States* (Cambridge, Mass., 2007); Larzer Ziff,

Writing in the New Nation: Prose, Print, and Politics in the Early United States (New Haven, Conn., 1991), chaps. 4–5. This pattern would only expand during the antebellum era, as these authors have shown.

15. "Ogilvie's Essays," *Richmond Enquirer*, Aug. 3, 1816, [4]. This ad reappeared hundreds of times in newspapers all over the country.

16. On the belletristic rhetorical style, see Michael T. Gilmore, "Letters of the Early Republic," in Sacvan Bercovitch and Cyrus R. K. Patell, eds., *The Cambridge History of American Literature, 1590–1820* (Cambridge, 1994), I, 541–547; Cynthia S. Jordan, *Second Stories: The Politics of Language, Form, and Gender in Early American Fictions* (Chapel Hill, N.C., 1989); and Michael Warner, *The Letters of the Republic: Publication and the Public Sphere in Eighteenth-Century America* (Cambridge, Mass., 1990), 12–38, 124–127.

17. I. Woodbridge Riley, *American Philosophy: The Early Schools* (New York, 1907), 560–561. The critic for the *Analectic Magazine* also points to these inconsistencies in the two-part essay, Review of James Ogilvie, *Philosophical Essays . . .* , *Analectic Magazine and Naval Chronicle*, VIII (December 1816), 486–506, and Review of James Ogilvie, *Philosophical Essays . . .* , Essay II, *Analectic Magazine*, IX (January 1817), 1–32. More recently, John R. Shook calls Ogilvie's book "notable for its epistemology, theory of scientific method, and its pragmatic version of Scottish common sense realism." See Shook, gen. ed., *The Dictionary of Early American Philosophers* (New York, 2012), II, 788–790.

18. Ogilvie, "Supplementary Narrative," PE, lxv.

19. Review of James Ogilvie, *Philosophical Essays . . .* , Port Folio, 4th Ser., II, no. 6 (December 1816), 502 ("permanent"), 511 ("sufficient evidence"); Review of Ogilvie, *Philosophical Essays, Analectic Magazine, and Naval Chronicle*, VIII (December 1816), 487 ("negligent habits"); Review of Ogilvie, *Philosophical Essays*, Essay II, *Analectic Magazine*, IX (January 1817), 32 ("Paradise Lost"). Richard Beale Davis claims that the author of the Port Folio review was William Cabell Rives, a former student of Ogilvie's. See Davis, *Intellectual Life in Jefferson's Virginia, 1790–1830* (Chapel Hill, N.C., 1964), 115; I have not been able to verify that claim.

20. [Ogilvie], "Addressed to the Intelligent and Candid Readers of the Port Folio and Analectic Magazine," *Boston Patriot*, Dec. 25, 1816, [2] ("putrescence"); "Mr. Ogilvie and His Reviewers," *Boston Patriot*, Jan. 15, 1817 [2] ("sincerely wish").

21. Lord Byron, *English Bards, and Scotch Reviewers; A Satire* (1809; rpt. Boston, 1811), [3] ("write better"); Clara Tuite, *Lord Byron and Scandalous Celebrity* (New York, 2015), chap. 4; Frederic V. Bogel, *The Difference Satire Makes: Rhetoric and Reading from Jonson to Byron* (Ithaca, N.Y., 2001), chap. 7. See also Dustin Griffin, *Satire: A Critical Reintroduction* (Lexington, Ky., 1994).

22. Ogilvie, "Addressed to the Intelligent . . . ," *Boston Patriot*, Dec. 25, 1816, [2] ("he has undertaken"); John E. Hall to William S. Shaw (editor of the *Monthly Anthology*), Jan. 2, 1817, Correspondence: Nineteenth Century, MS 15.117, Hay Library, Brown University, Providence, R.I. ("roast-meat"). Nineteenth-century writers often used Latin to cloak ideas most likely to shock, such as explicitly sexual material. Hall might have sought to

imply that the book ought to be used as toilet paper but reserved that implication only for those who knew the Latin (most likely educated men).

23. "Literary Controversies," *Massachusetts Spy* (Worcester), Jan. 15, 1817, [3] ("dull times"); "Ogilvie's Philosophical Essays," *National Register* (Washington, D.C.) III, 3 (1817), 34 ("do no good"); "Mr. Ogilvie," *Columbian* (New York), Jan. 3, 1817, [3] (defense of Ogilvie).

24. "Ogilvie's Philosophical Essays," *National Register*, III, no. 3 (Jan. 18, 1817), 35 ("mist and moonshine"); Review of Ogilvie, *Philosophical Essays*, Port Folio, 4th Ser., II, no. 6 (December 1816), 510–511 ("allotted to him").

25. Francis Walker Gilmer to William Wirt, Feb. 4, 1817, Francis Walker Gilmer Letters, Acc. No. 18763, Library of Virginia, Richmond.

26. P. Q. R., "To the Editor of the Charleston Times," *New-York Columbian*, May 7, 1821, [2–3] ("intellectual endowments"). In the literature on early modern celebrity, I have found only one scholar who has analyzed the phenomenon of public disenchantment with a celebrity, Giles Playfair, *The Prodigy: A Study of the Strange Life of Master Betty* (London, 1967), a book very much oriented around the rise and fall of a specific member of the British theater at the turn of the nineteenth century. More recent scholars have focused primarily on the questions of how the phenomenon arose. See, especially, Elizabeth Barry, ed., "Celebrity, Cultural Production, and Public Life," special issue of *International Journal of Cultural Studies*, XI (2008), 251–376; Páraic Finnerty and Rod Rosenquist, eds., "Transatlantic Celebrity: European Fame in Nineteenth-Century America," special issue of *Comparative American Studies*, XIV (2016), 1–89; Fred Inglis, *A Short History of Celebrity* (Princeton, N.J., 2010); and Tom Mole, ed., *Romanticism and Celebrity Culture, 1750–1850* (Cambridge, 2009).

27. These passages draw on Ari Adut, *On Scandal: Moral Disturbances in Society, Politics, and Art* (New York, 2008), chap. 1; and Victor Turner, "Social Dramas and Stories about Them," *Critical Inquiry*, VII (1980), 141–168, for concepts about transgression and backlash. For more on the complexities of scandal at the time, I have drawn on Norma Basch, "Marriage, Morals, and Politics in the Election of 1828," *Journal of American History*, LXXX (1993), 890–918; Elizabeth J. Clapp, *A Notorious Woman: Anne Royall in Jacksonian America* (Charlottesville, Va., 2016); Christopher L. Doyle, "The Randolph Scandal in Early National Virginia, 1792–1815: New Voices in the 'Court of Honor,'" *Journal of Social History*, LXIX (2003), 283–318; and Kirsten E. Wood, "'One Woman So Dangerous to Public Morals': Gender and Power in the Eaton Affair," JER, XVII (1997), 237–275.

28. This was not the first time that the American public had faced a form of identity crisis when they believed a public figure had betrayed them. As Charles Royster demonstrates, Benedict Arnold's treason during the Revolutionary War likewise prompted a thorough reassessment of a man previously considered a military hero. I would suggest that, although the crisis might have produced similar effects, the social position of a figure like Arnold made his situation a far cry from Ogilvie's fall from grace; the forms of their celebrity were quite different. See Royster, "'The Nature of Treason': Revolution-

ary Virtue and American Reactions to Benedict Arnold," *WMQ*, 3d Ser., XXXVI (1979), 163–193.

29. Veritas, "Mr. Ogilvie," *Southern Patriot, and Commercial Advertiser* (Charleston), Mar. 18, 1815, [2].

30. Adam Saul Gordon, "Cultures of Criticism in Antebellum America" (Ph.D. diss., University of California, Los Angeles, 2011). See also Jared Gardner, *The Rise and Fall of Early American Magazine Culture* (Urbana, Ill., 2012), chap. 2; James N. Green, "The Rise of Book Publishing," in Robert A. Gross and Mary Kelley, eds., *A History of the Book in America*, II, *An Extensive Republic: Print, Culture, and Society in the New Nation, 1790–1840* (Chapel Hill, N.C., 2010), 75–127; Heather A. Haveman, *Magazines and the Making of America: Modernization, Community, and Print Culture, 1741–1860* (Princeton, N.J., 2015), chap. 2; and Tim Lanzendörfer, *The Professionalization of the American Magazine: Periodicals, Biography, and Nationalism in the Early Republic* (Paderborn, Ger., 2013), chap. 3.

31. [Edward Channing], "Philosophical Essays," *North-American Review and Miscellaneous Journal*, IV, no. 12 (March 1817), 383, 385. A close reading of this review appears in Charles Paine, *The Resistant Writer: Rhetoric as Immunity, 1850 to the Present* (Albany, N.Y., 1999), 68–75. Many thanks to Alfred Brophy for a productive conversation that followed this line of thought.

32. Ralph Waldo Emerson to Edward Bliss Emerson, Jan. 5, 1817, in Ralph L. Rusk, ed., *Letters of Ralph Waldo Emerson*, I (New York, 1939), 32 ("*de oratore*"); "A Card," *Boston Daily Advertiser*, Dec. 30, 1816, [2] ("fatigue"); see also "Mr. Ogilvie," *Columbian*, Feb. 11, 1817, [2], in which he claims "debility occasioned by extreme exhaustion." Emerson refers to Cicero's *De Oratore* with this line. For Ogilvie's large audiences, see "The Rostrum," *New York Evening Post*, Dec. 4, 1816, [2]; for notices of the Forum, see "The Forum," *Kentucky Gazette* (Lexington), Dec. 23, 1816, [3]. See also Emerson, "Eloquence," *The Complete Works of Ralph Waldo Emerson . . .*, centennial ed., 12 vols. (Boston, 1903–1932), VII, 59–100.

33. Royster, "'The Nature of Treason,'" *WMQ*, 3d Ser., XXXVI (1979), 163–193; Jacob Katz Cogan, "The Reynolds Affair and the Politics of Character," *JER*, XVI (1996), 389–417; James E. Lewis, Jr., *The Burr Conspiracy: Uncovering the Story of an Early American Crisis* (Princeton, N.J., 2017); R. Kent Newmyer, *The Treason Trial of Aaron Burr: Law, Politics, and the Character Wars of the New Nation* (New York, 2012), esp. 198–200.

34. Ogilvie, "The following is an extract . . . ," *Richmond Enquirer*, Mar. 21, 1817, [3] ("little money"); "The Worthy Mr. Ogilvie," *Columbian*, Mar. 10, 1817, [2] ("amassed a fortune").

35. Washington Allston to Washington Irving, Mar. 13, 1818, in Pierre M. Irving, ed., *The Life and Letters of Washington Irving* (New York, 1862–1864), I, 399. I have found no other records of his resuming the habit except that in 1818 Allston acknowledged the seriousness of the problem.

36. Thomas Cooper to Thomas Jefferson, Aug. 17, 1814, Jefferson to Cooper, Sept. 10, 1814, both in James P. McClure and J. Jefferson Looney, eds., *Papers of Thomas Jefferson*, Retirement Series (Charlottesville, Va., 2008–2020), VII, 557–561 ("Earl of Findlater," 560), 649–655. "Livery and seisin" is a term from English common law; for Jefferson, it might

have indicated the grandeur of how he believed an earldom would be formally granted to an heir.

37. "Public Oratory," *Morning Post* (London), July 1, 1817, [3]. London was still slightly smaller than Beijing in 1818, though that would change within a few years.

CHAPTER TWELVE

1. "We understand . . . ," *Morning Post* (London), June 16, 1817, [3] ("probationary school"); "To correspondents," *Richmond Enquirer* (Virginia), Mar. 21, 1817, [3] ("I cannot imagine").

2. "The Rostrum," *Morning Chronicle* (London), June 23, 1817, [1] ("all denominations"); "The Rostrum," *Cheltenham Chronicle*, Sept. 4, 1817, [4] ("three or four hundred").

3. On the transatlantic differences in celebrity before the mid-nineteenth century, see Amanda Adams, *Performing Authorship in the Nineteenth-Century Transatlantic Lecture Tour* (Farnham, U.K., 2014); Páraic Finnerty and Rod Rosenquist, eds., "Transatlantic Celebrity: European Fame in Nineteenth-Century America," special issue of *Comparative American Studies*, XIV (2016), 1–89; Tom F. Wright, *Lecturing the Atlantic: Speech, Print, and an Anglo-American Commons, 1830–1870* (New York, 2017); and Wright, ed., *The Cosmopolitan Lyceum: Lecture Culture and the Globe in Nineteenth-Century America* (Amherst, Mass., 2013), esp. essays by Robert Arbour, Angela G. Ray, and Paul Stob.

4. Sharon Marcus lays out these dynamics in *The Drama of Celebrity* (Princeton, N.J., 2019), chap. 7; and in "Salomé!! Sarah Bernhardt, Oscar Wilde, and the Drama of Celebrity," *PMLA: Publications of the Modern Language Association of America*, CXXVI (2011), 999–1021.

5. The literature on patronage in Great Britain is vast, but the material I have found most valuable (and relevant to a figure like Ogilvie, rather than political, religious, or military patronage) includes J. M. Bourne, *Patronage and Society in Nineteenth-Century England* (London, 1986); Julie Cairnie, "The Ambivalence of Ann Yearsley: Laboring and Writing, Submission and Resistance," *Nineteenth-Century Contexts*, XXVII (2005), 353–364; Peter Fullerton, "Patronage and Pedagogy: The British Institution in the Early Nineteenth Century," *Art History*, V (1982), 59–72; Odai Johnson, *Absence and Memory in Colonial American Theatre: Fiorelli's Plaster* (Hampshire, U.K., 2006); Peter J. Jupp, "The Landed Elite and Political Authority in Britain, ca. 1760–1850," *Journal of British Studies*, XXIX (1990), 53–79; Paul J. Korshin, "Types of Eighteenth-Century Literary Patronage," *Eighteenth-Century Studies*, VII (1974), 453–473; and Betty Rizzo, "The Patron as Poet Maker: The Politics of Benefaction," *Studies in Eighteenth-Century Culture*, XX (1990), 241–266.

6. The members of Godwin's circle included the writer and orator William Hazlitt, essayist Charles Lamb, and the poet and critic Leigh Hunt, among many others. See Stephen Burley, "First Acquaintances: Hazlitt, Godwin, and the Trials of Authorship," *Bodleian Library Record*, XXIV (2011), 66–72; Jane Hodson, *Language and Revolution in Burke, Wollstonecraft, Paine, and Godwin* (Aldershot, U.K., 2007); Peter H. Marshall, *William Godwin* (New Haven, Conn., 1984). For an account of Godwin's diary, see James Grande, "Nineteenth-Century London in William Godwin's Diary," *Journal of Victorian Culture*, XV (2010), 201–211;

and David O'Shaughnessy and Mark Philp, "William Godwin Diary: An Introduction," *Bodleian Library Record*, XXIV (2011), 5–18. Ogilvie also introduced Godwin to the young actor John Howard Payne and the American artist Washington Allston, among others. See Richard Beale Davis, "James Ogilvie and Washington Irving," *Americana Illustrated*, XXXV (1941), 435–458; Katherine C. Hill-Miller, *"My Hideous Progeny": Mary Shelley, William Godwin, and the Father-Daughter Relationship* (Newark, Del., 1995); Donald H. Reiman, ed., *Shelley and His Circle, 1773–1822*, V (Cambridge, Mass., 1973), 232–236; William St. Clair, *The Godwins and the Shelleys: The Biography of a Family* (Baltimore, 1989). See also Barbara Taylor, *Eve and the New Jerusalem: Socialism and Feminism in the Nineteenth Century* (London, 1983). Finally, Ogilvie introduced Godwin to Joseph H. Bevan, one of his former students at the South Carolina College. Bevan had been a member of the college's Clariosophic Society, a debating society, and long remained fond of Ogilvie. Bevan looked on Godwin as a mentor (as he had been to Ogilvie) and enjoyed a correspondence with him. See Jack W. Marken, ed., "Joseph Bevan and William Godwin," *Collections of the Georgia Historical Society*, XLIII (1959), 302–318. In 1818, Godwin published a fifteen-page pamphlet entitled *Letter of Advice to a Young American: On the Course of Studies It Might Be Most Advantageous for Him to Pursue* (London, 1818), which subsequently appeared in the American *Analectic Magazine*, XII (August 1818), 128–135, and *Port Folio*, 4th Ser., VI, no. 3 (September 1818), 170–182.

7. [Anon.], "Recollections of Conversations, etc.," author's draft [undated; circa 1833], 7–8, 14, MS Abinger deposit 26, Bodleian Library, Oxford University (hereafter cited as BLOU) ("'great man'"). See Paula R. Feldman and Diana Scott-Kilvert, eds., *The Journals of Mary Shelley, 1814–1844* (Oxford, 1987), I, 170–171; Victoria Myers, David O'Shaughnessy, and Mark Philp, eds., *Diary of William Godwin* (Oxford, 2010), May–Aug. 1817, http://godwindiary.bodleian.ox.ac.uk.

8. Marshall, *William Godwin*, 273, 295; Andrew Cayton, *Love in the Time of Revolution: Transatlantic Literary Radicalism and Historical Change, 1793–1818* (Williamsburg, Va., and Chapel Hill, N.C., 2013).

9. John Quincy Adams diary 27 (Jan. 1, 1803–Aug. 4, 1809), Apr. 28, May 1, May 15, 1809, 400, 402, diary 30 (June 1, 1816–Dec. 31, 1818), May 24, 1817, 199, all in *The Diaries of John Quincy Adams: A Digital Collection*, Massachusetts Historical Society, Boston, 2005, www.masshist.org/jqadiaries/php. See Bourne, *Patronage and Society*, 56–85, 113–122. Irving would learn by early 1818 that his family's business was near bankruptcy, making it all the more important that his publications succeed. See Andrew Burstein, *The Original Knickerbocker: The Life of Washington Irving* (New York, 2007), 112–124; see also Pierre M. Irving, ed., *The Life and Letters of Washington Irving* (New York, 1862–1864), I, chaps. 24, 25.

10. "The Rostrum," *Morning Post*, Aug. 5, 1817, [3] ("uncommon plaudits"); "The Rostrum," *Cheltenham Chronicle*, Sept. 4, 1817, [3] ("all denominations"); Washington Irving to Henry Brevoort, Aug. 28, 1817, in George S. Hellman, ed., *The Letters of Washington Irving to Henry Brevoort* (New York, 1918), 260–261 ("well satisfied").

11. "The Rostrum," *Aberdeen Chronicle*, Dec. 6, 1817, [1]. Without any remaining Ogilvie family papers, I have reconstructed the Ogilvie family history from Hew Scott, *Fasti Eccle-*

siae Scoticanae: The Succession of Ministers in the Church of Scotland from the Reformation, new ed. (Edinburgh, 1926), VI, 38, 108–109, 124; obituary for Ogilvie's mother, "Margaret Reid," *Aberdeen Journal, and General Advertiser for the North of Scotland*, Sept. 26, 1804, [4]; obituary for Ogilvie's father, "Died in Scotland," *Boston Spectator*, Feb. 19, 1814, 30; "Misses Jane and Elizabeth Ogilvie," *Aberdeen Journal, and General Advertiser for the North of Scotland*, Jan. 1, 1851, [8]. The latter article records the enormous number of charitable donations made by the sisters to institutions in the community. They passed any remaining family belongings and papers, including something described only as "Ogilvie family portraits," to a cousin, according to the Aberdeen Sasine Registers at the National Records of Scotland (NRS), Edinburgh; although I traced the subsequent inheritance of those materials to a successive generation, any record of those materials was lost by the end of the nineteenth century.

12. "It rarely happens . . . ," *Aberdeen Journal, and General Advertiser for the North of Scotland*, Dec. 10, 1817, [3] ("so amply"); "Mr. Ogilvie," *Aberdeen Chronicle*, Dec. 13, 1817, [1] ("extraordinary attainments"); "Mr. Ogilvie," *Aberdeen Chronicle*, Jan. 3, 1818, [1] (honorary member).

13. George Brodie to William Godwin, Feb. 3, 1821, MS Abinger deposit, B. 214/2, BLOU.

14. Brodie to Godwin, Feb. 3, 1821, BLOU.

15. [Robert Mudie], *A Historical Account of His Majesty's Visit to Scotland*, 4th ed. (Edinburgh, 1822), 218–219 ("crystal lustres"). On the Assembly Rooms, see "Explanation of the Proposed Alterations of the Assembly Rooms," *Scots Magazine, and Edinburgh Literary Miscellany: Being a General Repository of Literature, History, and Politics for 1816* (Edinburgh), LXXVIII (1816), 363–365; see also "Anniversary of Mr. Pitt," *Scots Magazine*, LXXIX (1817), 476, for another kind of celebration there; and "History of the Building," www.assemblyroomsedinburgh .co.uk/about-us/history-of-the-building. On Edinburgh's literary reputation, see David Allan, *Virtue, Learning, and the Scottish Enlightenment: Ideas of Scholarship in Early Modern History* (Edinburgh, 1993); Jonquil Bevan, "Scotland," in John Barnard and D. F. McKenzie with Maureen Bell, eds., *The Cambridge History of the Book in Britain*, IV, *1557–1695* (Cambridge, 2002), 687–700; James Buchan, *Crowded with Genius: The Scottish Enlightenment, Edinburgh's Moment of the Mind* (New York, 2003); Ian Duncan, *Scott's Shadow: The Novel in Romantic Edinburgh* (Princeton, N.J., 2007); Antonia Forster, "Book Reviewing," in Michael F. Suarez and Michael L. Turner, eds., *The Cambridge History of the Book in Britain*, V, *1695–1830* (Cambridge, 2009), 631–648; Warren McDougall, "Edinburgh," in Stephen W. Brown and McDougall, eds., *The Edinburgh History of the Book in Scotland: Enlightenment and Expansion, 1707–1800* (Edinburgh, 2011), II, 271–296; and Mark R. M. Towsey, *Reading the Scottish Enlightenment: Books and Their Readers in Provincial Scotland, 1750–1820* (Leiden, 2010).

16. Washington Allston to Washington Irving, Mar. 13, 1818, in Irving, ed., *Life and Letters*, I, 399 ("full of health"); Brodie to Godwin, Feb. 3, 1821, BLOU ("catastrophe"); "Mr. Ogilvie," *Caledonian Mercury* (Edinburgh), Jan. 29, 1818, [3] ("repeatedly applauded"). The Allston letter was the first record I found regarding his opium use since his report during the fall of 1811 of having broken himself of the habit.

17. I explore these details in "The Transatlantic Celebrity of Mr. O: Oratory and the Networks of Reputation in Early Nineteenth-Century Britain and America," *Comparative American Studies*, XIV (2016), 7–20.

18. "On Friday evening last . . . ," *Caledonian Mercury*, Nov. 21, 1818, [2], reprinted from the *Portland Vase* ("numerous audience"); "Mr. Ogilvie," *Bath Chronicle & Weekly Gazette*, Dec. 9, 1819, [3] ("expressing a doubt"). Reports of his lectures in Bath and Bristol vacillated between describing "numerous and most respectable audience[s]" and a "thinness of the audience." See "Mr. Ogilvie," *Bath & Cheltenham Gazette*, Dec. 1, 1819, [3] ("numerous"); "Mr. Ogilvie," *Bath & Cheltenham Gazette*, Dec. 8, 1819, [3] ("thinness").

19. "Recitation and Criticism," *Bath Chronicle & Weekly Gazette*, Jan. 13, 1820, [3] ("Mr. O's Lectures"); "Mr. Ogilvie," *Bath & Cheltenham Gazette*, Jan. 26, 1820, [2] ("mental enjoyment"); "Mr. Ogilvie," *Bath Chronicle & Weekly Gazette*, Jan. 13, 1820, [3] ("indignation and shame"); see also A Friend to Merit, "To the Editor of the Bristol Gazette," *Bristol Gazette & Public Advertiser*, Jan. 13, 1820, [3]; and "Recitation and Criticism," *Felix Farley's Bristol Journal*, Jan. 15, 1820, [3].

20. William Hazlitt, *The Eloquence of the British Senate; or, Select Specimens from the Speeches of the Most Distinguished Parliamentary Speakers* . . . (London, 1807), I, iv–v ("giddy multitude"). The literature on British oratory is extensive, although it has tended to focus more on the development of adult education via lecture than on occasional lecturers like Ogilvie or on what later became lyceum-style lectures. See Penny Fielding, *Writing and Orality: Nationality, Culture, and Nineteenth-Century Scottish Fiction* (Oxford, 1996); Diarmid A. Finnegan, "Placing Science in an Age of Oratory: Spaces of Scientific Speech in Mid-Victorian Edinburgh," in David N. Livingstone and Charles W. J. Withers, eds., *Geographies of Nineteenth-Century Science* (Chicago, 2011), 153–177; Finnerty and Rosenquist, eds., "Transatlantic Celebrity," *Comparative American Studies*, XIV (2016), 1–89; Adam Fox, *Oral and Literate Culture in England, 1500–1700* (Oxford, 2000); Martin Hewitt, "Aspects of Platform Culture in Nineteenth-Century Britain," *Nineteenth-Century Prose*, XXIX (2002), 1–32; Thomas Kelly, *George Birkbeck: Pioneer of Adult Education* (Liverpool, U.K., 1957); Jon Klancher, *Transfiguring the Arts and Sciences: Knowledge and Cultural Institutions in the Romantic Age* (Cambridge, 2013); Paula McDowell, *The Invention of the Oral: Print Commerce and Fugitive Voices in Eighteenth-Century Britain* (Chicago, 2017); Joseph S. Meisel, *Public Speech and the Culture of Public Life in the Age of Gladstone* (New York, 2001); and Wright, *Lecturing the Atlantic*, chap. 1.

21. Mary Kupiec Cayton, "The Making of an American Prophet: Emerson, His Audiences, and the Rise of the Culture Industry in Nineteenth-Century America," *American Historical Review*, XCII (1987), 597–620; Kenneth Cmiel, *Democratic Eloquence: The Fight over Popular Speech in Nineteenth-Century America* (Berkeley, Calif., 1990); Carolyn Eastman, *A Nation of Speechifiers: Making an American Public after the Revolution* (Chicago, 2009), chap. 1; Sandra M. Gustafson, *Eloquence Is Power: Oratory and Performance in Early America* (Williamsburg, Va., Chapel Hill, N.C., 2000); James Perrin Warren, *Culture of Eloquence: Oratory and Reform in Antebellum America* (University Park, Pa., 1999); Donald M. Scott, "The Popular Lecture and the Creation of a Public in Mid-Nineteenth-Century America," *Journal of American History*,

LXVI (1980), 791–809; Scott, "The Profession That Vanished: Public Lecturing in Mid-Nineteenth-Century America," in Gerald L. Geison, ed., *Professions and Professional Ideologies in America* (Chapel Hill, N.C., 1983), 12–28.

22. Antoine Lilti, *Figures publiques: L'invention de la célébrité* (Paris, 2015); Marcus, *Drama of Celebrity*; Tom Mole, *Byron's Romantic Celebrity: Industrial Culture and the Hermeneutic of Intimacy* (Hampshire, U.K., 2007); Mole, ed., *Romanticism and Celebrity Culture, 1750–1850* (Cambridge, 2009); Judith Pascoe, *The Sarah Siddons Audio Files: Romanticism and the Lost Voice* (Ann Arbor, Mich., 2011); Stella Tillyard, "Celebrity in Eighteenth-Century London," *History Today*, LV, no. 6 (June 2005), 20–27.

23. "The Editor of the Enquirer will oblige . . . ," *Enquirer* (Richmond), Sept. 8, 1804, [3]; Thomas Cooper to Thomas Jefferson, Aug. 17, 1814, in James P. McClure and J. Jefferson Looney, eds., *The Papers of Thomas Jefferson Digital Edition*, Retirement Series (Charlottesville, Va., 2008–2020), VII, 557–561, https://rotunda.upress.virginia.edu/founders. When Ogilvie's father died in 1814, American obituaries had described him as "the younger branch of the whole family of Fin[d]later." See "Died in Scotland," *Boston Spectator*, Feb. 19, 1814, 30. The following passages on the law of succession for Scottish titles, a topic that appears thorny and contradictory to an American, have been compiled with the assistance of Alex Maxwell Findlater.

24. Kirsten McKenzie, *A Swindler's Progress: Nobles and Convicts in the Age of Liberty* (Sydney, Australia, 2009).

25. "The late Earl of Findlater's estates . . . ," *Cumberland Pacquet, and Ware's Whitehaven Advertiser* (Whitehaven, U.K.), Dec. 10, 1811, [3] ("£40,000"). For evidence of more orderly cases, see the Committee of Privileges record book, 1817–1818, HL/PO/DC/CP/2/14, Records of the House of Lords, Parliamentary Archives, Palace of Westminster, London. I'm grateful to archivist Catherine Hardman for guiding me through these materials. On complicated cases, see Iain Moncreiffe of that Ilk, *The Law of Succession: Origins and Background of the Law of Succession to Arms and Dignitaries of Scotland*, ed. Jackson W. Armstrong (Edinburgh, 2010); W. David H. Sellar, "Succession Law in Scotland: A Historical Perspective," in Kenneth G. C. Reid, Marius J. de Waal, and Reinhard Zimmermann, eds., *Exploring the Law of Succession: Studies National, Historical, and Comparative* (Edinburgh, 2007), 49–66. Dormant titles have occasionally been revived by the committee when a legitimate heir succeeds in making a claim. The committee has also declared titles "extinct" when all possible heirs have died out. To this day the earldom of Findlater remains dormant.

26. Alex Maxwell Findlater, email messages to author, Nov. 13, 2015, Jan. 22, 23, 2019 ("hold up one's head"); "Grant, Lewis Alexander (1767–1840), of Castle Grant, Elgin," in R. G. Thorne, ed., *The House of Commons, 1790–1820*, 5 vols., *The History of Parliament* (London, 1986), www.historyofparliamentonline.org/volume/1790-1820/member/grant-lewis-alexander-1767-1840 ("mental derangement"). The "deranged" earl's younger brother managed the estate. Some sources presume James Ogilvie entered suit for the earldom and was turned down but offer no evidence. See T. W. Bayne, revised by K. D. Reynolds, "Ogilvie, James (1760–1820), scholar," *Oxford Dictionary of National Biography Online* (Septem-

ber 2004), www.oxforddnb.com; Davis, "Ogilvie and Irving," *Americana Illustrated,* XXXV (1941), 448. See also Gordon Donaldson, "Peerage Cases and the Archivist: Presidential Address to the Scottish Record Society, 19 December 1985," in James Kirk, ed., *Scotland's History: Approaches and Reflections* (Edinburgh, 1995).

27. For examples of newspapers speculating on the Findlater inheritance, see *Morning Chronicle,* Nov. 30, 1811, [3] (War Office); *Salisbury & Winchester Journal,* Dec. 2, 1811, [3] (Inchmartine); *Aberdeen Journal, and General Advertiser for the North of Scotland,* Dec. 25, 1811, [3] (Inchmartine); *Caledonian Mercury,* Feb. 24, 1812, [3] (War Office); *Saunder's News-Letter* (Dublin), Sept. 16, 1820, [4] (Boyne); and "Mr. Canning and the Claimant to the Earldom of Findlater," *London St. James Chronicle and Evening Post,* Nov. 10, 1814, [2] (Canongate Jail). See Sir William Ogilvie letters, 1813, Add. MS 38252, vol. LXIII, fols. 261, 318, and Add. MS 38265, vol. LXXVI, fol. 72, Manuscripts and Archives, British Library, London (signing himself Findlater). Other family members continued to present unsuccessful claims. See the Memorial of James Ogilvie, Esq., for the Earldom of Findlater, 1819–1841, SCA BC/1/21/1, Special Collections, Sir Duncan Rice Library, University of Aberdeen, U.K., in which an advocate makes a careful (but unsuccessful) genealogical argument over the course of thirty-one pages for a different James Ogilvie.

28. Mole, *Byron's Romantic Celebrity,* chap. 5.

29. Theodore Gordon and James Ogilvie, sasine for Dunnydeer in Insch, Apr. 27, 1819, RS 8/73/241, NRS ("pendicles"); Irving to Brevoort, Sept. 27, 1818, in Hellman, ed., *Letters of Washington to Breevort,* 294 ("moderate wants").

30. In sasines of more than a decade later, his sisters sought confirmation and clarification of the terms by which he sold his half, suggesting that they had been ignorant of the sale. See Margaret, Elizabeth, and Jane Fletcher Ogilvie, sasine for Dunnydeer, Nov. 23, 1832, RS 8/142/277, NRS; John David Gordon of Wardhouse and Margaret, Elizabeth, and Jane Fletcher Ogilvie, sasine for Dunnydeer, Sept. 14, 1833, RS 8/147/55, NRS. These women, who lived together in Aberdeen throughout their adult lives, ultimately inherited their brother Simson's wealth as well as an evident facility for managing their funds, for they ultimately left a large estate to a wide range of Aberdeen charities. See "Misses Jane and Elizabeth Ogilvie," *Aberdeen Journal, and General Advertiser for the North of Scotland,* Jan. 1, 1851, [8].

31. Joseph Bevan to William Godwin, June 8, 1818, MS Abinger Deposit, B. 215/1, BLOU ("persevere"); Irving to Brevoort, Sept. 27, 1818, in Hellman, ed., *Letters of Washington and Breevort,* 294 ("most interesting").

32. Brodie to Godwin, Feb. 3, 1821, BLOU.

33. William Godwin to Joseph Bevan, June 29, 1818, MS Abinger Deposit, B. 215/ 1, BLOU ("would terminate"); Ogilvie to Godwin, Feb. 2, 1819, MS Abinger Deposit, B. 214/ 2, BLOU ("dissatisfaction"); Myers, O'Shaughnessy, and Philp, eds., *Diary of William Godwin,* February–September 1818 and October 1818–September 1819 (visits to Godwin).

34. Brodie to Godwin, Feb. 3, 1821, BLOU.

35. Ibid. ("dreadful effects"); Thomas De Quincey, *Confessions of an English Opium-Eater*

(1821; rpt. University Park, Pa., 2004), 79–80 ("throwing it off"). On De Quincey, see Frances Wilson, *Guilty Thing: A Life of Thomas De Quincey* (New York, 2016), 220. Scholars have turned increasing attention to the subject of the rise of the language of addiction. See, for example, Marcus Aurin, "Chasing the Dragon: The Cultural Metamorphosis of Opium in the United States, 1825–1935," *Medical Anthropology Quarterly*, XIV (2000) 414–441; David T. Courtwright, *Dark Paradise: A History of Opiate Addiction in America*, rev. ed. (Cambridge, Mass., 2001); Thomas Dormandy, *Opium: Reality's Dark Dream* (New Haven, Conn., 2012); Elizabeth Kelly Gray, *Habit Forming: Drug Addiction in America, 1776–1914* (New York, forthcoming); Lucy Inglis, *Milk of Paradise: A History of Opium* (New York, 2019); Jonathan S. Jones, "A Mind Prostrate: Opiate Addiction in the Civil War's Aftermath" (Ph.D. diss., Binghamton University, forthcoming); Joseph L. Zentner, "Opiate Use in America during the Eighteenth and Nineteenth Centuries: The Origins of a Modern Scourge," *Studies in History and Society*, V (1974), 40–54.

36. Robert Heron, *Scotland Described; or, A Topographical Description of All the Counties of Scotland . . .*, new and improved ed. (Edinburgh, 1799), 261.

37. Brodie to Godwin, Feb. 3, 1821, BLOU.

38. Ibid.

39. Information about the gun—what kind it was, how long Ogilvie had had it—has been lost. When he volunteered during the War of 1812, he purchased a musket and a pair of pistols; he might have continued carrying them, or at least the pistols, thereafter. Considering his itinerant life, it's entirely possible that he used a gun to protect himself against highwaymen. Yet, again, considering the gun culture of early modern England, he might have purchased one after arriving in Britain or even for the sole purpose of the suicide. See Ogilvie to Francis Walker Gilmer, Feb. 1, 1813, in Richard Beale Davis, *Francis Walker Gilmer: Life and Learning in Jefferson's Virginia* (Richmond, Va., 1939), 376; Lois G. Schwoerer, *Gun Culture in Early Modern England* (Charlottesville, Va., 2016). The matter of gun culture in the United States has been explored in Michael A. Bellesiles's controversial *Arming America: The Origins of a National Gun Culture*, rev. ed. (New York, 2003); Pamela Haag, *The Gunning of America: Business and the Making of American Gun Culture* (New York, 2016); Randolph Roth, *American Homicide* (Cambridge, Mass., 2009); and Roth, "Guns, Murder, and Probability: How Can We Decide Which Figures to Trust?" *Reviews in American History*, XXXV (2007), 165–175.

The Perth city burial registers characterized his death as "sudent"—a misspelling of *sudden*, and almost certainly a whitewashing of the facts in response to Ogilvie's siblings' campaigning to protect the family's reputation. Registering this as a sudden death rather than a suicide would have permitted them to bury his body in hallowed ground and avoid some of the shame associated with suicide. Ogilvie was buried in Greyfriars Burial Ground, Perth, on Sept. 13, 1820. See archives of Perth burgh burial registers, 1794–1855, Perth and Kinross Council, www.pkc.gov.uk. Thanks to Rab Houston for leading me to this source. On the topic of suicide, see Olive Anderson, *Suicide in Victorian and Edwardian England* (Oxford, 1987); Richard Bell, "The Moral Thermometer: Rush, Republicanism, and

Suicide," *Early American Studies*, XV (2017): 308–331; Bell, *We Shall Be No More: Suicide and Self-Government in the Newly United States* (Cambridge, Mass., 2012); R. A. Houston, *Punishing the Dead? Suicide, Lordship, and Community in Britain, 1500–1830* (Oxford, 2010); Andrew Lewis, ed., "Suicide in Medieval England: Proceedings of a Colloquium Held at Magdalen College, Oxford, July 1999," special issue of *Journal of Legal History*, XXI, no. 1 (April 2000), 1–65; Carol A. Loar, "'Go and Seek the Crowner': Coroners' Inquests and the Pursuit of Justice in Early Modern England" (Ph.D. diss., Northwestern University, 1998), chap. 3; Michael MacDonald and Terence R. Murphy, *Sleepless Souls: Suicide in Early Modern England* (Oxford, 1990); Georges Minois, *History of Suicide: Voluntary Death in Western Culture*, trans. Lydia G. Cochrane (Baltimore, 1999); Eric Vallee, "'A Fatal Sympathy': Suicide and the Republic of Abjection in the Writings of Benjamin Rush and Charles Brockden Brown," *Early American Studies*, XV (2017), 332–351; and John Weaver and David Wright, eds., *Histories of Suicide: International Perspectives on Self-Destruction in the Modern World* (Toronto, 2009), esp. essays by Rab Houston, Jeffrey Merrick, and Kevin Siena.

CHAPTER THIRTEEN

1. American women and men regularly asked their physicians for help with what only later became categorized as psychological or psychiatric conditions. For similar correspondence to Rush, see Ann Bigelow, "'My Damned Melancholy': Suicide in Frontier Ohio," *Timeline*, XXXI (2014), 32–43.

2. James Ogilvie to Benjamin Rush, Feb. 21, 1797, Benjamin Rush Correspondence, XXV, Rush Family Papers, 1748–1876, LCP.in.HSP.134, Historical Society of Pennsylvania (HSP), Philadelphia. Subsequent Ogilvie quotations come from this letter unless otherwise indicated.

3. I will use these terms interchangeably, given that writers today vary as to their preference. The writer and clinical psychologist Kay Redfield Jamison finds *bipolar* "strangely and powerfully offensive: it seems to me to obscure and minimize the illness it is supposed to represent. The description 'manic-depressive,' on the other hand, seems to capture both the nature and the seriousness of the disease I have, rather than attempting to paper over the reality of the condition." See Jamison, *An Unquiet Mind* (New York, 1995), 181–182. The current *Diagnostic and Statistical Manual of Mental Disorders* prefers *bipolar disorder*, which some suggest is less stigmatizing because it drops the term *manic* and, because it describes a chemical, physical, and cognitive condition rather than an emotional state, is more in keeping with the science. See *Diagnostic and Statistical Manual of Mental Disorders*, 5th ed. (Washington, D.C., 2013) (hereafter cited as DSM-5).

4. George Brodie to William Godwin, Feb. 3, 1821, MS Abinger Deposit, B. 214/2, Bodleian Library, Oxford University (hereafter cited as BLOU).

5. Kay Redfield Jamison, *Touched with Fire: Manic-Depressive Illness and the Artistic Temperament* (New York, 1993).

6. These passages characterizing mainstream twenty-first-century descriptions of manic depression have been compiled with the use of the DSM-5; Jay Griffiths, *Tristimania:*

A Diary of Manic Depression (Berkeley, Calif., 2016); David Healy, *Mania: A Short History of Bipolar Disorder* (Baltimore, 2008); Lisa M. Hermsen, *Manic Minds: Mania's Mad History and Its Neuro-Future* (New Brunswick, N.J., 2011); and Jamison's writing on the subject, including *Touched with Fire*, *Unquiet Mind*, and *Robert Lowell, Setting the River on Fire: A Study of Genius, Mania, and Character* (New York, 2017). Hermsen is particularly clear about the evolution of this diagnosis as it has changed over time. I have also drawn on Sheri K. Johnson, Charles S. Carver, and Ian H. Gotlib, "Elevated Ambitions for Fame among Persons with Bipolar I Disorder," *Journal of Abnormal Psychology*, CXXI (2012), 602–609; and Robert L. Leahy, "Decision Making and Mania," *Journal of Cognitive Psychotherapy*, XIII (1999), 83–105. The changes in the various editions of the DSM could be jarring and controversial for practitioners. See Gary Greenberg, *The Book of Woe: The DSM and the Unmaking of Psychiatry* (New York, 2013). See also Allen Frances, "The New Crisis of Confidence in Psychiatric Diagnosis," *Annals of Internal Medicine*, CLIX, no. 3 (Aug. 6, 2013), 221–222.

7. Jamison, *Unquiet Mind*, 67. For additional narratives of the condition, see Andy Behrman, *Electroboy: A Memoir of Mania* (New York, 2002); Terri Cheney, *Manic: A Memoir* (New York, 2008); John C. Forkasdi, *The Secrets Within: A Memoir of a Bipolar Man* (Tucson, Ariz., 2008); Griffiths, *Tristimania*; and Keith Allan Steadman, *The Bipolar Expeditionist* (Bloomington, Ind., 2008). I have particularly benefited from Hermsen's scrutiny of this genre of life writing in *Manic Minds*, chap. 4. Future revisions of the DSM might seek an entirely new formulation, as Hermsen signals, for it has continually based its categories on symptoms rather than a more thoroughgoing understanding of the causes of those symptoms. Imaging of brain activity in combination with neuropsychopharmacology have sought to find better means of treating specific manifestations of the highs and lows of the condition. See *Manic Minds*, 101–115; see also Nikolas Rose and Joelle M. Abi-Rached, *Neuro: The New Brain Sciences and the Management of the Mind* (Princeton, N.J., 2013). For a criticism of the DSM, see Greenberg, *Book of Woe*.

8. See Chapters 1 and 3, above; and [John] Ogilvie, "Ode to Melancholy," in *The Wreath: A Selection of Elegant Poems from the Best Authors* (New York, 1813), 97–101.

9. Annemarie Goldstein Jutel, *Putting a Name to It: Diagnosis in Contemporary Society* (Baltimore, 2011).

10. See, for example, Kathleen T. Brady and Susan C. Sonne, "The Relationship between Substance Abuse and Bipolar Disorder," *Journal of Clinical Psychiatry*, LVI (1995), 19–24; Seyed Vahid Shariat et al., "Mania Precipitated by Opioid Withdrawal: A Retrospective Study," *American Journal on Addictions*, XXII (2013), 338–343; Roger D. Weiss et al., "Substance Use and Perceived Symptom Improvement among Patients with Bipolar Disorder and Substance Dependence," *Journal of Affective Disorders*, LXXIX (2004), 279–283; Charles B. Schaffer et al., "Mood-Elevating Effects of Opioid Analgesics in Patients with Bipolar Disorder," *Journal of Neuropsychiatry and Clinical Neurosciences*, XIX (2007), 449–452; Anna Fels, "Can Opioids Treat Depression?" *New York Times*, June 5, 2016, 10 ("Sunday Review"; this essay appeared online as "Are Opioids the Next Antidepressant?" https://www .nytimes.com/2016/06/05/opinion/sunday/are-opioids-the-next-antidepressant.html).

11. Nathan Allen, *An Essay on the Opium Trade, Including a Sketch of Its History, Extent, Effects, Etc., as Carried on in India and China* (Boston, 1850), 23.

12. On historical perspectives on disease, see Andrew Cunningham, "Identifying Disease in the Past: Cutting the Gordian Knot," 13–34, and Jon Arrizabalaga, "Problematizing Retrospective Diagnosis in the History of Disease," 51–70, both in *Asclepio: Revista de historia de la medicina y de la ciencia*, LIV (2002); Allan Ingram and Leigh Wetherall Dickson, eds., *Disease and Death in Eighteenth-Century Literature and Culture: Fashioning the Unfashionable* (London, 2016), esp. essays by Heather Meck and Jane Taylor; Clark Lawlor, *Consumption and Literature: The Making of the Romantic Disease* (Houndmills, U.K., 2007), esp. parts 2 and 3; Randall M. Packard, "'Break-Bone' Fever in Philadelphia, 1780: Reflections on the History of Disease," *Bulletin of the History of Medicine*, XC (2016), 193–221; and Jonathan Sadowsky, "The Confinements of Isaac O.: A Case of 'Acute Mania' in Colonial Nigeria," *History of Psychiatry*, VII (1996), 91–112. Donna Trembinski takes a different but usefully cautious view in "Comparing Premodern Melancholy / Mania and Modern Trauma: An Argument in Favor of Historical Experiences of Trauma," *History of Psychology*, XIV (2011), 80–99. On the history of seeking institutional solutions for forms of mental disorders in America, see Norman Dain, *Disordered Minds: The First Century of Eastern State Hospital in Williamsburg, Virginia, 1766–1866* (Williamsburg, Va., 1971); Albert Deutsch, *The Mentally Ill in America: A History of Their Care and Treatment from Colonial Times*, 2d ed., rev. and enl. (New York, 1949); Stephen Fried, *Rush: Revolution, Madness, and the Visionary Doctor Who Became a Founding Father* (New York, 2018); Gary Greenberg, *Manufacturing Depression: The Secret History of a Modern Disease* (New York, 2010); Benjamin Reiss, *Theaters of Madness: Insane Asylums and Nineteenth-Century American Culture* (Chicago, 2008); David J. Rothman, *The Discovery of the Asylum: Social Order and Disorder in the New Republic* (Boston, 1971); and Nancy Tomes, *The Art of Asylum-Keeping: Thomas Story Kirkbride and the Origins of American Psychiatry* (Philadelphia, 1994). More widely, see Robert Castel, *The Regulation of Madness: The Origins of Incarceration in France*, trans. W. D. Halls (Berkeley, Calif., 1988); Michel Foucault, *A History of Madness*, ed. Jean Khalfa, trans. Jonathan Murphy and Khalfa (London, 2006); Andrew T. Scull, *Museums of Madness: The Social Organization of Insanity in Nineteenth-Century England* (London, 1979); and Edward Shorter, *A History of Psychiatry: From the Era of the Asylum to the Age of Prozac* (New York, 1997). On latter-day pharmacology and the pharmaceutical industry, see Andrew Lakoff, *Pharmaceutical Reason: Knowledge and Value in Global Psychiatry* (New York, 2005). Many men on the bipolar spectrum are initially misdiagnosed as schizophrenic (and women as having anxiety or major depressive disorder). See Healy, *Mania*; and George Winokur and Ming T. Tsuang, *The Natural History of Mania, Depression, and Schizophrenia* (Washington, D.C., 1996).

13. [Anonymous], "Bipolar Disorder and Stigma," National Alliance on Mental Illness, https://www.nami.org/Personal-Stories/Bipolar-Disorder-and-Stigma#. Discussions of stigma are common in the memoirs of mania cited in note 7.

14. James Ogilvie, "Supplementary Narrative," in *Philosophical Essays . . .* (Philadelphia, 1816), xxxvii. Recall from Chapter 11, above, that Ogilvie likewise described his disappointments in overheated terms when he could not persuade South Carolinians to estab-

lish a professorship of oratory and a hall of eloquence. He felt so crushed that he withdrew from society for a time and ultimately apologized for his behavior.

15. [John Armstrong], *The Art of Preserving Health: A Poem* (London, 1744), 108–109; Ogilvie to Charles Stewart Daveis, March 1810, Special MS Collection Daveis, Rare Book and Manuscript Library, Butler Library, Columbia University, N.Y. ("energy and animation"); Ogilvie to Francis Walker Gilmer, Oct. 8, 1813, Francis Walker Gilmer Correspondence, 1784–1826, Acc. no. 38–588, box 1, folder 44, Small Special Collections Library, University of Virginia, Charlottesville (hereafter cited as UVA) ("I now endure"). See Cunningham, "Identifying Disease in the Past," 13–34, and Arrizabalaga, "Problematizing Retrospective Diagnosis," 51–70, both in *Asclepio*, LIV (2002); and Rothman, *Discovery of the Asylum*. See also John Baker's riveting account of "'Strange Contrarys': Figures of Melancholy in Eighteenth-Century Poetry," in Allan Ingram et al., eds., *Melancholy Experience in Literature of the Long Eighteenth Century: Before Depression, 1660–1800* (Houndmills, U.K., 2011), 83–113. Ogilvie himself held forth on how poetry possessed a "magnetic attraction and immortal beauty" that touches "'with a master's hand' a chord in the human heart, strong and attuned by nature." See Ogilvie to Francis Walker Gilmer, Feb. 1, 1813, in Richard Beale Davis, *Francis Walker Gilmer: Life and Learning in Jefferson's Virginia* (Richmond, Va., 1939), 376 (hereafter cited as FWG).

16. "On Friday evening last . . . ," *Rhode-Island American, and General Advertiser* (Providence), Feb. 27, 1810, [3] ("admiration and delight"); "On Tuesday evening last . . . ," *Rhode-Island American*, Mar. 23, 1810, [3] ("at his command"). Nor was Ogilvie's propensity to discuss his melancholy unusual for the day, as shown in Leigh Wetherall-Dickson, "Melancholy, Medicine, Mad Moon, and Marriage: Autobiographical Expressions of Depression," in Ingram et al., eds., *Melancholy Experience in Literature*, 142–169.

17. Ogilvie to Francis Walker Gilmer, Oct. 8, 1813, Correspondence of Francis Walker Gilmer, 1784–1826, MS 38–588, box 1, folder 44, UVA ("my excursion"); Jamison, *Touched with Fire*, 105; see also "CXIX. Mr. Ogilvie," *American Anecdotes: Original and Select*, I (Boston, 1830), 151–154. One recent author and professor of psychiatry has characterized hypomania as a quality of being that has become associated with Americanness—a heightened state of energy, creativity, optimism, and "Yankee ingenuity"—all aspects of a national temperament. See John D. Gartner, *The Hypomanic Edge: The Link between (a Little) Craziness and (a Lot of) Success in America* (New York, 2005), 7, 11.

18. Washington Irving, "Mountjoy: Or Some Passages out of the Life of a Castle-Builder," *Knickerbocker, or New-York Monthly Magazine*, XIV (1839), 405; see also Richard Beale Davis, "James Ogilvie and Washington Irving," *Americana Illustrated*, XXXV (1941), 435–458.

19. "From the Boston Palladium: James Ogilvie," *Georgia Journal* (Milledgeville), June 5, 1821, [1] ("service of humanity"); P. Q. R., "To the Editor of the Charleston Times: Mr. Editor," *New-York Columbian*, May 7, 1821, [2–3] ("miserable man"). See also "Death of Mr. Ogilvie," *City of Washington Gazette*, Apr. 9, 1821, [2]; "Poetry: James Ogilvie," *Boston Daily Advertiser*, Apr. 16, 1821, [1]; "The Late Mr. Ogilvie, The Orator," *Georgian and Evening Advertiser* (Savannah), Apr. 25, 1821, [2]; "Mr. Ogilvie," *Richmond Enquirer*, May 1, 1821, [3]; H. of

Richmond [James Heath?], "Recollections of James Ogilvie, Earl of Fin[d]later," *Southern Literary Messenger*, XIV, no. 1 (January 1848), 534–537; and [John Peyton Little], "History of Richmond. Chapter VI. Resolutions of '98. Burr's Trial," *Southern Literary Messenger*, XVIII, no. 1 (January 1852), 8.

20. Quote comes from Jo[seph Vallence] Bevan to William Godwin, June 8, 1818, MS Abinger Deposit B. 215/1, BLOU. Nor is there clear evidence that he received a response from Benjamin Rush after writing the letter in 1797, although some Rush letters have survived in response to others with similar concerns about melancholy.

21. Meta Craig to Nicholas Biddle, Jan. 18, 1811, Biddle Family Papers, Coll. 1452A, box 3, folder 9, HSP ("recitations"); James Kirke Paulding to Peter Kemble, Jr., Jan. 8, 1809, in Washington Irving, *Letters*, ed. Ralph M. Aderman, H. L. Kleinfield, and Jenifer S. Banks, 4 vols. (Boston, 1978), I, 272 ("astounded"). At the time of the publication of this edited collection, the Paulding letter was owned by William Kemble of Bedford Hills, New York.

22. Irving, "Mountjoy," *Knickerbocker, or New-York Monthly Magazine*, XIV (1839), 405 ("improvement of society"); Review of *Fragment of a Journal of a Sentimental Philosopher . . . ," New-York Review; or Critical Journal* (March 1809), 117 ("visionary speculations"). As discussed in Chapter 6, above, this savage review of John Rodman's *Fragment of a Journal* was written by Irving and Paulding (and perhaps others in their circle). On portraits of Ogilvie, Irving wrote to Charles Robert Leslie in 1824, "I see among the pieces to be exhibited at the British Gallery, a 'Don Quixote' by [Gilbert Stuart] Newton, which I presume is the little picture made from poor Ogilvie." Leslie was developing his own Ogilvie-inspired images of Quixote at the same time. See Charles Robert Leslie, *Autobiographical Recollections*, ed. Tom Taylor (Boston, 1860), 260, 265–266. On interpretations of Quixote, see Fiona Evelyn Hamilton, "Don Quixote and Romanticism in Nineteenth-Century England: Irony in Duffield's, Ormsby's, and Watts' Translations" (Ph.D. diss., University of Edinburgh, 2016), chap. 2, conclusion. See also Rachel Lynn Schmidt, *Critical Images: The Canonization of Don Quixote through Illustrated Editions of the Eighteenth Century* (Montreal and Kingston, Canada, 1999). See also *Oxford English Dictionary Online*, s.v. "Visionary," www.oed.com.

23. G. J. Barker-Benfield, *Abigail and John Adams: The Americanization of Sensibility* (Chicago, 2010); Barker-Benfield, *The Culture of Sensibility: Sex and Society in Eighteenth-Century Britain* (Chicago, 1992); Naomi Booth, "Feeling Too Much: The Swoon and the (In)Sensible Woman," *Women's Writing*, XXI (2014), 575–591; Andrew Burstein, "The Political Character of Sympathy," *Journal of the Early Republic*, XXI (2001), 601–633; Andrew R. L. Cayton, "Insufficient Woe: Sense and Sensibility in Writing Nineteenth-Century History," *Reviews in American History*, XXXI (2003), 331–341; Markman Ellis, *The Politics of Sensibility: Race, Gender, and Commerce in the Sentimental Novel* (New York, 1996); Mike Goode, *Sentimental Masculinity and the Rise of History, 1790–1890* (Cambridge, 2009); Glenn Hendler, *Public Sentiments: Structures of Feeling in Nineteenth-Century American Literature* (Chapel Hill, N.C., 2001); Chris Jones, "Radical Sensibility in the 1790s," in Alison Yarrington and Kelvin Everest, eds., *Reflec-*

tions of Revolution: Images of Romanticism (London, 1993); Mary Kelley, Learning to Stand and Speak: Women, Education, and Public Life in America's Republic (Williamsburg, Va., and Chapel Hill, N.C., 2006), chap. 1; Sarah Knott, Sensibility and the American Revolution (Williamsburg, Va., and Chapel Hill, N.C., 2009); John Mullan, "Hypochondria and Hysteria: Sensibility and the Physicians," special issue of Eighteenth Century, XXV (1984), 141–174; Mullan, Sentiment and Sociability: The Language of Feeling in the Eighteenth Century (Oxford, 1988); Sarah M. S. Pearsall, "'The Power of Feeling'? Emotion, Sensibility, and the American Revolution," Modern Intellectual History, VIII (2011), 659–672; William M. Reddy, The Navigation of Feeling: A Framework for the History of Emotions (Cambridge, 2001); Janet Todd, Sensibility: An Introduction (London, 1986); Anne Vincent-Buffault, The History of Tears: Sensibility and Sentimentality in France, trans. Teresa Bridgeman (New York, 1991); and Dror Wahrman, The Making of the Modern Self: Identity and Culture in Eighteenth-Century England (New Haven, Conn., 2004). On medical responses, see Marina Benjamin, ed., Science and Sensibility: Gender and Scientific Enquiry, 1780–1945 (Oxford, 1991); Wayne Wild, "The Origins of a Modern Medical Ethics in Enlightenment Scotland: Cheyne, Gregory, and Cullen as Practitioners of Sensibility," Clio Medica, XCIV (2014), 48–73. It's also worth noting that many people today find a correlation between manic depression and the artistic temperament, claiming that this condition grants exceptional sensitivity to words, sounds, images, smells. "I honestly believe that as a result of it I have felt more things, more deeply; had more experiences, more intensely; loved more, and been more loved; laughed more often for having cried more often; appreciated more the springs, for the winters," Jamison writes in a long, eloquent passage (Unquiet Mind, 218); see also Griffiths, Tristimania, 39. Jamison sought to corroborate that correlation by collecting biographical information on thirty-six major British and Irish poets born between 1705 and 1805, showing evidence of how many of them suffered what Jamison terms recurrent depression or manic depression; some of these were confined to asylums or committed suicide. They include Ogilvie's contemporaries, the Romantic poets Robert Burns, Lord Byron, Samuel Taylor Coleridge, and William Wordsworth (Touched with Fire, chap. 3).

24. Clark Lawlor, "Fashionable Melancholy," in Ingram et al., eds., Melancholy Experience in Literature, 25–53. On this subject, see, among others, Baker, "Strange Contrarys," in Ingram et al., eds., Melancholy Experience in Literature; Allan Beveridge, "'Groaning under the Miseries of a Diseased Nervous System': Robert Burns and Melancholy," Clio Medica, XCIV (2014), 145–171; Ingram, The Madhouse of Language: Writing and Reading Madness in the Eighteenth Century (London, 1991); Ingram and Michelle Faubert, Cultural Constructions of Madness in Eighteenth-Century Writing: Representing the Insane (Houndmills, U.K., 2005); and Thomas Pfau, Romantic Moods: Paranoia, Trauma, and Melancholy, 1790–1840 (Baltimore, 2005).

25. On this subject, see, among others, Richard Bell, We Shall Be No More: Suicide and Self-Government in the Newly United States (Cambridge, Mass., 2012), chap. 2; Michelle Faubert and Nicole Reynolds, "Introduction," and the following articles in "Romanticism and Suicide," special issue of Literature Compass, XII (2015), 641–651; Faubert, "Werther Goes Viral:

Suicidal Contagion, Anti-Vaccination, and Infectious Sympathy," *Literature and Medicine*, XXXIV (2016), 389–417; and Stuart Sim, "Despair, Melancholy, and the Novel," in Ingram et al., eds., *Melancholy Experience in Literature*, 114–141.

26. Benjamin Rush, *Medical Inquiries and Observations; to Which Is Added an Appendix, Containing Observations on the Duties of a Physician, and the Methods of Improving Medicine*, 2d ed. (London, 1789), 255. On this subject, see W. F. Bynum, Roy Porter, and Michael Shepherd, eds., *The Anatomy of Madness: Essays in the History of Psychiatry*, 3 vols. (London, 1985–1988); Joseph F. Kett, *The Formation of the American Medical Profession: The Role of Institutions, 1780–1860* (New Haven, Conn., 1968); Kathryn Shively Meier, *Nature's Civil War: Common Soldiers and the Environment in 1862 Virginia* (Chapel Hill, N.C., 2013); and John Harley Warner, *The Therapeutic Perspective: Medical Practice, Knowledge, and Identity in America, 1820–1885* (Cambridge, Mass., 1986).

27. Ogilvie to Francis Walker Gilmer, July 12, 1813, FWG, 378–380.

28. Stanley W. Jackson, *Melancholia and Depression: From Hippocratic Times to Modern Times* (New Haven, Conn., 1986), esp. chaps. 7–8; Jackson, "Melancholia and Mechanical Explanations in Eighteenth-Century Medicine," *Journal of the History of Medicine and Allied Sciences*, XXXVIII (1983), 298–319; Jackson, "Melancholia and Partial Insanity," *Journal of the History of the Behavioral Sciences*, XIX (1983), 173–184; Jackson, "Melancholia and the Waning of the Humoral Theory," *JHMAS*, XXXIII (1978), 367–376; Jackson, "Two Sufferers' Perspectives on Melancholia: 1690s to 1790s," in Edwin R. Wallace IV and Lucius C. Pressley, eds., *Essays in the History of Psychiatry: A Tenth Anniversary Supplementary Volume to the Psychiatric Forum* (Columbia, S.C., 1980), 58–71; G. A. Lindeboom, *Herman Boerhaave: The Man and His Work* (London, 1968); John C. Powers, *Inventing Chemistry: Herman Boerhaave and the Reform of the Chemical Arts* (Chicago, 2012); Warner, *Therapeutic Perspective*.

29. Information about Rush's prescriptions in Bigelow, "'My Damned Melancholy,'" Timeline, XXXI (2014), 41.

30. S. A. [D.] Tissot, *An Essay on Diseases Incident to Literary and Sedentary Persons . . .* , 2d enlarged ed. (London, 1769), 11, 13 ("perpetual labours"), 23 ("degenerate into melancholy"), 53 ("voided a mass"), 56–57 ("may be useful"). For others who believed melancholy was common among the literati, see Mullan, "Hypochondria and Hysteria," *Eighteenth Century*, XXV (1984), 144–149.

31. George Edward Male, *An Epitome of Juridical or Forensic Medicine; for the Use of Medical Men, Coroners, and Barristers* (London, 1816), 166. Other Americans suffering from melancholy likewise received advice that centered on exercise and improving their digestion. See Robert E. Shalhope, *A Tale of New England: The Diaries of Hiram Harwood, Vermont Farmer, 1810–1837* (Baltimore, 2003), esp. chap. 9; and Bertram Wyatt-Brown, *The House of Percy: Honor, Melancholy, and Imagination in a Southern Family* (New York, 1994).

32. Robert Whyte, *Observations on the Nature, Causes, and Cure of Those Disorders Which Have Been Commonly Called Nervous Hypochondriac or Hysteric . . .* , 2d ed., corr. (Edinburgh, 1765), 357 ("flesh-brush"); Jack Larkin, *The Reshaping of Everyday Life, 1790–1840* (New York, 1988), 163–166 (baths in the early United States).

33. Rush's notes on the verso of the letter from Matthew Backus, June 29, 1807, Benjamin Rush Correspondence, II, 2, Rush Family Papers, 1748–1876, LCP.in.HSP.134, HSP. No response from Rush to Ogilvie has survived, and his papers do not indicate whether he responded.

34. William Buchan, *Domestic Medicine; or, A Treatise on the Prevention and Cure of Diseases by Regimen and Simple Medicines*, 2d ed. (London, 1772), 72 ("discourses in public"); Whyte, *Observations*, 520 ("variety of amusements"); Rush, *Medical Inquiries and Observations, upon the Diseases of the Mind* (Philadelphia, 1812), 153 ("every Sunday").

35. "Mr. Ogilvie's Discourses," *Washington Federalist*, June 16, 1808, [2] ("persevering"); Thomas Jefferson to Rev. John Glendy, June 21, 1808, in *Founders Online*, National Archives, https://founders.archives.gov ("considerations"); Jefferson to Thomas Cooper, Sept. 10, 1814, in James P. McClure and J. Jefferson Looney, eds., *The Papers of Thomas Jefferson Digital Edition*, Retirement Series (Charlottesville, Va., 2008–2020), VII, 649–655 ("tour of health," 649), https://rotunda.upress.virginia.edu/founders.

36. Ogilvie to Francis Walker Gilmer, July 12, 1813, FWG, 378–380.

EPILOGUE

1. For examples of eulogies that offer explanations for his suicide, see [William Crafts], "The Late Mr. Ogilvie, the Orator," *Georgian and Evening Advertiser* (Savannah), Apr. 25, 1821, [2]; and P. Q. R., "To the Editor of the Charleston Times," *New-York Columbian*, May 7, 1821, [2–3]. For those that claim he had received the title (and died on his estate), see "Died," *New-York Evening Post*, Apr. 4, 1821, [2]; "Death of Mr. Ogilvie," *City of Washington Gazette*, Apr. 9, 1821, [3]; see also H. of Richmond [James E. Heath?], "Recollections of James Ogilvie, Earl of Finlater," *Southern Literary Messenger*, XIV (1848), 534–537.

2. "Mr. Hazelton," *Saratoga Sentinel*, July 25, 1821, [3] ("distinguished model"); "Mr. Walter," *Alexandria Herald*, Jan. 10, 1823, [3] ("his friend"); "Literary Notice," *Haverhill Gazette* (Mass.), Dec. 26, 1823, [3] ("in imitation"); "We rather think . . . ," *National Intelligencer* (Washington, D.C.), Oct. 16, 1823, [3] ("large audiences"). For more on the imitator Mr. Huntington, see 179, above, and *Mr. Huntington's Address to the Public: An Address to the Public, by Mr. Huntington, on the Renewal (for a Limited Season) of His Lectures and Recitations* (n.p., [1841?]).

3. [Josiah Holbrook], *American Lyceum; or, Society for the Improvement of Schools, and Diffusion of Useful Knowledge* (Boston, 1829), 5 ("elevated character"); Academicus, "For the Courier. The Lyceum," *Country Courier*, II, no. 4 (December 1816), 60 ("Schools of improvement"); [Josiah Holbrook, ed.], "Astronomy . . . ," *Family Lyceum . . . ,* I (1833), [1] ("nation's glory"). Schoolbooks that taught elocution to youth enhanced their claim to teach *American* oratory by anthologizing speeches by a limited list of authors. Some of these retrospectively declared Ogilvie to be an outsider to the United States and breezed past his name to sing the praises instead of those they claimed as American (which could include other naturalized American citizens like Alexander Hamilton). See Samuel L. Knapp, *Lectures on American Literature, with Remarks on Some Passages of American History* (New York, 1829), 213–227. A writer for *Blackwood's Edinburgh Magazine* did the same thing, except in reverse, by calling Ogilvie

an "American Writer." "A declaimer of wonderful powers, if we may believe what is told of him," the author explained. "He was a man of genius, destroyed by opium-eating." See X. Y. Z., "American Writers, No. V," *Blackwood's Edinburgh Magazine*, XVII (1825), 198. More recent scholars often display a gap between celebrating the eloquence of the Revolutionary generation and that of orators beginning in the 1820s and afterward. See William Norwood Brigance, ed., *A History and Criticism of American Public Address* (New York, 1960), I, 55–110; and Lawrence Buell, *New England Literary Culture: From Revolution through Renaissance* (Cambridge, 1986), esp. chap. 6. On lyceums and their popularity, see [Holbrook], *American Lyceum*, 5.

The story of Josiah Holbrook's lyceum is usually told in triumphal terms and framed as something new. "Ordinary citizens," one historian wrote in the 1950s, "commenced to seek for themselves and for their neighbors a fuller life, a better society, and a wider understanding of the world beyond the horizon," answers for which, he states, they found in the lyceum movement. More recently, a scholar has proclaimed that "the American Lyceum Movement became a pivotal foundation of U.S. adult education during the nineteenth-century." See Waldo W. Braden, "The Beginnings of the Lyceum, 1826–1840," *Southern Speech Journal*, XX (1954), 125; Vyacheslav Khrapak, "Reflections on the American Lyceum: The Legacy of Josiah Holbrook and the Transcendental Sessions," *Journal of Philosophy and History of Education*, LXIV (2014), 60. See also Carl Bode, *The American Lyceum: Town Meeting of the Mind* (New York, 1956); Gregory Clark and S. Michael Halloran, "Introduction: Transformations of Public Discourse in Nineteenth-Century America," in Gregory Clark and S. Michael Halloran, eds., *Oratorical Culture in Nineteenth-Century America: Transformations in the Theory and Practice of Rhetoric* (Carbondale, Ill., 1993), 1–26; Joseph F. Kett, *The Pursuit of Knowledge under Difficulties: From Self-Improvement to Adult Education in America, 1750–1990* (Stanford, Calif., 1994); Angela G. Ray, *The Lyceum and Public Culture in the Nineteenth-Century United States* (East Lansing, Mich., 2005); Donald M. Scott, "The Popular Lecture and the Creation of a Public in Mid-Nineteenth-Century America," *Journal of American History*, LXVI (1980), 800; Scott, "Print and the Public Lecture System, 1840–1860," in William L. Joyce, David D. Hall, and Richard D. Brown, eds., *Printing and Society in Early America* (Worcester, Mass., 1983), 278–299; Scott, "The Profession That Vanished: Public Lecturing in Mid-Nineteenth-Century America," in Gerald L. Geison, ed., *Professions and Professional Ideologies in America* (Chapel Hill, N.C., 1983), 12–28; Leah G. Stambler, "The Lyceum Movement in American Education, 1826–1845," *Paedagogica Historica*, XXI (1981), 157–185; and James Perrin Warren, *Culture of Eloquence: Oratory and Reform in Antebellum America* (University Park, Pa., 1999). Not all scholars have insisted that Holbrook's lyceum represented a new order for the ages. See, especially, Tom F. Wright, *Lecturing the Atlantic: Speech, Print, and an Anglo-American Commons, 1830–1870* (New York, 2017).

4. Ralph Waldo Emerson, "Eloquence," in *The Complete Works of Ralph Waldo Emerson . . .*, centennial ed., 12 vols. (Boston, 1903–1932), VII, 63 ("to agitate"), 66; Emerson to Edward Bliss Emerson, Jan. 5, 1817, in Ralph L. Rusk, ed., *Letters of Ralph Waldo Emerson*, 6 vols. (New York, 1939), I, 32. See also Lawrence Buell, *Emerson* (Cambridge, 2003), 22–31; Buell, *New*

England Literary Culture, 158–163; and Mary Kupiec Cayton, "The Making of an American Prophet: Emerson, His Audiences, and the Rise of the Culture Industry in Nineteenth-Century America," *American Historical Review*, XCII (1987), 597–620. Emerson began giving the lecture on eloquence during the 1840s and continued to rework it for decades afterward (Buell, *Emerson*, 29). On civic enchantment, see Michelle Sizemore, *American Enchantment: Rituals of the People in the Post-Revolutionary World* (New York, 2017).

5. Before the 1820s, newspapers reprinted speeches but did so by requesting the text from the orator. See Will Slauter, *Who Owns the News: A History of Copyright* (Stanford, Calif., 2019), chaps. 3–4.

6. On abolitionists infusing their speeches with references to the sounds of slavery, see Mark M. Smith, *Listening to Nineteenth-Century America* (Chapel Hill, N.C., 2001), 172–197; and Shane White and Graham White, *The Sounds of Slavery: Discovering African American History through Songs, Sermons, and Speech* (Boston, 2005). On abolitionist tactics and their references to what they called the "slave power," see Julie Roy Jeffrey, *The Great Silent Army of Abolitionism: Ordinary Women in the Antislavery Movement* (Chapel Hill, N.C., 1998); Aileen S. Kraditor, *Means and Ends in American Abolitionism: Garrison and His Critics on Strategy and Tactics, 1834–1850* (New York, 1969); W. Caleb McDaniel, *The Problem of Democracy in the Age of Slavery: Garrisonian Abolitionists and Transatlantic Reform* (Baton Rouge, La., 2013); Stacey M. Robertson, *Hearts Beating for Liberty: Women Abolitionists in the Old Northwest* (Chapel Hill, N.C., 2010); and Ronald G. Walters, *The Antislavery Appeal: American Abolitionism after 1830* (Baltimore, 1976).

7. David Crockett, *The Life and Adventures of Colonel David Crockett of West Tennessee* (Cincinnati, Ohio, 1833), 153 ("half horse"). On Crockett, see Mark Derr, *The Frontiersman: The Real Life and Many Legends of Davy Crockett* (New York, 1993); Richard Boyd Hauck, "The Man in the Buckskin Hunting Shirt: Fact and Fiction in the Crockett Story," in Michael A. Lofaro, ed., *Davy Crockett: The Man, the Legend, the Legacy, 1786–1986* (Knoxville, Tenn., 1985), 3–20; and Sharon Marcus, *The Drama of Celebrity* (Princeton, N.J., 2019), 215. On the Know-Nothings, see Tyler Anbinder, *Nativism and Slavery: The Northern Know-Nothings and the Politics of the 1850s* (New York, 1992); A. Cheree Carlson, "The Rhetoric of the Know-Nothing Party: Nativism as a Response to the Rhetorical Situation," *Southern Communication Journal*, LIV (1989), 364–383; Dale T. Knobel, "Beyond 'America for Americans': Inside the Movement Culture of Antebellum Nativism," in Timothy Walch, ed., *Immigrant America: European Ethnicity in the United States* (New York, 1994), 7–28; and Bruce Levine, "Conservatism, Nativism, and Slavery: Thomas R. Whitney and the Origins of the Know-Nothing Party," *JAH*, LXXXVIII (2001), 455–488.

8. "Explanations," *New-York Evening Post*, May 8, 1810, [2] ("this country"). See also Trish Loughran, *The Republic in Print: Print Culture in the Age of U. S. Nation Building, 1770–1870* (New York, 2007); Angela G. Ray and Paul Stob, eds., *Thinking Together: Lecturing, Learning, and Difference in the Long Nineteenth Century* (University Park, Pa., 2018).

9. Ray, *Lyceum and Public Culture*, 40–42; see also the organs that turned actors into stars in Sara Lampert, *Starring Women: Celebrity, Patriarchy, and American Theater, 1790–1850* (Urbana,

Ill., forthcoming); and Renée M. Sentilles, *Performing Menken: Adah Isaacs Menken and the Birth of American Celebrity* (New York, 2003), esp. chap. 4; Matthew Fox-Amato, *Exposing Slavery: Photography, Human Bondage, and the Birth of Modern Visual Politics in America* (New York, 2019), 121–125; Richard Wightman Fox, *Trials of Intimacy: Love and Loss in the Beecher-Tilton Scandal* (Chicago, 1999); Charles L. Ponce de Leon, *Self-Exposure: Human-Interest Journalism and the Emergence of Celebrity in America, 1890–1940* (Chapel Hill, N.C., 2002); Jeremy C. Young, *The Age of Charisma: Leaders, Followers, and Emotions in American Society, 1870–1940* (New York, 2017).

10. James Rush annotation, Apr. 24, 1832, on James Ogilvie to Benjamin Rush, Feb. 21, 1797, Benjamin Rush Correspondence, XXV, Rush Family Papers, 1748–1876, LCP.in .HSP.134, Historical Society of Pennsylvania, Philadelphia. Like his father, James Rush was later praised for his early work on what would come to be called psychiatry. See Stephen G. Kurtz, "James Rush, Pioneer in American Psychology, 1786–1869," *Bulletin of the History of Medicine*, XXVIII (1954), 50–59. James Rush's *Philosophy of the Human Voice* . . . (Philadelphia, 1827), a scientific tract, found numerous admirers from the worlds of oratory and rhetoric.

{ INDEX }